English Language Learning in the Digital Age

English Language Learning in the Digital Age

Learner-Driven Strategies for Adolescents and Young Adults

Mark Dressman
University of Illinois at Urbana-Champaign, IL

Ju Seong Lee
Education University of Hong Kong, Hong Kong

Laurent Perrot
University of Strasbourg, Strasbourg, France

Registered Office(s)
John Wiley & Sons, Inc., 111 River Street, Hoboken, NJ 07030, USA
John Wiley & Sons Ltd, The Atrium, Southern Gate, Chichester, West Sussex, PO19 8SQ, UK

Editorial Office
9600 Garsington Road, Oxford, OX4 2DQ, UK

For details of our global editorial offices, customer services, and more information about Wiley products visit us at www.wiley.com.

Wiley also publishes its books in a variety of electronic formats and by print-on-demand. Some content that appears in standard print versions of this book may not be available in other formats.

A catalogue record for this book is available from the Library of Congress

Paperback ISBN: 9781119810353; ePub ISBN: 9781119810360; ePDF ISBN: 9781119810377

Cover image: © filo/Getty Images
Cover design by Wiley

Set in 9.5/12.5pt STIXTwoText by Integra Software Services Pvt. Ltd, Pondicherry, India
Printed and bound by CPI Group (UK) Ltd, Croydon, CR0 4YY

C9781119810353_250123

For our mothers

Contents

List of Figures

List of Tables

Acknowledgments

We wish to express our deep gratitude to the following individuals who read parts of this book as it was being written and contributed valuable ideas and feedback across multiple stages of conceptualization, writing, and editing: Siobhán O'Sullivan, Khalifa Ahmed Al Shehhi, Fazal Rizvi, Christian Torres, Sydney Sadler, Carrie James, Chen Chen Lu, Mohamed Mahna, Rao Dingxin, Samy Hassim, Ian Westbury, Robb Lindgren, Lynn Burdick, Yassine Hamdane, and Mohamed Ezzghari. Thank you, dear and generous friends.

Part I

Introduction: Informal Digital Learning of English and Its Implications

1

The Age of IDLE and the IDLE Age

Four independent digital learners of English (IDLERs) at a university library in Morocco. Note the combined use of smartphones and notebooks and the computer with plug-in modem.

Introduction and Plan for the Book

Taking a Learner-Driven Approach

This book is about the integration of instructional technology, often abbreviated as IT, or sometimes ICT (information and communications technology) with English language instruction in classroom settings, but it takes a different approach from most books on the subject. In a typical Computer-Assisted Language Learning (CALL) or Mobile-Assisted Language Learning (MALL) approach, the focus is "top-down" and often technology-driven, with additional concern for research-derived theories and principles of language acquisition and learning, almost exclusively within formal classroom settings.

English Language Learning in the Digital Age: Learner-Driven Strategies for Adolescents and Young Adults,
First Edition. Mark Dressman, Ju Seong Lee, and Laurent Perrot.
© 2023 John Wiley & Sons Ltd. Published 2023 by John Wiley & Sons Ltd.

Our approach in this book is quite different and somewhat unique. It takes a "bottom-up" view of how, over the past two decades, learners across the globe have increasingly relied on the informal use of information and communications technology to both acquire and learn English outside classroom settings. Inspired by our own research and that of others, this book takes a "learner-driven" approach, focusing on strategies adapted from what adolescents and young adults tell researchers about how they are learning English while playing video games, watching television and movies, and chatting with others online when they are not in the classroom, and how this learning contributes to their success in the classroom. These strategies are powerful, not only because their grounding in the interests and social behaviors of learners makes them highly motivating, but because they effectively solve many of the logistical issues that have persistently challenged formal language instruction for over a century, such as regular, inexpensive access to authentic sources of input, and opportunities for interaction with more proficient speakers.

In keeping with this bottom-up, learner-driven approach, each chapter begins with a series of fictional but research-based, authentic portraits of English learners and their teachers using digital technologies in the early twenty-first century. We follow these portraits with a discussion of current research and theory in second language acquisition and CALL and conclude the chapters of Part II and the first three chapters of Part III with three scenarios for teaching at the middle, secondary, and tertiary levels. Although the specific focus of these is on the learning of adolescents and young adults, many of the scenarios (especially those in middle schools) are easily adaptable for primary school settings.

Our goal in writing this book, then, is to provide an approach to the integration of CALL and MALL that is naturalistic in focus, highly readable and engaging, and grounded in cutting-edge research and theory on second language acquisition and learning. We welcome you, our readers, into a world of English language learning and teaching that embodies the full potential of ubiquitous technologies and autonomous learning in the early twenty-first century.

Imagine This

Team Teaching in Taipei

Li Mei (Liz) Wang is a middle-school English teacher in Taipei, Taiwan. Li Mei was born in Taiwan, but when she was nine, she emigrated with her family to the United States and settled in Chicago, where she became known by her schoolmates and teachers as Liz. Li Mei graduated from the University of Illinois with a degree in primary education but in her early 20s her family returned to Taiwan and Li Mei followed them, lured by a new program aimed at increasing the English proficiency of students by teaming teachers from English-speaking countries with Taiwanese teachers.

Li Mei is enjoying her return to Taiwan and is charmed by her new students, who are fascinated not only by her bilingualism but by her bicultural habits, and who shyly quiz her about life in the United States. However, she is troubled by the English curriculum, which is focused more on grammatical rules than on communication, and by some of her colleagues who lack Li Mei's fluency and insist on continuing to teach English from the textbook.

In her conversations with students, which are conducted partly in Taiwanese dialect and partly in English, Li Mei has discovered that her students are gaining quite a bit of English receptively from online sources, especially video streaming, online gaming, and music videos. Along with Japanese anime, Hallyu, and Taiwanese stars, her students are avid fans of Ariana Grande, Justin Bieber, and Drake. They tell her they grew up watching *My Little Pony* and *SpongeBob SquarePants* and now watch *The Voice* on television every week, and that they "try to understand without reading the subtitles." Moreover, she has discovered that her students' curiosity and engagement with these sources of English contrast sharply with their demeanor and performance in formal English classes, where they are reluctant to speak and seem to struggle with English grammar exercises.

In weekly meetings, Li Mei has suggested finding ways to use materials from popular culture or even trying to use captioned videos in classes, but her ideas have not been accepted. One colleague suggested that she should "save those ideas for the English club." Another was more direct. "That is not good English," the teacher told her. "We teach correct English." Another asked Li Mei why teachers should "take time for SpongeBob" in their classrooms when students were "doing that on their own." Class time, she was told, was "for serious study, not playing around." Li Mei also discussed the matter with her school director, who smiled and told her, "Your job is to help students with their fluency and pronunciation. Leave the rest of the teaching to the older teachers."

A Bilingual Bachillerato in Spain

Miguel Días teaches English and physics in a bilingual *bachillerato*, or upper-grades high school, located on the outskirts of Cordoba, Spain. The school only opened in 2019 and is part of the Spanish national government's efforts to increase the English proficiency of students, especially those intending to major in the sciences at university. Miguel, who studied physics as an undergraduate, spent three summers with relatives in Miami as a teenager and "picked up" English during those visits, from high school and a few university English classes, and from playing massively multiplayer online role-playing games (MMORPGs) through much of his time at the university. For the past two summers, he has participated in a TESOL certification program at a British university, where his fluency and ability to write in English have increased dramatically.

Miguel has thought deeply about his own learning processes as part of his professional development. His position is 50% in the English department and 50% in physics, and he is required to teach at least 30% of physics content in English. He typically introduces subjects in Spanish but later reviews and tries to extend the same concepts in English through a variety of means, including video clips and articles from *Scientific American*, *National Geographic*, and other popular sources. Khan Academy, which offers videos on much of the content in his classes in both English (with captions) and Spanish, has become an important resource for him and for his students, especially for review.

However, Miguel's teaching as well as the bilingual program of the school have recently come under criticism, not only in the press and popular opinion but from some parents and from his colleagues in both English and physics. Miguel has heard that some of his colleagues in English have mocked his "gringo" (American) accent and occasional errors in usage and grammar. They also cite recent articles in Spanish newspapers about the failure of Spanish schools to teach a British standard of

English—despite their own frequent lack of a Castilian accent in Spanish. His colleagues in physics, on the other hand, have challenged the "rigor" of his teaching, arguing that the "simplification" of content required for instruction in English is a disservice to students preparing to study science and engineering at university. In addition, some parents have complained that their children's poor background in English places them at a disadvantage compared to other students whose parents can afford to send their children to English-speaking countries on holiday or pay for private classes at English centers.

These complaints have left Miguel distracted and discouraged, but they have not weakened his determination or enthusiasm for teaching his students. He has noticed that a number are learning to speak "California dialect," nurtured by their fondness for pirated television series like "Breaking Bad," "Buffy the Vampire Slayer," or the "Fast and Furious" movie franchise, as well as several Latinx and Caribbean hip-hop artists and pop singers who move effortlessly in their lyrics from Spanish to English and back. They, in turn, are embracing highly communicative forms of English expression that, Miguel knows, may or may not help them in their future university careers, but in the meantime offer them release from the inauthenticity of the topics in their English textbooks, such as "A Trip to the Bakery" or "The Story of the Premier League."

Preparatory English in Abu Dhabi

Rakel de Silva has been a lecturer in the English preparatory program at a major private university in Abu Dhabi, United Arab Emirates, for more than a decade. Her family was originally from Kerala, on the southwest coast of India, but Rakel's father attended university in the United States to study engineering when she was a small child and she grew up speaking both Malayalam and English. She and her husband, who is a physician, have been expatriates living in Abu Dhabi since 2005. Rakel has degrees in English and applied linguistics from US universities. She was hired in 2008 as one of the first English instructors shortly after the university was founded, and she feels deeply invested in the education of her students, in her colleagues, and in the preparatory program.

However, Rakel is worried that Prep English is in danger at her university and that her program may soon be discontinued or reduced in size and impact. For over two decades, preparatory programs in Abu Dhabi and across the UAE served as "bridges" for high school graduates with weak skills, mostly in English and mathematics, to meet the entrance requirements of four-year university programs. These English programs were TESOL-based, in which students would be assessed and grouped according to their level, and the instructor would focus on specific skill areas such as vocabulary, writing, and general speaking skills in an effort to raise students' general IELTS score to a level of 6.0.

In recent years, however, fewer students have entered the university needing Prep English, and those who do enter have significantly higher scores than students of a decade before. As a result, the government has begun to reduce funding for preparatory programs and plans to eliminate them entirely in the coming years.

Rakel, her colleagues, and the program's director are unsure about how to respond to these developments. Some of her peers joke bittersweetly that they have "taught themselves out of a job," while the government attributes students' improved scores to reforms in secondary schools and more English-curriculum high schools. Rakel, who frequently talks with her students about how they have learned English both in and out of class, has noticed an alternative pattern: Her most proficient and fluent students spend significant amounts of time listening to western music in English, watching programs in English on YouTube, Netflix, or MBC, or playing MMORPGs. She has also watched over the years as English has become the lingua franca of Abu Dhabi, allowing the emirate's large expatriate community of Filipino and South Asian workers to communicate with each other, with native Emiratis, and with westerners with relatively few problems.

Rakel's concern for the decline of Prep English extends beyond worries about job security or the loss of colleagues. She has long wondered if the remedial nature of the program has not "pumped up" test scores without providing students with the additional skills they will need to succeed in their later university careers and professionally. Professors in the sciences and humanities routinely describe the challenges their students face in reading and writing in their disciplines. They point out that the simple term papers or group writing assignments on general topics offered in the undergraduate English program do not prepare students to write in professional contexts, such as reports or proposals in which hard data, charts, graphs, and language must be integrated, and in which the form of presentation is digital and visual rather than simply print- and paper-based.

During the Covid-19 pandemic, Rakel's university moved to online instruction, which provided Rakel with a laboratory and the incentive to redesign her assignments and her teaching. Instead of a general focus on "communication," Rakel created assignments in which students were required to do online research and data-based writing about specific, disciplinary-related topics and to write in new genres, creating reports for authentic academic and work-related contexts. Technical issues and a prohibition against students turning on their cameras from home led to presentation assignments in which students produced animated, narrated PowerPoint videos and uploaded them to YouTube (unlisted) for Rakel and classmates to watch. Rakel discovered that several of her students already had their own YouTube channels and were producing content, and that all her students were unable to create informative, lively, multimodal texts on their own.

Rakel counts her experiment with redesigning English at her university a major success and has shared her process and examples of student work with her colleagues. She has argued in meetings that this is the path forward for the continued relevance of English at her university. But now that the university is slowly reopening and some classes are being taught face to face again, it is uncertain whether her colleagues and director will redesign the program as a whole and make the case to university administrators for its continuation.

A Brave New World for English Learning and Teaching

These three fictional scenarios, all based on authentic developments in their country settings and worldwide, illustrate both challenges and opportunities for learning and teaching English as a second or additional language in the early twenty-first century (Menárguez 2021; Nagarajan 2021; Tzu-ti 2021). Less than thirty years ago in most parts of the non-English-speaking world, it was typical for an English teacher and a textbook to be a student's primary if not only sources of English. Instruction often did not begin until middle or high school, and classrooms were considered well-equipped if each had its own overhead projector and screen. Communicative Language Teaching (CLT; Richards 2005) was an innovation in some countries, whereas in others Grammar-Translation methods (Benati 2018) prevailed. If a teacher wanted to use some additional media, they might bring a cassette or CD player to class to teach a song or sometimes show an educational film. In the best-equipped schools there might be a language lab, with individual audio tapes for listening, and/or reading along, to stories, essays, or conversations written to teach specific vocabulary and grammatical structures. In these conditions, a student might never hear or read English spoken or written in authentic, naturalistic language unless they watched an imported television program or movie with subtitles, or listened to the BBC or Voice of America on shortwave radio.

Revolutions in digital communications and affordable intercontinental travel from the early 1990s onward at first slowly and then very rapidly changed the context of English education globally (World101 n.d.). Satellite television first brought English-language programs and movies into many homes on a daily and sometimes hourly basis. Students in more affluent homes might be able to spend summer holidays with their relatives in English-speaking countries, or their English-speaking cousins might visit them. As the internet spread across the globe from the early 1990s onward, internet cafes sprang up, offering access to a growing range of websites, chat rooms, and games to play. Digital Subscriber Lines (DSL) brought the internet into people's homes, first through telephone lines and later through optic cable, and as bandwidth improved it became increasingly feasible to stream video on YouTube (late 2005) and later through a wide range of streaming services such as Netflix, Hulu, Viki Rakuten, TenCent, and others.

Did You Know?

The first form of electronic communication, the telegraph (invented 1844), used the same binary system of dots and dashes (zeroes and ones) as all computer-based communication systems today.

Source: Eschner 2019

When the iPhone and then Android smartphones debuted in 2007, the internet became available to anyone with a smartphone, and almost anywhere (for a price). Today, for anyone with a smartphone and a data plan, nearly all the world's games, movies, television shows, books, shopping, languages, and much of its population, are accessible at a moment's search. There are of course some limitations: in some parts of the world, services are limited and others are banned, smartphones and data plans are not affordable in others, and in some places the internet may still be difficult to access; but these limitations pale in the face of what is available to most people most of the time globally.

Differences in perception and world view between those born before and after 1995 are enormous and should not be underestimated. The world simply looks different to most people born since 1995, and if the world does not often function differently and its institutions typically operate as though they were still in the 1970s, that is because they originated in the pre-digital era and are largely controlled by people who were born in that era as well. So, too, it is with schools and the education system in most parts of the world, and so, too, with the curriculum, including the teaching of languages, and in particular, English.

Take, for example, the TESOL Technology Standards Framework, to which the scenarios and activities of this textbook are referenced (Healey et al. 2008). They were published in 2008, a year after the introduction of smartphones, and were authored by scholars who were most certainly born before 1995. Although over a decade old, for the most part they remain relevant; yet as we worked through the Standards, we could not help but notice how they also seem tentative and to be permeated with fear about the lack of availability of resources in some cases, and in others, of how technology will be used. For example, it is stated, "To sum up, the Technology Standards *can provide* an opportunity for the ELT community to *clarify expectations* regarding the integration of technology in teaching and learning" (our italics; 10). There is a focus on "basic operational skills" (Goal 1, Standard 1), as though most teachers and students had never browsed the internet or word processed before and needed instruction in how to use the equipment, and the admonition to "use appropriate caution when using online sources" (Goal 1, Standard 3), as well as understanding "that communication conventions differ across cultures, communities and contexts" (Goal 2, Standard 1), and finally to "respect" and "appropriately use and evaluate" technology tools (Goal 3). The general implication is that technology is a new and possibly useful but also possibly dangerous "tool" that must be approached with care, something *outside* the classroom that might offer value, but that must be brought under control.

The view that digital technology is more than simply a tool—that it is a principal medium and increasingly the source itself of English language instruction and learning—is not anticipated in these Standards, but it is the perspective of this book, and, we have strong reason to believe, the reality in which all English language teachers in the coming decades will work. This is primarily for two reasons.

The first is the Covid-19 pandemic, which has driven classroom teaching online across much of the world. It is very true that during this period educators, students, and parents all over the world have discovered how unprepared education was for a move to formal digital education: that is, how limited in terms of human contact, instructional interaction, and opportunities for socialization online teaching can be, and how time-consuming preparation of materials for delivery is. Yet at the same time it has also become clear how digital technology made formal instruction possible at all during shutdowns, how easy it is to make and archive materials that can be revised and used again and again, and how critical learner motivation is for any learning to occur at all. For innovative teachers and curriculum developers during this period, other important lessons about the need to combine visual images and speech during instruction as well as how digital tools facilitate this process, have become clear. It seems unlikely that, post pandemic, formal education will go back to exactly the way it was before, and, more likely, some hybridization will develop in which perhaps the more didactic aspects of teaching and learning like lecturing stay online while class time is used for more process-oriented activities.

During the Covid-19 Pandemic

- 188 countries closed schools.
- More than 90% of countries adopted digital/broadcast remote learning.
- Only 69% of primary and secondary schoolchildren were reached by digital or broadcast means.
- 75% of children not reached were from rural or impoverished backgrounds.
- 1 billion+ students risked falling behind in their education.

Source: Adapted from UNICEF Education and Covid-19, 2020

A second and perhaps more lasting and significant reason for English language education is that, well before the pandemic, many students across the globe were already learning as much if not more English digitally and/or through sustained contact with other more proficient speakers than in classrooms. These learners, as studies across the world have shown, develop, larger vocabularies, and greater spoken fluency in English than peers who have less access to these resources or who are less motivated to seek them out. The findings of these studies challenge some basic assumptions of English language instruction, such as the difficulty of learning English as a foreign language and the need for structured, logically ordered language curricula; and it is perhaps for this reason or perhaps because many of the studies are very recent that their implications or the approaches to learning have not, until now, been featured in textbooks on instructional technology and language learning.

To introduce the implications of these studies, and especially to introduce their focus on *learner-driven strategies* for learning English, we will briefly describe studies from five countries, followed by an introductory discussion of their implications and finally, the plan for this book.

Chapter Objectives

The central goal of this chapter is to introduce readers to the global phenomenon of Informal Digital Learning of English (IDLE) and its implications for classroom teaching. A subgoal is to understand the global implications of IDLE as a topic of research in five countries. A second subgoal is to introduce how IDLE promotes language learning/acquisition through five features. A third subgoal is to begin to imagine new roles for teachers and students in classrooms that integrate IDLE into their instructional practices. The final subgoal of the chapter is to introduce readers to the organization of the book. By the end of this introductory chapter, readers should be able to:

1) Describe the extent of digital technology's impact on English language education globally.
2) Describe research studies in five countries on IDLE and its implications for formal education.
3) Explain the role of five features of IDLE as a practice in learning the English language.
4) Describe ways that IDLE can positively impact formal English language education.
5) Describe the organization of the book as a map for integrating IDLE and IDLE-like practices into classroom teaching, now and into the future.

Key Words

informal digital learning of English (IDLE); learner-driven strategies; social connection; authenticity; autonomy; multimodality; ubiquity; co-learner

English Learners Today: Studies from Five Countries

Brazil

In Brazil, where Portuguese is the predominant language, students choose to study either English or Spanish in school, with English being offered in most private and some public schools, according to Bambirra (2017). Bambirra concluded that learning English is a "middle class aspiration" but also cited findings from a 2014 study by Data Popular Institute that "Brazilians believe that they do not learn English at regular schools and also that it is too expensive to pay for English private courses" (2). Overall, Brazil ranks Low (53/100 countries) on the English Proficiency Index (EF EPI 2021) and the average total score on the TOEFL iBT in 2019 was 87/120 (72.5/100; ETS 2019).

A study by Cole and Vanderplank (2016) suggests that an alternative source of English learning for many Brazilians derives increasingly from a wide range of digital resources, and that, in fact, Fully Autonomous Self-Instructed Learners (or FASILs), learn English *better* than Classroom-Trained Learners (or CTLs). Their study was a remarkable and convincing one, because unlike many studies, their participants (age 18–24) were either almost completely self-taught (having studied English in a classroom no more than a year) or they had studied at a private institute for a minimum of four years and reported not using digital media to learn English. The participants were all university students, and the two groups were matched in terms of their age, economic status, education, and professional goals.

Seven different measures of English proficiency were given to participants in both groups, including reading comprehension, vocabulary, grammar and usage, and fluency. A particular interest of the researchers concerned differences between the two groups' use of "fossilized" structures, indicating the continuing influence of Portuguese on English communication. Finally, the participants were interviewed and answered a questionnaire about their motivation and attitudes about learning English.

Cole and Vanderplank found that FASILs scored significantly higher on all measures than did CTLs. Surprisingly, although no FASILs had been taught grammar formally, their ability to find and correct grammatical errors greatly exceeded the ability of formally taught CTLs. For one specific structure, "there is/are," which is problematic for Portuguese speakers, 88.2% of FASILs demonstrated an acquired knowledge of the structure compared to 55.1% of CTLs. They concluded, "The linguistic tests showed that while FASILs often acquire the nuances of the second language, CTLs frequently persist in deficiencies in acquisition common in Brazilian English learner dialect, seemingly hitting a barrier in terms of development" (40).

When Cole and Vanderplank compared the amount of time spent learning to proficiency, they found this made a difference in proficiency for CTLs but not FASILs, suggesting that it was not the time spent on the task but the *mode of learning* that accounted for FASILs better performance. Overall, three factors contributed to the differences between the two: internal extrinsic motivation; mode of learning; and number of years spent learning, as opposed to number of hours per week. They concluded, "Taken together, these findings challenge the current orthodoxy on the limitations of naturalistic language learning and highlight the extent to which the affordances of the internet have transformed the opportunities for informal, independent, high level foreign language acquisition" (41).

France

Although the French have a long-standing reputation for not speaking English well within Europe (where on the English Proficiency Index they rank 23rd of 34 countries), worldwide they rank 28th of 100 countries, second highest among the five countries discussed here. Foreign language education begins in the primary grades, where English competes with German and Spanish. Recent education reforms have called for the expansion of English in the curriculum. However, attitudes toward the French language (e.g., as a marker of cultural identity and a focus on stringently correct pronunciation) have traditionally raised a high affective filter (Krashen 1982) for learners of any foreign language in France.

There is evidence, however, that among some French university students, resistance to communicating in English is fading. Since the early 2010s, a team of researchers led by Geoffrey Sockett and Denyze Toffoli have studied the Online Informal Learning of English (OILE) by university students across multiple universities. In a pioneering study, Toffoli and Sockett (2010) surveyed 222 non-specialist students of English at the University of Strasbourg. Of the 222 students, only six reported not regularly using the internet in English. Ninety percent reported listening to English online at least once a month and 50% reported listening at least once a week. Most of the listening occurred while watching TV and movies in English, aimed at young adults from the United States. These programs were not dubbed or subtitled and were obtained largely through peer-to-peer networks in which pirated original materials (that were not dubbed or subtitled in French) predominated. These materials differed sharply, they noted, from instructional materials, in that they were far more engaging and that the motivation to comprehend them was for pleasure rather than specifically to study and learn English.

In terms of literacy, interaction through social media predominated, with most students reporting that they read or wrote on their own and other's social media sites on a weekly or monthly basis. Few students reported problems with understanding what others wrote and agreed that they often used expressions and phrases in English they had picked up from others in their own posting online.

Sockett and Kusyk (2015) analyzed the fanfiction written by 45 computer science students in a French university. They found that students who were heavy viewers of US television series in English used more than twice as many "4-grams" (four-word phrases) commonly found in TV series as students who were infrequent viewers, and that more frequent viewers scored higher on tests of vocabulary knowledge. The students themselves also attributed much of their knowledge of, and proficiency in, English to frequent television viewing.

Republic of Korea

With its close ties to the United States and an export-driven economy, foreign-language education and especially English education is a cornerstone of the Republic of Korea's education system. English is one of three principal subjects on the College Scholastic Ability Test (CSAT), the national college admissions exam. It is the focus of many *hagwon* or cram schools, which, along with the Ministry of Education, employ thousands of native speakers yearly. Korea ranks fourth among 24 Asian countries on the English Proficiency Index but only 32nd worldwide, and there are many cultural and historical factors that impede the use of English within Korea, including a fear of "showing off" and concerns about speaking with a Korean accent (Lee 2014). Generally, it is rare to encounter a Korean English speaker outside Seoul, and then only among some youth.

Anecdotally, however, it is equally rare to enter a coffee shop or convenience store near a university in Korea and meet a young adult worker who is not fully conversational in English. Ju Seong Lee (2019) interviewed 94 students at three Korean universities. He found that the diversity of the students' online activities correlated positively with both their fluency and use of productive vocabulary when speaking. As a case study, Lee described the strategies of Su-ja, a student from a provincial capital, from a working-class background, who had received no formal English instruction beyond public school, but who had achieved 900 of 990 points on the Test of English for International Communication (TOEIC). Su-ja reported that she had engaged in 21 different online English activities in the previous six months. As a child, she learned English through playing World of Warcraft and watching movies and television shows in English. She attributed 30% of her English learning to formal education and 70% to online activities.

Morocco

English is unofficially one of three "prestige languages" in the Kingdom of Morocco, along with Standard Arabic and French, but unlike them, it has no official standing. It has been taught in *lycées*, or high schools, since the early 1970s, and is now taught for two hours per week in the last year of college, or middle school. These factors account for its rank of 74/100 on the English Proficiency Index (but sixth of thirteen African countries). Nevertheless, English is very popular in Morocco, especially among many working-class youths who prefer it to French, which is spoken primarily among the upper class in major urban centers.

Dressman (2020) interviewed 107 students specializing in English at three universities about how they had learned English. On average, the students attributed nearly 60% of their English learning to informal activities. Students from urban homes (with greater access to digital media) attributed the highest percentage (64%) and students from rural areas the least (30% for females; 50% for males). There was a significant positive relationship between students' reported percentage of informal learning and their TOEFL speaking scores, and between students' reported use of social media and watching movies in English and their TOEFL speaking scores.

Students named 18 different types of English resources, most of them internet-based, from music to informational videos to lessons on grammatical points of English on YouTube to chat rooms, social media to satellite television, and live contact with English-speaking international friends and relatives. On average, students named more than five different sources they regularly used.

In some cases, their acquisition of English was incidental and in others very deliberate. One student described watching an American TV series, *Zack and Cody*, in English with Arabic subtitles for months until one day he turned his head from the screen, and still listening, realized he understood what was being said. Another student described listening to music lyrics and attempting to write them down, then checking what she had written against the official lyrics. A third student began to watch R-rated Hollywood movies to learn swear words that he would use in "battles" with friends in the street; his pronunciation and fluency were recognized by teachers at his high school, and he became a star of his debate club. In many cases, students described a long, slow process of listening and reading subtitles in Arabic, building a repertoire of phrases through repetition and rehearsal, followed by a knowledge base that took form and rapidly grew once formal instruction began in the last year of middle or first year of high school.

Sweden

Sweden ranks fourth in the world on the English Proficiency Index and is also fourth among European nations. Study of English begins early in primary school and English is one of three subjects that students are required to pass (along with Swedish and mathematics) to graduate from compulsory education. Yet, English is not a national language in Sweden, and although Swedes may use English to communicate with non-Swedish speakers, among themselves they speak almost exclusively in Swedish, especially at home.

Among Swedish researchers, the out-of-school English activities of students are described as Extramural English (or EE; Olsson 2012; Sundqvist 2009; Sundqvist and Sylvén 2012). Olsson (2012) studied 37 teenagers in their last years of compulsory schooling (aged 15–16) in Sweden. She found that nearly all students in the school engaged in some EE, but that those who engaged in higher amounts demonstrated significantly better writing ability. Sundqvist and Sylvén studied the relationship between online gaming by 86 students of English aged 11–12 in Sweden and found that students who were frequent gamers (five or more hours per week) outperformed students who gamed only moderately, and moderate gamers outperformed non-gamers on tests of English proficiency.

It's Not "Magic": How Informal Learning Works

Research into informal language learning worldwide is no more than 15 years old and still in its early stages. However, this brief review of studies from five different countries provides compelling evidence of its effectiveness in the acquisition of English by students across a wide variety of first languages, cultures, and educational systems. In addition, these studies suggest how robust informal, primarily digital sources are in the learning process, and how varied students' processes of acquisition can be.

Digital Media Facts

- The internet is used by 4.66 billion people—59.5% of the world population.
- 4.2 billion people use social media.
- 4.15 billion access social media with a mobile device.
- 2.9 billion people use Facebook; 2.56 billion use YouTube; 2 billion use WhatsApp (owned by Meta).
- In a single minute on the internet:
  - 5,700,000 Google searches are conducted
  - 2,000,000 SnapChat messages are sent
  - 452,000 hours of Netflix are streamed
- 60% of the top 10 million websites are in English.

Source: Adapted from Statista Social Media, 2020

In some studies, such as in France and Sweden, acquisition of English seemed to be an incidental by-product of pleasure-driven activities, whereas in others such as Brazil, Korea, and Morocco, a combination of incidental and often highly deliberate strategies for learning predominated (in Morocco, some students described taking notes as they watched television or seeking online videos to learn grammar points). Cole and Vanderplank's (2016) study in Brazil suggested that informal digital learning of English (or IDLE, as coined by Lee and Dressman 2018) on its own can produce more proficient speakers of English than classroom instruction. However, in their concluding discussion they do not discount the value of classroom-based input for most learners, and the students in all other studies had acquired English through a combination of formal classroom instruction and informal engagement with English.

Why and how does informal learning of English work? Based on a survey of the research to date, the process is not as "magical" as it seems, and a range of theoretical and analytical explanations are under development. The reasons why informal learning "works" is discussed in greater detail in Chapter 2 of this book. For now, here are five main features of IDLE:

1) **Social Connection.** Opportunities for meeting and identity construction apparent from one's close circle of friends through international affinity groups such as fan clubs, gamers, and issues-oriented groups in which the lingua franca is English.
2) **Authentic, Compelling, and Varied Input.** English input that is non-didactic (not created for educational purposes), that responds to the personal interests of a learner, and that is offered in a variety of formats, topics, and platforms.
3) **Autonomy.** The opportunity for self-directed study at a pace and through processes created by the learner for specific purposes.
4) **Multimodality.** The purposeful coordination of multiple modes of input (sound, speech, visual images, motion) within a single text to create an enhanced, supralinguistic experience.
5) **Ubiquitous Access.** The ability to access and engage with input in English on demand, almost 24 hours per day and 7 days a week, often with control of the medium itself.

In summary, these five features are frequently named by informal learners as central to their learning experiences and success with English acquisition. In combination, they account for a very high percentage of the differences between formal and informal learning and are the focus of the learner-driven strategies in the methodological chapters of this book.

It's Not a Panacea, Either

As revolutionary and exciting as the research on informal digital learning of English is, it is not our position, or the position of any researchers we are aware of, that it is time to abandon classroom teaching of English or any additional language and simply turn students loose with digital media, now or in the foreseeable future. Such a move would be irresponsible and unwarranted, because although recent research demonstrates beyond a doubt that it is possible to learn English solely through engagement with digital media, it is just as certain that for many other learners a totally informal path is not feasible, either because these learners lack the motivation, the time, or the talent for learning English on their own. In most studies, even the most successful informal learners have attributed a significant portion of their learning to classroom instruction, which provided structure, order, and accountability to their learning.

Reimagining English as a Learner-Driven Activity

Rather than abandoning classroom instruction, our position in the following chapters will be that digital media and the learner-driven strategies identified in current research on informal language learning are more complementary than conflicting with formal classroom instruction and curriculum. A digitally oriented, learner-driven approach offers an organic response to many of the serious limitations of classroom instruction that have troubled English language educators for decades. These are, namely, the need for authentic communicative materials and situations; greater autonomy on the part of learners and less dependence on teachers as the source of input; a need to embed and use language within a wide variety of contexts; and severe limitations on contact time in terms of both exposure to and practice with English.

Reimagining English as a learner-driven activity will entail more, however, than adopting a few teaching ideas adapted from the practices of self-taught English learners. At a very fundamental level, it will require educators to abandon the view that English is an extremely challenging and difficult language to learn, one that requires decades of study to develop any significant level of fluency, grammatical correctness, or accuracy in pronunciation. Certainly, languages that are more closely related to English have some advantage; but research shows that even speakers whose native language is Korean or a variety of Arabic benefit dramatically from engagement with digital resources that are authentic, of a wide variety, that are highly multimodal and ubiquitous, and that offer a great deal of choice and self-direction.

Additionally, it simply is not true, as we enter the third decade of the twenty-first century, that textbooks and other classroom or teacher-developed materials are likely to be the primary sources of English language input for learners anymore, or that a highly controlled sequence of instruction is likely to achieve anything but severe boredom for students who have been spending their evenings watching *Game of Thrones* or *Breaking Bad* or *Friends* for hours on end with English captioning. Flexibility and openness to what students already know and, just as important, what they are curious about or don't fully understand are key to developing a curriculum that keeps pace with and even anticipates and challenges learners at all levels of acquisition and access to informal learning opportunities.

Your Role as Teacher

Finally, it is not true that because increasing numbers of students are learning English on their own that the profession of English education has suddenly become obsolete and that English teachers will soon be out of a job, especially if the lessons of the digital revolution in language acquisition are incorporated into formal education in meaningful, consequential ways.

The greatest challenge facing English language teachers interested in taking advantage of the revolution in digital self-directed learning of English is the shift in role this requires. In the United States, L1 English teachers are often urged to become "guides on the side" rather than "sages on the stage"; but the role we foresee for L2 English teachers is much more complex and sophisticated than that of a guide on the side of students. In this book, we won't be asking teachers to give up authority or pretend they know less about English than they do so that they can play the role of a "guide" or, in another cliché, to become "facilitators of learning." Clearly, teachers are in charge in their classrooms, and they must take charge for any integration of learner-driven strategies to be effective.

However, for authentic digital input to become *compelling* for students and to engage their full interest and learning, teachers must themselves first become participants in digital youth culture in English, which varies from country to country, and sometimes between genders, sociocultural groups, rural vs. urban areas, and so on. Teachers must take steps, in other words, to see the digital world from their students' points of view, and to build on what they learn about that world from their students. Second, the learner autonomy that characterizes informal language learning is not automatic and must be acquired. Some students in a class may already be avid learners of English informally; but many others may not, and they may need help in learning to become more autonomous and less dependent on their teacher as the source of English knowledge.

Third, conventional English language teaching tends to focus largely on written and spoken language, with only a few or occasional uses of realia or images. But informal digital learning of English is highly multimodal and requires teachers to become semiotically aware of the quality and uses of video, audio, captioning, and how their artful combination can exponentially raise students' receptive and productive capabilities. This is especially true when students are invited to compose multimodally, combining images, narration, writing, and music into video presentations—which will also require teachers to become experts not only in English but in the basics of digital production.

Finally, the ubiquity of 24/7 digital resources and learning poses great opportunities for teachers but also some challenges. Ubiquity requires teachers to be constantly aware of what new videos and social media platforms may offer, and what their students may be learning from. "Going digital" also means that teachers need to become aware and responsive to their students' uses of media and learning management systems 24 hours a day. These will need to be maintained and updated regularly for students to use them from their homes, and teachers may need to get used to students messaging them outside class or working hours and expecting responses. Some boundaries will obviously need to be set, but generally, digital learning will also require teachers to become more adaptive and responsive outside instructional time.

Summing up, the role shift that the integration of informal digital learning with formal classroom instruction requires is from deliverer of knowledge to knowledgeable co-learner. Teachers interested in taking advantage of the gifts of informal digital learning of English in their teaching will need to become much better informed about their students' online lives, and this will require both entering that world themselves and learning how to talk with their students and learn from them informally as well. In the end, teachers will still be The Boss in their classrooms; but they must become bosses who are empathetic and responsive to the realities of life and learning in the Digital Age.

Plan for the Book

This book is written for English language educators in general and especially English teachers who have an interest in adapting lessons acquired from research on the informal digital learning of English, or IDLE, into their classroom curriculum. It is not a curriculum guide or a "cookbook" with precise directions or "recipes" for teaching, but rather is written as a resource for teachers with scenarios that may be modified to fit the needs of students in specific countries and situations where English is taught as a second or additional language. The book is divided into three main sections:

- **Part I: Introduction: Informal Digital Learning of English and Its Implications.** Introduces and provides background on IDLE, its characteristics, and its complementarity with formal classroom teaching.

  Chapter 1: The Age of IDLE and the IDLE Age: Introduction and Plan for the Book. Introduces IDLE as a research and pedagogical activity, its implications for classroom teaching and for the role of teachers, and the plan for the book.

  Chapter 2: Seeing and Hearing the English All Around Us. This chapter describes who informal digital learners of English (IDLERs) are and provides a more detailed discussion of each of the four characteristics of IDLE discussed in Chapter 1.

  Chapter 3: Complementarity: Tradition and Innovation in English Learning and Teaching. Discusses the opportunities and challenges of integrating IDLE with traditional, conventional language instruction.

- **Part II: IDLE in the Classroom.** Provides concrete, hands-on teaching ideas based on the major types of digital media that students learn from worldwide. Each chapter focuses on one digital medium and includes a discussion of that medium's opportunities and challenges for learning and adaptation, followed by three scenarios in which a fictional teacher at the middle, secondary, or university level adapts a digital format to their classroom instruction. Each of these scenarios also includes a narrative of the instruction, a sequenced plan, and rubrics for evaluating outcomes. The activities of the scenario are also referenced to the TESOL Technology Standards Framework and to the Common European Framework of Reference for Languages (CEFR), and each scenario concludes with a discussion of possible modification or extension of the activities.

  Chapter 4: Songs, Video, and Vlogging. Begins with a review of why and how video and music promote language acquisition before moving into discussions of how teachers can extend these affordances through watching and then making vlogs. Additional topics focus on shooting and editing videos and on how to protect the privacy of students online.

  Chapter 5: Audiobooks, E-Books, and Podcasting. Describes opportunities for learning by pairing of audiobooks with print books and podcasts with their transcripts. Downloadable audiobooks in the public domain can be paired with print versions of the audiobooks from open online sources. A wide range of podcasts with transcripts are also downloadable for simultaneous listening/reading.

The chapter discusses the possibilities for students to make their own audiobook recordings and podcasts using open-source editors.

Chapter 6: Social Networking and Ethical/Safety Considerations. Acknowledges that a powerful source of language input is through social media. The attractions and affordances of these must be weighed against their inherent danger to students' safety and wellbeing. The chapter discusses these issues and ways of making social media "safe" without completely eliminating their "coolness" for learners.

Chapter 7: Games and Other Virtual Learning Environments. Discusses the merits and uses of gamification and online language learning through video games and virtual reality sites such as Second Life. The merits of nonformal learning programs like Babbel, Duolingo, and Rosetta Stone as additions to language programs are also considered.

Chapter 8: Mobile Apps: Translation, Vocabulary, and Grammar. Reviews the rise of mobile apps for translation and practice of vocabulary, grammar, and other structural components of language learning. The chapter includes a discussion of how mobile applications can complement and add innovation to traditional curriculum and instruction.

- **Part III: Language Curriculum in the Digital Age.** Focuses on general language curriculum rather than on individual classroom lessons and units, from the perspective of conventional educational practice, with special focus on changes in teaching during the Covid-19 pandemic. Chapters 9–11 begin with three portraits of teachers and their students at middle, secondary, and university levels and include teaching scenarios after a discussion of research and pedagogy.

  Chapter 9: Beyond the Pandemic: Online and Flipped Learning. Marks a shift from a focus on learner-driven strategies to the integration of IDLE-like uses of technology in the wake of the pandemic. A specific focus of this chapter is on the merits and pitfalls of online learning and hybrid "flipped" learning.

  Chapter 10: From IDLE to Academic Literacy. Presents ways to bridge the gap between the colloquial and informal uses of English and more formal, academic modes of language use in light of the pandemic. The focus of this chapter is on complementarity and overlap between informal and formal practices.

  Chapter 11: Curriculum, Assessment, and Professional Development in the Age of IDLE. Addresses mandated curricula and the need for test preparation that teachers face in many nations with centralized curriculum and high-stakes tests. This chapter draws from the strategies of all previous chapters to demonstrate how learner-driven strategies can enhance mandated curricula and preparation for national exams.

  Chapter 12: Autonomous, Informal Learning and the Future of English Education. Considers the future of English language education in light of the pandemic, advances in digital technologies for communication, and developments in the role of English as a global language. A special focus of the chapter is on the future of English teaching as a profession.

Let's Discuss

1) What is your experience with IDLE? If you are an educator who learned English as an additional language; what do you remember of your exposure to and engagement with English outside of school? Does your experience relate to recent research findings about how students around the world are lea rning English digitally and informally today?

2) If you are a current English teacher, have you discussed with your students how they may be learning English outside your classroom? Have you noticed signs of informal learning in your students' writing or speaking? Have you considered incorporating, or have you already begun to incorporate, digital resources into your teaching that complement or build on the informal digital learning of English?

References

Bambirra, Raquel. "Motivation to Learn English as a Foreign Language in Brazil – Giving Voice to a Group of Students at a Public Secondary School." *Linguagem em (Dis)curso* 17, no. 2 (May–August 2017): 215–236. https://doi.org/10.1590/1982-4017-170204-5316.

Benati, Alessandro. "Grammar-Translation Method." In *The TESOL Encyclopedia of English Language Teaching*, 1–5, 2018. https://doi.org/10.1002/9781118784235.eelt0153.

Cole, Jason, and Robert Vanderplank. "Comparing Autonomous and Class-Based Learners in Brazil: Evidence for the Present-Day Advantages of Informal, Out-of-Class Learning." *System* 61 (July 2016): 31–42. https://doi.org/10.1016/j.system.2016.07.007.

Dressman, Mark. "Informal English Learning among Moroccan Youth." In The Handbook of *Informal Language Learning*, edited by Mark Dressman and Randall William Sadler, 303–318, Mark Dressman and Randall William Sadler, 303–318., Hoboken, NJ: John Wiley & Sons, Inc., 2020. https://doi.org/10.1002/9781119472384.ch20.

EF EPI. *EF English Proficiency Index: A Ranking of 112 Countries and Regions by English Skills*. 2021. www.ef.com/epi.

Eschner, Kat. "The Roots of Computer Code Lie in Telegraph Code." *Smithsonian Magazine* (October 30, 2019). https://www.tweentribune.com/article/tween56/roots-computer-code-lie-telegraph-code/#:~:text=%22Baudot's%20Printing%20Telegraph%20was%20an, %2C%20tablets%20and%20mobiles%20today.%22.

ETS. "TOEFL iBT® Test and Score Data Summary 2019." 2019. www.ets.org/toefl.

Healey, Debra, Volker Hegelheimer, Phil Hubbard, Sophie Ioannou-Georgiou, Greg Kessler, and Paige Ware. *TESOL Technology Standards Framework*. TESOL. Alexandria, VA: Teachers of English to Speakers of Other Languages, Inc, 2008. http://www.tesol.org.

Krashen, Stephen D. "Acquiring a Second Language." *World Englishes* 1, no. 3 (1982): 97–101.

Lee, Claire. 2014. "[Eye on English] Complex Perceptions of Korean English-Speakers." *The Korea Herald*. http://www.koreaherald.com/view.php?ud=20140416001223.

Lee, Ju Seong. "Quantity and Diversity of Informal Digital Learning of English." *Language Learning & Technology* 23, no. 1 (February 2019): 114–126. https://doi.org/10125/44675.

Lee, Ju Seong, and Mark Dressman. "When Idle Hands Make an English Workshop: Informal Digital Learning of English and Language Proficiency." *TESOL Quarterly* 52, no. 2 (November 2018): 435–445. https://doi.org/10.1002/tesq.422.

Menárguez, Ana Torres. "Defenders of Bilingual Education in Spain: 'It's a Mistake to Think that Students Will Speak English like They Do Spanish'." *EL PAÍS*, 2021. https://english. elpais.com/society/2021-07-14/defenders-of-bilingual-education-in-spain-its-a-mistake-to-think-that-students-will-speak-english-like-they-do-spanish.html.

Nagarajan, Nisthula. "Educating Graduate Students for a Digital-Driven Future." *Khaleej Times*, 2021. https://www.khaleejtimes.com/business-technology-review/educating-graduate-students-for-a-digital-driven-future.

Olsson, Eva. *"Everything I Read on the Internet Is in English": On the Impact of Extramural English on Swedish 16-Year-Old Pupils' Writing Proficiency*. Göteborg: Institutet för svenska som andraspråk, Institutionen för svenska språket, Göteborgs universitet, 2012.

Richards, Jack C. *Communicative Language Teaching Today*. New York, NY: Cambridge University Press, 2005.

Sockett, Geoffrey, and Meryl Kusyk. "From Informal Resource Usage to Incidental Language Acquisition: Language Uptake from Online Television Viewing in English." *ASp* 62 (2012): 45–65. https://doi.org/10.4000/asp.3104.

Sockett, Geoffrey, and Meryl Kusyk. "Online Informal Learning of English: Frequency Effects in the Uptake of Chunks of Language from Participation in Web-Based Activities." *Usage-Based Perspectives on Second Language Learning* (2015): 153–178. https://doi.org/10.1515/9783110378528-009.

Statista. "Social Media—Statistics & Facts." 2022. https://www.statista.com/topics/1164/social-networks/#dossierKeyfigures.

Sundqvist, Pia. "Extramural English Matters: Out-of-School English and Its Impact on Swedish Ninth Graders' Oral Proficiency and Vocabulary." diss. Karlstad University, 2009. http://kau.diva-portal.org/smash/record.jsf?pid=diva2:275141.

Sundqvist, Pia, and Liss Kerstin Sylvén. "Gaming as Extramural English L2 Learning and L2 Proficiency among Young Learners." *ReCALL* 24, no. 3 (September 2012): 302–321. https://doi.org/10.1017/s095834401200016x.

Toffoli, Denyze, and Geoffrey Sockett. "How Non-Specialist Students of English Practice Informal Learning Using Web 2.0 Tools." *ASp* 58 (2010): 125–144. https://doi.org/10.4000/asp.1851.

Tzu-ti, Huang. "Taipei Adopts 6 Approaches to Promoting English Education." *Taiwan News*, 2021. https://www.taiwannews.com.tw/en/news/4140734.

UNICEF. 2020. "Education and Covid-19." https://data.unicef.org/topic/education/covid-19.

World101. "Two Hundred Years of Global Communications." Council on Foreign Relations, n.d. https://world101.cfr.org/global-era-issues/globalization/two-hundred-years-global-communications.

2

Seeing and Hearing the English All Around Us

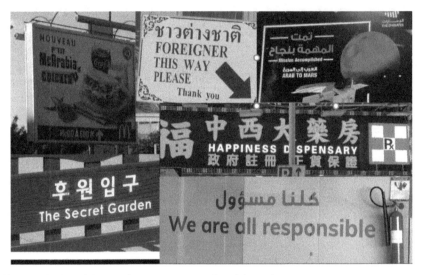

English co-mingles with many languages across the globe today.

Introduction

In Chapter 1, we introduced Informal Digital Learning of English (IDLE) as a global phenomenon with the potential to address many of the most persistent problems for the teaching and learning of English in formal classrooms, especially the lack of authentic input and opportunities to learn and practice outside of class. In this chapter we take a deeper look into the growth of digital communications, who Informal Digital Learners of English (or IDLERs) are, and how they use digital media to learn and use English for a variety of purposes.

We also review research that challenges three popular beliefs about adolescents' and young adults' use of digital media, explore digital media's dynamics, and look at how it enables student learning. Finally, we suggest three activities that will challenge readers to explore their own use of digital media and the internet.

English Language Learning in the Digital Age: Learner-Driven Strategies for Adolescents and Young Adults, First Edition. Mark Dressman, Ju Seong Lee, and Laurent Perrot.
© 2023 John Wiley & Sons Ltd. Published 2023 by John Wiley & Sons Ltd.

Chapter Objectives

The central goal of this chapter is to develop a research-based understanding of the role of digital telecommunications in English language learning today. A first subgoal is to understand the role that smartphone technology plays in the informal English language learning of students, as well as how widespread the phenomenon is globally. A second subgoal is to consider the positive and negative impact of digital telecommunications and especially social media for youth, in contrast to messages in popular journalism and media. A final subgoal is to understand the role of digital technology in the informal learning of English for individual learners. By the end of this chapter, readers should be able to:

1) Describe the advance of telecommunications technology in the last 40 years and its implications for English language learning.
2) Explain how the growth of smartphones and 4G technology has contributed to informal language learning.
3) Describe the role of English as a global medium of communication via social media and entertainment.
4) Describe issues in the sociology of adolescence and the rise of digital media, especially social media.
5) Discuss three common beliefs in the media about the relationship between youth culture and digital media.
6) Describe the "typical" informal digital learner of English (IDLE).
7) Explain the efficacy of digital media in promoting informal English language learning through five features of IDLE.
8) Consider three activities to develop an understanding of the power of IDLE within the English language classroom.

Key Words

IDLE/IDLERs; global youth culture; digital apprentice; authenticity; multimodality; autonomy; ubiquitous access

---

Telecommunications and the English Language in the Early Twenty-first Century

If the field of English language education has not yet fully embraced the digital revolution, it is likely because that revolution has come so suddenly that its full impact is just recently beginning to be grasped. Worldwide, the internet and satellite television have been present since the early to mid-1990s, but in the early years, satellite offerings were limited and limits in bandwidth often prevented the easy exchange of audio or video, often allowing only text messages to be sent. In its first fifteen years of practical use, the internet was also largely computer-based and expensive, requiring users to connect via internet cafes, at workplaces, or for the fortunate, at home over an often very slow ADSL (telephone) connection. The advent of Wi-Fi in the early 2000s expanded the ease and locations for connection but until 2010, even in the developed world, signals were often weak and unreliable, especially in public spaces.

If you are under 30 years of age, you may not be aware of how very recent the use of smartphones is. Early mobile phones allowed texting and audio exchange but little more. Not until the introduction of the iPhone in 2007 did the internet become fully available, and it was then only possible with a strong 3G connection. LTE (4G) connectivity was not introduced until 2011 and was at first expensive and available only to a privileged few. In most parts of the world—even in Western Europe, North America, or Australasia—relatively inexpensive data plans and reliable, strong connectivity to the internet almost anywhere, anytime, have only existed since 2015 or later in many locations (Galazzo 2022).

Advances in Instructional and Communications Technology (ICT)

For many practicing educators over the age of 30, ourselves included, the promises of the digital revolution for teaching and learning have always seemed something just on the horizon—something that was "coming" and that we should be preparing for, but that was also in reality always out of reach due to limitations in infrastructure or budgets, or lack of content, or restrictions on use in school; and most often due to glitches that prevented things from ever working properly in classrooms when we needed them to.

This was all true "back in the day" (as recently as 2019)—but not now. To understand how rapidly educational opportunities are expanding and why the reasons for dismissing the role of digital technology in teaching and learning are fading away, here are some recent statistics and reports from the International Telecommunication Union (ITU 2020a and 2020b), which is the United Nations specialized agency for global ICT statistics. Between 2005 and 2019, use of the internet increased by 373%. In 2019, when the world population was estimated at 7.674 billion, more than half (3.952 billion or 51.49%), were using the internet, and over the previous 14 years, usage increased on average over 208 million users per year. The greatest increases in the period were in (Sub-Saharan) Africa (1,573%) and in Arab states (900%), but in Asia and the Pacific and the Commonwealth of Independent States (all the states of the former Soviet Union) the rate of growth was over 500% and at least doubled in Europe and North America.

It might seem, if only 51.49% of the world is using the internet, that many people are still without that experience or its benefits. However, the total population includes many children and elderly people. In 2019, only 65.252% of the world population, or 5.007 billion people, were between 15 and 64 years of age. The number of youth and working adults who use the internet was 78.924% of that age bracket, or roughly 4 of 5 individuals, age 15–64, and in many parts of the world, including the Americas, Europe, the Arab States, and the Asian Pacific, a likely much higher ratio.

Smartphone Technology

The growth of internet usage worldwide has not come through the expanding use of desktops or laptops in relatively fixed locations but instead by the exponential growth of smartphone access and ownership. In 2020, there were 8.152 billion mobile phone subscriptions in the world—more than one per person globally. Of these, 6.575 were LTE (4G) subscriptions capable of streaming video and audio. This is an astounding figure because it approaches, at least in theory, high-quality internet coverage for nearly all populated areas of the planet. The growth of LTE connectivity is especially impressive in developing countries and regions of the world. Between 2005 and 2020, subscriptions more than doubled worldwide, but in (Sub-Saharan) Africa they increased by a factor of more than 5, in the Arab states by more than 3, and in Asia and the Pacific by more than twice. The World Advertising Research Center (WARC) in 2021 estimated that by 2023, 75% of internet users would access the internet primarily through a mobile device (McDonald 2021).

How Mobile Phones Have Changed Life in Africa

Around the world, mobile phones have made life more convenient, but in many parts of Africa since 2010, they have opened up opportunities for development and growth that never existed before (Ogunlesi and Busari 2012). Here are seven sectors where mobile phones are revolutionizing life in Africa today:

1) **Banking and Money Transfer.** Purchases, payments, and exchange online are safer, quicker, and make economic growth possible.
2) **Political and Cultural Activism.** From the Arab Spring to elections across the continent, governments are now much more accountable than before.
3) **Education.** Opportunities for basic education, not only English, are now available in remote areas, around the clock.
4) **Culture and Entertainment.** Mobile phones make it possible for people to record their own music and videos and share these locally and globally.
5) **Disaster Management.** Mobile phones make it possible to instantly communicate and update information about ongoing floods, earthquakes, famines, and other disasters, increasing responsiveness and coordination of resources.
6) **Agriculture.** Mobile phones allow farmers to be informed and communicate about weather conditions, crop prices, and micro-insurance.
7) **Health.** In remote areas where health care is scarce, mobile phones allow for consultation, information, and to check the authenticity of medications.

Among youth (ages 15–24), 69.4% used the internet worldwide in 2019. The percentage of youth using the internet was highest in developed countries (97.6%) compared to developing (65.6%) and least developed (38.3%) countries, and regionally was highest in Europe (96.2%), followed by the Americas (89.9%), the Commonwealth of Independent States (84.5%), Asia and the Pacific (70.3%), the Arab states (67.2%), and (Sub-Saharan) Africa (39.6%). By gender, usage was roughly equivalent (but slightly higher for males than females) in developing countries and in Europe, the Americas, and the Commonwealth of Independent States; however, it was significantly higher for males than females elsewhere.

Globally, smartphone usage is very widespread among youth. A survey conducted by the Pew Research Center found that among 17 countries with the most advanced economies (e.g., the United States, Japan, the United Kingdom, South Korea, Russia, Canada, Australia), at least 90% of individuals aged 18–34 owned or had access to a smartphone (Silver 2019). Smartphone ownership for 18–34-year-olds in countries with emerging economies was lower and more variable: Brazil (85%); Philippines (74%); Indonesia

(66%); Kenya (51%); India (37%). However, in these countries, smartphone ownership among young adults rapidly increased between 2013 and 2018: in Brazil by 62%; in the Philippines by 53%; in Indonesia by 49%; in Kenya by 26%; and in India by 21%. In nearly every country surveyed, the 19–34 age group led in ownership and the pace of increase in smartphone acquisition.

The astronomic increase of LTE (4G) availability and smartphone use worldwide since around 2010, especially among youth, has produced changes in media distribution and the number of ways in which people access not only websites and social media but television/video and audio (music; podcasts). Nielsen (2021a), a multinational group based in the United States and a major source of data on viewership and advertising, noted that although linear (conventional) television remains the primary source of video worldwide, its share of the market has decreased by 2–3% annually, to be replaced by viewing on a wide variety of other devices, such as smartphones, tablets, and laptops. In its video report, "The State of Global Media" (Nielsen 2021b), it noted "five tectonic shifts" in media: 1) a strong increase in online advertising, primarily on Google/YouTube, Facebook/Instagram, and Amazon; 2) a shift in viewing to subscription services and a focus on the purchasing of new hardware (i.e., mobile devices) by consumers; 3) the introduction of "influencers," or personalities to market goods; 4) a shift in social media from consumption to production of content; and 5) a new focus on privacy and embedded systems within social media for controlling privacy. The report noted that television viewership was increasingly digitized and occurred largely through streaming.

Finally, let us note that all the data described trends in digital communications prior to the recent introduction of 5G technology, with its promises of much higher performance and greater efficiency (see Chapter 12 for a discussion of 5G's potential).

English on the Internet

According to Statista (2021), English is by far the most widely used language on the internet, with 25.9% of users, followed by Chinese (Mandarin, 19.4%), Spanish (7.9%), and Arabic (5.2%). In 2021, ten languages accounted for 76.9% of internet usage. The share of the internet in English as a percentage of total usage is declining, but English remains its lingua franca, and video and music streaming are overwhelmingly in English. English was also the most common gaming language (33.56%) followed by Simplified Chinese (30.12%), Russian (9.46%), and Spanish (4.93%). According to IMDB (2019), the 25 most-watched television series in the world are all in English and captioned in English, with subtitles available in a wide variety of languages. English is so popular among gamers in South Korea that at Seoul National University, students wrote a manual for players of the game Starcraft to teach them English through the game (Lee 2018).

Summing Up

To summarize:

1) The growth of LTE (4G) technology and smartphone ownership by youth worldwide has been exponential in recent years.
2) These technologies will soon provide nearly every student in the developed and developing world with the capacity to both consume and produce text, video, and audio for a limitless audience.

3) English remains the lingua franca of the internet and by an overwhelming margin the first language of the most popular games, video series, and audio downloads.

Much of this content is free, such as videos streamed through YouTube, and many Massive Multiplayer Online Role-Playing Games (MMORPGs), while most television series and movies are accessed through relatively inexpensive subscription services or are pirated (we do not condone or recommend this practice).

For educators of English as a foreign, second, or additional language this means that very shortly nearly all students will have access to English language input that is:

1) Socially engaging
2) Authentic and compelling to watch, and whose content is varied enough to catch and hold any interest
3) Multimodal, combining images, text, movement, and audio in engaging and meaningful ways
4) Ubiquitous, meaning that it can be viewed on a wide range of devices on demand, at any time of day or night
5) Comprehensible at almost any level, through translation apps and captioning (in English) or subtitling (in many languages), allowing students to autonomously both *use and acquire* English on their own.

Youth Culture and Digital Media

In *Technology and the Global Adolescent* (2020), Judith Gibbons and Katelyn Poelker surveyed research on recent use of digital technologies, especially smartphones, the internet, and social media, on adolescent life and development worldwide. One critical point of their review was that although digital media are often held responsible in the popular press as the *cause* of problems with bullying, low self-esteem, and other social ills among adolescents, digital media are more typically a new medium, or pathway, for problems that already existed in the population prior to the coming of smartphones and the internet. These problems, in other words, are not new; adolescents have engaged in bullying and circulating rumors, and some but by no means all have also suffered from problems with body image, low self-esteem, and depression throughout history.

Additional research supports this view. Shankleman, Hammond, and Jones (2021) conducted a meta-analysis of 19 qualitative research studies and found four ways in which the use of social media promotes adolescent well-being, but also noted that internet use could be problematic for some youth. A survey of adolescents in 29 countries (Boer et al. 2020) found that "intense" users of the internet reported more support from friends than non-intense users. They distinguished "intense" users (who could refrain from internet use when required) from "problematic" users (who felt compelled to be online constantly, regardless of circumstances) and found that problematic users did report lower well-being. Similarly, Kelly et al. (2018) found that greater use of social media (more than three hours per day) was associated with higher rates of depression, especially for girls in the United Kingdom, but it was unclear whether the association was causative. Finally, Rutledge, Dennen, and Bagdy (2019) acknowledged concerns about the dangers of social media but also found that the adolescents they surveyed understood these dangers and knew how to deal with them. They concluded, "Our study suggests that the kids are doing just fine" (23).

One area that digital media are largely responsible for is the development, according to Gibbons and Poelker, of a "global youth culture," based not only on shared holidays (e.g., Valentine's Day and Halloween) and the development of affinity groups around music or issues, but also on core values. They cited surveys and interviews conducted with thousands of adolescents worldwide, whose "most important goals were not materialistic but instead the desire to do good. They were especially concerned with addressing climate change and economic inequity ... adolescents most valued kindness, honesty, and prosocial behavior in the ideal person; having a lot of money or being sexy were rated as much less important" (Gibbons and Poelker 2020, 21).

Digital media and global youth culture also play an important role in identity formation. Gibbons and Poelker cited research noting that as they engage with digital media globally, youth are often confronted by values that may conflict with those of their families and traditional cultures and religions. In these cases, the most radical options were to reject traditional values and assimilate or to reject the values of the global culture and adhere more strongly to traditional values, or to feel marginalized by either option. However, the most common approach was to integrate what may be acceptable or not in direct conflict with tradition. In this "hybrid" approach and following the work of Goffman (1959) on identity, youth opt to play one role and adopt one identity in one situation, such as when gaming online, but to adopt another very different identity and set of behaviors in the presence of friends or in public, or at family gatherings. Gibbons and Poelker noted that digital media may play a vital role in developing a strong sense of self in relation to others, and in exploring and experimenting with identity safely. This is particularly true in the case of youth who are socially marginalized, such as among the LGBTQ community, those living with disabilities, or youth who are oppressed ethnic minorities, refugees, or orphans and seeking support and a platform for (often anonymous) self-expression.

Another way that digital media have affected youth culture is through the capacity to mobilize and organize for civic engagement quickly, especially to raise awareness of global issues like global warming. Gibbons and Poelker cited incidents of social advocacy (e.g., Malala's online advocacy for girls' education in Pakistan) as well as studies of how youth organize themselves to share information, to spread awareness, and sometimes to raise money for important causes. For example, in Moroccan public universities, students within a single course often create a Facebook page that is used to share information about class meetings, assignments, and the scheduling of exams and other events in lieu of formal university-based learning management systems. The effectiveness of youth mobilization globally is such that many governments now seek to monitor and occasionally censor the activities of youth online as they mobilize to raise awareness or to protest government policies.

Not surprisingly, Gibbons and Poelker concluded that the effects of digital media and the internet on adolescents globally are "complex" (65). The opportunity for immediate access to an unprecedented amount of information (and misinformation) and to connect with others instantly, driven by one's own beliefs and desires, poses equally unprecedented opportunities for connection and learning that could be very positive but also dangerous. However, again, it also seems there is no retreat for youth or adults from digital media in the world, and in the case of language learning, the benefits would seem to far outweigh the dangers, and even to provide resourceful educators with opportunities for teaching about the ethical and productive use of digital media. This is a problem that can best be addressed through education rather than by ignoring or denying its effects, or worse yet, trying to ban or prohibit use, which only increases media's attraction and effects.

Challenging Three Common Beliefs

Although, as Gibbons and Poelker (2020) noted, research on adolescents' use of digital media typically provides a relatively positive view of its social and individual benefits, a quite different view is presented in the popular media and through online searches. Google "adolescent smartphone use" or "adolescents and social media" and thousands if not millions of links appear, nearly all of them suggesting that the world's youth would be much happier, much healthier, and much better educated without the internet.

Our investigation of peer-reviewed research on the subject, in line with the review of Gibbons and Poelker, suggests a very different view from Google searches or the popular media. With respect to language acquisition, we cite research evidence that challenges three commonly held and frequently expressed beliefs about adolescents and their use of digital media.

Media Coverage of Adolescents' Mobile Use

Although there are clearly both positive and negative aspects to teenagers' use of mobile phones, to read about this on the internet is to become convinced that mobile phones are the source of nothing but danger, disease, and disaster for teenagers today, especially but not only in the United States. Here are a few of the headlines we found in our research:

- Have Smartphones Destroyed a Generation?
- Teenage Cell Phone Addiction: Are You Worried About Your Child?
- The Teenagers So Addicted to Cellphones (in South Korea) They're Going to Detox Centers
- What Do Mobile Phones Do to Teenage Brains?
- Teenagers' Sleep Quality and Mental Health at Risk Over Late-Night Mobile Phone Use
- Almost a Third of Teenagers Sleep with Their Phones, Survey Finds
- New Study Reveals More Teens in Mexico Feel "Addicted" to Their Mobile Devices Than Teens in Other Countries Surveyed
- Can Too Much Cell Phone Usage Hurt Your Family Bond?
- Teens Around the World Are Lonelier Than a Decade Ago. The Reason May Be Smartphones

---

Belief #1: Adolescents use social media and the internet only for recreation. Most studies of adolescent media use are conducted by sociologists or communications researchers interested in media consumption and identity formation. For this reason, hedonistic, pleasure-seeking uses of the internet are often foregrounded in these studies, which then make headlines in the media itself. However, studies conducted by researchers in education tell a very different story.

Rutledge, Dennen, and Bagdy (2019) in the United States, for example, surveyed 48 students in a Florida high school and interviewed 37 students and 18 administrators and teachers. They found that although both adults and students used social media for both recreational and informational purposes, adults assumed that the students were only using social media to chat with friends or entertain themselves. The students told a very different story: 70% reported making extensive and intentional use of the internet for self-regulated learning entirely outside of learning taking place in school. Uses included knowledge building and hobbies; college planning; building knowledge on future careers; entrepreneurship; and networking with communities, such as sharing poetry and short stories or connecting with people in Germany interested in videos.

Pires, Masanet, and Scolari (2021) surveyed 1633 teenagers (aged 11–19) and interviewed 311 of them in eight countries globally about their uses of YouTube. They described five categories of use: radiophonic (listening to music and podcasts); televisual (being entertained and informed); productive (creating personal content for sharing); social (co-producing; commenting on other videos); and educative (learning from Massive Open Online Courses [MOOCs]; watching tutorials). They described teenagers' use of YouTube as very active and purposeful. Many of them used the search engine on YouTube before using Google, preferring the audio and visual aspects of YouTube to the primarily print-based format of other search engines. Similarly, Tso (2019) surveyed 30 high school students in Hong Kong about their use of social media in learning English and found that 90% reported using YouTube for this purpose. Tso also found that teachers reported using YouTube and other social media extensively in their planning for lessons, but they disapproved of students' use of it, arguing that YouTube and social media in general would lead to students writing ungrammatically and using slang. However, students disagreed, noting that they could distinguish among registers in the use of English in social media.

Many other studies have also reported students' use of social media and the internet educationally, both for formal school subjects and informally for personal purposes. Tan and Kim (2019) presented two case studies of students in southeast Asian country who used social media to connect with others in order to teach themselves photography and marketing. These cases "suggested that the adolescents' pursuit of their passions on online affinity spaces gave rise to intellectual friendships and the development of personal pedagogies" (196). Jurkovič (2019) found that Slovene university students used their smartphones to learn English but they used social media to chat with friends in Slovene. Elias and Lemish (2008) and Li, Snow, and White (2015), in Israel and the United States respectively, found that immigrant adolescents frequently used the internet both to stay in touch with their original culture and friends and as a source of English language learning in their new country.

Belief #2: Anyone born since the development of the internet is a "digital native."
The term "digital native" was coined by Prensky (2001) to describe individuals born before 1984 who presumably "pick up" knowledge of technology and how to use the internet "naturally," just as humans acquire language as children, through exposure and interaction. Since 2001, the term has become a mass media cliché, used to divide current generations from those born before 1984 and explain the relatively greater attraction of youth to the internet than (some) adults.

However, research evidence suggests otherwise. Gibbons and Poelker (2020) were highly critical of the concept of a digital native, citing multiple research studies showing that skill in using the internet as a tool varies widely among youth, depending on the quality and quantity of access youth have, and also on the purposes to which they put digital technology. Adolescents who blog or create content for broadcast, for example, have a very different and likely more elaborated set of skills than students who primarily chat with friends on social media or use Google or YouTube to search for information. Among content creators, knowledge may be limited to specific platforms or the software they use, and, among others, to specific websites rather than to the entirety of the World Wide Web. Based on a study of two schools in Barcelona, Masanet, Guerrero-Pico, and Establés (2019) argued that the term "digital apprentice" better describes the learning *about* digital technology and how to use it that youth acquire while using online media for a wide variety of purposes.

These findings are critical for teachers interested in using digital media instructionally. It cannot be assumed that, because students are "digital natives," they will automatically know how to use all digital media to produce content or learn from it efficiently or effectively. Although many students may be familiar with or learn new technologies quickly, instruction in the media itself must therefore be included as part of the assignments and learning activities within a classroom setting.

Belief #3: The digital world and the "real" world are largely separate domains. An implication of the discourse around "digital natives" is that the digital world and the "real" world are two different places, in which people live two different lives: a life of work, family, and obligation in the "real" world, and a life of pleasure seeking and open relationships in the digital world. However, research on adolescents' use of digital media and the internet shows a high degree of integration and overlap between the two, in which adolescents use social media to connect with family and friends from school *and* with others they have never met in person, and to play video games in fantasy worlds *and* to do research for both school assignments and self-initiated projects and learning.

Perhaps the assumption of a digital world separated from the physical one is an artifact of older adults' lingering habits from the days before the internet or even computers. As recently as the first decade of this century, it was possible to imagine living in the world without also going online, and so that separation was conceivable. But today, and especially since the Covid-19 pandemic, that division largely no longer exists. Online mass education has eliminated that divide for many societies, along with online shopping and the premier of first-run movies on subscription services like Netflix, Viki Rakuten, and Amazon Prime, and music streaming through services like Spotify. Even in academia, library research is more likely to be digital, with articles and books downloaded from Google Scholar far more often than they are located and copied or borrowed in hard copy (nearly all the references for this chapter, for example, were downloaded).

This integration of digital and real-life worlds has enormous implications for education in general and for language learning, especially English, yet we will note in conclusion that in most studies teachers and administrators were unaware of the extent of this shift in their own or their students' life worlds. With this paradox in mind, we now move in this and the next chapters to a more focused and detailed discussion of the potential of digital media for learning English, not only informally but through recognition and adaptation, in formal classroom learning as well.

Who Are Informal Digital Learners of English (IDLERs)?

Based on studies from a wide range of cultural and geographic regions, Informal Digital Learning of English (IDLE) appears to be a global phenomenon and one that embraces all genders, nearly all economic levels, and the rural–urban divide. Access and privilege, however, create clear differences in the quality and quantity of acquisition or learning. During the pandemic, UNICEF (2020) reported that two-thirds of youth under the age of 25 did not have internet access at home, meaning a computer with a DSL (telephone line) or fiber optic connection in their residences, and so were hampered from attending school online. The one-third of the population that had home internet access was largely in the developed world. Within the developing world, youth in cities typically also have more access than youth in rural areas, and in some countries, poverty and a lack of electricity also prevent access to basic digital communication services, such as satellite television. The use of smartphones does provide access to the internet for many youths without land-based connectivity, but as noted previously, there are slight differences in access for males and females in Europe, the Americas, and the Commonwealth of Independent States (CIS) but significant elsewhere.

The question of prevalence, or how many youths actively acquire English informally, is more difficult to answer because no formal statistics exist for the phenomenon globally. However, surveys of IDLE conducted by independent university researchers in Europe, North Africa, Brazil, and East Asia, and North America suggest that it is a quite common feature of students' learning of English, although it is often unrecognized, even by the students themselves. Anecdotally, we have spoken over the years with many university students who do not have English as a first language who, on prompting, tell us that their first and perhaps most engaging and powerful exposure to English was through a television series, a movie, or a song they heard in English in their early adolescence.

Rather than divide the English-learning population into two contrasting groups, Informal vs. Formal Learners, we note that nearly all learners have had some exposure to English both informally and formally, in school. We therefore suggest that the informal–formal distinction is better described as a continuum, with two main factors, exposure and engagement, determining the quality and quantity of outcomes for learners. Exposure on this continuum refers to the frequency and quality of English input learners receive. On the formal end, learners who receive more and better-quality instruction in school than through media are likely to learn English more formally. Engagement on this continuum refers to how active and deliberate learners are in the classroom or informally. At the informal end, learners who actively watch, listen, and/or interact with others through English, possibly taking notes or practicing words and phrases they have acquired, are likely to learn more English informally than those whose engagement is more incidental and limited by time or effort.

Four Portraits of IDLERs from Morocco

IDLERs in Morocco, on the northwest coast of Africa, provide an interesting cross-section of the factors influencing the acquisition of English informally and, equally important, their frequent complementarity with formal instruction. Morocco is a developing country with a relatively strong telecommunications system, a stratified socioeconomic system, and many major cities, mid-sized towns, and rural villages. English is not a national language, but it is widely taught from the last year of middle school through high school, and it is one of the most popular subjects of study in public universities there. For these reasons, Morocco is an interesting microcosm of the demographic and educational conditions behind the rise of IDLE.

Here are four portraits of IDLERs in Morocco, taken from a recent research study (Dressman 2020a). These learners are actual individuals, although their names have been changed. They were selected from a group of 117 university students and represent a range of learners along the continuum of informal–formal learning of English in Morocco.

Missed Opportunities. Salwa Bouchra grew up in a major Moroccan city where her father worked as a laborer in a factory and her mother worked at home. She attended public high school in the same city and first became interested in English as a student there. She also described watching English-language movies on television with subtitles in Arabic. Salwa's family did not have a computer or internet connection at home, but she did have a smartphone, which she said she "used a lot" to chat with friends on Facebook and WhatsApp, but usually in Arabic. She also had an app on her smartphone for translation and she named Avril Lavigne as her favorite singer. She used YouTube to listen to Lavigne and other music in English.

Salwa said that she did not begin to study English before her classes at school. She was interested in English because it was a global language and she said she might like to teach it. She attributed 30% of her knowledge of English to digital media and 70% to formal instruction in school. In her first semester at the university her rating on the TOEFL Speaking Rubric by three evaluators was 1.32/4.0. Salwa is currently studying at a vocational school for hospitality workers in her hometown.

A Casual Learner. Basma Khaldi grew up in a provincial capital of 90,000 people on the eastern plains of Morocco. Her father was a nurse at a public hospital and her mother worked at home. The family was, by Moroccan standards, middle class. She first began using the internet in middle school, when she went to a cybercafe with friends to complete an assignment for school. Her family owned a laptop computer connected to the internet through a 3G streaming "stick," but Basma relied more on her smartphone, which she used to chat with friends on Facebook and WhatsApp, usually in Arabic but sometimes in English (her Facebook page is almost exclusively in English). She said she had friends in Morocco, in Egypt, and in England. She also used her smartphone for school assignments and in fact had recently used it to research social media.

Basma stated that she first began to study English in high school and had good teachers. She also watched movies in English and was particularly interested in English-language pop singers, naming the Spanish/English singer Enrique Iglesias as a favorite. She described English as a "universal language" but did not have specific plans for a career in English. Basma attributed 50% of her English knowledge to informal sources and 50% to formal education. She was rated 2.0/4.0 on the TOEFL Speaking Rubric by three evaluators. She graduated from the university in 2017 and returned to her home town.

Socially Motivated. Youness Hafidi never had a formal English lesson until he began to attend university. He grew up in the medina (old city) of one of Morocco's major cultural centers and attended a high school where the foreign language program was Italian, not English. His father's tailor shop for traditional clothing was located in an area frequented by tourists, and Youness grew up hearing them speak English. He began to teach himself at age 15 by watching English-language movies and series on MBC, a group of satellite television channels broadcasting from Dubai. He described his parents as moderately prosperous and himself as a good student in high school, where he studied in the science (not letters) track. He began using the internet in his early teens at cybercafes, where he played video games and chatted with people on Yahoo!. His family later purchased a computer with a DSL connection, and he described surfing the net to study chemistry, mathematics, and biology in English. He described English as "a door to a new world" and decided to focus on studying it rather than the sciences at university because of his fascination with the language and his interest in society.

Youness was an active user of social media and described his use of multiple platforms, including Twitter, Facebook, and Instagram to chat with many friends, including tourists he had first met in the medina. He used EngVid, a YouTube channel for learning English, to teach himself the English grammar he had not learned in high school. He attributed 70% of his English to informal sources and 30% to formal instruction at the university. On the TOEFL Speaking Rubric, he was rated 3.0/4.0 by three evaluators during his first year at the university.

Youness was a very extroverted student with many friends and connections in the city and internationally. He volunteered at a center for disabled children and was a talented athlete with an interest in martial arts. He completed his university studies in 2019 and currently works as an instructor at a Hapkido center in the city.

Scholarship. Mustapha El Moudni grew up in poverty in a small village on the edge of the Middle Atlas Mountains where his parents were subsistence farmers. He was educated in a one-room primary school in his village. When he was 13, he became a boarder at a middle school 50 km from his home and later also boarded at a high school in the same provincial capital. Mustapha began to use the internet to learn English in his second year of high school. He owned a second-hand, Blackberry-like mobile phone that was physically cracked and held together with transparent tape. He described sitting with the phone near a café to pirate its Wi-Fi signal and surf topics on Wikipedia and Google. Mustapha was excited by literature in English. He was inspired by a fable, *The Wind and the Sun*, that a high school teacher shared with his class and had learned to use the internet to search for other stories to read and imitate as a writer. He also used Facebook Zero, a stripped-down, text-only version of Facebook that allowed access without bandwidth charges to interact with friends in Morocco and seek connections abroad.

Over the summer between high school and entering the university, Mustapha earned enough money to purchase a small, off-brand tablet with a 10 cm screen and 8 GB of memory. He used this device to download and practice writing stories in English and to sit outside cafes and watch a wide range of videos on YouTube, including captioned TED Talks. In his second year at the university, he attributed 55% of his English to formal instruction and 45% to informal learning.

Mustapha's speaking ability averaged 3.68/4.0 when rated by three evaluators on the TOEFL Speaking Rubric. Shortly after his interview he was accepted as a student at a prestigious third-year English program in Rabat and continued there for a master's degree in applied linguistics. He taught for a year until the onset of the Covid-19 pandemic and works today as a cultural liaison for TikTok in Casablanca.

Discussion

These four brief portraits of IDLERs in Morocco are representative of the range of opportunities and circumstances in which English is acquired informally in Morocco and, with a few differences, worldwide. For example, in countries with higher-speed internet, video games often play a larger role in adolescents' acquisition than in Morocco; but as is also the case globally, smartphones are common and more frequently relied on for interacting with friends, finding information quickly, and watching videos on YouTube.

Two points are critical here. First, as noted in Chapter 1, there is nothing "magical" about the relationship between opportunities for learning through digital media and its outcomes. It is no coincidence that Salwa, who owned a smartphone and used it to chat with her friends mostly in Arabic, and who watched English-language movies with Arabic subtitles, was rated 1.32/4.0 on the TOEFL Speaking Rubric, whereas Mustapha, who could not afford a data plan for his smartphone or tablet but who focused on reading and writing in English and watched videos captioned in English, scored 3.68/4.0. Interestingly, for many (but not all) of the 117 students interviewed in Dressman's (2020a) study, the quality and quantity of access to digital media did not correlate with learning outcomes; however, there was a significant correlation between the degree of active engagement with English through media that learners described and their TOEFL scores. In some but again not all cases, students from very impoverished rural backgrounds outscored students from urban, working-class settings. The exception in this case were the few students from homes with professional and wealthier backgrounds not included here whose combination of access and motivation made a clear difference in their speaking ability.

The second point is the clear relationship in these four portraits between the proportion of informal acquisition and formal instruction and learning that students reported and their TOEFL Speaking Scores. Again, it is no coincidence that Salwa, who attributed 70% of her learning to school, had the lowest TOEFL score of the group; Basma, who attributed 50% to each had a middle-range speaking score; and Youness, who attributed 70% of his learning to informal sources, had the second-highest score of the four students. This positive relationship between the quantity and quality of engagement with digital media in English and measured proficiency was also found among the 117 students in Dressman's (2020a) study and, as we again noted in Chapter 1, is a consistent finding in many studies worldwide.

The exception, again, was Mustapha, who attributed only 45% of his ability to informal learning but received the highest score of the four students in speaking. In this case, Mustapha's attribution is an honest reflection of his relative lack of access to media but also a tribute to his capacity to take advantage of every opportunity he was afforded, opportunities such as Facebook Zero that, in the developed world, might not even have been recognized as such.

The Internet as a Communicative Space: Five Features of IDLE

The internet as a communicative space is very different from a classroom. Not only are classrooms three-dimensional as opposed to the two dimensions of a computer screen, but classroom language is far more focused on language itself, and even when task-based approaches are used, classroom instruction is far more teacher-directed than informal learning. Opportunities for language use are also much narrower in classrooms, and time constraints require teachers to condense a great deal of content into a short amount of time with limited use of visual aids (realia) and other extralinguistic materials. Students may be given out-of-class assignments but usually they are to review and drill content presented in class rather than to explore new dimensions of English.

Studies of IDLE suggest five features that promote language learning through digital/ social media. These features are also found to some degree in other contexts for language learning, such as classrooms and nonformal, programmed learning, but they are prevalent, identifying features of IDLE. See Table 2.1 for a comparison of these five features

Table 2.1 Comparison of learning contexts by five features of IDLE.

Factors	Traditional classrooms	Digital/social media	Self-instruction (no digital/social media)
1. Social connection	Limited to teacher and peers within the classroom	Almost limitless potential through chatrooms, messaging, and forums for comments on social media platforms	Limited to the textbook author
2. Authentic, Compelling, and Varied Input	Use of realia and innovative, motivating resources gathered by the teacher; otherwise, didactic situations from textbook and worksheets	Almost limitless source of video, news websites, informational platforms, social media sites, etc., usually composed for non-didactic purposes	Limited to environmental print and textbooks, dictionaries, practice booklets, perhaps live meetings with speakers (tourists and family members)
3. Autonomy	Opportunities for self-motivated students to study independently; mostly teacher-initiated and directed activities	Highly autonomous; learners choose materials and times and pace for learning; high variation in incidental vs. intentional learning	Highly autonomous and self-directed; learners choose textbooks or other sources; high intentionality typically required
4. Multimodality	Live, classroom-limited, 3-dimensional interaction between teacher and students and among students; highly language-focused, with sporadic coordination of visual and comprehensible speech/print inputs	Potential coordination of comprehensible speech, print, visual images, motion, music, and sound effects; language is one among many inputs	Limited coordination of print and visual input within textbooks through captions; focus on print-based input with possible input through audio recordings
5. Ubiquity	Limited; scheduled class meetings with options for students to meet outside class or study independently	Potential availability of materials and input 24/7; options to stop and rewind video and other materials for review	Availability of textbooks, recordings, other materials 24/7 at the discretion of the learner

across three contexts: traditional classrooms, learning with digital and social media, and self-instruction without digital or social media.

1) **Social Connection.** Digital media provide learners with a range of opportunities to connect with others and the world. Much of this connection is with family and peers from school or other places in their daily lives through texting and posts on social media such as Facebook, Instagram; or in the United States, SnapChat. In these cases, users typically communicate in their home language. In other cases, however, learners may reach outside their own culture and language to join larger "affinity groups" such as fan clubs for pop idols (for example, BTS's Army) or to play MMORPGs, for which the lingua franca is often English (Sauro 2017). For adolescents worldwide, the glamor of being part of a "scene" much larger than themselves associated with high-status figures can be both a motivational force and a source of authentic and compelling English input.

2) **Authentic, Compelling, and Varied Input.** "Authentic input" in this case refers to materials for learning whose purposes and language are not instructionally driven. Such materials do not have controlled vocabulary or linguistic structures, and their content is typically audience oriented (Wong and Looi 2010). "Compelling input" refers to input that is both generally authentic and that learners of a specific gender, age group, culture, national setting, and so on find especially engaging (Krashen 2011). Learners have often reported across studies that only English input with a special personal or social appeal engages their interest and motivates them to learn. In addition, "varied input" refers to the wide variety of formats and content available also serves as a gateway to learning English. Attraction to different types of media may vary by country and gender: In France, television series are typical gateways, whereas in Sweden, Korea, and Brazil games are very popular. Attraction also varies by gender in some cases, as in Morocco, where females are often first attracted by pop music in English and males by satellite television programs subtitled in Arabic or captioned in English.

3) **Autonomy.** An additional feature of informal learning that is also closely related to the quality and quantity of input is autonomy (Benson 2011; Godwin-Jones 2019). Autonomous learning is self-directed. Compared to learning that is directed by a teacher, autonomous learners choose where, when, how much, and what materials they will learn from. Autonomous learners develop metacognitive skills and confidence, although at times their content knowledge can be idiosyncratic, and learning can be haphazard. A possible compromise is offered by non-formal language programs (for example, Babble or Duolingo) which offer didactically ordered content to learners at a time and place of their own choosing.

4) **Multimodality.** Multimodality refers to the coordination of multiple modes of communication—photos, movement, subtitles, captions, sound effects, music—across a single field or text to create a unified message for a listener/viewer/reader (Dressman 2020b). The use of multiple forms of input simultaneously creates a more authentic message for which comprehension is much easier, because the different modes both compensate for, and reinforce, each other, making it easier for gaps in linguistic understanding to be filled in and remembered. Informal learners often describe first learning English through subtitled programs or captioned music lyrics. Of course, classrooms are also multimodal; teachers write on boards as they speak or show photos of what they are talking about; however, the coordination of written and

spoken language and images in classrooms is often less coordinated and more limited than in a well-produced video or podcast accompanied by a transcript.

5) **Ubiquitous Access.** Ubiquitous access is related to autonomous learning and refers to the availability of media to learners at their discretion rather than at times fixed by a classroom schedule (Chen and Li 2010; Chen et al. 2019). Informal learners often cite their ability to access English input not only at times of their own choosing but on devices of their choice, and typically through more hours of contact per week than a classroom. Ubiquity in some cases can approximate an "immersion experience," similar to visiting an English-speaking country or living with English speakers.

In conclusion, it may seem that we are comparing and contrasting IDLE with formal classroom instruction to set up an analysis in which IDLE "wins." But that is not the case. In this book, we are arguing for the power of IDLE to develop levels of proficiency in English that often far exceed what can be learned through formal instruction alone, but it is our position that formal instruction also offers features of language learning that are not prevalent in IDLE, such as systematicity and accountability. It is through the integration of the features of IDLE with classroom instruction that the greatest number of students are likely to become powerful users of the English language for a wide variety of personal and academic purposes.

Discovering and Building on the Strengths of IDLE

Throughout this chapter we have presented evidence showing the transformative power of IDLE globally, especially among youth. However, our own introduction to its power and potential was initially not through formal research but through the experiences of students who told us and showed us how they were learning English outside the classroom. On the principle that, oftentimes, seeing and hearing are both more persuasive and more energizing than reading, we invite readers to informally explore the potential of IDLE activities for themselves, through three activities.

Activity #1: Interview Three Friends

In this activity, we invite you to have an informal but structured conversation with three students or friends about their use of digital media in learning English or another language. These individuals should be regular users of the internet and formally students of an additional language, preferably English. With their permission, you may record your conversation, but at a minimum you should take notes about what they tell you. We suggest you plan your conversation and make a list of questions. These may include:

- Do you remember when you first saw or heard English (or the target language)? Was it online or possibly on television?
- Why did you notice the language? What intrigued you?
- Do you remember specific words? How did you learn their meaning?
- Where else have you experienced English through digital media? How have your experiences changed over time?
- Can you describe your learning of English through digital media? Do you use digital media to learn English on a regular basis?

- Do you think informally engaging with English on digital media has helped your formal learning of English in classrooms? How?
- What percentage of your current English proficiency would you say is from informal learning, and what percentage is from formal study?

Once you've interviewed three (or you may choose to interview more) people, try to compare and contrast their experiences and relate them to the quality of each person's English. Do you see any patterns? What are the implications of what you have learned for teaching English, do you think?

Activity #2: Self-Study of Language Learning on YouTube

For this exercise, choose a language that you are somewhat familiar with but do not speak or read/write with fluency. Do a search on YouTube for five to seven videos (two hours in length, in total) in which this language is used and for which there are captions in the video. The videos should be a combination of lessons in the language (but exclusively in the target language) and non-didactic videos in the target language. Take a few hours and see how much more about the language you can learn from these videos. Be sure to take notes as you study, noting new words, phrases, or other new information or practices you are acquiring (for example, new grammar points or tips on pronunciation) as you study, along with any specific strategies for learning that you are devising as you watch and learn from the videos.

Now, compare your experience of learning through self-study on YouTube to studying based on formal classes in the language over the same amount of instructional time. What differences/similarities do you notice? Think about how much you have learned in the two modes and about the quality of the learning. Which mode was more pleasurable? Which felt like it took longer? What differences in the type of learning do you notice? Was your learning more receptive in one mode and more productive in the other? What do you think the implications are for teaching that language, based on your experience of both modes?

Activity #3: 30-Day IDLE Challenge

For this activity you will need either a blank notepad with at least 30 pages or set up an Excel spreadsheet or Word doc with 30 units left blank for recording your informal experience of English digitally over 30 days. Date each page or unit and begin to systematically record, as though you were keeping a diary, your informal engagement with English input over 30 days. Each day, record where you experienced English, what medium or platform you were using, and how long your experience lasted. Also record any insights about English that you received, words, phrases, or concepts you were introduced to, and the context in which this learning occurred. You may also want to record your formal, classroom-based, experiences of English during the same time.

At the end of 30 days, return to the beginning of your record keeping and begin to note any patterns you see in your use of digital media and learning of English, compared to the progress made in the same period from formal classroom sources of English. What patterns do you note? What do you think the implications of what you have learned from this activity can or should be for teaching English formally?

Conclusion

Since 2010, the world has seen an explosion in the expansion of digital media globally, both in terms of the availability of internet connections and the ownership of computers, tablets, and especially smartphones, for connecting with, and learning from, others both locally and worldwide. Within this revolution of the ways that people increasingly connect, inform, and entertain themselves, youth are leading the way.

The lightning speed of this revolution—and the past failure of educational technology often to keep its promises—may explain why many classroom teachers, and especially teachers of English as an additional language in most parts of the world have not until now incorporated digital media and technology into curriculum and instruction. However, that situation may also rapidly begin to change, as students themselves begin to demonstrate just how much and how well they are learning English through IDLE activities.

What, then, are the implications of IDLE for formal classroom language teaching? This is the central question to be addressed in the next chapters of this book. The situation at present, in which increasingly large numbers of students are acquiring increasingly large percentages of their English informally and largely without acknowledgment of recognition by the English teaching profession, may persist for some time, but it will not do so without an erosion of faith in—and in some cases—purpose, for that profession.

We believe that would be unfortunate for both English learners and the profession, and that it should be avoided. To maximize learning, there is a need for both formal instruction and informal acquisition/learning of English. The real question, then, is how both modes of acquisition and learning can be integrated, so that the strengths of one mode complement the needs and challenges of the other. Answering that question will be the focus of Chapter 3 and the implementation of that answer are the focus of the remaining chapters of this book.

Let's Discuss

1) Where would you locate yourself within the discussion of global internet usage at the beginning of this chapter? How do you generally access digital media? Through your laptop, your tablet, or your smartphone? How much time per day would you estimate you spend online? What types of activities do you engage in online? How do you think your online activities compare to your peers and/or your current or future students?

2) How would you describe your learning of English, in terms of informal vs. formal acquisition and learning, both early in your process and now? How would you relate your experience of learning English digitally to the four Moroccan students in this chapter? What percentage of your English proficiency would you attribute to informal learning practices and what percentage would you attribute to formal learning experiences?

3) What do you imagine are the implications of IDLE for your own teaching career? If you are currently a practicing, certified teacher, do you foresee any changes in your curriculum or your instruction that will build on the strengths of IDLE? If you are a preservice teacher, how do you think you might incorporate IDLE activities into your teaching?

4) What long-term impact do you see the pandemic and the shift to online learning will have for teaching English in your country or locality? In two years, do you think you will still offer some instruction online? What has been your experience as a teacher or student during this period? Are there aspects of online education you hope or think will remain?

References

Benson, Phil. "What's New in Autonomy?" *The Language Teacher* 35, no. 4 (July 2011): 15–18. https://doi.org/10.37546/jalttlt35.4-4.

Boer, Maartje, Regina J.J.M. van den Eijnden, Meyran Boniel-Nissim, Suzy-Lai Wong, Joanna C. Inchley, Petr Badura, Wendy M. Craig, Inese Gobina, Dorota Kleszczewska, Helena J. Klanscek, and Gonneke W.J.M. Stevens."Adolescents' Intense and Problematic Social Media Use and Their Well-Being in 29 Countries." *Journal of Adolescent Health* 66, no. 6 (February 2020): S89–S99. https://doi.org/10.1016/j.jadohealth.2020.02.014.

Chen, Chih-Ming, and Yi-Lun Li. "Personalised Context-Aware Ubiquitous Learning System for Supporting Effective English Vocabulary Learning." *Interactive Learning Environments* 18, no. 4 (December 2010): 341–364. https://doi.org/10.1080/10494820802602329.

Chen, Yi-Wen, Gi-Zen Liu, Vivien Lin, and Hong-You Wang. "Needs Analysis for an ESP Case Study Developed for the Context-Aware Ubiquitous Learning Environment." *Digital Scholarship in the Humanities* 34, no. 1 (July 2019): 124–145. https://doi.org/10.1093/llc/fqy019.

Dressman, Mark. "Informal English Learning among Moroccan Youth." In *The Handbook of Informal Language Learning*, 303–318, Hoboken, NJ: John Wiley & Sons, Inc., 2020a. https://doi.org/10.1002/9781119472384.ch20.

Dressman, Mark. "Multimodality and Language Learning." In *The Handbook of Informal Language Learning*, edited by Mark Dressman and Randall William Sadler, 39–56. Hoboken, NJ: John Wiley & Sons, Inc., 2020b. https://doi.org/10.1002/9781119472384.ch3.

Elias, Nelly, and Dafna Lemish. "When All Else Fail: The Internet and Adolescent-Immigrants." In *Informal Learning and Digital Media*, edited by Kirsten Drotner, 139–157. Cambridge: Cambridge University Press, 2008.

Galazzo, Richard. "Timeline from 1G to 5G: A Brief History on Cell Phones." 2022. https://www.cengn.ca/information-centre/innovation/timeline-from-1g-to-5g-a-brief-history-on-cell-phones.

Gibbons, Judith L., and Katelyn E. Poelker. "Technology and the Global Adolescent." In *Elements in Psychology and Culture*. Cambridge: Cambridge University Press, 2020. https://doi.org/10.1017/9781108639538.

Godwin-Jones, Robert. "Riding the Digital Wilds: Learner Autonomy and Informal Language Learning." *Language Learning & Technology* 23, no. 1 (February 2019): 8–25. https://doi.org/10125/44667.

Goffman, Erving. *The Presentation of Self in Everyday Life*. Palatine, IL: Anchor, 1959.

IMDB. "Top 100 Most Watched TV Shows of All Time." 2019. https://www.imdb.com/list/ls095964455.

International Telecommunication Union. "ITU_regional_global_Key_ICT_indicator_aggregates_Nov_2020." *Spreadsheet*, 2020a. https://docs.google.com/spreadsheets/d/1FF6u0EYJXnOQzEuQc8hb6K8Dg2Cdgj6L/edit#gid=1793901290.

International Telecommunication Union. "Measuring Digital Development Facts and Figures 2020." *ITU Publications*, 2020b. https://www.itu.int/en/itu-d/statistics/pages/facts/default.aspx.

Jurkovič, Violeta. "Online Informal Learning of English through Smartphones in Slovenia." *System* 80 (October 2019): 27–37. https://doi.org/10.1016/j.system.2018.10.007.

Kelly, Yvonne, Afshin Zilanawala, Cara Booker, and Amanda Sacker. "Social Media Use and Adolescent Mental Health: Findings from the UK Millennium Cohort Study." *EClinicalMedicine* 6 (December 2018): 59–68. https://doi.org/10.1016/j.eclinm.2018.12.005.

Krashen, Stephen. "The Compelling (Not Just Interesting) Input Hypothesis." *The English Connection* 15, no. 3 (Autumn 2011): 1. Korea Teachers of English to Speakers of Other Languages.

Lee, Ju Seong. "Informal, Digital Learning of English: The Case of Korean University Students." PhD dissertation, University of Illinois at Urbana-Champaign, 2018.

Li, Jia, Catherine Snow, and Claire White. "Urban Adolescent Students and Technology: Access, Use and Interest in Learning Language and Literacy." *Innovation in Language Learning and Teaching* 9, no. 2 (2015): 143–162.

Masanet, Maria-Jose, Mar Guerrero-Pico, and María-José Establés. "From Digital Native to Digital Apprentice. A Case Study of the Transmedia Skills and Informal Learning Strategies of Adolescents in Spain." *Learning, Media and Technology* 44, no. 4 (July 2019): 400–413. https://doi.org/10.1080/17439884.2019.1641513.

McDonald, James. 2021. "Almost Three Quarters of Internet Users Will Be Mobile-Only by 2025." https://www.warc.com/content/paywall/article/warc-datapoints/almost_three_quarters_of_internet_users_will_be_mobileonly_by_2025/124845.

Nielsen. "The State of Global Media." 2021a. https://www.nielsen.com/us/en/insights/video/2021/the-state-of-global-media.

Nielsen. "The State of Global Media." *Online Video*, 1:34:57, 2021b. https://www.nielsen.com/us/en/insights/video/2021/the-state-of-global-media.

Ogunlesi, Tolu, and Stephanie Busari. "Seven Ways Mobile Phones Have Changed Lives in Africa." *CNN*, September 14, 2012. https://www.cnn.com/2012/09/13/world/africa/mobile-phones-change-africa.

Pires, Fernanda, Maria-Jose Masanet, and Carlos A. Scolari. "What Are Teens Doing with YouTube? Practices, Uses and Metaphors of the Most Popular Audio-Visual Platform." *Information, Communication & Society* 24, no. 9 (2021): 1175–1191. https://doi.org/10.1080/1369118x.2019.1672766.

Prensky, Marc. "Digital Natives, Digital Immigrants." *On the Horizon* 9, no. 5 (October 2001): 1–6. Bingley: MCB University Press.

Rutledge, Stacey A., Vanessa P. Dennen, and Lauren M. Bagdy. "Exploring Adolescent Social Media Use in a High School: Tweeting Teens in a Bell Schedule World." *Teachers College Record: The Voice of Scholarship in Education* 121, no. 14 (November 2019): 1–30. https://doi.org/10.1177/016146811912101407.

Sauro, Shannon. "Online Fan Practices and Call." *CALICO Journal* 34, no. 2 (2017): 131–146. https://doi.org/10.1558/cj.33077.

Shankleman, Michael, Linda Hammond, and Fergal W. Jones. "Adolescent Social Media Use and Well-Being: A Systematic Review and Thematic Meta-Synthesis." *Adolescent Research Review* 6, no. 4 (April 2021): 471–492. https://doi.org/10.1007/s40894-021-00154-5.

Silver, Laura. "2. In Emerging Economies, Smartphone Adoption Has Grown More Quickly Among Younger Generations." 2019. https://www.pewresearch.org/global/2019/02/05/in-emerging-economies-smartphone-adoption-has-grown-more-quickly-among-younger-generations.

Statista. "Most Common Languages Used on the Internet as of January 2020, by Share of Internet Users." 2021. https://www.statista.com/statistics/262946/share-of-the-most-common-languages-on-the-internet.

Tan, Lynde, and Beaumie Kim. "Adolescents' Agentic Work on Developing Personal Pedagogies on Social Media." *Literacy* 53, no. 4 (November 2019): 196–205. Oxford: John Wiley & Sons Ltd.

Tso, Anna Wing-bo. "Learning English as a Foreign Language through Social Media: Perspectives from Hong Kong Adolescents." In *Shaping the Future of Education, Communication and Technology*, edited by Will W. K. Ma, Wendy Wing Lam Chan, and Cat Miaoting Cheng, 107–116. Singapore: Springer, 2019.

UNICEF. *How Many Children and Young People Have Internet Access at Home?* New York: UNICEF, 2020.

Wong, Lung-Hsiang, and Chee-Kit Looi. "Vocabulary Learning by Mobile-Assisted Authentic Content Creation and Social Meaning-Making: Two Case Studies." *Journal of Computer Assisted Learning* 26, no. 5 (April 2010): 421–433. https://doi.org/10.1111/j.1365-2729.2010.00357.x.

3

Complementarity: Tradition and Innovation in English Learning and Teaching

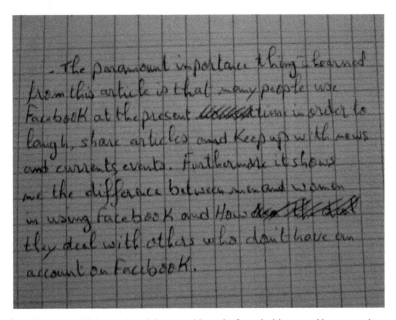

Facebook is the most widely used social networking platform in Morocco. Here a student responds to an article about Facebook after a class discussion.

Introduction

In the previous chapters, we introduced and provided research evidence of the revolution in language acquisition and learning that is occurring globally, driven by rapid advances in speed and access to the internet and the affordability of new (or often used) smartphones, offering access to streamed content on demand. We also discussed the emergence of a global youth culture and introduced IDLE, or Informal Digital Learning of English, as a recent social phenomenon, described its use in multiple countries, and provided four portraits of users, or IDLERs, in Morocco. Finally, we briefly

English Language Learning in the Digital Age: Learner-Driven Strategies for Adolescents and Young Adults,
First Edition. Mark Dressman, Ju Seong Lee, and Laurent Perrot.
© 2023 John Wiley & Sons Ltd. Published 2023 by John Wiley & Sons Ltd.

discussed features of IDLE that contribute to language acquisition/learning of English and argued that informal and formal language learning were not oppositional but complementary features of a reconceptualized approach to English education in the digital age.

In this chapter, we build a framework for reconceptualizing and redesigning English language curriculum and instruction at the classroom level, to develop proficiency in all four modes of communication: speaking, listening, reading, and writing. Our focus will be on the integration of the principles and features of IDLE within the context of classroom instruction in English globally. We will take a practical approach, acknowledging the need for accountability and systematicity that is a critical aspect of modern education in public and private schools, universities, and language centers worldwide. In conclusion, we look to Parts II and III of this book, which focus on integrating digital media and technology with classroom instruction. Within each chapter we provide three scenarios in which fictional teachers address realistic practical, instructional challenges.

Chapter Objectives

The central goal of this chapter is to examine the complementarity of IDLE and conventional classroom English language instruction. A subgoal is to understand formal distinctions between language acquisition and learning, and to consider how IDLE blurs these distinctions for learners. A second subgoal is to consider how the practices of informal learning might be adapted within a formal classroom setting, without destroying the integrity or engagement factor of those informal practices. A final subgoal of the chapter is to consider how the use of informal practices in classrooms might relate to two sets of standards: the TESOL Technology Standards and the Common European Framework of Reference (CEFR 2020) level descriptors. By the end of the chapter, readers should be able to:

1) Describe the traditional difference between language acquisition and learning, with respect to the research and theory of Krashen.
2) Explain how and why the use of IDLE-based practices blurs this distinction.
3) Describe points of complementarity between IDLE and classroom instruction.
4) Explain with concrete examples how IDLE-based practices can be adapted to formal classroom settings.
5) Describe possible threats to authenticity of adapting IDLE for the classroom and how these threats might be avoided or mitigated.
6) Describe the correlation of IDLE-based practices to formal standards, including the TESOL Technology Standards and the CEFR level descriptors.

Key Words

language acquisition; language learning; language acquisition device (LAD); monitor model; affective filter; complementarity

Language Acquisition and Language Learning: Opposition or Overlap?

Although digital aspects of informal language acquisition/learning are recent, appearing approximately a decade ago in the research literature, discussions of informal vs. formal language acquisition/learning are nearly as old as applied linguistics and TESOL themselves. In the early days, the conventional view was that children *acquired* language informally but that, with rare exceptions, above the early teenage years, adults needed to formally *learn* languages by studying them. In the 1960s Noam Chomsky postulated a Language Acquisition Device (LAD; Chomsky 1967) as a feature of early cognitive development in humans that became inactive in adulthood. The LAD offered an explanation for why most adults seemed to require instruction to learn a new language and also for why children could acquire additional languages with "native" pronunciation, but adults always seemed to retain the accent of their first language when speaking a second language. Over time, distinctions between informal acquisition and formal learning of languages grew. Acquisition was described as an almost effortless, unconscious, and natural process resulting in mastery and was contrasted with learning, which was considered difficult, required conscious effort, and was nearly always imperfect. Although cases of adults acquiring a new language without formal instruction were documented, these were rare and considered exceptions to the rule.

Challenging Conventional Views

However, not all researchers accepted this view. In a now classic paper, Stephen Krashen (1976) reviewed the extant research of the time to consider two hypotheses: 1) informal environments were sufficient for language acquisition in adults; or 2) formal learning was significantly more efficient than informal learning for adults. In studies of university students in the United States whose first language was not English (e.g., international students in summer programs), students in enrolled in programs including formal ESL instruction scored no better on end-of-program exams than those without formal ESL instruction. There was a significant positive relationship between time spent abroad by the students and their test scores: students studying abroad for a year scored better than those who studied for a summer, and all students who studied abroad scored better than those who had only studied formally in their home countries; moreover, if the target language was spoken in the students' home, those students outperformed students who spoke only their original language at home. These studies appeared to confirm the first hypothesis, that informal environments provide sufficient context for learning by adults.

Krashen also reported studies that seemed to confirm the second hypothesis, that adults learned better with instruction than with informal language input. In these studies, however, the quality of the informal environment was questionable, because although students were exposed to the target language in their environment, they were often not required to use it. From this analysis, Krashen concluded that exposure alone was not a sufficient condition within informal environments; what made the difference was the extent to which students were required to use the target language daily.

Stephen Krashen and Five Influential Hypotheses

- Stephen Krashen (born 1941) is a linguist and Emeritus Professor of Education at the University of Southern California.
- He is known for five hypotheses in language education:
  - input hypothesis
  - acquisition-learning hypothesis
  - monitor hypothesis
  - natural order hypothesis
  - affective filter hypothesis.
- Krashen's work is highly influential but controversial because he argues that languages are only acquired through comprehensible input and can't be "taught" or "learned." Critics also argue that his hypotheses are untestable and lack empirical support.
- He is also a proponent of free voluntary reading for second-language acquisition (see Chapter 5 for a discussion of Extensive Reading).

Krashen concluded: "Formal and informal environments contribute to second language competence in different ways, or rather, to different aspects of second language competence" (162–163). To account for these different aspects, Krashen proposed the "monitor model," in which knowledge about language acquired in formal instruction was used strategically by students to monitor and correct errors made in the use of language acquired informally. Krashen cited differences in testing formats for students who were primarily informal or formal learners as evidence in support of monitoring: On tests in which students were required to rapidly respond, informal students scored better than formally taught students; but on tests in which students had time to consider (and monitor) their responses, formally taught students performed better.

In the intervening years, innumerable articles have debated Krashen's conclusions and his recommendations regarding classroom curriculum and instruction (Gregg 1986; Higgs 1985; Ioup 1984; Krashen 1991). Many scholars would agree that the "best" (if not the only) way to develop proficiency in a new language is through acquisition, in which individuals are required to interact purposefully with the language (and other users), whereas the formal learning of grammatical, syntactic, morphological, and phonological "rules" serves only to develop students' ability to monitor and correct their performance.

Do You Believe These About Language?

- **Some languages are harder to learn than others.** This is only true relative to the languages you speak. Languages with more cognates and grammatical similarities to a known language may be easier to learn than languages with fewer cognates, dissimilar grammar, or phonemes.
- **You are never as proficient in a second or third language as in your first.** Your most proficient language is the one you've used the most often and in the most contexts. It is possible that you learned a language as a child but now rarely speak

---

(Continued)

(Continued)

it or only in limited contexts, so that you are more proficient in your second or third well-used language.

- **Only native speakers fully understand a language and can write well in it.** Tell that to Joseph Conrad, Vladimir Nabokov, Yiyun Li, Eva Hoffman, Jack Kerouac, and Samuel Beckett, among many others—literary figures who achieved greatness writing in a language other than their first.

It is also widely accepted that human beings possess an innate capacity for language acquisition, and that this capacity does not disappear with age, although it may be mitigated by cultural variables and adult self-consciousness, described by Krashen as the "affective filter" (Krashen 1982). Similarly, innumerable examples of actors worldwide acquiring impeccable accents to match the regional dialects and national languages of the characters they are playing, or native speakers of one language singing convincingly in another, suggest that it is not puberty but other social psychological factors surrounding speakers' sense of cultural identity that explain many adults' retention of a native accent when speaking another language.

The Research-Practice Divide: Continuing Challenges for Formal Language Education

Yet, while Krashen's and others' revision of the conventional story of language acquisition in children vs. learning in adults is widely known and accepted by researchers and educators today, this appears not to have lessened the struggle of students and teachers in language classrooms or led to sizable increases in English language proficiency for many students around the world. Surely instructional approaches such as Communicative Language Teaching (CLT; Richards 2005) or Task-Based Language Teaching (TBLT; Nunan 2004) present a radical improvement over the Grammar-Translation method (Benati 2018); but it is seldom the case that these new approaches have radically improved the efficiency or outcomes of English language education globally.

Why is this? One reason often given is Krashen's affective filter: Students are often too shy or self-conscious to risk making a mistake when trying to speak, and so they resist the very activities that would improve their proficiency. Another reason given in some countries and educational systems is that high-stakes testing, and especially tests that are given in paper-and-pencil format, rather than formats requiring students to use language functionally, emphasize aspects of language that need to be learned rather than acquired, thus reducing the emphasis placed by teachers and students on acquisition-type activities in classroom.

However, as plausible as the affective filter and test-driven explanations are, we strongly suspect that these are, in fact, the symptoms of a far more intractable and fundamental problem: classrooms themselves are inherently inauthentic and awkward spaces for the development of communicative contexts geared to the backgrounds, personal interests and needs of individual students. From this perspective, the affective filter is raised for students when they are given tasks that might on the surface seem relevant and be of interest to them, but are in fact, artificial and meaningless. Similarly, if students and teachers are certain in their minds that performance of a particular task will have no bearing either on their test performance or any other aspect of their lives, they may perform the task but without engagement, forgetting everything as soon as it is no longer needed.

It might seem that all is lost, then. Locked in an inauthentic environment that lends itself more to test prep and artificiality than to the authentic communication required for its acquisition, what are students and teachers of the English language to do?

Bridging the Gap between Acquisition and Learning in Classrooms

But all is not lost, for two reasons. First, the differences between acquisition and learning are exaggerated by both conventional wisdom and research. For example, children do not acquire language for its own sake; they acquire it because they must understand what others are saying and speak to have their needs met. Anyone who has communicated with a toddler knows that this process is often not easy or straightforward and involves struggle and frustration, albeit without the affective filter. Moreover, multiple studies of parents interacting with infants and toddlers demonstrate the large amount of "scaffolding" of language parents do to shape their child's speech (Behrend, Rosengren, and Perlmutter 1989; Khaliliaqadam 2014; Vygotsky and Cole 1978). Scaffolding is surely a form of teaching, and so in these cases the child is both acquiring *and learning* language from a parent, even if the lessons are not formal in nature.

Moreover, in the research literature what is described as "learning" is often caricatured as what students take from grammar lessons or repetitive skill-and-drill activities ("What's your favorite sport?"; "My favorite sport is ..."). But this represents a very mediocre and limited range of the activities possible in a typical language classroom, which could also include learning songs, reading stories or informative articles, debates, or even learning vocabulary and grammatical structures in the course of studying a cognate subject such as history or science, as in Content-Based Instruction (CBI; Snow 2010) or Content and Language Integrated Learning (CLIL; Dalton-Puffer 2011) approaches. In these cases, acquisition and learning are often blended and sometimes indistinguishable from each other.

Second, the argument can be made that classrooms and formal education have several advantages over informal environments in terms of time, efficiency, and focus. Consider, for example, that it usually takes nearly a year of human interaction after birth before a child speaks their first word, another year before that child begins to speak in short sentences, and four or more years before children become conversational, with a vocabulary of 1000 or more words; and this is with near-constant daily engagement with the language. By comparison, most adults placed in the same situation of input and need would acquire an equivalent level of proficiency in much less time; and with the added focus and structure of high-quality, engaging formal instruction they would also learn to read and write and to monitor the correctness of their language use across multiple contexts. Krashen's (1976) conclusion still holds true:

> The classroom can contribute in two ways: As a formal linguistic environment, providing rule isolation and feedback for the development of the monitor, and, to the extent language use is emphasized, simultaneously as a source of primary linguistic data for language acquisition. (167)

But there is a caveat: "language use" and "primary linguistic data" do not exist in a vacuum; they come alive in meaningful, consequential exchanges among speakers that are typically integrated into other, nonverbal forms of input, such as music, sound, images, motion, and so on. And these complex, multimodal forms of input have proven very often difficult if not impossible for teachers to arrange on a regular, reliable basis. Moreover, the requirements of scheduling and the need to condense information transfer within one- or two-hour sessions provides little time for students to explore language on their own or to practice with others within a classroom setting.

Are These Examples of Language Acquisition or Learning?

- A friend corrects your pronunciation of a word, and you make a note of it.
- You watch an instructional video on YouTube about a grammatical structure and, in the process, you understand several new terms and phrases in English.
- You listen to songs on the radio and try to write down the lyrics that you hear.
- You notice a new word in a book you're reading and realize you understand the meaning from the context.
- As a child, you have an argument with your mother about something and when you begin to cry, she realizes you misunderstood her meaning. She rephrases her statement to clarify what she has said, and you stop crying and begin to cooperate with her.
- You watch a YouTube video in your class and afterwards the teacher has a conversation with the class about it.

This is why the revolution in digital communications of the previous decades, accelerated by the development of affordable smartphones and high-speed connectivity, is also revolutionary for language education. It is why the learner-driven strategies of IDLERs, especially those who claim to have acquired 50% or more of their English from digital media, must be taken seriously by language educators now and into the future: Because digital media and learner-driven strategies dissolve the gap between language acquisition and learning and offer a realistic, ubiquitous, affordable response to the previously inherent limitations of classrooms as spaces for language education.

We know from global research evidence that on their own youth around the world are teaching themselves English on their laptops and smartphones, and so the question remaining for language educators is not, "Can it be done?" but "How do we take advantage of this phenomenon and solve the problem that has plagued classroom educators since formal language education began?" In other words, not why but *how* do we combine digital media with conventional curriculum? Or more precisely, how do we combine these in proportions and in ways that complement each other and that maximize acquisition/learning outcomes for students?

The Complementarity of IDLE and Classroom Teaching

Just as the difference between language acquisition and learning becomes more nuanced and complex in practice than in theory or research, so too the complementarity of IDLE with conventional classroom instruction requires complex analysis and consideration of both approaches. It would be simplistic and unfeasible to declare schools obsolete and call for the replacement of all the traditional elements of education by expensive technologies and the unfiltered, unedited transfer of the extramural media practices of youth into classrooms. However, it would be equally ill-conceived and destructive if the educational opportunities of the digital age were reduced to online, often highly programmed learning of mandated content, accompanied by panoptic (Foucault 2012) tools for the assessment of students and the monitoring of teachers. Since the Covid-19 pandemic it has become obvious that this alternative's limitations are serious and not sustainable. What is required, then, is not a "balance" of these two extremes but rather a close reading of the educational strengths and weaknesses of both IDLE and conventional second-language instruction, leading to a reconceptualization of learner-driven, digitally integrated strategies for English education, now and into the future.

Analyzing the Learning Potential of Classroom Practices

Table 3.1 provides an analysis of ten common learning tasks in conventional language classrooms along four dimensions. The tasks are roughly arranged from the simplest to the most complex, considering the number of communication modes, degree of (likely) self-monitoring and rehearsal, and amount of time and materials needed to complete them. The last column describes the likely amount of student autonomy and engagement each is task is likely to generate.

Table 3.1 Analysis of academic/formal English activities across modes, monitoring/rehearsal, time and materials, and autonomy/engagement.

Academic/formal English activities	Mode (speak, listen, read, write)	Self-monitoring/ rehearsal (none, possible, or required)	Time and materials requirements	Learner autonomy and engagement
1. Reading silently	Read	None	In class/assigned; books/hard copies	Dependent on text quality, level
2. Listening and reading along	Listen, read	None	In class; recordings and books/hard copies	Typically teacher directed; dependent on text quality, level
3. Taking lecture notes	Listen, write	Possible	In class; paper or digital writing	Teacher directed; dependent on text quality, level
4. Writing about a personal topic	Write	Possible	In class/assigned; paper or digital writing	Dependent on whether the topic is student or teacher nominated
5. Researching and writing a report	Read, write	Required	In class/assigned; library or online materials; paper or digital writing	Dependent on whether the topic is student or teacher nominated

(Continued)

Table 3.1 (Continued)

Academic/formal English activities	Mode (speak, listen, read, write)	Self-monitoring/ rehearsal (none, possible, or required)	Time and materials requirements	Learner autonomy and engagement
6. Researching and composing a PowerPoint	Read, write	Required	In class/assigned; school or home digital computing	Dependent on whether the topic is student or teacher directed
7. Rehearsing and performing a skit or dialogue	Listen, speak, read, write	Required	In class/assigned; books/hard copies	Dependent on the content of the skit and whether teacher or student directed
8. Speaking in a debate	Listen, speak	Required	In class; possible assigned prep.	Dependent on topic and whether teacher or student nominated
9. Small group conversation on a topic	Listen, speak	Possible	In-class	Dependent on topic and whether teacher or student nominated
10. Small group problem solving and presentation	Listen, speak, write	Required	In-class; teacher-produced materials	Dependent on topic and whether teacher or student nominated

These tasks are "authentic" in the sense that they authentically reflect the types of speaking, listening, reading, and writing activities necessary in academic and formal settings. However, they do not reflect tasks typical of students' everyday lives, or, increasingly, of workplaces, and they are also frequently not topical or culturally relevant but instead generic and most lack any intrinsic interest for youth. They are, in effect, inherently unmotivating for the majority of learners. Only one of them (#7: Rehearsing and performing a skit or dialogue) requires more than two of the four modes of communication (although if the higher-end tasks were completed in small groups they would require all four modes; but without stringent monitoring by a teacher these might not be in English).

The third column, Self-monitoring/rehearsal, is important because as Krashen (1976) noted, to the extent that students check and revise their production of language their metacognition develops, along with their accuracy and learning. One might argue that the successful completion of all these tasks requires a level of monitoring and rehearsal. Teachers may insist on this with students but, practically, many times students simply "go through the motions" of completing school tasks without reflection or self-monitoring. Only in the more complex tasks is monitoring likely to be a requirement for completion of tasks.

The fourth column refers to the time and material requirements of the task. It points to the significant in-class time requirements of many activities, especially the simplest, and to the limitations on materials when they must be purchased by schools or photocopied and distributed to students; in addition, most materials are only available in-class, limiting their length and time of engagement with them. We might assume that many schools have computer labs or banks of tablets available for students or that students can write at home on laptops or smartphones and upload work to learning management systems, but these "advances" may only increase the efficiency of production and assessment of work, not its relevance, engagement, or learning outcomes.

The last column contains notes on the level of learner autonomy and engagement for each of the ten activities typical of conventional classrooms. Again, lacking student choice of materials or topics, this level is strikingly low across nearly all activities. It may be argued that a more "student-centered" approach, in which students are provided greater opportunity to choose among materials and topics for work, may increase autonomy and engagement, but only somewhat; in the end, teachers typically direct most of these activities with little deviation from the rubric permitted while the tasks themselves remain academic and formal in nature.

As negative and critical of conventional language classroom activities as this analysis is, however, conventional language education and formal education in general have some necessary strengths. Formal education offers systematicity and regularity, as well as accountability to students, parents, and the public. These elements are critical for social and cultural stability and sustained support of education. Equally important, the curricular focus of conventional education on academic skills and on the formal uses of language is a critical element in students' preparation for higher education and for the workplace. Although an uncritical and exclusive focus in formal education on the conventions of language use does privilege the already privileged in most societies, its abandonment in schools is unlikely to change conditions in society at large rather than leading to equity and social justice. A far more pragmatic solution is to look for ways to bridge the gap between vernacular, local uses of language and formal, "elite" ways of speaking and writing.

Analyzing the Learning Potential of IDLE Activities

Table 3.2 provides a list of ten common ways that IDLERs acquire English through digital media along four dimensions, roughly from simplest activity to most complex. The first three of these dimensions are the same as in Table 3.1; the fourth is different, to reflect the challenges of IDLE not for Learner Autonomy and Engagement (these are givens for IDLE) but for Transferability to Formal Learning.

Overall, the analysis demonstrates significant differences between IDLE and formal English education. With respect to the first column of analysis, Mode, only one activity (Using non-formal language programs) requires more than two modes of communication. Across all activities, reading is the most common mode (8 of 10 activities), followed by listening (5 of 10 activities), and then speaking and writing (3 of 10 activities each). Reception, then, seems to predominate over production of language even more than in formal education.

However, the second column, Self-monitoring/rehearsal, suggests that the reception activities of IDLE are more active and engaging for IDLERs than in formal

Table 3.2 Analysis of extramural/informal English activities across modes, monitoring/rehearsal, time and materials, and transferability.

Extramural/informal English activities	Mode (speaking, listening, reading, writing)	Self-monitoring/ rehearsal (none, possible, or required)	Time and materials requirement	Transferability to formal learning
1. Using translation and dictionary apps	Read	Possible	Classroom or home; personal devices	Very common currently among students
2. Self-initiated searching for information	Read	Required	Classroom or home; personal devices, internet	Dependent on whether search is teacher or student directed
3. Using non-formal language programs (e.g., Duolingo)	Speak, listen, read	Required	Home; personal devices, internet	Possible use for practice
4. Watching music videos in English with lyrics	Listen, read	Required	Home; personal devices, internet	Possible but dependent on fit to curriculum, teacher openness, and student autonomy
5. Watching captioned video	Listen, read	Required	Home; personal devices, internet	Possible but dependent on fit to curriculum, teacher openness, and student autonomy; time constraints may require extension outside classroom
6. Reading/writing asynchronous comments on conversation boards	Read, write	Possible	Home; personal devices, internet	Possible but dependent on fit to curriculum, teacher openness, and student autonomy

Extramural/informal English activities	Mode (speaking, listening, reading, writing)	Self-monitoring/ rehearsal (none, possible, or required)	Time and materials requirement	Transferability to formal learning
7. Listening to podcasts/ audiobooks with transcripts	Listen, read	Required	Home; personal devices, downloaded from internet	Very possible, dependent on fit to curriculum, teacher openness, and student autonomy; time constraints require students to work outside classroom
8. Chatting (written) on social media in English	Read, write	Possible	Home; personal devices, internet	Possible but the artificiality of school-based platforms will reduce student engagement and autonomy
9. Chatting live via digital platforms and videogames	Listen, speak	Required	Home; personal devices, internet	Possible connection with classrooms overseas? Difficult to arrange but "gaming" format may be transferred within classroom
10. Vlogging, podcasting	Write, speak	Required	Home; personal devices, internet	Possible but time constraints require students to work outside classroom

education. In seven of the ten activities, self-monitoring is required at some level. A learner who is searching online for information in English must pay close attention to that process, sifting through multiple hits on a search engine, generating key words, and so on. This would also be necessary, perhaps, in a formal classroom, but typically to save time teachers provide students with sources or links in advance, thus reducing the amount of engagement required of learners. Similarly, live chat requires IDLERs to pay close attention to what is being said to them to respond appropriately. The same process might occur in a classroom setting, but it is not typical for students to have an extended conversation in English unless prompted and coached by their teacher.

The third column, Time and materials requirement, suggests marked differences between IDLE and formal classrooms. For IDLE activities, all tasks require materials procured by IDLERs themselves, whereas in formal education the onus for procurement of materials is on the school and on teachers. In cases where all or nearly all students have smartphones and the school has Wi-Fi connectivity in classrooms, this represents enormous opportunities for creative instruction using authentic materials from the internet and a wide variety of platforms; with the provision of a few smartphones for students without them, the world online is literally at the teachers' and learners' fingertips. In other cases, students may need to use data plans or schools may need to purchase tablets or smartphones for student use. If students have home connectivity, the opportunities for expanding activities beyond classroom meeting times—assigning viewing of videos or collaboration among students—also becomes possible.

The fourth column, Transferability to formal learning, is more complex. Some activities do not directly lend themselves to classroom learning contexts creatively or appropriately, such as playing video games or using non-formal language learning programs to practice grammar exercises or watching extended television series or movies. However, many of the features of games are quite feasible, and the viewing of extended video programs can be assigned for homework. Again, we do not advise simply bringing the same IDLE activities students are using on their own into formal learning contexts without carefully considering how they can best be adapted to serve the purposes of language acquisition/learning within the classroom.

In summary, IDLE activities present both challenges and opportunities for learning, especially within formal learning contexts. Additional issues not named in the analysis include the haphazard nature of informal learning and time-related issues: informal learners who become proficient English speakers often do so by spending many hours per day—often five or more—online, and almost every day of the week. IDLE, in other words, may be effective for many learners, but it is also inefficient. Finally, not all IDLE activities are appropriate for classroom contexts and would not be tolerated in most schools. These are activities in which violence, displays of multiple forms of abuse, and inappropriate, crude language may be present, elements that may be accepted at home or tolerated by parents, but that pose serious problems for schools. In short, the internet, smartphones, and IDLE present enormous opportunities for language acquisition, but their adoption within classroom settings requires significant adaptation as well.

Table 3.3 Hybrid, blended academic/formal and extramural/informal English language activities across modes, monitoring, format, autonomy/engagement, and transferability.

Academic/formal English activities	Mode (speak, listen, read, write, compose)	Self-monitoring/ rehearsal (none, possible, or required)	Time and materials requirement	Learner autonomy and engagement, fit within formal education
1. Commenting on a classroom blog about a student-nominated issue	Read, write	Possible	Classroom or home; school or personal devices; internet	High autonomy, some teacher monitoring; in-class or homework
2. Listening/reading along with audiobooks/transcribed podcasts of student choice and commenting on class blog	Listen, read, write	Possible	Classroom or home; school or personal devices; internet, online materials downloaded or streamed	Medium autonomy, teacher sets pace, amount of reading, monitors and assesses outcome
3. Reading/listening to audiobooks in a group chosen by students and participating in classroom and online discussions	Listen, read, speak, write	Required	Classroom or home; school or personal devices; internet, online materials downloaded or streamed	Medium autonomy; teacher sets pace, amount of reading, monitors and assesses outcome
4. Watching a series of captioned YouTube videos on a topic of student choice and taking notes for a presentation	Listen, read, write	Required	Classroom or home; school or personal devices; internet, online materials streamed	Medium autonomy; teacher sets pace, amount of work, monitors and assesses outcome
5. Keeping a student-produced blog individually for posting reviews of poetry, music, and movies	Write/compose, read, listen	Required	Classroom or home; school or personal devices; internet, online platform	High autonomy; teacher sets pace, number of posts, monitors and assesses outcome
6. In small groups, using a testing app (Quizlet/Kahoot) to write multiple choice questions for readings found by students online on topics of their choice	Listen, speak, read, write	Required	Classroom or home; school or personal devices; internet, online platform	Medium autonomy; teacher sets pace, number of questions, gives feedback on questions and monitors use of Quizlet and playing

(Continued)

Table 3.3 (Continued)

Academic/formal English activities	Mode (speak, listen, read, write, compose)	Self-monitoring/ rehearsal (none, possible, or required)	Time and materials requirement	Learner autonomy and engagement, fit within formal education
7. Working in small groups to present a response to a problem or task from a teacher composed WebQuest	Listen, speak, read, write	Required	Classroom or home; school or personal devices; internet, online platform	Low autonomy; teacher composes the WebQuest, monitors student work, assesses student responses for the task
8. In small groups, writing/choosing a poem, reciting it chorally, and recording and editing a video for sharing privately on a class YouTube channel	Read, listen, speak, write/compose	Required	Classroom or home; school or personal devices; internet, online platform	Medium autonomy; teacher monitors selection process, supervises process, assesses final video presentations
9. Individually or in small groups, researching a student-chosen topic and writing a report with graphs and images on a webpage	Listen, speak, read, write/compose	Required	Classroom or home; school or personal devices; internet, online materials and platform	Medium autonomy; teacher monitors topic selection, supervises process, assesses final project
10. Composing a narrated PowerPoint presentation and converting it to a video for sharing and feedback from students on a class YouTube channel	Write/compose speak	Required	Classroom or home; school or personal devices; internet, online materials and platform	Medium autonomy; teacher monitors topic selection, supervises process, assesses final project

Analyzing a Hybrid, Blended Approach to IDLE within Formal Learning Contexts

Table 3.3 presents an analysis of ten hybridized activities in which IDLE activities have been adapted to formal learning contexts. These ten activities are representative of the approach taken to the integration of IDLE with formal learning in Chapters 4–12.

Our design of the ten hybridized activities (and of all the scenarios in this book) is the result of a practical, three-step process. In the first step, we reviewed current studies of IDLE and from these we made a list of the digital media identified by learners in the studies as helpful for their acquisition/learning of English, noting any challenges these might present within a formal classroom context. For each type of media activity (e.g., watching captioned YouTube videos; watching music videos; key word searching) we also listed modes of communication (listening, speaking, reading, writing) used in each activity, noting also whether the use of a mode was brief or extended.

In the second step, we revisited the tasks of classroom English language learning and made a short list of the basic, essential tasks and products that a student in middle, high school, or university should be able to perform and produce. This list did not include specific, detailed assignments but rather was a list of basic things an educated user of English should be able to do, such as collaborate with others to solve a problem, write a report from multiple sources, or give a persuasive presentation. This list was similar to the scales and activities of the Common European Framework of Reference (CEFR 2020), but with an academic focus.

In the third step, we compared the two lists and began inductively to match the opportunities of different types of digital media and the modes of communication they facilitated with the basic tasks of classroom English language learning. This was a very creative process, in which we focused first on a particular type of digital media and how it was used by youth to acquire English and then looked for an academically oriented task that fitted the media. This step of the process was in some critical ways the opposite of conventional approaches to instructional design, in which outcomes ("write a persuasive essay"; "practice new vocabulary in a presentation") drive the development of tasks and assignments. However, it was also a critically necessary shift in direction if the strategies that were designed were to remain learner-driven and authentic to the practices of IDLE and IDLErs.

As a result of this three-step process, the activities of Table 3.3 are generally more complex than either the activities of formal learning or IDLE because they involve at least two and typically three or all four modes of communication. As the first column indicates, each typically involves both reception (listening, reading) and production (speaking, writing) activities. In addition, four of the activities are multimodal, requiring students to coordinate written text with images, video, sound, and sometimes narration—to *compose* texts instead of only writing them. Many of these activities are thus *supralinguistic*: They extend beyond learning language in isolation from other types of sign systems, in keeping with the communication practices of digital media today.

The second column indicates that in eight of ten activities, self-monitoring/rehearsal is required of learners, and in the first two (least complex) activities, it is possible. Again, self-monitoring and rehearsal do not guarantee durable, consequential learning, but they are essential elements for it. A learner who is not engaged in an activity may of course "go through the motions" to complete any activity, but the complexity of the activities and the relatively high levels of autonomy required to complete them (and the authenticity of materials found on the internet) reduces the likelihood that students will not be engaged as learners.

The third column describes the origin of materials and time required for completion of the activities. As in the case of IDLE activities, the materials used in these activities are largely taken from online sources and platforms that require a relatively high-speed internet connection. Ideally, that connection is through school-based Wi-Fi rather than an LTE (4G) signal dependent on student data plans. The activities also assume a 1:1 ratio of devices per student, although in small group activities the ratio could be increased. In addition, it is likely that some relaxation of typical school restrictions on access would need to be allowed, in order for students to search the internet freely and watch YouTube videos. Overall, however, it is likely that were student smartphones permitted in classrooms, less hardware would be required of schools and the resources available to teachers and students that were of high quality and authenticity would significantly increase.

The fourth column indicates the relative levels of autonomy allowed to learners and the role and activities of teaching for the completion of each activity. For all activities, some decrease in autonomy over unmonitored IDLE is indicated, to allow for management, monitoring, and assessment by teachers; but the level of autonomy and potential authenticity of activities is significantly higher than in exclusively formal instruction, allowing for higher levels of motivation and engagement.

Discussion

In summary, the potential of ten activities typical for formal classroom instruction in Table 3.1 and ten for IDLE in Table 3.2 were compared. Both formal instruction and IDLE were found to have significant strengths but also showed problems for language acquisition/learning. Most important, although the strengths of each approach seemed to complement the weaknesses of the other, it was also found that combining the approaches required significant modification and adaptation of features of each. The redesigned activities in Table 3.3 were found to be more complex, to require greater integration of reception and production, greater dependency on the integration of school and student resources, and to yield greater learner autonomy and motivation while retaining opportunities for teacher supervision and assessment.

However, the success of implementing the curricular activities of Table 3.3 is also dependent on other important factors. These include the use of materials and platforms that are relevant, authentic, and engaging for students, and equally important, on teachers who remain The Boss in their classrooms but who also understand, empathize with, and most of all trust and respect the intelligence of their students as learners. These teachers are also able to act as co-learners, acknowledging their students' own extramural strategies for language acquisition/learning and sources of knowledge—from their peers, from family members, popular culture, and the internet—as legitimate and of value educationally. Without this recognition, the affective filter will be raised, and the hybrid activities of Table 3.3 will quickly become as formalized and lacking in engagement and motivation for students as formal classroom learning often is.

The Coming Chapters

The conclusion of this chapter marks the end of Part I of this book and its focus on the *potential* of learner-driven strategies adapted from IDLE to transform English language learning and teaching, and the transition to a focus on methods, or the *implementation* of learner-driven strategies in classrooms.

To remain as close to the activities of IDLE as possible, Chapters 4–8 in Part II are organized not by formal categories typical of methods textbooks but instead by the ways and means that informal learners typically use in their acquisition/learning of English, supplemented by additional issues, such as ethical and safety considerations. Chapters 9–12 in Part III focus on curricular issues such as "flipped" classrooms and the impact of the pandemic on language education, the teaching of academic literacy through IDLE-based activities, and assessment. These chapters begin with scenarios focusing on teachers rather than learners, but the activities discussed in the scenarios of these chapters are consistent with the learner-driven approach of Part II.

Each chapter in Part II and Part III, Chapters 9–11, begins with a discussion of research and an assessment of the learning potential of a learning strategy, such as music (Chapter 4) or flipped classrooms (Chapter 9), followed by three detailed scenarios that might be used as lesson plans: one at the middle school, one at secondary/high school, and one at university level; however, in many cases scenarios written for one level are easily modified for learners at higher or lower grades. These scenarios are largely focused on learners at the advanced beginner to advanced intermediate /early advanced levels who require opportunities to develop proficiency. They assume that students have had some experience with English, or in cases of advanced proficiency, that learners are already so autonomous that they can create their own scenarios for digital learning. Chapter 12 of Part III offers a vision of the future of English language education in the coming 15 years.

Connecting Learner-Driven Acquisition/Learning and Standards-Driven Outcomes

Although the organization of this book does not present a formal curriculum for English education at any single level, the activities of Chapters 4–11 in total offer broad coverage of both the TESOL Technology Standards (2008) and the Common European Framework of Reference Level Descriptors (CEFR 2020). A list of standards and scale levels met is provided at the end of each scenario in Chapters 4–11 and in Tables 3.4 and 3.5.

IDLE and Chapter Topics: TESOL Technology Standards

Table 3.4 IDLE and chapter topics: TESOL Technology Standards for Language Learners coverage, Chapters 4–11.

TESOL Goals and Standards	Chapter 4 Scenarios			Chapter 5 Scenarios			Chapter 6 Scenarios			Chapter 7 Scenarios			Chapter 8 Scenarios			Chapter 9 Scenarios			Chapter 10 Scenarios			Chapter 11 Scenarios		
	1	2	3	1	2	3	1	2	3	1	2	3	1	2	3	1	2	3	1	2	3	1	2	3
Goal 1: Foundational knowledge and skills																								
Standard 1: Basic operational skills			✓	✓						✓						✓	✓							
Standard 2: Use of devices			✓	✓	✓	✓			✓	✓						✓	✓							
Standard 3: Exercise caution							✓	✓	✓															
Standard 4: Comp. use of technology			✓	✓	✓				✓	✓					✓		✓		✓			✓		✓
Goal 2: Appropriate social and cultural use of technology																								
Standard 1: Comm. convent.	✓											✓	✓		✓						✓			
Standard 2: Respect for others	✓							✓													✓			

TESOL Goals and Standards	Chapter 4 Scenarios			Chapter 5 Scenarios			Chapter 6 Scenarios			Chapter 7 Scenarios			Chapter 8 Scenarios			Chapter 9 Scenarios			Chapter 10 Scenarios			Chapter 11 Scenarios		
	1	2	3	1	2	3	1	2	3	1	2	3	1	2	3	1	2	3	1	2	3	1	2	3
Goal 3: Effective, critical use of tools																								
Standard 1: Eval. product. tools		✓	✓		✓				✓	✓			✓	✓	✓	✓	✓	✓				✓	✓	✓
Standard 2: Eval. skill-build tools		✓	✓		✓	✓			✓	✓	✓	✓	✓	✓	✓	✓	✓		✓	✓	✓	✓		
Standard 3: Eval. commun. tools	✓	✓	✓	✓	✓				✓	✓	✓	✓	✓	✓	✓	✓	✓		✓	✓	✓	✓	✓	✓
Standard 4: Eval. research tools	✓	✓						✓					✓	✓	✓	✓			✓	✓				✓
Standard 5: Tech. for autonomy ...	✓		✓	✓	✓	✓	✓		✓	✓		✓	✓	✓	✓	✓	✓	✓	✓	✓				✓

IDLE and Chapter Topics: Common European Framework of Reference (CEFR) Level Descriptors

Table 3.5 IDLE and chapter topics: Common European Framework of Reference (CEFR) scales, Chapters 4–11.

CEFR scales	Chapter 4 Scenarios			Chapter 5 Scenarios			Chapter 6 Scenarios			Chapter 7 Scenarios			Chapter 8 Scenarios			Chapter 9 Scenarios			Chapter 10 Scenarios			Chapter 11 Scenarios		
	1	2	3	1	2	3	1	2	3	1	2	3	1	2	3	1	2	3	1	2	3	1	2	3
1.1: Global scale	A2	B1	B1	B1	B1	B1	A2	B2	B1	A2	B2	A2	A2	B2	B2	A2	A2	B2	A2	B2	B1	B1	B2	B2
2.1: Communicative activities																								
Overall listening comp.		B1		B1	B1							A2						B2						
Understand native speaker																								
Listening as live audience																								
Listen to announce, instr.										B1						B1								
Listen to radio, recordings				B1	B1	B1												B2						
Watching TV and film	A2	B1	B1															B1						
Overall read. comp.		B1	B2	B1	B1		A2	B1		A2	A2	B1	B1	B2	B1	A2			A2	B2	B1		B2	B2

CEFR scales	Chapter 4 Scenarios			Chapter 5 Scenarios			Chapter 6 Scenarios			Chapter 7 Scenarios			Chapter 8 Scenarios			Chapter 9 Scenarios			Chapter 10 Scenarios			Chapter 11 Scenarios		
	1	2	3	1	2	3	1	2	3	1	2	3	1	2	3	1	2	3	1	2	3	1	2	3
Reading correspondence							A1																	
Reading for orientation											B1			B2	B1	B1			A2					
Read. info. and argument		B2	B1	B2	B1	B1	A1	B2		A2		A2	A2	B2		A2				B2	B1		B1	B2
Reading instructions								B1		B1					B1	B1								
Overall spoken interaction	A2		B1					B1	B1	A2	B1	A2			B1	A2						A2		
Understand native interloc.												B1	A2		B1									
Conversation												A2										B1		
Informal discuss, friends																								
Formal discuss, meetings		B1	B2					B2	B2	A2	B1		A2	B2	B2	A2	A2	B2		B2	B1	A2		
Goal-oriented co-op	A2	B2	B2		B1	B2		B1	B1	B1		A2	A2	B2	B2	B1	A2		A2	B2	B2	A2		

(Continued)

Table 3.5 (Continued)

CEFR scales	Chapter 4 Scenarios			Chapter 5 Scenarios			Chapter 6 Scenarios			Chapter 7 Scenarios			Chapter 8 Scenarios			Chapter 9 Scenarios			Chapter 10 Scenarios			Chapter 11 Scenarios		
	1	2	3	1	2	3	1	2	3	1	2	3	1	2	3	1	2	3	1	2	3	1	2	3
Transact. goods, services												A2			B1									
Information exchange		B1	B1		B1				B1		B1	B1	A2		B1		A1	B2		B1	B1	A2	B1	
Interview, be interviewed								B1					A2											
Overall written interaction							A2			B1						B1					B1			
Correspondence							A1																	
Notes, messages, forms				B1																				
Overall spoken production	A2		B2		B1	B1		B1	B1	A2	B2		A2	B2	B1	A2					B1			
Monologue: Describe exp.	A1		B1			B1		B1			B2													
Monologue: Putting a case																								
Public Announcements					B1																			

CEFR scales	Chapter 4 Scenarios			Chapter 5 Scenarios			Chapter 6 Scenarios			Chapter 7 Scenarios			Chapter 8 Scenarios			Chapter 9 Scenarios			Chapter 10 Scenarios			Chapter 11 Scenarios		
	1	2	3	1	2	3	1	2	3	1	2	3	1	2	3	1	2	3	1	2	3	1	2	3
Addressing audiences	A1	B1				A2	A2	B1	B1	A2			A2	B2		A2								B2
Overall written production	A2	B2	B2		B1	B2	A2	B2	B1		B2			B2	B1		A2		A1	B2	B1	B1	B1	B2
Creative writing							A1										A2							
Reports and essays						B1		B2	B1		B1								A2		B1	B1		B2

2.2 Communication strategies

CEFR scales	Chapter 4 Scenarios			Chapter 5 Scenarios			Chapter 6 Scenarios			Chapter 7 Scenarios			Chapter 8 Scenarios			Chapter 9 Scenarios			Chapter 10 Scenarios			Chapter 11 Scenarios		
	1	2	3	1	2	3	1	2	3	1	2	3	1	2	3	1	2	3	1	2	3	1	2	3
Identify clues and infer				B1									B1	B1					A2	B1				
Taking the floor																					B1			
Cooperating								B2					B1			B1					B2	B1		
Asking for clarification												A2	A2						A2		B1			
Planning	A2										B1				B2						B2			
Compensating												B1	B1		B1						B1			
Monitoring and repair												B1	B1								B2			

(Continued)

Table 3.5 (Continued)

CEFR scales	Chapter 4 Scenarios			Chapter 5 Scenarios			Chapter 6 Scenarios			Chapter 7 Scenarios			Chapter 8 Scenarios			Chapter 9 Scenarios			Chapter 10 Scenarios			Chapter 11 Scenarios		
	1	2	3	1	2	3	1	2	3	1	2	3	1	2	3	1	2	3	1	2	3	1	2	3
2.3 Working with text																								
Note-taking, sem. lect.				B1	B1	B1					B1							B2						
Processing text	B2	B2	B2	B1	B1			B2	B1		B2		A2	B2	B1			B1	A2	B1	B2	B1	B1	B2
2.4. Communicative language competence																								
General linguistic range	A2	B1	B1	B1	B1	B1	A2	B1	B2	A2	B2	A2	A2	B2	B2	A2	A2	B2	A2	B2	B2	B1	B2	B2
Vocabulary range						B1	A2		B1	A2	B2		B1	B2	B2		A2	B2				A2		B2
Grammatical accuracy		B1	B2		B1	B1	A2		B1		B1	A2			B1		A2		A2	B1	B2	B1	B1	B2
Vocabulary control					B1	B1								B2	B2			B2					B1	
Phonological control												A2				A2								
Orthographic control									B1	B1					B2				B1				B1	B2

CEFR scales	Chapter 4 Scenarios			Chapter 5 Scenarios			Chapter 6 Scenarios			Chapter 7 Scenarios			Chapter 8 Scenarios			Chapter 9 Scenarios			Chapter 10 Scenarios			Chapter 11 Scenarios		
	1	2	3	1	2	3	1	2	3	1	2	3	1	2	3	1	2	3	1	2	3	1	2	3
Socioling. appropriateness	A2											A2									B1			B2
Flexibility					B1					A2		B1							B1				B2	
Taking the floor												A2												
Thematic development	A2	B1				B1		B1			B2						A2							B2
Coherence					B1	B1		B1	B1					B2		A2			A2		B1	B1	B1	
Propositional precision		B1			B1		A2	B1	B1	A2	B2				B2	A2						B1	B1	B1
Spoken fluency	A					B1					B1													B2

Level of proficiency:
A1, A2: Beginning level
B1, B2: Intermediate level
C1, C2: Advanced level

Conclusion

In Chapter 3, we have presented a discussion of the history of research and beliefs about language acquisition and learning to demonstrate the complementarity of informal, acquisition-focused approaches and formal, learning-focused approaches in education. We argued that distinctions between acquisition and learning were much more blurred in practice than in research and theory, and that this presented an opportunity for the redesign of language education through a hybrid, blended redesign of activities that combined the authenticity and learner autonomy of IDLE with the systematicity and accountability of formal instruction.

Through an analysis of the strengths and weaknesses of IDLE and traditional, formal approaches to English education, we further established the complementarity of these approaches and presented examples of activities that combined the strengths of both approaches. Finally, we demonstrated that the activities presented in scenarios from Chapters 4 to 11 broadly covered both the TESOL Technology Standards and the Common European Framework of Reference Scales. Chapter 12 reviews the history of English language education since the start of the twentieth century and offers a vision of how advances in technology will impact the field in the coming 15 years.

We will conclude with the admonition, again, that as instructionally powerful a tool for learning and teaching learner-driven strategies are, they remain dependent on a reconceptualized role for teachers, in which the autonomy of students and their own strategies and means of learning are respected, and in which teachers act as knowledgeable co-learners with their students.

Let's Discuss

1) What is your opinion about language acquisition vs. language learning? Do you think that children have an advantage in learning languages over adults? If so, what do you think are the implications of this for your own acquisition/learning of languages and for your future teaching of English?

2) What is your experience of the affective filter? As a language learner, how reluctant have you been to take risks in your speaking and writing? How have you overcome any hesitancy you might have? What advice will you give or what strategies will you share with students who express reluctance to speak in class?

3) What is your opinion of the potential of learner-driven strategies and digital media use to lower the affective filter of language learners? In your experience, have you been less reluctant to engage others in the use of English when it was through digital media? Why do you think this has or has not been true for you?

4) Where do you stand on the call for teachers to rethink their role as teachers? Do you think the new role described in this chapter will be effective? Would it be effective without a shift to learner-driven strategies? As a teacher, how do you think you will adapt to this role, and to a greater level of autonomy for your students in the classroom than is traditional in many countries? Or, is this already the way you see yourself teaching now and into the future?

References

Behrend, Douglas A., Karl Rosengren, and Marion Perlmutter. "A New Look at Children's Private Speech: The Effects of Age, Task Difficulty, and Parent Presence." *International Journal of Behavioral Development* 12, no. 3 (1989): 305–320.

Benati, Alessandro. "Grammar-Translation Method." In *The TESOL Encyclopedia of English Language Teaching*. 2018. https://doi.org/10.1002/9781118784235.eelt0153.

CEFR. "The CEFR Levels." 2020. https://www.coe.int/en/web/common-european-framework-reference-languages/level-descriptions.

Chomsky, Noam. "Recent Contributions to the Theory of Innate Ideas." In *A Portrait of Twenty-five Years*, edited by Robert S. Cohen and Marx W. Wartofsky, 31–40. Dordrecht: Springer, 1967. https://doi.org/10.1007/978-94-009-5345-1_3.

Dalton-Puffer, Christiane. "Content-and-Language Integrated Learning: From Practice to Principles?" *Annual Review of Applied Linguistics* 31 (2011): 182–204. https://doi.org/10.1017/S0267190511000092.

Foucault, Michel. *Discipline and Punishment: The Birth of the Prison*. New York: Knopf Doubleday Publishing Group, 2012.

Gregg, Kevin R. "Review of Krashen: the input hypothesis." *TESOL Quarterly* 20, no. 1 (1986): 116–122.

Healey, Debra, Volker Hegelheimer, Phil Hubbard, Sophie Ioannou-Georgiou, Greg Kessler, and Paige Ware. *TESOL Technology Standards Framework*. TESOL. Alexandria, VA: Teachers of English to Speakers of Other Languages, Inc., 2008. http://www.tesol.org.

Higgs, Theodore V. "The Input Hypothesis: An Inside Look." *Foreign Language Annals* 18, no. 3 (1985): 197–203. https://doi.org/10.1111/j.1944-9720.1985.tb01791.x.

Ioup, Georgette. "Two Readers Comment on Stephen Krashen's Input Hypothesis: Testing the Relationship of Formal Instruction to the Input Hypothesis." *TESOL Quarterly* 18, no. 2 (1984): 345–350. https://doi.org/10.2307/3586703.

Khaliliaqdam, Salam. "ZPD, Scaffolding and Basic Speech Development in EFL Context." *Procedia—Social and Behavioral Sciences* 98 (2014): 891–897. https://doi.org/10.1016/j.sbspro.2014.03.497.

Krashen, Stephen D. "Formal and Informal Linguistic Environments in Language Acquisition and Language Learning." *TESOL Quarterly* 10, no. 2 (1976): 5–16.

Krashen, Stephen D. *Principles and Practice in Second Language Acquisition*. Oxford: Pergamon Press Inc., 1982.

Krashen, Stephen D. "The Input Hypothesis: An Update." In *Georgetown University Round Table on Languages and Linguistics (GURT) 1991: Linguistics and Language Pedagogy: The State of the Art*, edited by James E. Alatis, 409–431. Washington, DC: Georgetown University Press, 1991.

Nunan, David. *Task-Based Language Teaching*. Cambridge: Cambridge University Press, 2004.

Richards, Jack C. *Communicative Language Teaching Today*. Singapore: SEAMEO Regional Language Centre, 2005.

Snow, Marguerite Ann. "Trends and Issues in Content-Based Instruction." *Annual Review of Applied Linguistics* 18 (2010): 243–267. https://doi.org/10.1017/S0267190500003573.

Vygotsky, Lev Semenovich, and Michael Cole. *Mind in Society: Development of Higher Psychological Processes*. Cambridge, MA: Cambridge, MA: Harvard University Press, 1978.

Part II

IDLE in the Classroom

4

Songs, Video, and Vlogging

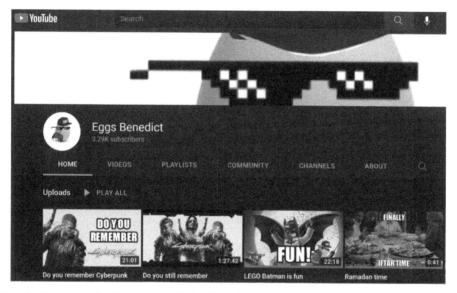

The YouTube page of a vlogger in the United Arab Emirates.

Introduction

Ouissal Id Hajji: Teenage Vlogger

Ouissal Id Hajji is a Moroccan teenage vlogger (*video blogger*) from a small town in the southern part of Morocco. She began recording her experiences learning English when she was 10 years old and quickly became a celebrity, appearing on the "Momo Morning Show" on Hit Radio, a station broadcasting from Rabat.

English is not taught in schools in Morocco until the last year of middle school, and so at age 10 Ouissal was entirely self-taught. In an early video on her YouTube channel, she explained her "secret" to learning English in five steps. First, she suggested that viewers find cartoons and movies in English that they enjoy and watch these regularly.

English Language Learning in the Digital Age: Learner-Driven Strategies for Adolescents and Young Adults, First Edition. Mark Dressman, Ju Seong Lee, and Laurent Perrot.
© 2023 John Wiley & Sons Ltd. Published 2023 by John Wiley & Sons Ltd.

For Ouissal, the US children's series, *My Little Pony*, broadcast on satellite television with Arabic subtitles, was her gateway to English. Over repeated viewings, she began to learn repeated phrases and words, and practiced them with her older sister, who was studying English in high school. This was Ouissal's second tip: Find someone close to you who knows a little bit more than you do and practice with them, getting help with things you don't understand.

Ouissal's third tip was to create a "fun world" through imaginary play, in which, for example, she might see her mother cooking a tagine (stew) for lunch, and pretend she was a food critic on television, offering suggestions for seasoning or alternative cooking methods to an imaginary audience, stretching her capacity for description in English. Her fourth tip was to push beyond speaking and learn to read and write in English, locating books and other materials online or locally in bookstores and libraries, to develop vocabulary and more formal modes of expression. Finally, Ouissal urged her viewers to begin to listen to music in English, studying the lyrics to practice both pronunciation and to pick up new ways to phrase ideas.

Nan Shinawatra: Adele Super Fan

Nan Shinawatra is a 16-year-old Thai student enrolled in Matthayom 5 (Grade 11) in a public school in Phuket Province, Thailand. Her family owns a small restaurant that caters to tourists, mostly from the UK and United States, who are drawn by English language menus and her father's English as host. Her grandfather served in the Thai Royal Air Force in the 1970s and learned English from US pilots stationed at Thai bases. When he retired to Phuket in the 1990s, he opened a restaurant and used his English to attract tourists, later teaching Nan's father—who now manages the restaurant—the basics of English as well.

Nan's knowledge of English comes through a combination of school and her family's restaurant. As a child, she listened attentively to tourists as they dined and stared at the strange English translations beneath the photos and descriptions of menu items in Thai. English remained distant and largely incomprehensible to her, however, until her teenage years, when the family installed speakers in the restaurant and began to play British and US pop music at lunch and dinner.

The voice of one British singer in particular, Adele, caught her attention. While her friends at school focused their attention on K-pop Stars like Rain and bands such as EXO and BTS, the Korean-language lyrics of most of this music were elusive. Nan and her classmates had studied English in school since their primary years, but instruction was largely focused on rote exercises about topics that did not catch her interest. Adele, however, seemed to have a voice and a message that was powerful. One day in passing, as "Rolling in the Deep" was playing in the restaurant, the phrase, "We could have had it all," began to repeat itself in Nan's mind.

From then on, Nan was hooked. She downloaded several of Adele's songs from Spotify and sat down to study them. Her strategy was to listen to a lyric again and again and try to transcribe it; then she would look up the English lyrics online and compare her transcription to the published lyric. When she didn't understand the meaning of a lyric, she used translation apps on her smartphone to try to figure it out. At first Nan struggled, but soon she became increasingly accurate and able to identify English words when she heard them in songs. From Adele, she moved to other singers like Ed Sheeran and Justin

Bieber, and soon found that with only a few repetitions she was picking up more and more of the lyrics.

Nan also found that it was not only fun to practice singing and repeating the lyrics to herself, but useful for her own pronunciation. This emboldened her to have brief conversations with customers at the restaurant, who complimented her and made her even more confident. Her major moment of triumph, however, came when the K-pop group BTS dropped their first all-English single, "Dynamite," and the next year "Butter" and "Permission to Dance." Nan's friends knew of her knack for learning English song lyrics and they came to her for help with learning the lyrics of these BTS songs. Soon she was teaching her techniques to classmates, and they began to share each other's transcriptions and information about singers they found on the internet in English.

"Friends Don't Lie": Stranger Things in France

Didier, Marc, Jean, and Paul are a group of friends who grew up together, attended a lycée (high school) in the Grand Est region of France and now study at the University of Strasbourg. They are studying different subjects at university but remain united by their years of friendship and mutual love of one long-running US television series, *Stranger Things.*

In their pre-university days, Didier, a computer geek, would find ways to stream-watch episodes of the series from websites that were part of a network of sites in unnamed countries hosting series copied from US-based streaming services. These pirated copies were available only in English, but the language was basic enough that with a few years of secondary-school English they were able to follow the episodes. If a challenge arose, they could combine their knowledge and Paul, who had spent a few summers with cousins in Virginia, could usually figure out what was being said.

Part of the initial attraction of *Stranger Things* was its quirky characters and plotline, combined with its exotic small-town setting in Indiana that, they decided, had some "strange things" in common with the town in Alsatian France where they lived. Over time they began to pick up catchphrases in English that were repeated by characters and, among themselves, they would infuse these into their conversations. The joking became so involved that whenever they met, they would assume the personas of characters in the series. Eventually they were able more and more to mimic the characters in their speech, coming to a point at which they held extended conversations in an imagined midwestern American dialect. Almost without noticing it, the four friends' proficiency in English began to increase to the point where, even after the series became available to them dubbed in French, they still preferred to watch the original with English captions rather than French subtitles as they believed the subtitles distracted them and spoilt their fun.

Discussion

These three vignettes provide our starting point for this chapter's focus on adapting learner-driven strategies for using music, videos, and vlogging as resources within English language classrooms. The first vignette is a real-life portrait of a recent YouTube vlogger in Morocco (Id Hajji 2014) and the second and third are composites of learners drawn from research and our own experiences as teachers. Although all three accounts are very different in terms of location, age, and types of media, they also share several characteristics that are critical to their adaptability within classroom settings.

The first characteristic is that in all three vignettes the learners came to English through content that was compelling and that drew them into the content and the need to learn English to fully enjoy it. In other words, it wasn't English itself that motivated the learners initially; it was the message, and English was "merely" the medium. However, this also changed over time. Ouissal, for example, could have continued to watch *My Little Pony* with Arabic subtitles; Nan could have enjoyed the melody and sound of Adele's voice and looked up the Thai translation of "Rolling in the Deep" if she'd been curious about its meaning; and the four French friends could have muddled through their pirated episodes and then switched to the dubbed or subtitled French version when it became available; but none of them did. Why not? We suspect it was because as they became immersed in the multimodal experience of these media, they also began to sense that the full pleasure of their experiences could not be had without learning the language.

Second, they quickly developed strategies for learning. Ouissal was able to articulate a five-step plan for learning English from a television series; Nan quickly figured out that trying to transcribe the lyrics was key to developing her listening comprehension and ability to memorize and understand them; and the four university friends found that extending the world of *Stranger Friends* as a metaphor for their own was not only a source of new insights but also provided a meaningful context for rehearsing the English they had heard in their viewing. These strategies were pedagogically very sound and even innovative and would easily correlate with TESOL Technology Standards or CEFR Reference Level Descriptors.

Third, and as discussed in Chapter 2, these learners made very little distinction between the world of their everyday lives and the digital world of the media they engaged. This is especially true in the case of the students' formal learning of English in school, which in the case of Nan and the French friends directly provided a foundation for their initial informal activities, and in the case of Ouissal, through her sister's learning of English in school. It was this dissolution of barriers between school and extramural English that spurred their learning. As Ouissal's English proficiency developed it was no doubt noticed by her family, who then helped her find outlets for its expression that led to her appearance on one of Morocco's most popular national radio shows. The connection between Nan's family's restaurant and her interest in its music eventually led her to practice her English with the customers and to the recognition of her achievement by her friends. And although the four university students did not "go public" with their role-playing, it certainly blurred differences between *Stranger Things* and their daily lives.

Chapter Objectives

The central goal of this chapter is to explore the potential of digital media that combine music, spoken and written language, images, and movement for learning English both informally and, with some adaptation, formally in classroom settings. As subgoals, readers will learn about recent research in the use of music and videos in language education, as well as basic semiotic principles and how these contribute to language acquisition. By the end of this chapter, readers should be able to:

(Continued)

1) Explain the features of songs that make them a powerful gateway to early and intermediate language learning.
2) Explain the need for intentionality in learning English from songs.
3) Distinguish between *subtitled* and *captioned* video.
4) Apply research findings to judge the quality of video for language learning.
5) Describe the benefits of vlogging for language learners.
6) Describe the *semiotic* differences between an *icon*, an *index*, and a *symbol*.
7) Describe the theoretical and practical aspects of the principle of *reciprocal indexicality* in learning from songs, video, and vlogs.
8) Describe three approaches to adapting learner-driven strategies for learning from songs, video and vlogs to classroom contexts.
9) Consider how the research, theory, and three scenarios in this chapter can be applied to the reader's pedagogical context.

Key Words
caption; subtitle; vlogging; multimodality; semiotics (icon, index, symbol); reciprocal indexicality

Research and Theory

Learning from Songs and Music

The combination of chant or music with a rhythmic text has long been a powerful technique for memorization and learning, from sung recitations of Homer's Iliad and Odyssey in ancient Greece to the present time and the continuing tradition of Navajo healing ceremonies that last for days (Matthews 1894; Minchin 2001). Today, the music of global recording artists ranging from K-pop to Euro-pop to North American and British stars like Ed Sheerhan, Taylor Swift, Beyoncé, and Drake to Spanish crossover artists Shakira, Enrique Inglesias, and Ricky Martin are often a gateway to English for youths around the world.

Research Findings. Much of the research on informal learning of English through songs comes from surveys of students (Toffoli and Sockett 2014) and through first-hand accounts of learners. One of the best archives of these accounts is the Hall Project (2014), which contains many narratives of students from Hong Kong learning English through music and other media. This research suggests that songs are most effective in the early through intermediate (CEFR: A1-B1) levels of language proficiency. Reviews of the literature on the use of songs both informally and in classrooms indicate that not only listening to songs but practicing them by singing either to oneself or in a group can significantly improve learners' pronunciation, speaking confidence, fluency, vocabulary, and use of grammar (Albaladejo, Coyle, and de Larios 2018; Aquil 2012; Diakou 2013; Jarvis 2014; Ludke, Ferreira, and Overy 2014).

Music and Language: Research Findings

Recent research at Stanford University has found a direct link between musical training and language ability (Trei 2005). People who play a musical instrument are better able to:

- Distinguish among sounds (minimal pairs)
- More efficiently process sound (make distinctions immediately)
- Increase phonetic (sound-print) processing skills
- Reproduce tonal sequences they have heard

Four factors contribute to songs' effectiveness in language learning. First, the rhythm of the lyrics and music introduces learners to patterns of intonation in speech. Second, the catchy repetitiveness of a song's chorus provides opportunities for practicing pronunciation, vocabulary, and grammatical structures. Third, the condensed language of songs means that they are relatively easy to memorize and to repeat. Finally and crucially, the "coolness" of a current singer or group, their ubiquity on the radio and online streaming services, and especially artists' function as markers of social identity for adolescents (e.g., membership in BTS's "Army") is highly motivational for youth, compelling many learners to listen over and over again to songs and to study lyrics and to seek out and read materials in English about their favorite singers that they otherwise would not.

Songs are not only a gateway to learning to speak but also to literacy in a language. Many learners report their attempts to learn song lyrics by listening to them, attempting to transcribe them, and then checking their transcriptions against published lyrics. This practice assists in learning the orthography and phonetics of a language. In addition, attention to the poetic quality of song lyrics and often their inventiveness provides early access for learners to some of the most advanced literary features of a language.

The Power of Intentionality. Simply listening over and over to the same song, however, does not automatically lead to learning its language. Karen Ludke (2020) notes that learning from music requires the same intentionality and attention to lyrics as learning from any other medium, including a textbook. The critical difference, it seems, is the motivation that comes from studying a song or lyric sung by a singer with influence in learners' social lives. That is why it is also critically important for songs used in classrooms to, again, reflect the interests of learners and their life worlds.

Language Learning Through Video

A second very popular gateway for English is through *subtitled* (translated in the speaker's language) or *captioned* (transcribed in the original language) video. Many times, learners become "hooked" on English through a favorite subtitled satellite or streamed television series. These feature familiar, recurring characters and settings and episodic storylines whose redundancy makes them predictable and easy to follow. The characters may also repeat the same expressions across episodes, which are easily learned and practiced with friends, reinforcing the social "coolness" of the series and of English among youth.

In addition to television series, online streaming services like YouTube offer an extraordinary range of free, ubiquitous, and sometimes high-quality programs on a vast array of topics, from documentaries to short comedy videos to how-to programs (including many series on learning English), informational programs like TED Talks, and so on. In addition, there are many young vloggers sharing their lives across the globe in both their native languages and in English, such as Darcie in the Republic of Korea (Darcie 2018) or Mohamed (Mohamed Talks 2021) in Algeria. Most YouTube videos are captioned in their original language, and many are subtitled in one or more additional languages, although the quality of the subtitling, especially if it is automatic, can vary. These videos can be paused, and sections can be replayed, allowing listeners to watch/listen to a confusing line multiple times to figure it out.

Five English-Speaking YouTube Vloggers

Eggs Benedict. This Emirati vlogger posts reviews of movies, video games, and other media on his YouTube channel.

Acholi Pride. Eunice posts in English about her life in a village in Northern Uganda and the Acholi language.

KrisTells Vlogs. Kristel Fulgar is a trilingual Filipina vlogger in English, Filipino, and Korean who posts about her life in the Philippines and travel to South Korea.

Miaslifestyle. Mia is a German university student and YouTube "influencer" who vlogs about school, travel, cooking, and fashion.

Joonkik. This Korean vlogger lived in Canada for some years and speaks both Korean and English. He vlogs about cross-cultural relationships with people in South Korea.

However, not all videos are equally effective resources. A key element of an effective video for learning is the degree to which its visual content illustrates the spoken content and reciprocally, the degree to which the spoken content of a video accurately aligns with the visual content. Many times, the visual content is a "talking head," that is, someone on screen talking to the viewer with few visual references to what is being talked about. When this happens, the visual channel of the video for learning is significantly reduced to the facial expressions and gestures of the speaker.

Reception: Captioning vs. Subtitling. Most videos today combine images that are still or moving with audio recordings of speech, music, or other acoustic sounds. The benefits of learning a wide range of subjects through a combination of well-coordinated modes are well documented in the research literature, and the addition of a written transcription of speech within the videos is especially critical for language acquisition. But which is better for language learning: *captions*, which are transcriptions of speech in the original (L1) language, or *subtitles*, which are translations of the original language of a video into another language more familiar to a learner? Robert Vanderplank (2010; 2020) in two seminal reviews of the research literature, has made a clear case for the superiority of captions over subtitles for language learning; however, this also depends on two factors. The first factor is the proficiency level of the learner: someone with little or no understanding of the target language will probably need subtitling for input to be comprehensible (in which case they may only pick up a few words or phrases), while an intermediate learner may be able to both follow and learn more from captioned video. The second factor is the viewer's purpose and motivation: viewers interested in learning a language will tend to focus more on captions and the language of the video than viewers who are watching solely to be entertained. Vanderplank concludes: "The most successful language learners ... are certainly those who put time and effort into actively engaging with others in the foreign language, consciously drawing on the language of video resources to enhance and further communication" (Vanderplank 2020, 198).

Production: Vlogging as Writing/Composing. One of the most popular genres for language learning is vlogging, in which typically young and engaging individuals share their lives in many different nations with viewers in English or in their original languages. Vloggers provide an engaging resource for English and other language learners receptively, but as Tatiana Codreanu and Christelle Combe (2020) explain, vlogging also provides an extraordinary opportunity for language learners to create their own vlogs using smartphones and basic editing equipment and to share these on YouTube, either with the world or, if privacy is an issue, through unlisted channels available only to classmates and their teachers. Vlogging requires learners to write a script in English, to practice reading or using that script as the basis for speaking extemporaneously, to compose and present themselves publicly (again, worldwide or to a limited group), and to extend the experience of the vlog through written comments from viewers and responses to those comments. YouTube provides excellent tutorials on vlogging on its YouTube Creators channel (YouTube 2022). Vlogs can be produced by learners of almost any age and level of proficiency. There may be no more comprehensive or more engaging way for learners to practice and develop listening, speaking, reading, and writing/composing skills in English than through making a vlog and sharing it with a (safe) community.

A Critical Factor: Multimodality

Songs, videos, and vlogging, especially when offered digitally online, offer a powerful response to some of the most intractable problems in formal language education, namely, the lack of authentic, compelling, and limitless content, filled with opportunities for social connection and self-directed selection and learning at almost any time. But these media's most outstanding and yet least understood feature may be their multimodality, or their wide range of visual and auditory input, which when well coordinated, produce messages whose complexity and comprehensibility far exceeds their individual parts.

Multimodality is a feature that is often noted by researchers of songs and video in language education but seldom explained. Dressman (2020) has noted the challenges inherent in describing the interactions among the various modes of a song or video, comparing these to our evolving physical understanding of gravity, both in complexity and importance for language education. The *semiotic* theory of Charles Sanders Peirce (Parmentier 1994; Peirce 2007), an American philosopher and scientist of the late nineteenth/early twentieth century, offers some basic insight into the questions at hand. Peirce's work is grounded in the work of medieval European philosophers who asked, fundamentally, how input to our senses was received and processed into meaningful information about the world. These philosophers and Peirce held that we understand the data of our senses in three ways: *iconically*, through resemblance to objects already experienced; *indexically*, through paired association or contiguity with previous experience; and *symbolically*, through conventional systems of understanding. A photograph of a dog, for example, is an *icon*, because it resembles other animals within a category; a dog's bark from behind a door is an *index*, because through past experiences of contiguity the bark indexes, or "points to" a dog; and everything that might be said about dogs in general, such as laws within a city about dog ownership, is a *symbol*, or codified conventional knowledge presented through an abstract system of codes, i.e., language.

What is a Sign?

Semiotics is the study of how we perceive and interpret sensory input, through "signs," which connect what we see, hear, touch, smell, and taste with our conscious and unconscious understanding.

There are two major semiotic theories. Ferdinand de Saussure proposed a theory of signs based on language, in which "signifiers" (speech) are arbitrarily paired with "signifieds" (concepts) to create meaning. His theory is best used to describe linguistic systems, but it has been used also for cultural analysis.

However, not all connections between input and meaning are arbitrary, as in language. For example, we know what a chair is when we see it because it resembles a category of objects known as chairs, and we know that a sign on a door tells us what is behind the door because of its physical placement. These connections are not arbitrary.

Charles Sanders Peirce, an American philosopher in the late nineteenth and early twentieth centuries, developed a theory of signs based on medieval philosophy, in which relations between an object, its sign, and its interpretation are determined by whether the connection is conventional or arbitrary (as in language), iconic or through resemblance (as when we recognize objects in a photo), or indexically connected in space or time (as in the placement of a stop light at an intersection).

Peirce's theory includes language, but it is most useful in describing non-linguistic signs. Its complexity and Peirce's writing style have prevented it from being frequently used in multimodal research.

For Peirce, our formal, articulated knowledge not only of dogs but everything else in the world is contained within symbolic systems, usually either linguistic or mathematic; yet that knowledge originates in experiences that are pre-lingual and grounded in types of signs and signification that are non-linguistic and much more primary to our being in the world. This, notes Dressman, is where and why formal language education has traditionally faltered: "If ... learning begins in and with experience of the world, then to learn a language as an abstracted system of meaning with only very limited access to the world is an almost pointless and ultimately dreary and very frustrating enterprise. Yet that is how languages for years were, and in most places still are, formally taught" (Dressman 2020, 47). Informal learners, in contrast, have learned to harness the resource of multimodality ... (of) multiple types of signs working in coordination with three relational principles of resemblance, contiguity, and convention to produce an articulated experience that is whole and that encompasses all our ways of knowing, from the visceral and qualitative to the relational and rational to the cerebral and intellectual. (48)

As different types of signs (icon, index, symbol), images, speech, and captions are not the same, and do not replace each other; but they do point to, or index each other, building a whole out of their parts. Dressman describes this as the principle of *reciprocal indexicality*, whereby music and rhythm complement the lyrics of a song to make it both memorable and more easily remembered, or visual images, speech, and transcribed captions fill in or compensate for gaps in the understanding of each to create a unified, fully comprehensible message.

Practical Applications in the Classroom

Scenario One: Vlogging at a Parisian Collège (Middle School)

The Scene. Justin Lacombe teaches English and German in a collège (middle school) in a working-class arrondissement of Paris. Most of his students, who are 14–15 years old, were born in France but speak the language of their parents' birth nations at home. They are a lively, gregarious group who have little enthusiasm for learning English at school, although many of them love to insert English words and phrases picked up from songs, television shows, and films into their speech.

The collège has a strict policy regarding the use of smartphones at school and bans them from being used in classrooms, but Justin frequently sees his students holding them in their laps beneath their desks, texting and sometimes watching videos. Rather than create an ongoing distraction in his classes, he has announced that he will not confiscate smartphones if he sees them, but will reserve the right to share with the rest of the class what the students are watching. He has hoped that the humor of the warning and potential danger of embarrassment would reduce students' use.

However, recently, during a class in which students were supposed to be working on a short essay in English, he noticed Leila, who sat toward the back of the room on the left, deeply engaged with watching something beneath her desktop. Quietly slipping around the periphery of the desks, he walked up behind her and said aloud, "Ah, Leila! What are you watching that's so interesting? Let's all have a look!"

Leila jerked around, shocked and a bit embarrassed, but then she recovered. "Monsieur Lacombe, excuse me, but I've finished my essay and I'm watching a YouTube video about this American student who is teaching himself French," she said. She giggled as she handed Justin her phone. "Ah, Michael!" another girl said, then another and another: "Michael! Michael! His accent's so cute!" Justin had expected that Leila was perhaps watching a music or comedy video, but never one about an American learning French. He held the phone up and increased the volume as the entire class turned and laughed, hearing Michael mangle one French vowel after another. "He's a vlogger?" Justin asked. "Learning French?" "Yes!" a chorus responded. "Oh, that guy," Simon groaned from a desk in front.

As the discussion continued, Justin learned that Michael (Texfrancais 2012) was a very popular YouTube vlogger among the students and that they were fans of several other teenage vloggers as well who spoke French, English, and other languages, including Jules (GoingbyJules 2022) from Norway, and Em (Em's Other Side 2021), a French vlogger living in Korea. He was surprised by his students' deep interest in these vloggers' lives and languages, and even more by their excitement to share their interest with him. He wondered if, perhaps, this was exactly what he needed to ignite a similar passion in his students for speaking English and sharing their life worlds with an audience.

Analysis: Challenges and Opportunities. As we have discussed in this chapter, vlogging provides an extraordinary opportunity not only for students to access authentic English language content that is highly engaging but also to produce English language videos of their own for an audience. With little more than a smartphone, access to basic editing equipment (iMovie, Windows Video Editor, an open-source editor, or YouTube Studio Editor), and an internet connection, students can create their own YouTube channels.

One serious consideration, especially for students in middle and high school, is privacy. However, YouTube offers three levels of visibility that will protect the privacy of students, their families, and communities: Private (the composer lists the emails of people who may view); Unlisted (the video is unsearchable but anyone with the link may view it); and Public (searchable and anyone can view). In addition, it is advisable for teachers to screen videos to be sure that activities such as bullying or revealing private information are avoided; and it may be necessary to allow administrators and parents to have access to all vlogs produced by students under class supervision. These precautions are not demanding or difficult to take, however, and in most cases should not prevent students from creating engaging, inspiring vlogs in English.

Instructional Plan. Justin's announcement that the students would be composing a vlog in pairs in English and uploading it to YouTube was met with cheers. He began by asking for the names of three vloggers the students enjoyed and overnight previewed these, noting the key elements of a good vlog. In the morning, he showed the students three vlogs and brainstormed key attributes of an interesting vlog, recording these on the board. He organized the students into pairs and then brainstormed topics with the students, including settings and other content features, and explained that by the following week each pair would complete "an original vlog of 3–5 minutes in English on a topic related to their lives." He also explained that both students would need to share the narration and speak equally in the video.

Justin also distributed a simple storyboard format consisting of a sequence of blocks, in which the students sketched in shots they would use with their written narration underneath. These were due in two days. Once all storyboards were turned in and Justin had checked them for completion and the feasibility of their plans, the students began to produce the vlogs. The students used their own smartphone cameras. Shooting of the videos was completed in another two days.

To edit the videos, the class moved to the school's computer lab. Justin provided the students with a brief tutorial in how to use Windows Video Editor. He allowed several students who had experience with other software to use it, provided they could bring it on laptops or tablets from home or access the software online (but not download it on school computers). Working in pairs, the students quickly figured out how to import clips from their phones, add them in sequence to the Video Editor storyboard, and begin to trim them, adding transitions, and title and end frames. He announced that students would receive extra credit for including theme music and captions in English.

Within three days, most of the students had completed their vlogs. Justin showed the students how to upload them to a class channel he had created on YouTube, making sure that each video uploaded was listed as "Private." As a few pairs continued editing, he directed the remaining students to begin viewing and commenting on each other's vlogs. Within two weeks, the project was completed, and Justin was able to send his school director and parents a link for viewing the vlogs.

1) Materials:
   a) Student smartphones
   b) Storyboard handout for planning
   c) Computers with editing software
   d) Internet connection to YouTube
   e) Class YouTube channel.

2) Learning Mode: Whole class and dyads
3) Time: Ten days; 50-minute periods
4) Sequence of Activities:
   a) On Day 1, announce the project
   b) Show three vlogs and discuss features; record on board
   c) Brainstorm vlogging topics; organize student pairs
   d) On Day 2, introduce and demonstrate storyboarding
   e) Have students write storyboards
   f) Teacher circulates among pairs
   g) On Day 3, continue storyboarding
   h) Check completed storyboards
   i) On Day 4, students begin to shoot their vlogs
   j) Shooting continues for homework
   k) On Day 5, shooting continues
   l) Students are instructed to complete shooting over the weekend
   m) On Day 6, class meets in the computer lab
   n) Teacher demonstrates editing software briefly
   o) Students begin to edit
   p) On Days 7–8, editing continues
   q) Days 9–10, students upload and view each other's vlogs
   r) Remaining pairs complete editing
   s) Remaining pairs view vlogs and comment.

Assignments and Assessment. This activity has one assessment for the students' process and their final vlogs (see Table 4.1).

Table 4.1 Rubric for process and final vlog.

Achievement level	Descriptor
Excellent	The students worked well as a team and prepared a careful, detailed storyboard with a full English text. The vlog was complete, of 3–5 minutes in length, and included all elements brainstormed by the class. Editing was clear with solid transitions. The topic was appropriate; both students spoke equally and shared narration. The English in the video was grammatical with good word choice and clear pronunciation. Overall, the vlog was attractively edited and engaging for viewers. For extra credit, students added theme music and well-written captions in English.
Very good	The students worked as a team and prepared a detailed storyboard with an English text. The vlog was complete and of appropriate length, and included nearly all elements brainstormed by the class. The editing was clear with transitions. The topic was appropriate; both students spoke in the video. The English in the video had few errors and was comprehensible. Overall, the video was attractive and engaging. For extra credit, students added theme music and well-written captions in English.
Satisfactory	The students worked together and prepared a storyboard with English text. The vlog was complete and nearly met the 3–5 minute limits. It included most of the elements brainstormed by the class, with a beginning, a middle, and an end. There was evidence of editing, but some transitions were not smooth. The topic was appropriate and both students spoke, but one student may have dominated. Despite errors, the English in the video was comprehensible. Overall, the video was complete and interesting. For extra credit, students added theme music and well-written captions in English.
Unsatisfactory	The students did not work well as a team. The storyboard was incomplete with an incomplete English text. The vlog did not meet the 3–5 minute limits and lacked many elements brainstormed by the class. Editing was poor, with rough transitions. The topic may not have been appropriate and only one student may have spoken. The English was challenging to understand. Overall, the vlog was incomplete and needed major editing and/or reshooting. Extra credit was not allowed.

Relation to TESOL Technology Standards for Learners and CEFR Reference Level Descriptors

TESOL Technology Standards:

- Goal 2 (Use technology in appropriate ways)
  - Standard 1 (Understand that conventions differ across contexts)
  - Standard 2 (Demonstrate respect for others).
- Goal 3 (Effectively use and evaluate tools)
  - Standard 3 (Use and evaluate tools for communication and collaboration)
  - Standard 4 (Use and evaluate tools appropriately)
  - Standard 5 (Recognize the value of technology to support autonomy, creativity, and collaboration).

CEFR Reference Level Descriptors:

- Global Scale: A2 (Can understand and use familiar expressions/Can understand sentences and frequently used expressions)

- Watching TV and Film: A2 (Can identify the main point of TV news)
- Overall Spoken Interaction: A2 (Can interact with reasonable ease in structured situations)
- Goal-Oriented Cooperation: A2 (Can ... manage simple, routine tasks)
- Overall Spoken Production: A2 (Can give a simple description or presentation)
- Sustained Monologue: A1/A2 (Can describe him/herself; can tell a story or describe something in a simple list of points)
- Addressing Audiences: A1/A2 (Can read a very short, rehearsed statement; can give a short, rehearsed presentation)
- Overall Written Production: A2 (Can write a series of simple phrases and sentences)
- Planning: A2 (Can recall and rehearse an appropriate set of phrases)
- General Linguistic Range: A2 (Can use basic sentence patterns and communicate with memorized phrases)
- Sociolinguistic Appropriateness: A2 (Can socialize simply but effectively)
- Thematic Development: A2 (Can tell a story or describe something in a simple list of points)
- Spoken Fluency: A2 (Can construct phrases on familiar topics with sufficient ease).

Analyzing and Extending the Lesson: Application to Additional Contexts. In this scenario, a teacher in a collège (middle school) in France found a way to turn his students' interest in YouTube vloggers into a project in which pairs of students created a 3–5 minute vlog and uploaded it to a private YouTube channel for viewing by themselves and parents. In the process, students practiced writing and speaking as well as recording and editing videos in English to present themselves to the world of their friends and family. They also practiced listening and responding in writing to each other's videos and used online tools to look for appropriate vocabulary and check on the grammatical accuracy of their productions.

Perhaps the greatest challenge to completing this exercise successfully, beyond assuring parents and administrators that the privacy of the students would not be violated, is the editing process. In this case, the teacher chose to have students edit in the school's computer lab and upload to a private class channel, but other ways might be to have students edit the videos directly on their smartphones or to use an online editor; this would allow them to edit outside of class time, and the videos might be used for future projects.

Beyond vlogging, there are many uses of video within an English language classroom. Instead of vlogging, students might make videos narrating and making short presentations on school sporting or other events, or subjects of personal interest. They might also create a presentation using PowerPoint, record a narration of the presentation and then save it as a video to upload to the class's channel.

Scenario Two: "Rewilding" an Afterschool English Program with TED Talks

The Scene. Lu Dingxin teaches high school English in Taichung, Taiwan, and is an active hiker and outdoor sportsman in his spare time. He studied abroad in the United States as an undergraduate at Montana State University, where he made many hiking and camping trips in the Rocky Mountains and Yellowstone National Park.

Mr. Lu has been inspired by the story of the reintroduction of the grey wolf into Yellowstone and its impact on the ecology there, which has led to his interest in "rewilding," or the reintroduction of megafauna, or large species, to ecosystems where they have disappeared internationally, and especially from Taiwan. When he was asked by parents and students to form an afterschool English study club, he decided that he would combine his skills as an English teacher with his interest in ecology, to form a club in which the content of language activities would focus on ecological issues.

Because this is an afterschool club, Mr. Lu knows that he must keep the activities engaging and open-ended to keep students working. Parents and the principal of his school have expressed concern that the focus on ecology will distract the students from learning the English skills they need to succeed in upcoming exams, but Mr. Lu has argued that he can keep students more engaged and develop all the requisite skills in academic English that are on the test if he uses English language materials that build vocabulary and activities that require students to use English to write and talk about topics that are academic in focus but that also appeal to their idealism and interest in the natural world.

Mr. Lu also knows that his students are avid users of technology, not only to play games but for informal learning through videos. He remembers his own experiences learning English through captioned TED Talks on YouTube, and he has decided to make TED Talks on ecology and "rewilding" the center of his students' afterschool learning.

Analysis: Challenges and Opportunities. The challenges of conducting an afterschool program for students in their final years of secondary school can be overwhelming. Pressure from parents and a combination of anxiety and boredom experienced by students, as well as the extra workload imposed on teachers, can create a high-pressure system for all concerned that reduces rather than energizes teaching and learning.

Rather than rely on test-prep packets and endless drill of grammar rules and vocabulary out of context, an alternative method is to use high-quality videos focusing on academic subject matter of interest to students and use this content to review grammar and develop vocabulary and writing skills. TED Talks on YouTube are an excellent source of material for teachers interested in designing an afterschool program that is interesting for them and their students but which also provides opportunities for review and practice of important skills tested in English exams. The videos are relatively short (usually 15–20 minutes) and are presented by English speakers who are not only leading academics in their fields but are also engaging story tellers and lecturers. They are carefully captioned in English and on a broad range of engaging topics which are sure to catch the interest of students.

In terms of language curriculum and pedagogy, TED Talks lend themselves to the teaching of not only critical academic vocabulary but also practice in key grammatical structures, such as conditionality, passive vs. active voice, and mass vs. countable nouns, depending of course on the topic and the speaker selected. Most important, the engagement of the speakers with their audience and topic provides a platform for practice in conceptualizing ideas and expressing them solely in English.

Instructional Plan. Mr. Lu spent an hour or so over the weekend browsing the TED Talks channel on YouTube for an appropriate video to introduce his afterschool review sessions. He knew he wanted to focus on a topic that was regaining the popular imagination in a number of East Asian countries, including South Korea, Japan, and

Taiwan: "Rewilding" abandoned or unpopulated rural and wilderness areas. After watching several videos on this topic, he chose one by British journalist George Monbiot (2013), "For More Wonder, Rewild the World," featuring Monbiot's review of several successful rewilding programs framed by his personal story.

Mr. Lu's analysis of this video was that although it lacked supporting images of the topics and places Monbiot described, the text of the talk was filled with key concepts and vocabulary. It also lent itself to the review of one of the main elements of the national exam in English, conditionality. With the development of vocabulary and practice in the use of conditionals and modals in mind, he set about designing a series of activities that would practice these.

Mr. Lu's plan was to begin by showing the video to the students as a class, pausing to introduce a few key concepts and vocabulary words as they occurred in the video, and writing them on the board with some notes. He then placed the students in groups of three or four and had them watch the video again in their groups, noting additional vocabulary. In whole-class discussion the students shared their additional vocabulary and Mr. Lu then asked the students to write a one-page summary of the video using at least five of the new vocabulary words, to check their comprehension. Each group shared its summary with the class, and they discussed the key concepts and worked to peer-edit each other's summaries.

Next, Mr. Lu introduced conditionality and the use of modals by asking the students, "What if rewilding were introduced to Taiwan? Where would the best locations be, and what animals should be reintroduced?" To provide the students with more information, he provided them with links to stories about Taiwanese wildlife from newspapers such as *The China Post* and the *Taiwan News*. Each small group was given one article and asked to summarize it. The students then brainstormed possible species to reintroduce in specific areas, such as the Formosan black bear, Taiwan's three indigenous species of deer, the Taiwanese Leopard Cat, and smaller species of birds, reptiles, and amphibians. From this list, each group chose one topic and began to research possible locations for rewilding and, most important, to consider the consequences and implications of reintroducing a species for both the ecology of the location and the human population in the area.

In addition, Mr. Lu provided a quick review at the beginning of each class of conditional structures, including the use of modals and the subjunctive "were," as in "If the Taiwanese Leopard Cat were reintroduced to ..." Each group was given an assignment to create a PowerPoint presentation about the reintroduction of their species with a narrative script in which they practiced the use of conditional structures and key concepts.

In a concluding activity, the students narrated their PowerPoint presentations and saved them as videos for uploading to an unlisted channel he had created for the purpose. He then invited his principal and the students' parents to view the students' videos, along with a video of his own reviewing the vocabulary and grammar the students had learned and practiced during the activities.

1) Materials:
   a) Teacher's computer, projector, internet connection (or downloaded videos)
   b) Student computers (one per group) and internet connection (or paper, pencils, and hard copies of reference materials)
   c) YouTube TED Talk Channel
2) Learning Mode: Whole class and small group
3) Time: 8–10 days (depending on degree of elaboration/sharing/discussion), 50-minute sessions

4) Sequence of Activities:
   a) On Day 1, introduce the topic of "rewilding"
   b) Show the selected YouTube video, pausing to record key concepts and vocabulary
   c) Students rewatch the video in small groups of 3–4, taking notes
   d) Groups share their vocabulary and notes with the whole class; teacher records
   e) On Day 2, students write a short summary of the video from their group and class notes, including 5–10 vocabulary/concept words
   f) Students share their summaries; class discusses and edits
   g) On Day 3, teacher introduces rewilding as a concept in Taiwan
   h) Review grammatical structures of conditionality
   i) Small groups read online or downloaded articles about wild species in Taiwan
   j) Small groups report their findings to the class
   k) On Day 4, student groups choose a species as a topic for research and begin researching
   l) On Day 5, researching continues
   m) Review of conditionality
   n) Groups are asked to write notes in response to a series of "What if?" questions using conditionality about effects on ecology and human populations
   o) On Day 6, students begin to create PowerPoint presentations with written narrative phrased in conditional statements
   p) On Day 7, students narrate and record their PowerPoint presentations and save as video files (MP4, WMV, or Mov)
   q) On Day 8, students view each group's video presentations and discuss; teacher shares links with principal and parents to view.

Assignments and Assessment. This activity has two assessments: (1) focusing on groups' use of conditional structures and development of conceptual thinking and language in the PowerPoints; and (2) focusing on individual student participation and performance (see Tables 4.2 and 4.3).

Table 4.2 Group use of conditionals and conceptual thinking in PowerPoint presentations.

Achievement level	Descriptor
Excellent	The PowerPoint presentation was carefully and clearly narrated and included most of the key vocabulary and concepts discussed in class, and contained relevant images as well as text. There was strong evidence of research in the information and ideas presented. The PPT showed clear evidence of conceptual thinking about the impact of reintroduction of the species ecologically and on humans, noting positive changes and possible problems. Each student was seen to contribute during the process speaking English.
Very good	The PowerPoint presentation was fully narrated with few errors in grammar or use of terms and contained a majority of vocabulary and concepts introduced in class as well as some images. There was clear evidence of research in the information and ideas presented. The PPT showed evidence of conceptual thinking about the human and ecological impact of reintroduction. Students noted positive changes and briefly discussed possible problems. Each student contributed to the process and was observed to speak and use English.

(Continued)

Table 4.2 (Continued)

Achievement level	Descriptor
Satisfactory	The PowerPoint presentation was fully narrated with some errors in grammar or use of terms, but was comprehensible, with the use of some vocabulary and concepts introduced in class, with a few images. There was evidence of research in the information and ideas presented. The PPT showed some conceptual thinking about human and ecological impacts, but this was not elaborated. All students were observed to use some English but some students' contributions were stronger than others.
Unsatisfactory	The PowerPoint presentation was narrated but not fully and contained few if any images. The use of terms was limited and the grammar contained significant errors. There was limited evidence of research and little development of concepts, with only brief mention of human and ecological impact. Some students did not participate or only very minimally. The students spoke very little English during the process.

Table 4.3 Individual participation and performance.

Achievement level	Descriptor
Above expectations	The student asked relevant questions and offered comments during whole class discussion. They contributed in every aspect of the project, from class discussions to research to the writing of the narrative and production of the PPT. The student spoke English through the process and helped others with their speaking. The student demonstrated strong conceptual thinking and expression in English about the impact of reintroduction.
Meets expectations	The student participated in all aspects of the process and was attentive during class discussion, answering in Englsh when called on. They contributed throughout the project and was attentive, speaking English when needed. The student demonstrated some conceptual thinking and expression in English about the impact of reintroduction.
Below expectations	The student participated in only some aspects of the process and seemed inattentive at times. They did not, or could not, answer in English when called on. The student spoke little English and did not attempt to contribute to the PPT, showing little evidence of conceptual thinking.

Relation to TESOL Technology Standards for Learners and CEFR Reference Level Descriptors

TESOL Technology Standards:
- Goal 3 (Effectively use and critically evaluate technology-based tools)
  - Standard 1 (Effectively use productivity tools)
  - Standard 2 (Use and evaluate language skill-building tools)
  - Standard 3 (Use and evaluate tools for communication and collaboration)
  - Standard 4 (Use research tools appropriately).

CEFR Reference Level Descriptors:
- Global Scale: B1 (Can understand the main points of clear standard input; can understand the main ideas of complex text on both concrete and abstract topics)

- Overall Listening Comprehension: B1 (Can understand main points of clear standard speech)
- Watching TV and Film: B1 (Can understand a large part of many TV programmes)
- Overall Reading Comprehension: B1 (Can read straightforward factual texts)
- Reading for Information and Argument: B2 (Can understand specialized articles outside their field)
- Overall Spoken Interaction: A2 (Can interact with reasonable ease in structured situations)
- Formal Discussion: B1 (Can put over a point of view clearly)
- Goal-Oriented Cooperation: B2 (Can help along the progress of the work by inviting others to join in)
- Information Exchange: B1 (Can exchange, check and confirm accumulated factual information)
- Addressing Audiences: B1 (Can give a prepared straightforward presentation on a familiar topic)
- General Linguistic Range: B1 (Has enough language to get by)
- Grammatical Accuracy: B1 (Communicates with reasonable accuracy)
- Thematic Development: B1 (Can reasonably fluently relate a straightforward narrative)
- Prepositional Precision: B1 (Can explain the main points in an idea or problem with reasonable precision).

Analyzing and Extending the Lesson: Application to Additional Contexts

In this scenario, a teacher built on an interest of his own to design a review session in vocabulary development, conditionality, and conceptualization in English that used a video from the TED Talk channel as its main text. Rather than beginning with the review topic, the teacher found materials that were relevant and engaging for his students and that provided an opportunity for reviewing and developing key elements on the national English exam.

Some parents and administrators might be suspicious of such approaches to review, noting that such activities might short-change review of critical topics for the sake of "entertaining" students. However, if the lessons themselves are carefully tied to curriculum guides and focus specifically on key points, and if these parties can be brought into the process through briefings and evidence of learning outcomes such as the videos made from student PowerPoints in this instance, doubts can often be assuaged.

Or course, review is not the only use for TED Talks or other videos from YouTube or other streaming services. The number of available videos and video channels on the internet is enormous and the range of topics is remarkable. Most of these videos are captioned, and some are captioned in the students original language, allowing beginners to also have access to these. A few channels, such as TED-Ed, also include teaching plans.

Scenario Three: Integrating Songs into a Korean EFL University Classroom

The Scene. Ms. Hana Lee has been teaching English to first-year intermediate EFL students (ages 18–19) for eight years at a private university in Busan, South Korea. Last semester, she was assigned to teach the course, "English Grammar in Context," to 30 freshmen who were not majoring in English. She taught English from the textbook published by a commercial publisher. At the beginning of each lesson, she set out clear learning objectives and sequencing activities. For each lesson (lasting 90 minutes), she mainly asked students to take turns reading aloud and translating sentence by sentence from English to Korean. Ms. Lee did interact with students, but only to provide corrective feedback about students' translation performance. When a student's translation was incorrect, she immediately stopped the reading and provided the correct translation. Ms. Lee explained key grammar points using grammatical terms and relevant examples. But the grammatical terms were often so technical that students struggled to understand.

A few weeks into the semester, Ms. Lee began to sense that students were not actively engaged in the class sessions, and to verify this she video-recorded one of her classes. In the video, most students were passively sitting in the classroom. Some of them were busy taking notes of what Ms. Lee said. But almost all students, especially toward the back of the room, were not paying attention. Some were texting via phone, others were sleeping with their heads covered, and quite a few were giggling at videos on their smartphones or seemed to be listening to music. The following week, Ms. Lee gave her students a questionnaire, asking them anonymously to describe their feelings about the class honestly and to tell her what they were watching or listening to on their phones while she lectured.

To her surprise, the students told her that they mainly were watching and listening to English language songs and videos. Some of them told her they were watching videos that described the same grammar concepts she was presenting! At the next class, Ms. Lee presented the findings of the questionnaire to the students and admitted that she had not been aware of what was going on. The students shyly admitted that they didn't understand the textbook or the lessons very well, but that they seemed to understand more when they watched videos or listened to songs. Ms. Lee then asked the students if they thought they could find songs that contained the grammar structures she was teaching and videos that explained the same concepts within the context of a song or popular television series. The students, sensing an opportunity, quickly said yes. This gave Ms. Lee an idea.

Analysis: Challenges and Opportunities. It is not at all unusual—and, in fact, it has happened to us in our own teaching—for teachers not to know what is going on in their classrooms as they teach until they video-record their own class. In this case, Ms. Lee was open and honest enough to see that many of her students were not paying attention and, instead of blaming them, asked the students why this was happening, so that she could find ways to address her students' learning needs and interests. It was also fortuitous that the students were honest enough to anonymously report their informal use of songs and video to learn the same or similar concepts that she was teaching.

Instructional Plan. The questionnaire showed three things. First, the students wanted to learn English in a fun and positive atmosphere. Second, they wanted to improve not only their grammar skills but also communicative competence. Third, they all had mobile phones and listened to English songs or watched music videos on the mobile phones for hours every day. Based on these findings, Ms. Lee decided to challenge her students to demonstrate their autonomy in learning "grammar in context" by finding examples of the grammar concepts from the textbook and course syllabus in popular English songs and videos and present them to the class, as an experiment.

Ms. Lee began her revised lesson by placing the students in her class into groups of three. She identified five grammar concepts from the next chapter of the textbook and assigned one each to two groups, announcing that each group would find a video or song in English that used the grammar concept and use that song or video as part of presentation in which the group would teach the concept to the class. In addition, the two groups with the same concept would act as each other's editors, giving their presentation to each other first to verify its accuracy and "polish" the presentation before giving it to the entire class. In this way, students also had a chance to rehearse their presentations in English in a lower-stakes context and build confidence.

Preparation for each presentation began in class but, Ms. Lee noted, each group would need to meet outside class to complete their preparations before the next class meeting the following week. The next week, the paired groups presented to each other and edited their presentations. The students uploaded their presentations with links to songs and videos on the class's Learning Management System (LMS) site. In the next class session, the groups presented in pairs, teaching the class the grammar concept. Ms. Lee followed each paired presentation with a quick lesson summarizing key points about each grammar structure and inviting students to take notes based on the songs and videos presented. The presentations took an additional class session, for a total of four 90-minute sessions—exactly as much time as she would have spent to teach the five concepts if she were simply lecturing. At the end of the exercise she gave the students a short quiz and was amazed to find that students showed mastery of the concepts at a level of 90% or greater. She decided that this would be the structure of the remaining lessons of her course.

1) Materials:
    a) Student smartphones
    b) Internet connection
    c) Learning Management System (LMS)
    d) Projector and computer for presentations.
2) Learning Mode: Whole-class for introduction and presentations; small groups of 3 for the activity
3) Time: Four 90-minute sessions plus the quiz to check comprehension
4) Sequence of Activities:
    a) In Session 1, teacher announces the lesson, places students in groups of three, and distributes grammar concepts
    b) Students begin to work in groups to learn the grammar concept using the textbook, videos, and finding examples online of the concept in context
    c) Students meet outside of class in groups to complete a draft of the assignment
    d) In Session 2, the paired groups (with the same grammar concept) meet together to share their presentations, give feedback to each other, and revise
    e) Teacher circulates among the students during the session, providing feedback and troubleshooting

f) Before the next session, each group uploads its presentation and link to the song or video they are using

g) In Sessions 3 and 4, the students begin to present in paired groups

h) Teacher discusses each grammar concept with the students before the next paired group presents

i) At the end of Session 4, the teacher debriefs with the students about the success of the activity

j) A week after Session 4, the teacher gives the students a quiz to check their understanding of the concepts.

Assignments and Assessment. There are two assessments for this activity: (1) an assessment of each group's accuracy and quality of the presentation; and (2) a quiz to check for student understanding of the concepts; however, this quiz would be teacher made and depend on the exact grammar structures chosen and so is not provided here (see Table 4.4).

Table 4.4 Rubric to assess accuracy and quality of the group presentation.

Achievement level	Descriptor
Excellent	The group accurately described the grammar concept/structure that was assigned and provided an accurate example of it in the form of a song lyric and/or a video scene, with additional supporting details and examples. The language used in the presentation was clear, fluent, and itself grammatical, and all students in the group spoke in a coordinated and clear manner. The group additionally demonstrated creativity in their example and was able to provide additional accurate examples of the concept's use in context when requested, without teacher support.
Very good	The group accurately described the grammar concept/structure that was assigned and provided an accurate example of it in the form of a song lyric and/or a video scene. The language used in the presentation was clear and relatively fluent, and all students in the group spoke. The group additionally was able to provide examples of the concept's use in context when requested, but with some teacher support.
Satisfactory	The group accurately described the grammar concept/structure that was assigned and provided a relatively accurate example of it in the form of a song lyric or a video scene. The language used in the presentation was relatively clear, and all students spoke, although one or two spoke most of the time. The group could provide additional examples with support of the teacher or help to explain the teacher's additional examples.
Unsatisfactory	The group's description of the grammar concept/structure that was assigned was inaccurate or confused, and their example was lacking or inaccurate. The language used in the presentation was not clear and only one or two students spoke. The group could not provide additional examples when prompted, even with teacher support.

Relation to TESOL Technology Standards for Learners and CEFR Reference Level Descriptors

TESOL Technology Standards:

- Goal 1 (Foundational knowledge and skills in technology for a multilingual world)
  - Standard 1 (Basic operational skills in using various technology tools and internet browsers)
  - Standard 2 (Use available input and output devices)
  - Standard 4 (Basic competence as users of technology).
- Goal 3 (Effectively use and critically evaluate technology-based tools as aids in the development of their language learning competence)
  - Standard 1 (Effectively use and evaluate available technology-based productivity tools)
  - Standard 2 (Appropriately use and evaluate available technology-based language skill-building tools)
  - Standard 3 (Appropriately use and evaluate available technology-based tools for communication and collaboration)
  - Standard 5 (Recognize the value of technology to support autonomy, lifelong learning, creativity, metacognition, collaboration, personal pursuits, and productivity).

CEFR Reference Level Descriptors:

- Global Scale: B1 (Can ... briefly give reasons and explanations for opinions and plan)
- Watching TV and Film: B1 (Can understand a large part of many TV programs on topics of personal interest)
- Overall Reading Comprehension: B2 (Can read with a large degree of independence)
- Reading for Information and Argument: B1 (Can recognize significant points in straightforward newspaper articles)
- Overall Spoken Interaction: B1 (Can communicate with some confidence on familiar routine and non-routine matters related to his/her interests)
- Formal Discussion (Meetings): B2 (Can participate actively in routine and non-routine formal discussion)
- Goal-Oriented Cooperation: B2 (Can outline an issue or a problem clearly)
- Information Exchange: B1 (Can exchange, check, and confirm accumulated factual information)
- Overall Spoken Production: B2 (Can give clear, detailed descriptions and presentations)
- Monologue: Putting a Case: B1 (Can briefly give reasons and explanations for opinions, plans, and actions.)
- Overall Written Production: B2 (Can write clear, detailed texts on a variety of subjects)
- Addressing Audiences: B1 (Can give a prepared straightforward presentation on a familiar topic)
- Processing Text: B2 (Can summarize a wide range of factual and imaginative texts)
- General Linguistic Range: B1 (Has enough language ... to express themselves with some hesitation)
- Grammatical Accuracy: B2 (Shows a relatively high degree of grammatical control)
- Propositional Precision: B1 (Can explain the main points in an idea or problem with reasonable precision).

Analyzing and Extending the Lesson: Application to Additional Contexts. In this scenario, a teacher who noticed that her students were not attending to her lectures on grammar discovered through video recording her own teaching and a student questionnaire that her students were learning much of their English grammar from videos and songs. She took this opportunity to redesign her instruction using popular music and videos, providing her students with greater autonomy for their learning than previously.

This scenario provides an interesting example of how to teach grammar in context, but more important, perhaps, it demonstrates the need for teachers to observe both themselves and their students during teaching, and to build on the unexpected insights provided by students about their own learning. This lesson has many, many applications across more than the teaching of grammar, and is in fact foundational to building strong and effective pedagogical practice.

Let's Discuss

1) If you are a speaker of a second or additional language, what has been your experience in learning that language informally from songs, videos, and/or vlogs? Did you learn from these at the early, intermediate, or advanced stages of your acquisition? Did you learn from these in a classroom setting? What was that experience like?

2) Do you agree or disagree with the finding reported in this chapter that intentionality is critical for learning from songs, video, and vlogging? In your own experience, has it been true that intentionality accounts for differences in the quality and quantity of your learning? What intentional strategies have or haven't you used in learning from these media?

3) What differences, if any, do you see between the type of intentionality of informal learning and the intentionality that is assumed by teachers and learners in a classroom?

4) In this chapter, multimodality is described as a critical distinguishing factor between learning from digital media and learning in the classroom. Do you agree or disagree with this view? How do you think multimodality could be enhanced within classroom settings beyond the use of digital media?

5) Which of the three scenarios for adapting songs, videos, and vlogs to classroom instruction do you think is most appropriate for the context in which you are teaching or will teach? What adaptations will you make, and what other possible uses of these media do you see being adaptable to your classroom context?

References

Albaladejo, Sara, Yvette Coyle, and Julio Roca de Larios. "Songs, Stories, and Vocabulary Acquisition in Preschool Learners of English as a Foreign Language." *System* 76 (May 2018): 116–128. https://doi.org/10.1016/j.system.2018.05.002.

Aquil, Rajaa. "Revisiting Songs in Language Pedagogy." *Journal of the National Council of Less Commonly Taught Languages* 11 (Spring 2012): 75–95.

Codreanu, Tatiana, and Christelle Combe. "Vlogs, Video Publishing, and Informal Language Learning." In *The Handbook of Informal Language Learning*, edited by Mark Dressman and Randall William Sadler, 153–168. Hoboken, NJ: John Wiley & Sons, Inc., 2020. https://doi.org/10.1002/9781119472384.ch10.

달씨Darcie. "A Day in KOREAN High School Vlog EXPOSED." YouTube video, 24:04, 2018. https://www.youtube.com/watch?v=aj_n_C_uadI. ***Cite whole channel or specific video?***.

Diakou, Maria. "Using Songs to Enhance Language Learning and Skills in the Cypriot Primary EFL Classroom." Open Research Online. Thesis. The Open University, 2013. oro.open.ac.uk.

Dressman, Mark. "Multimodality and Language Learning." In The Handbook of Informal Language Learning, edited by Mark Dressman and Randall William Sadler, 39–56. Hoboken, NJ: John Wiley & Sons, Inc., 2020. https://doi.org/10.1002/9781119472384.ch3.

Em's other side. "How I Truly Study Korean + Chatting with You | Koreanwithem." YouTube video, 10:28, 2021. https://www.youtube.com/watch?v=XVkPntIPpHs. ***Cite whole channel or specific video?***.

Goingbyjules. "VLOG:Buying a Vintage Designer Item, Curtain Bangs + Styling – New Hair -70's Hair? Healthy Pancakes." YouTube video, 17:39, 2022. https://www.youtube.com/watch?v=7V5zzQoAujE. ***Cite whole channel or specific video?*** Youtube"

"طفلة مغربية تعلمت الإنجليزية بدون معلم وتدعو لتدريسها في التعليم االبتدائي العمومي". 2014. Ouissal.

Id Hajji video, 5:09, 2014. https://www.youtube.com/watch?v=6dz_KHUSyag.

Jarvis, Sarah. "How Effective Is It to Teach a Foreign Language in the Foundation Stage through Songs and Rhymes?" *Education 3–13: International Journal of Primary, Elementary and Early Years Education* 41, no. 1 (September 2014): 47–54. https://doi.org/10.1080/03004279.2012.710099.

Ludke, Karen M. "Music and Songs." In *The Handbook of Informal Language Learning*, edited by Mark Dressman and Randall William Sadler, 203–214. Hoboken, NJ: John Wiley & Sons, Inc, 2020. https://doi.org/10.1002/9781119472384.ch13.

Ludke, Karen M., Fernanda Ferreira, and Katie Overy. "Singing Can Facilitate Foreign Language Learning." *Memory & Cognition* 42, no. 1 (July 2014): 41–52. https://doi.org/10.3758/s13421-013-0342-5.

"LyricsTraining." Elasthink. https://lyricstraining.com.

Matthews, Washington. "Songs of Sequence of the Navajos." *The Journal of American Folklore* 7, no. 26 (July–September 1894): 185–194. https://doi.org/10.2307/532830.

Minchin, Elizabeth. *Homer and the Resources of Memory: Some Applications of Cognitive Theory to the Iliad and the Odyssey.* South Melbourne: Oxford University Press, 2001. https://books.google.com.au.

Mohamed Talks. "Trailer." YouTube video, 3:35, 2021. https://www.youtube.com/watch?v=Fgz-790xCiE ***Cite whole channel or specific video?***.

Monbiot, George. "For More Wonder, Rewild the World." TEDGlobal video, 14:57, 2013. https://www.ted.com/talks/george_monbiot_for_more_wonder_rewild_the_world#t-2939.

Parmentier, Richard J. "Peirce Divested for Nonintimates." In *Signs in Society: Studies in Semiotic Anthropology*, 3–22. Bloomington, IN: Indiana University Press, 1994.

Peirce, Charles Sanders. "What is a Sign?" Essay. In *Theorizing Communication: Readings across Traditions*, edited by Robert T. Craig and Heidi L. Muller, 177–182. Los Angeles, CA: Sage, 2007.

Texfrancais. "Mots Imprononçables Pour Nous les Américains." YouTube video, 5:09, 2012. https://www.youtube.com/watch?v=uJ3X7Zjy2iM.

Toffoli, Denyze, and Geoffrey Sockett. "English Language Music: Does It Help with Learning?" *Recherche et pratiques pédagogiques en langues de spécialité* XXXIII, no. 2 (2014): 192–209. https://doi.org/10.4000/apliut.4450.

Trei, Lisa. "Musical Training Helps Language Processing, *Studies Show*." Stanford News, November 15 2005. https://news.stanford.edu/news/2005/november16/music-111605.html#:~:text=The%20findings%20reveal%2C%20for%20the,for%20learning%20language%20and%20reading.

Vanderplank, Robert. "Déjà Vu? A Decade of Research on Language Laboratories, Television and Video in Language Learning." *Language Teaching* 43, no. 1 (January 2010): 1–37. https://doi.org/10.1017/s0261444809990267.

Vanderplank, Robert. "Video and Informal Language Learning." In *The Handbook of Informal Language Learning*, edited by Mark Dressman and Randall William Sadler, 183–201. Hoboken, NJ: John Wiley & Sons, Inc., 2020. https://doi.org/10.1002/9781119472384.ch12.

YouTube Creators. "Welcome to the Youtube Creators Channel." YouTube video, 0:30, 2022. https://www.youtube.com/watch?v=fzBTvDraO5U.

5

Audiobooks, E-Books, and Podcasting

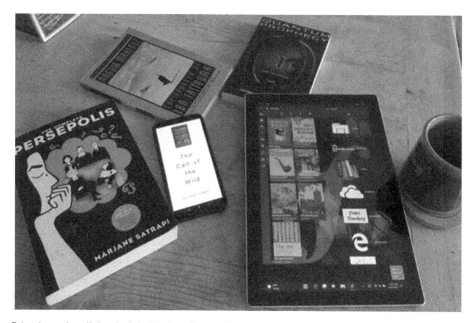

E-books and audiobooks join hard copies on the coffee table.

Introduction

Lars Kristiansen: Avid Reader

Lars Kristiansen is a 13-year-old eighth-grade student in Ungdomsskole (middle school) in Tromsø, Norway, above the Arctic Circle. An avid reader and dog sledder in the winter, Lars has heard of two books by Jack London, *The Call of the Wild* and *White Fang*, and is eager to read them. These books are available in Norwegian, but to challenge himself Lars has decided to download them from Project Gutenberg on his smartphone and read them in English. Lars has been studying English since primary school and enjoys watching English-language television series, sometimes with captions and other times

English Language Learning in the Digital Age: Learner-Driven Strategies for Adolescents and Young Adults, First Edition. Mark Dressman, Ju Seong Lee, and Laurent Perrot.

with Norwegian subtitles, but as he began to read, he struggled with London's writing style. When his older sister suggested that he find an audiobook version to listen to as he read, Lars was excited to see audiobooks for both novels were also available on the Project Gutenberg site. He downloaded both on his smartphone to read/listen on the bus to and from school. The combination of print text and audio has dramatically increased the ease of his comprehension. Lars has also begun to copy London's style in his essays for school, using new vocabulary and expressions that his teacher has noticed in her comments on his work.

Meryem Al Hosni: Podcasting in Dubai

Meryem Al Hosni is a 17-year-old student in Dubai, UAE, with a strong interest in Emirati cultural traditions and sustainability in the twenty-first century. She speaks Gulf Arabic as her home language but is also fluent in Standard Arabic and has attended a British-curriculum private school since middle school, where she studied in English. Meryem describes her English as "good but not great." She has few problems with studying in English but finds writing difficult.

Meryem dreams of having a career as a journalist, but she knows that she must improve her writing skills in both English and Standard Arabic if she is to achieve that dream. One of her science teachers suggested that she should listen to Radiolab (n.d.), a program from the United States with podcasts about science in English along with their transcripts, to follow along with the audio. Meryem downloaded several podcasts and transcripts and as she listened, she began to wonder if she could create podcasts herself about Emirati culture and sustainable technology, using the GarageBand application on her iPhone. She quickly created a podcast in Arabic about Emirati coffee culture and shared it with her older sister and some friends. They enjoyed it and suggested Meryem produce an English-language version to help her own English and to share with "the world." Meryem translated her Arabic script into English with the help of some friends and has launched her own channel on Spotify featuring a series of podcasts about life in Dubai.

Pragasit Chanthara: University Engineering Student in the UK

Pragasit Chanthara is a third-year engineering student in a semester-abroad program in the UK. He was a gifted student in Thailand and worked hard to learn English, knowing that some day he would need it for his work as a structural engineer. Pragasit dreams of building skyscrapers and other large buildings and is in the UK to learn more about advanced construction techniques and to improve his English. He has had little trouble following lectures in his classes, but the reading assignments have been very difficult for him. One of his classmates from Hong Kong has suggested that he get the e-book version of his textbooks or research articles and either use the built-in read-aloud feature or the computer-based feature (Narrator for Windows; Siri on Macintosh) to listen as he reads, saying it has helped him a lot. Pragasit has found that the combination of reading and listening has dramatically increased his comprehension and ability to use technical terms on homework assignments and group projects with classmates.

Discussion

In Chapter 4, the role of popular digital media as a gateway, or introduction, to the English language was considered for the application of learner-driven strategies within formal classroom instruction. In this chapter, the focus shifts from gateway applications to intermediate and advanced uses of digital media to develop listening and reading comprehension, vocabulary, and syntactic and phonological acquisition through statistical learning (Ellis 2005; Ewert 2020; Seidenberg 2017).

The three vignettes that introduce this chapter provide fictional but authentic portraits based on accounts from our own experiences as teachers and researchers of how students combine audio recordings and *extensive reading* of print texts for the explicit purpose of content learning and, incidentally and implicitly, to improve their English. Extensive reading is a practice that mirrors informal reading done outside of formal instruction of extended (multiple page) texts such as novels, lengthy periodical, and journal articles, and chapter- or book-length informational texts that are typically authentic in that they are not produced for educational purposes, are of high interest for the reader, and were individually chosen.

Among L1 English speakers, audiobooks, podcasts, and e-books are usually unimodal texts, in which language is received through one channel, either audio (listening) or visual (reading). However, each of these media also allows for simultaneous listening and reading through downloadable transcripts or original (book) versions and in e-books, through text-to-speech apps frequently embedded in the text. E-books also provide the additional resource of hypertext, allowing readers to click on a word or phrase to find its definition or learn more about its meaning. The dual-channel experience of being able to listen and read the same text simultaneously not only doubles the amount of input, through the principle of reciprocal indexicality in which "gaps" in the comprehension of one channel are compensated for through the other (see Chapter 3), it also lowers the threshold for L2 listeners/readers of what would typically be comprehensible for them, essentially scaffolding their experience to produce Krashen's (1983) "input + 1" condition for language acquisition. Finally, as the preceding portrait of Meryem Al Hosni suggests, podcasts also provide a model not only for improving language through receptive processes, but also through writing and production of original materials.

Audiobooks, e-books, and podcasting thus provide powerful tools for both content learning and language acquisition, but their successful adaptation within English language classrooms also requires close attention to the five features of IDLE discussed in Chapter 2: Social Connection; Authentic, Compelling, and Varied Input; Autonomy; Multimodality; and Ubiquitous Access. This is especially the case for the relationship between Autonomy and Authentic, Compelling, and Varied Input. For the listening to and reading of texts to be successful, learners must be able to choose materials that are both of compelling interest to them *and* at or slightly above their level of proficiency. This means that conventional classroom practices in which the entire class reads/listens to the same book or in which teachers prescribe reading materials for students based less on interest than on an assessed level of proficiency are likely not to achieve positive results. As in the case of all IDLE activities, learners must have the freedom to choose their own materials and digital formats and to proceed at their own pace and use their own strategies for the learning and management/monitoring of their processes.

Chapter Objectives

The central goal of this chapter is to consider the opportunities that digital books, audiobooks, and podcasting, especially when combined with corresponding audio or print versions, present for developing a wide range of language skills, from vocabulary development and reading comprehension to writing, spelling, and even pronunciation. Subgoals include understating the role of statistical learning in language acquisition and the implications of listening and literacy for the development of vocabulary, reading comprehension, writing, and pronunciation. In addition, readers will be presented with three instructional models applying the use of e-books, audiobooks, and podcasting in classroom settings. By the end of this chapter, readers should be able to:

1) Explain how the combination of print and audio versions of the same text expand learners reading comprehension, vocabulary development, and pronunciation.
2) Describe the role of multimodality in developing literacy in a second or other language.
3) Explain the role of statistical learning through extensive reading in language learning and its implications for classroom instruction.
4) Explain the key features of an extensive reading program.
5) Identify and be able to access online open-source resources for e-books, audiobooks, and podcasts.
6) Describe three approaches to adapting learner-driven strategies for learning from e-books, audiobooks, and podcasts to classroom contexts.
7) Consider how the research, theory, and three scenarios in this chapter can be applied to the reader's pedagogical context.

Key Words
extensive reading; e-book; audiobook; podcast; hypertext; statistical learning

---

Research and Theory

Research on Print-Only Extensive Reading

Research on extensive reading in L2 contexts consistently points to positive gains for learners across a wide range of areas, including fluency, vocabulary development, comprehension, and "general reading ability" (Chang 2011; Ewert 2020; Robb and Susser 1989; Suk 2017; Yamashita 2008). Explanations of the effect of extensive reading are varied, however. Yamashita, for example, argued that Japanese learners improve their general ability in reading English by transferring skills of comprehension from reading Japanese to English. In a context in which the L1 script was very different from the L2 script, extensive reading provided an opportunity mainly for practice to develop fluency. Yamashita argued that she did not find gains in vocabulary or other subskills because the readers in her study were focused on general meaning rather than explicitly focusing on vocabulary and other linguistic subskills. However, in a similar Korean context, Suk found significant gains in vocabulary for students who received a combination of intensive instruction in those subskills with extensive reading. Robb and Susser compared students in Japan who used a self-paced reading program with some choice (they termed this "extensive" reading) and students who received a very directed, skills-based reading program. They found that the students in the self-paced program outperformed the skills-instructed students on measures of vocabulary acquisition and comprehension. They attributed their findings to significant differences in motivation and the level of engagement for the self-paced group, measured by a post-test questionnaire.

E-Books or Paper Copies?

According to *CNBC* (Handley 2019):
- Paper books still outsell e-books 10 to 1.
- People prefer paper copies over e-books to display and as status items.
- Readers prefer books about cooking, nature, and children's books in paper, but crime novels, romances, and thrillers as e-books.
- Younger people prefer paper books more than older readers.
- Some literary authors have resisted electronic versions of their books.

A significant methodological problem for the study of extensive reading, according to Ewert (2020) appears to be its defining features, namely the requirement for students to choose their own materials and to pace themselves. The naturalistic "looseness" of the practice means that gains in vocabulary, comprehension, and ultimately the ability to speak and write with greater proficiency are difficult to trace directly to a learner's extensive reading, especially in cases in which students are receiving other forms of input from classroom instruction and other informal sources such as songs, environmental print, and video. Ewert has cited the concept of *statistical learning* (Seidenberg 2017) as key to understanding the processes and success of extensive reading in second-language acquisition. Statistical learning is a term used to describe the capacity of human beings to learn about and understand the world simply through immersion and repeated experience. It is how we learn to dress ourselves, to understand family relationships, to know what to eat and not to eat, and so on. It is basic, fundamental learning, including first-language acquisition in childhood.

In second language acquisition, statistical learning accounts for informal language acquisition—everything that learners "pick up" about a language that was not explicitly taught to them—and it is often the principal means by which engaged learners develop communicative proficiency (Ellis 2002). Because the knowledge acquired through statistical learning is implicit, incidental, and experiential, it is often unnoticed, complex, and difficult to isolate from knowledge that is more explicitly taught, and therefore it is also more difficult to measure. In a seminal paper on the relationship between implicit and explicit learning, Ellis (2005) notes that although researchers and theorists may rightfully separate these two for theoretical and research purposes, for the learner (and in many cases for teachers) the two are indistinguishable and function reciprocally.

Research on Listening Only: Audiobooks and Podcasting

A second set of research studies focuses on listening to audiobooks and podcasts rather than reading print text. In this condition, learners may take notes on what they listen to under a range of extensive conditions, from unstructured self-selected to highly structured, in-class listening. The most frequent finding of these studies is that learners report that they are highly motivational, due to rich content, variety of topics to choose from, and portability, and that they help mainly with listening comprehension (Abdous, Camarena, and Facer 2009; Hegelheimer and O'Brien 2007; Rosell-Aguilar 2013; Ting 2014; Tusmagambet 2020).

Studies also point to the use of podcasting to develop fluency, vocabulary, and pronunciation. Ting (2014), in a study conducted in Taiwan with adult learners, found that when permitted to choose from a wide range of informational audiobooks, learners were highly motivated and reported an increase in vocabulary, pronunciation, speaking, and listening comprehension. These learners reported actively using vocabulary and phrases they had "picked up" from listening in their daily interactions with English speakers.

Research on Multimodal Reading, Writing, Listening, and Speaking

Audiobooks and E-Books. Evidence for the power of multimodal combinations of reading, listening, writing, and speaking is even more compelling than the evidence of English language development through reading or listening alone. Lin (2010) found that the use of audiobooks with multimodal enhancements (audio narration, music/sound effects, animation) was highly motivating for middle school learners. In a highly controlled study, Chang (2011) reported an increase in fluency and vocabulary among Taiwanese high school students who combined reading with listening, and that they were able to read English books of greater difficulty following one semester of this practice. Similarly, Chang and Millett (2015) found that learners improved their reading fluency and comprehension in two conditions, reading and reading + audio support, but that the group receiving audio support improved substantially more than the reading-only group. Woodall (2010) also found that university students in Puerto Rico increased their efficiency (fluency) and reading comprehension when they read and listened to books simultaneously.

Sources of Free Audiobooks

Lit2Go. Thousands of books in the public domain are available in both audio and print versions.

ThoughtAudio. Classic literature and philosophy are presented in a YouTube video format with closed captions.

Storynory. This is a children's literature site featuring audio and print versions of classic and contemporary books as well as stories written by children for children.

Open Culture. The focus of this site is on recordings of humanities-focused readings from a wide variety of authors. Transcripts are not always available.

Project Gutenberg. One of the oldest sources of e-books and audiobooks. Not all books on the site have an audio recording but many do.

(Continued)
YouTube. Go to YouTube.com and search for "audiobooks." A vast amount and variety of captioned recordings are available.
Librivox. This site offers thousands of books in the public domain read by volunteer readers.

Podcasting. A separate but related set of research studies has focused on the combination of listening to audio recordings, typically in the form of podcasts, and the production of podcasts by learners, by recording speech (either extemporaneous or read from learner-written scripts; Godwin-Jones 2005). Marchetti and Valente (2018), for example, detailed three case studies of students and teachers engaged in producing podcasts in three instructional formats. They argued that rather than have students simply listen (and sometimes take notes), developing interactive features in which students no only listen but produce, share, and then comment on each other's work can dramatically increase student motivation, engagement, and learning. Saka (2015) and Ducate and Lomicka (2009) reported improved engagement and pronunciation when second-language learners listened to and then recorded their own podcasts.

Sources of Podcasts with Free Transcripts
LeonardoEnglish. This site offers access to a limited number of podcasts with free transcripts. Access to all the podcasts requires a paid membership.
StoryCorps. These are short, personal stories told by people, with simple animations and transcripts. They are available on the StoryCorps channel of YouTube.
National Public Radio. This is ad-free public radio programming produced in the United States. Go to npr.org and click on "Podcasts & Shows" for an extraordinary range of programs, many downloadable with transcripts.
This American Life. These are extraordinary, ironic stories with a twist. Search for This American Life to download or listen to many free stories with transcripts.
Radiolab/HappyScribe. Radiolab is a series of podcasts produced by WNYC studios. Transcripts and recordings of some podcasts are available through HappyScribe at happyscribe.com/public/radiolab.

Discussion: Classroom Implications

In summary, research on language-only (no images or video) digital formats for English language learning has shown that extensive reading of books and e-books, and listening to audiobooks and podcasts, can have positive effects on learners' motivation, fluency, listening and reading comprehension, and vocabulary development. Multimodally pairing reading of print text with listening to audio versions of the same text and pairing listening with opportunities to produce audio representations of text extends the upward range of reading comprehension for learners.

In addition, research suggests some important conditions to keep in mind when introducing e-books, audiobooks, and podcasting into a classroom. First, it is important to remember that the success of extensive reading depends largely on *allowing students to select their own reading materials* and to *read in quantity*. Many times, teachers may be concerned that students will choose materials beyond their level, and will focus on intensive reading instruction of shorter passages, or assume that students will not actually read without intensive supervision in the form of quizzes, essays, and other measures. However, statistical learning requires that students read in quantity and assumes that if allowed freedom of choice, students will not select materials above (or well below) their reading level. Allowing students the freedom to choose and then discussing those choices with them is the best way to teach students to self-monitor and to assess whether they are reading and how much they are learning through reading or listening.

Second, it is important to remember that *the reading/listening materials should be authentic and varied*, rather than designed specifically for teaching students about language. Motivationally, research indicates that this is critical, especially if the reading/listening assignments are to be completed outside of class. Learners at the beginning or lower-intermediate (CEFR A1–B1) levels may be challenged to find and understand authentic materials at their level, especially for audiobooks and podcasts; but combining listening with the reading of print text through e-books, hard copies, or transcripts of podcasts can significantly extend the range of learners' comprehensible input.

Third and finally, research shows that *the multimodal combination of reading/listening with production of written or spoken texts* provides an enormous boost to learners' engagement and capacity to both understand and produce language meaningfully. The three scenarios that follow provide powerful examples of teachers adapting learner-driven strategies for their classrooms through multimodal applications of reading, listening, writing, and speaking.

Practical Applications in the Classroom

Scenario One: An E-Book Reading Workshop in Ottawa

The Scene. Marie McDermott teaches eighth-grade language arts in a middle-grade French immersion program (50% French and 50% English language instruction) at an elementary (Grades 1–8) school in Ottawa, Ontario, Canada. A third of her students come from primarily French-speaking homes and a third are from primarily English-speaking homes; the remaining third are international students from the city's diplomatic corps or are refugees or immigrants born in Syria, the Democratic Republic of Congo, Morocco, or Nigeria. Her students translanguage regularly in her classes, not only in English and French but a variety of other languages. Marie is fully bilingual in English and French and has learned to divide her instructional time between these languages. Her students are conversational in both French and English, but she has noticed that they struggle with reading and writing exclusively in one or the other language, especially those not born in Canada.

Marie and her fellow language arts teachers use the reading and writing workshop approach to literacy advocated by Nancie Atwell in *In the Middle* (1987), in which students individually choose their own reading materials from the school or class library, write on topics of their own choosing, and regularly conference with their teacher on what they are reading and writing. Although Atwell's approach was originally not a bilingual approach to literacy and assumed that students would be reading and writing in their first language, Marie and her colleagues have found that its focus on individual choice in reading and writing were easily adaptable to a bilingual context if resources, especially the classroom library, are equal in French and English. However, they are also concerned that some students, especially those from abroad, are struggling with literacy tasks in both languages.

Recently, Marie found that one of her students had brought a digital tablet to school and had asked permission to read *The Hunger Games* (Collins 2008) using it instead of the copy from the class library because "I can listen and read at the same time and it's easier for me." Marie was intrigued and asked for a demonstration. She found that not only could a reader listen to the e-book as she read but she could also stop and, by clicking on an unknown word, find its definition. Excited by this possible solution to her multilingual students' English/French reading needs, Marie has asked for a meeting of her colleagues with the school librarian.

Analysis: Challenges and Opportunities. A major challenge for developing reading comprehension in a second language is that many books that are authentic and of likely interest to readers are also linguistically beyond their reach, especially at the beginning and early intermediate stages. As a result, teachers often rely on "leveled" readers with controlled vocabulary and syntax that are readable but not interesting or engaging, with the result that students resist or avoid reading them beyond class assignments.

However, as discussed in this chapter, reading and listening to the same text simultaneously creates opportunities for reciprocal indexicality, in which each channel reinforces or compensates for gaps in understanding of the other, and significantly increases the capacity of readers to understand materials that would be too difficult for them if they only read or listened. In addition, reading and listening simultaneously builds both fluency in reading and comprehension in both modes. The feature available on many e-book readers to pause, reread, and to look up unknown words by clicking on them also increases readability.

Of course, there are limits to the advantages of e-books. It is important for readers to be fully literate in their first language before attempting to become literate in a second or third, and it is unlikely that a beginning speaker of a language will be able to read advanced material easily simply by reading and listening together. Finally, interest and engagement in the content—and the sense of urgency and need to know that comes with these—are critical. For this reason, it also important for extensive reading to also be self-selected reading, or at least for students to have significant input and choice in what they read.

Finally, the logistics of reading e-books may pose some challenges, but these are often easily solved. This may require investment by schools (such as a Kindle reader program with tablets and the opportunity to select texts), or many school libraries may offer e-book versions of many new books. A challenge for Kindle users may be that many texts do not have accompanying audiobooks; however, readers can download an open-source text reader to their smartphones, copy chapters from Kindle books, and paste them into the reader. Finally, there are many opportunities to download books free of charge (for example, Project Gutenberg, which also provide free downloads of audiobook versions of the same texts).

Instructional Plan. Marie explained her idea and its possible benefits to the students, to her colleagues, and the librarian, who thought it had merit and should be given a trial at their school. The librarian had been acquiring e-book versions of recent adolescent fiction and had a class set of tablets for students to use. However, Marie suggested that it might be more engaging for students (and they would be more likely to read outside of class as well) if they could download books from the library to read on their smartphones. She also suggested that some students might already have tablets or digital readers of their own that they could use to borrow e-books from the library or elsewhere, and that some students might prefer to use their smartphones.

After much discussion, the teachers and librarian decided that they should allow three options for the students: (1) download books with audio versions from the internet on their own devices; (2) download books from the library on their own devices and use Speechify or another text-to-speech app to listen; or (3) use tablets from the library to download library books and audio versions to read. At least one of these options would give every student access to e-books with audio recordings.

The teachers were already using a reading workshop approach in their classrooms (Curriculum Corner n.d.), in which each class began with a mini-lesson, moved to independent reading and conferencing with students, and ended with journaling and a short wrap-up discussion. To introduce the e-book/audio option for readers, they scheduled one session in the school library in which all three options were demonstrated to the students, along with links to sites such as Bookriot and Lifewire, where free books and audiobooks could be downloaded, including Marie's favorite, Project Gutenberg. With some individual help, within a class session most of the students had selected an e-book and audio version and were reading/listening in class, with many students reporting that they listened on the bus to and from school and at home.

1) Materials:
   a) Digital devices (students' or the library's)
   b) Projector and link to e-book and audio websites
   c) Links to download e-books and audio.
2) Learning Mode: Whole class (for discussion); individual (for reading)
3) Time: Two days for introduction and one reading session of 50 minutes
4) Sequence of Activities:
   a) On Day 1, class meets in the library for introduction to e-books and audio
   b) Using a smartphone or tablet and projector, teacher demonstrates downloading and reading/listening to books
   c) Students are surveyed about ownership of devices; each chooses one of three options
   d) Students begin to download apps and select e-books with audio files
   e) Teacher circulates to help
   f) On Day 2, teacher surveys students to learn which students have successfully downloaded a book and audio file
   g) Whole-class discussion of student processes
   h) Students begin to read independently as teacher helps students who have not succeeded
   i) Workshop process of independent reading and teacher conferencing begins.

Assignments and Assessment. This activity has two assessments: 1) an assessment of students' reading comprehension and vocabulary development; and 2) an assessment of the e-book and audio pairing within a reading workshop (see Tables 5.1 and 5.2).

Table 5.1 Rubric for assessment of students' reading comprehension.

Achievement level	Descriptor
Excellent	The student reports increased ease of reading using paired written and audio books and can retell information in detail and identify multiple new vocabulary learned both in speech and writing. Notebooks and journals recording reading are detailed and demonstrate full clarity of information. The student reports interest in reading outside of school and can identify and demonstrate use of software to select books in written and audio format.
Very good	The student reports some increased ease of reading using paired written and audio books and can retell information and identify some new vocabulary learned in speech and/or writing. Notebooks and journals are kept and demonstrate clear understanding of what was read. The student reports interest in reading outside of school and demonstrates use of software to select books.
Satisfactory	The student reports using paired written and audio books but may have some challenges in selecting books at an appropriate level. The student is able to recall and retell information read clearly in speech and/or writing and identifies some new vocabulary words. Notebooks and journals demonstrate understanding of what was read. The student reports some interest in reading beyond class time and can select books for reading with assistance from others.
Unsatisfactory	The student reports continued difficulty in using paired written and audio books and is frequently unable to select books at an appropriate level. The student is unable to recall what was read in any detail. Notebooks and journals are kept slightly or not used at all. The student reports little interest in reading beyond class time and has difficulty selecting books with the help of others.

Table 5.2 Rubric for assessment of the e-book and audio pairing within a reading workshop.

Achievement level	Descriptor
Above expectations	Nearly every student in the class can identify written and audio books at an appropriate level and demonstrates strong comprehension and vocabulary development in conferences and in notebook and journal entries. Students widely report improvement in the ease of reading, are reading books at a higher level than previously, and report reading outside class more than before.
Meets expectations	Most of the students can identify written and audio books at an appropriate level and nearly all are able to do so with slight assistance from others. Students demonstrate comprehension and vocabulary development in conferences with the teacher and in their notebook and journal entries. Some students report reading more outside of class using their digital devices.
Below expectations	More than a few students report continuing difficulties in selecting books and using the software to read them in print and audio formats. Students continue to have significant problems with reading comprehension and vocabulary and cannot recall what they've read in conferences or in notebooks and journals. Only a few students may report using their devices outside of class for reading/listening.

Relation to TESOL Technology Standards for Learners and CEFR Reference Level Descriptors

TESOL Technology Standards:

- Goal 1 (Demonstrate foundational knowledge)
  - Standard 1 (Demonstrate basic operational skills)
  - Standard 2 (Use available input and output devices)
  - Standard 4 (Demonstrate basic competence)
- Goal 3 (Effectively use and critically evaluate technology-based tools)

  - Standard 3 (Use and evaluate tools for communication)
  - Standard 5 (Value technology to support autonomy and lifelong learning)

CEFR Reference Level Descriptors:

- Global Scale: BI (Can understand the main points of clear standard input)
- Overall Listening Comprehension: B1 (Can understand the main points of clear standard speech)
- Listening to Radio Audio and Recordings: B1 (Can understand the information content of recorded audio material on topics of personal interest)
- Overall Reading Comprehension: B1 (Can read straightforward factual texts on subjects related to interest)
- Reading for Information and Argument: B2 (Can understand articles and reports in which the authors adopt particular stances)
- Notes, Messages, and Forms: B1 (Can write notes conveying simple information)
- Identifying Clues and Inferring: B1 (Can identify unfamiliar words on topics related to interest)
- Note-Taking: B1 (Can take notes as a list of key points)
- Processing Text: B1/B2 (Can paraphrase short written passages/Can summarize a wide range of factual and imaginative texts)
- General Linguistic Range: B1 (Has enough language to get by)

Analyzing and Extending the Lesson: Application to Additional Contexts. In this scenario, a group of bilingual language arts teachers implemented the use of e-books supported by audio recordings to boost the reading and listening comprehension of their students in English. The teachers were already using the reading workshop approach, in which students self-select reading materials and conference with their teachers. That approach may be used with e-books and audio recordings, or a teacher may choose to perhaps select a book with students and read it together as an entire class, allowing greater control over vocabulary introduction and the explicit development of comprehension skills. However, this approach is not advised for extensive reading, and is unlikely to develop students' use of e-books and audio recordings outside of class. Perhaps the most effective approach in this case is to combine or alternate the reading of a book with an entire class with independent reading (two weeks whole class/two weeks independent reading), to build both explicit knowledge about reading and implicit, statistical learning from reading.

Scenario Two: Secondary-Level Audiobooks in Hong Kong

The Scene. Albert Lo has been teaching English in a private secondary school in Hong Kong for four years. Overall, the students are capable readers of English and have performed well on previous English reading assessments; however, they do not speak English fluently. Mr. Lo has had a visitor to his class and has observed his students in an English conversation led by her. The teacher was young and very enthusiastic, and so it was surprising to him that the students were not more conversational. Some raised their hands only when they knew an answer to a question or to talk about Asian entertainment. Even then, they provided brief responses and used simple English sentences, such as the subject-verb-object pattern. Only a few students were proficient in the use of various complex structures. They did, however, make mistakes in tense, modality, and subject-verb agreement.

Mr. Lo has attributed their lack of communication skills to both personal and environmental factors. Some students are shy or introverted by nature, while others are nervous about speaking English in front of their teacher or peers. He also knows that his students, like other Asian EFL learners, spend most of their day-today time with classmates and family members who speak the same first language (e.g., Cantonese). As a result, they have only a limited number of opportunities to speak English at school or at home. Finally, his students have been hesitant to speak English in class because they are aware that high-stakes English tests assess receptive skills such as reading.

To be sure that his students were able to speak English, Mr. Lo gave his students a two-minute speaking test to determine their basic speaking skills and invited his visitor to participate. They noticed that overall, the students' pronunciation was much better than expected, although they made some grammatical errors, such as with prepositions and subject-verb agreement, and spoke in short sentences that often did not follow one another. The visiting teacher also mentioned that she had noticed some interesting behavior from students while they were waiting their turn for the speaking test. Several of the students were surreptitiously looking at their phones beneath their desks and cupping their hands over one of their ears. Thinking the students were listening to music, she approached them and discovered that instead they were reading *in English* and *listening* to the text as they read. After class, she approached one of the boys, Chen, and asked him what he had been reading. The student was embarrassed at first, but then laughed and explained in English that he was reading about the last game of the NBA Finals in *The Standard* and had pasted the article into a text reader because "it helped me understand."

Analysis: Challenges and Opportunities. One of the greatest challenges in teaching is assuming that students are not motivated to learn a subject or that they lack basic skills when they show reluctance to participate in class. This is true in many countries, where fear of losing face or standing out can prevent students from volunteering to speak. And yet, teachers who are patient and observant in these situations may find that outside of class or even in hidden ways during class students are, in fact, using what they have been taught to achieve their own goals and objectives based on their own interests.

In these cases, there are enormous opportunities for creatively harnessing student interests and their own technological innovations within classroom settings. If Mr. Lo's students have learned to read English on their smartphones and paste texts into readers to help them with their comprehension, this is also a more powerful way to achieve accurate pronunciation and confidence in the use of more complex grammatical constructions than they could generate on their own. The challenge in this case is to find a way to build on students' interests and use of technology to coax them to become more public and fluent in their classroom uses of English.

Instructional Plan. Mr. Lo was surprised by what his visitor told him and decided to see just how many of his students were reading in English on their smartphones with help from text-to-speech apps. The next day, he asked the class to raise their hands if they had ever done this. To his surprise, again, nearly half the students' hands went up. He shared this information with his visitor the next time they met, and she remarked that perhaps this explained the students' better than expected pronunciation.

This gave Mr. Lo an idea. He approached the student who had confessed his love of the NBA to the visitor and asked if the student could show him "how he did it." Chen was reluctant but when he realized he wasn't in trouble, he was happy to show Mr. Lo the app and how to use it. Mr. Lo downloaded the same app and after some experimenting, he saw how much listening and reading helped him stay focused as he read.

On Friday, Mr. Lo asked his students to all bring their smartphones to class on Monday and to have them fully charged. He also suggested they install the speech-to-text app that Chen had recommended, and find an English-language article online about a topic they were interested in. The students were excited about this "assignment" and asked for more information, but Mr. Lo said he would tell them more on Monday, "if they all came prepared."

On Monday, to his amazement, every student brought a smartphone to class with the app installed and an article. Mr. Lo asked students to use earphones or, if they had none, he quickly distributed some cheap pairs he had picked up in the market over the weekend, and then he instructed them to read their article and listen to it, taking notes as they did. Withing 15 minutes, the students had completed the task. Mr. Lo then instructed the students to write a summary of the article they had read of approximately 100 words and told them they would each be reading their summaries aloud to the class. The students quickly wrote their summaries and seemed eager to read them aloud.

"Now," he told the class, "I want you to reduce the length of your summaries by half but leave nothing important out." To demonstrate, he projected the summary of an article he had written with many of the errors the students made in their summaries on the class whiteboard, and together they cut the length in half, combining sentences and correcting errors. He asked one student to read the new version aloud and summarized the editing strategies they had used. Finally, one student read the new summary aloud and the class agreed it was now better written "and left nothing out."

The next day, Mr. Lo placed the students in groups of three and instructed them to edit each other's summaries by reducing them to half again and then rehearse reading them. By the end of the class, each group had reduced each of the three essays to half its original length. Mr. Lo circulated among the students as they edited, noting both successes and problems, and periodically interrupted the students to demonstrate successful edits or to offers instruction on how to correct a problem he had seen.

On the third day, each student read their shortened essay aloud to the class, and then the students discussed their learning with Mr Lo. The students agreed that summarizing and reading what they had listened to helped their writing and pronunciation. "But," one student admitted, "it is still hard to speak on my own." Mr. Lo agreed, but he suggested that if the students were speaking in small groups about what they had read and recording themselves, "it might be easier." He instructed the original groups of three to move to different corners of the classroom, to the outside hall, or to an empty classroom and to record each other not reading but speaking on their own about what they had read, ask each other at least one question, record each speech, and upload it to a central file on the class's Learning Management System.

To the students' surprise, their writing, editing, and rehearsed reading made it much easier for them to speak extemporaneously about their topics. Each group was easily able to record its members speaking and to upload the recording. Mr. Lo was impressed by the improved quality of speech in the final recordings, as was his visitor. "Now," he told her, "the next step will be to do this as a whole class."

1) Materials:
   a) Smartphones
   b) Earphones
   c) Text-to-speech app
   d) School wifi or 4G connection.
2) Learning Mode: Individual for listening and summary writing; groups of three for editing; whole class for discussion
3) Time: Three 50-minute sessions
4) Sequence of Activities:
   a) On Day 1, teacher instructs students to read their article and listen to it simultaneously with the text-to-speech app
   b) Students read and listen, taking notes
   c) Students write a summary of the article of approximately 200 words
   d) On Day 2, students are placed in groups of three
   e) Students are instructed to read each other's summaries in groups and reduce each to half its length, "leaving nothing important out"
   f) Students complete reducing length of summaries
   g) Teacher circulates and provides guidance to groups
   h) On Day 3, students rehearse reading their summaries aloud, recording their discussions and reading on their smartphones
   i) Students upload their recordings to the class LMS.

Assignments and Assessment. There are two assessments for this activity: (1) an assessment of the group work to reduce the original summaries and then record their reading; and (2) an assessment of students' individual, original summaries (see Tables 5.3 and 5.4).

Table 5.3 Assessment of group work to reduce summaries and record discussions and reading.

Achievement level	Descriptor
Excellent	The group collaboratively read each other's summaries and reduced them by 50% of their original length. The reduced summaries were grammatically correct and included all essential details of the original text. Each student contributed actively to the editing process. The recordings also reflected a fully collaborative process, with each student taking part. The reading was fluent, and pronunciation of words was accurate. Overall, the group collaboration was highly effective.
Very good	The group collaboratively read each other's summaries and reduced them to approximately 50% of their original length. The reduced summaries showed few grammatical errors and included most essential details of the original text. Each student contributed to the editing process. The recordings showed collaboration, with contributions from all members. The reading was mostly fluent and most words were pronounced accurately. Overall, the group collaboration was effective.
Satisfactory	The group collaboratively read each other's summaries and reduced them by at least 30% of their original length. The reduced summaries were comprehensible with some grammatical errors and included essential details of the original text. All students contributed to the editing process, but some contributed more than others. The recordings showed evidence of collaboration, and all voices could be heard. The reading was mostly fluent and comprehensible, with errors in pronunciation. Overall, the group showed evidence of collaboration.
Unsatisfactory	The group struggled to collaborate in reading each other's summaries and reducing them. Some summaries were not comprehensible and had many grammatical errors. Critical details of the original text were missing in some summaries. Not all members contributed to the editing process, with some making few contributions. The recordings were completed by one or two group members and not all voices were heard. The reading was not fluent and there were many errors in pronunciation. Overall, the group's collaboration was not successful.

Table 5.4 Assessment of students' individual, original summaries.

Achievement level	Descriptor
Above expectations	The original summary was complete and covered all main points of the article that was read. It was approximately 200 words in length. The writing was clear and contained few grammatical, stylistic, or spelling errors.
Meets expectations	The original summary was complete and covered most of the main points of the article that was read. It was shorter or longer than 200 words by a significant margin, but still summarized, rather than restating, the article. The writing was mostly clear and contained some grammatical, stylistic, and spelling errors, but these did not impede meaning.
Below expectations	The original summary was incomplete and did not cover important main points of the article that was read. It was much shorter or longer than 200 words and did not summarize but recopied parts of the article. The writing was confusing and contained many grammatical, stylistic, and spelling errors which impeded meaning.

Relation to TESOL Technology Standards for Learners and CEFR Reference Level Descriptors

TESOL Technology Standards:

- Goal 1 (Foundational knowledge and skills in technology for a multilingual world)
  - Standard 2 (Use available input and output devices)
  - Standard 4 (Basic competence as users of technology).
- Goal 3 (Effectively use and critically evaluate technology-based tools as aids in the development of their language learning competence)

  - Standard 1 (Effectively use and evaluate available technology-based productivity tools)
  - Standard 2 (Appropriately use and evaluate available technology-based language skill-building tools)
  - Standard 3 (Appropriately use and evaluate available technology-based tools for communication and collaboration)
  - Standard 5 (Recognize the value of technology to support autonomy, lifelong learning, creativity, metacognition, collaboration, personal pursuits, and productivity).

CEFR Reference Level Descriptors:

- Global Scale: B1 (Can understand the main points of clear standard input)
- Overall Listening Comprehension: B1 (Can understand straightforward factual information)
- Listening to Radio Audio and Recordings: B1 (Can understand the information content of the majority of recorded or broadcast audio material)
- Overall Reading Comprehension: B1 (Can read straightforward factual texts on subjects related to his/her field and interest)
- Reading for Information and Argument: B1 (Can recognize significant points in straightforward newspaper articles)
- Goal-Oriented Cooperation: B1/B2 (Can make opinions and reactions understood/ Can outline an issue or a problem clearly)
- Information Exchange: B1/B2 (Can exchange, check, and confirm accumulated factual information/ Can synthesize and report information and arguments from a number of sources)
- Note-taking, Seminars and Lectures: B1 (Can take notes during a lecture)
- Overall Spoken Production: B1 (Can reasonably fluently sustain a straightforward description)
- Overall Written Production: B1/B2 (Can write straightforward connected text)
- Public Announcements: B1 (Can deliver short, rehearsed announcements on a topic)
- Processing Text: B1/B2 (Can collate short pieces of information/ Can summarize a wide range of factual and imaginative texts)
- General Linguistic Range: B1/B2 (Has enough language to get by/ Has a sufficient range of language to be able to give clear descriptions)
- Grammatical Accuracy: B1 (Communicates with reasonable accuracy)
- Vocabulary Control: B1 (Shows good control of elementary vocabulary)
- Flexibility: B1 (Can adapt expression to deal with less routine, even difficult, situations)

- Coherence: B1 (Can link a series of shorter, discrete simple elements)
- Propositional Precision: B1 (Can explain the main points in an idea or problem with reasonable precision.)

Analyzing and Extending the Lesson: Application to Additional Contexts. In this scenario, a teacher built on one student's strategy for reading and listening to design an activity in which students read and listened to an article using their smartphones, wrote a summary of what they had read, and then worked collaboratively to revise their summary and record a discussion and reading of it. The use of text-to-speech apps has many applications, especially in scaffolding students' reading comprehension of materials that may be slightly above their reading level.

Scenario Three: University-Level Podcasting in Turkey

The Scene. Özge Eryaman is a doctoral student teaching second-year students in the English department of a major university in central Turkey. Her students are avid users of social media, especially English-language television shows and YouTube channels about life in Turkey produced by expats and Turks in English. However, although they enjoy consuming media in English, they are less enthusiastic about producing written and spoken English and, in addition, large class sizes at her university of 40 or more students reduce opportunities for students to speak in class. Özge remembers her own struggles with speaking English via social media and has decided to build on her students' interest in an exercise to improve her students' confidence, fluency, and pronunciation.

Özge has decided that an excellent medium for developing spoken and written English skills in her large classes is an assignment in which her students will create a podcast reviewing one of their favorite television shows or YouTube channels. For this assignment, students will work in small groups to create a 5–10-minute podcast in which they discuss the merits and their concerns about a popular television show or YouTube channel. They must conduct an analysis, choose a format and speaking roles, and then write a script. To check their pronunciation, they will use a speech-to-text dictation program.

Analysis: Challenges and Opportunities. A very familiar challenge for English teachers in many countries is the reluctance of students to speak in class, as well as finding time in class for speaking practice and ensuring that all students in a class do, in fact, speak extended English during class meetings. In addition, the teaching of pronunciation can be fraught with frustration and embarrassment for both students and teachers.

Podcasting, in which students write a script on an engaging topic and then record it for presentation, can provide students with the opportunity to practice both extended speaking and pronunciation skills. The technology is fairly simple to use and it is ubiquitous, allowing students to practice at home using laptops, tablets, or their smartphones, and to easily upload and share files that are relatively small. The use of digital dictation devices allows students the chance to auto-correct gross pronunciation errors that impede accurate speech-to-text production and avoid the embarrassment of public errors. Finally, because there is no visual aspect to podcasting, the entire focus of the activity is on producing meaning exclusively through language.

Instructional Plan. Özge introduced the assignment to her classes by engaging them in a conversation about their favorite television shows and YouTube channels, recording the students' choices on the board and then quickly narrowing their selections to 10 choices. She announced that the students would be conducting an analysis of one of these and then writing and producing a 10-minute podcast in which they presented their analysis. She then organized the 45 students in her class into groups of three, according to the program or channel of their choice. To introduce podcasting, the students listened to a podcast and read along with the transcript as a class.

Özge instructed the students to watch at least three episodes of their chosen program or channel for homework. As they watched, the students were also instructed to take notes organized around a set of analytical questions, developed in discussion. These questions included:

- Why is this program/channel interesting to you? What connections do you make with the program or channel?
- How would you describe the host or characters? Why are they appealing or not appealing to you?
- What is the typical structure of a program/channel? What are the positive or negative qualities of this structure?
- What is your evaluation of the titles, graphics, and music used by the program or channel?
- Why is this program/channel effective in helping you learn English? Can you give any examples of words, grammar, or concepts you have learned by watching?
- In summary, what does this program or channel do very well? What changes would you make if you were the producer?

Over the next three class sessions, the students worked in groups to complete their analysis and write the script for their podcast. At Özge's direction, each group divided the narration of the text into three parts, each student chose one part, and began to rehearse. During this time each group also prepared to produce the recording. Using their smartphones and/or laptops, each group downloaded Audacity (or another) open-source software program for recording and editing audio. They also perused theme music from Free Music Archive (or another) copyright-free source and downloaded it.

As the students rehearsed, they checked their pronunciation in two ways. First, they read their section to Özge, who gave them some initial feedback on their grammar, word choice, speed, and pronunciation. They also used dictation programs, either online, as Google extensions, or downloaded open-source programs, to obtain feedback on their pronunciation.

In the last stage, the students found quiet spaces in empty classrooms, the library, or in their living quarters to record their podcasts. Using editing software, they combined their separate recordings, brief introduction and conclusion, and theme music into a single file. They saved their files as MP3 files on flash drives along with the transcripts and delivered them to Özge, who uploaded them to the class's Learning Management System (LMS). Each group gave a brief introduction for their podcast to the class, and each student then downloaded three of the podcasts assigned to them by Özge, listened to them for homework, and wrote a brief, 50–100 word review of each podcast. The students uploaded their reviews on the LMS for both Özge and the podcasters to read.

1) Materials:
    a) Audacity or another open-source audio recording and editing program
    b) A speech-to-text program included on Windows or Mac, a Google extension, or other open-source program
    c) Digital devices for students (laptops, tablets, smartphones)
    d) Learning Management System.
2) Learning Mode: Primarily small group but also individual
3) Time: Three weeks; three hours per week
4) Sequence of Activities:
    a) On Week One, Hour 1, teacher announces the assignment
    b) Teacher brainstorms programs with the students and assigns them to groups
    c) Teacher introduces and plays a podcast for students along with a transcript
    d) Students are assigned to listen to three more podcasts for homework and to take notes in response to a list of analytical questions
    e) On Hour 2, students meet in their groups and begin to share their notes about the program they chose and the podcasts they listened to
    f) Teacher circulates in the room, checking progress and students' notes
    g) In a whole class discussion, teacher checks student understanding of the assignment and answers questions about the podcasting process
    h) On Hour 3, students begin to write the scripts for their podcast in small groups
    i) Teacher circulates to troubleshoot and provide feedback on the scripts
    j) Students complete the transcripts working outside class and submit their drafts to the teacher on the LMS
    k) On Week Two, Hour 1, teacher returns the transcripts with feedback; students revise and begin work on podcast production, downloading software if needed and choosing theme music
    l) Students divide their transcripts into three parts with assigned parts for reading, and begin to practice reading, using a dictation program to check their pronunciation
    m) On Hour 2, students begin to practice record their parts
    n) Students record their parts at home in a quiet, isolated space
    o) On Hour 3, students combine and edit their recordings, including theme music
    p) Students complete the assignment outside class and upload their final podcast to the LMS, for the teacher to assess and share with the class for listening.

Assignments and Assessment. This activity has two assessments: (1) an assessment of the group's podcast; and (2) an individual assessment of student pronunciation and speaking fluency (see Tables 5.5 and 5.6).

Table 5.5 Assessment of the group podcast.

Achievement Level	Descriptor
Excellent	The podcast has a clear, well-articulated topic and the response to the questions presented to the groups is highly analytical and well grounded in evidence. The transcript is well written with few errors and moves engagingly between subtopics, with good use of theme music that is appropriate. Each student speaks clearly and fluently with relatively accurate pronunciation. In combination, the podcast and transcript are well produced and a pleasure to listen to.
Very good	The podcast has a clear topic and the response to the questions presented to the groups is strong, analytical, and grounded in evidence. The transcript is well written but contains some errors. Transitions between subtopics are marked, and the theme music is appropriate. Each student speaks fluently and pronunciation errors do not impede understanding. In combination, the podcast and transcript are complete and easy to understand.
Satisfactory	The podcast has a clear topic and the response to the questions presented to the groups is somewhat analytical and grounded in some evidence. The transcript is complete but contains some errors. There are recognizable transitions between subtopics and some use of theme music. Each student speaks intelligibly but there may be hesitancy and some pronunciation errors. The podcast and transcript are complete and can be followed.
Unsatisfactory	The podcast's topic may not be clear or announced and the response to the questions presented to the groups lacks analysis or grounding in evidence. The transcript may be incomplete and/or contain errors that impede meaning. Transitions between subtopics are not marked and there may be little or no use of theme music. Not all students may speak, or their speech may contain many errors with hesitancy and significant pronunciation errors. The podcast and transcript pose significant challenges to reading and listening with understanding.

Table 5.6 Individual assessment of student pronunciation and speaking fluency.

Achievement Level	Descriptor
Above expectations	The student speaks fluently with few hesitations. Pronunciation is very clear with a slight accent that does not impede understanding of individual words or complete utterances. The speaker projects confidence and command of English in spoken communication.
Meets expectations	The student speaks fluently with some hesitations that do not obstruct understanding. Pronunciation is clear with a discernible accent but understanding is not impeded overall. The speaker projects a competent command of English in spoken communication.
Below expectations	The student speaks with many hesitations and repetitions of words or phrases and meaning is obstructed. Pronunciation is not clear and there may be systematic errors in the pronunciation of phonemes that impedes understanding at the word and utterance level. The speaker struggles and projects a lack of confidence in spoken English communication.

Relation to TESOL Technology Standards for Learners and CEFR Reference Level Descriptors

TESOL Technology Standards:

- Goal 1 (Demonstrate foundational knowledge)
  - Standard 2 (Use available input and output devices)
- Goal 3 (Effectively use and critically evaluate technology-based tools)
  - Standard 2 (Use and evaluate language skill-building tools)
  - Standard 5 (Recognize value of technology to support autonomy).

CEFR Reference Level Descriptors:

- Global Scale: B1 (Can understand main points and produce simple, connected text/ Can produce clear, detailed text on a wide range of subjects and explain a viewpoint)
- Listening to Radio Audio and Recordings: B1 (Can understand the information content of the majority of recorded or broadcast audio material)
- Reading for Information and Argument: B2 (Can understand articles and reports concerned with contemporary problems)
- Goal-Oriented Cooperation: B2 (Can outline an issue or a problem clearly)
- Overall Spoken Production: B1 (Can reasonably fluently sustain a straightforward description of one of a variety of subjects)
- Sustained Monologue (Describing Experience): B1 (Can reasonably fluently relate a straightforward narrative or description)
- Addressing Audiences: A2 (Can give a short, rehearsed presentation)
- Overall Written Production: B2 (Can write clear, detailed texts on a variety of subjects)
- Reports and Essays: B1 (Can summarize, report and give an opinion about accumulated factual information)
- Note Taking: B1 (Can take notes during a lecture)
- General Linguistic Range: B1 (Has enough language to get by, with sufficient vocabulary to express themselves)
- Vocabulary Range: B1 (Has sufficient vocabulary to express themselves)
- Grammatical Accuracy: B1 (Communicates with reasonable accuracy)
- Phonological Control: B1 (Pronunciation is clearly intelligible even if a foreign accent is sometimes evident)
- Thematic Development: B1 (Can reasonably fluently relate a straightforward narrative)
- Coherence: B1 (Can link a series of shorter, discrete simple elements)
- Spoken Fluency: B1 (Can express themselves with relative ease).

Analyzing and Extending the Lesson: Application to Additional Contexts. In this scenario, a teacher struggling with a large class of students reluctant to speak in class finds a way to use podcasting that requires all students to speak and to practice their pronunciation and writing on a topic of interest to them. Some educators may be concerned that reading aloud from a written script does not provide the same level of authentic practice in speaking that interactive conversation or presenting before a class does. However, given large class sizes and the reluctance of the students to speak, even when called on, having students work together on a podcast is a very feasible alternative.

In addition, producing a podcast in groups, especially within a large class, has additional benefits. First, working in groups collaboratively—and requiring all students to participate—extends the Zone of Proximal Development (Vygotsky 1978) for all students and allows them to produce much more complex forms of language than would be the case individually. A single group assignment significantly reduces the time a teacher spends assessing student work, but more important, it also provides teachers with an optimal sample of individual speech for assessment. Third, the use of ubiquitous, easily familiarized software makes it possible for students to work together collaboratively and individually outside of class. Finally, the combination of written and spoken texts, both receptively and productively, again raises the level at which English students are able to listen, read, write, and speak.

In this case, students worked collaboratively in small groups, but once students become familiar with the process, it can become an individual assignment as well, in which, for example, a student might write a report on a topic and then create a podcast by recording their reading of it for a teacher to listen to as well as read. Although this scenario is set in a university classroom, the simplicity of the technology means that students at lower levels of proficiency and in high school or even middle school could use a simplified version of the assignment to boost their listening, reading, writing, and speaking skills as well.

Let's Discuss

1) What has been your experience learning to read in a second language? Do you agree with the argument that reading and listening to the same text help to raise the reading level of what one can read, and helps with fluency? Have you ever read and listened to the same text before?

2) Statistical learning has proven to be a powerful way to make gains not only in the development of fluency as a reader but also comprehension and vocabulary development. Advocates of extensive reading are also insistent that readers must be able to choose their own materials and read at their own pace, without instructional interference. What is your view about requiring students to keep lists of new vocabulary words as they read, or keep a journal of their reading? Do you think this is likely to help them or will it slow them down and reduce their motivation?

3) What is your experience with podcasting? Do you listen to podcasts, and if so, how would you describe their benefits and challenges? Do you think that having students create their own podcasts is something your current or future students would be able to do? Do you think they would enjoy the process, and what expectations would you have of them in terms of learning?

4) What is your response to the three scenarios presented in this chapter? Can you see yourself implementing them in your teaching; how would you revise them instructionally to fit your context?

References

Abdous, M'Hammed, Margaret M. Camarena, and Betty Rose Facer. "MALL Technology: Use of Academic Podcasting in the Foreign Language Classroom." *ReCALL* 21, no. 1 (2009): 76–95. https://doi.org/10.1017/S0958344009000020.

Atwell, Nancie. *In the Middle: Writing, Reading, and Learning with Adolescents.* Portsmouth: Heinemann Educational Books, 1987, 295. https://eric.ed.gov/?id=ED315790.

Chang, Anna Ching-Shyang. "The Effect of Reading While Listening to Audiobooks: Listening Fluency and Vocabulary Gain." *Asian Journal of English Language Teaching* 21 (2011): 43–64.

Chang, Anna C.-S., and Sonia Millett. "Improving Reading Rates and Comprehension through Audio-assisted Extensive Reading for Beginner Learners." *System* 52 (2015): 91–102. http://dx.doi.org/10.1016/j.system.2015.05.003.

Collins, Suzanne. *The Hunger Games.* New York: Scholastic Inc., 2008.

The Curriculum Corner. "Launching Your Reader's Workshop." n.d. https://www.thecurriculumcorner.com/thecurriculumcorner456/launching-your-readers-workshop.

Ducate, Lara, and Lara Lomicka. "Podcasting: An Effective Tool for Honing Language Students' Pronunciation?" *Language Learning & Technology* 13, no. 3 (October 2009): 66–86.

Ellis, Nick C. "At the Interface: Dynamic Interactions of Explicit and Implicit Language Knowledge." *Studies in Second Langauge Acquisition* 27 (2005): 305–352. https://doi.org/10.1017/S027226310505014X.

Ellis, R. "Does Form-focused Instruction Affect the Acquisition of Implicit Knowledge? A Review of the Research." *Studies in Second Language Acquisition* 24 (2002): 223–236.

Ewert, Doreen E. "Extensive Reading for Statistical Learning." In *The Handbook of Informal Language Learning*, edited by Mark Dressman and Randall William Sadler, 395–404. John Wiley & Sons Ltd, 2020. https://doi.org/10.1002/9781119472384.ch26.

Godwin-Jones, Robert. "Emerging Technologies." *Language Learning & Technology* 9, no. 3 (September 2005): 9–12.

Handley, Lucy. "Physical Books Still Outsell E-Books—And Here's Why." *CNBC*, September 19, 2019. https://www.cnbc.com/2019/09/19/physical-books-still-outsell-e-books-and-heres-why.html.

Hegelheimer, Volker, and Anne O'Brien. "Integrating CALL into the Classroom: The Role of Podcasting in an ESL Listening Strategies Course." *ReCALL* 19, no. 2 (2007): 162–180. https://doi.org/10.1017/S0958344007000523.

Krashen, Stephen D. "The Din in the Head, Input, and the Language Acquisition Device." *Foreign Language Annals* 16, no. 1 (1983): 41–44. https://doi.org/10.1111/j.1944-9720.1983.tb01422.x.

Lin, Chih-Cheng. "'E-book Flood' for Changing EFL Learners' *Reading Attitudes*" 7, no. 11 (2010): 36–43.

Marchetti, Emanuela, and Andrea Valente. "Interactivity and Multimodality in Language Learning: The Untapped Potential of Audiobooks." *Universal Access in the Information Society* 17 (2018): 257–274. https://doi.org/10.1007/s10209-017-0549-5.

Project Gutenberg. n.d. https://gutenberg.org.

Radiolab. n.d. https://www.wnycstudios.org/podcasts/radiolab.

Robb, Thomas N., and Bernard Susser. "Extensive Reading vs Skills Building in an EFL Context." *Reading in a Foreign Language* 5, no. 2 (1989): 239–251.

Rosell-Aguilar, Fernando. "Podcasting for Language Learning through iTunes U: The Learner's View." *Language Learning & Technology* 17, no. 3 (October 2013): 74–93.

Saka, Zeynep. "The Effectiveness of Audiobooks on Pronunciation Skills of EFL Learners at Different Proficiency Levels." MA thesis. İhsan Doğramacı Bilkent University, 2015.

Seidenberg, M. *Language at the Speed of Sight.* New York, NY: Basic Books, 2017.

Suk, Namhee. "The Effects of Extensive Reading on Reading Comprehension, Reading Rate, and Vocabulary Acquisition." *Reading Research Quarterly* 52, no. 1 (2017): 73–89. https://doi.org/10.1002/rrq.152.

Ting, Kuang-yun. "Blended Learning as a Theoretical Framework for the Application of Podcasting." *English Langauge Teaching* 7, no. 5 (2014). http://dx.doi.org/10.5539/elt.v7n5p128.

Tusmagambet, Botagoz. "Effects of Audiobooks on EFL Learners' Reading Development: Focus on Fluency and Motivation." *English Teaching* 75, no. 2 (2020): 41–67.

Vygotsky, Lev. *Mind in Society: The Development of Higher Psychological Processes,* edited by Vera John-Steiner, Michael Cole, Sylvia Scribner, and Ellen Souberman. Cambridge, MA: Harvard University Press, 1978.

Woodall, Billy. "Simultaneous Listening and Reading in ESL: Helping Second Language Learners Read (and Enjoy Reading) More Efficiently." *TESOL Journal* 1, no. 2 (2010): 186–205.https://doi.org/10.5054/tj.2010.220151

Yamashita, Junko. "Extensive Reading and Development of Different Aspects of L2 Proficiency." *System* 36 (2008): 661–672. https://doi.org/10.1016/j.system.2008.04.003.

6

Social Networking and Ethical/Safety Considerations

A coffee shop in Tangier.

Introduction

PHAM Hoa Lanh: Twitter K-Pop Follower

PHAM Hoa Lanh is 13 years old and lives in Ho Chi Minh City (formerly Saigon), Vietnam. She is in the seventh grade and is an ardent fan of K-pop bands, especially BTS and Super Junior. Lanh is a member of several Twitter fansites for these groups, which feature the latest photos and comments about the groups' appearances and new releases.

Lanh uses the Twitter handle, @bigkpopfan, to protect her identity and privacy when she posts. After a conversation with her older sister about safety, she created a cartoon avatar to use as a photo and was careful never to post personal information or photos. Although her tweets are public, she never identifies herself and only follows groups or individuals whom she knows and trusts.

There are several Twitter fansites for these groups in Vietnamese, but Lanh has discovered that most new information is on English language sites. She has been studying

English Language Learning in the Digital Age: Learner-Driven Strategies for Adolescents and Young Adults, First Edition. Mark Dressman, Ju Seong Lee, and Laurent Perrot.
© 2023 John Wiley & Sons Ltd. Published 2023 by John Wiley & Sons Ltd.

English for two years and has a very basic grasp of vocabulary and grammar. At first, she struggled with some posts but has slowly begun to acquire a better grasp of expressions and words, and even to post some of her own favorite pictures with captions. These activities on her smartphone have given her new interest in English at school, where her teacher has begun to notice Lanh's new-found interest in the language and her increasing improvement in writing.

Saïd Lamsaoui: Chatting with Sofía on Facebook

Saïd Lamsaoui is a 17-year-old Baccalauréat I (eleventh grade) science student in Kasba Tadla, a small town in central Morocco. He began studying English in ninth grade but since entering the science track at his *lycée*, English has become a minor subject for him, with only three hours of instruction per week. In addition to Darija, or Moroccan Arabic, and Standard Arabic, Saïd is also proficient in French, which is the language of instruction in all his mathematics and science classes. Saïd and his friends are avid watchers of Hollywood action movies on the satellite channel MBC Action, from which they have picked up a wide range of Americanisms, but they have watched these shows with Arabic subtitles and have not focused on the language.

Saïd's interest in English has grown over the past year, however, since he began chatting regularly on Facebook with Sofía, a *bacchillerato* student in Málaga, Spain. They met on Instagram through Moad, the older brother of a friend and neighbor of Saïd in Kasba Tadla who now works in Málaga, and have begun to chat regularly in the evening, at first in writing, then through recording voice messages, and now more frequently on live video. Their conversations at first were limited because Saïd speaks hardly any Spanish and Sofía no French; however, Sofía's second language is English, which she has studied since primary school, and so that has become their primary language.

Sophía has opened a new world of English language media and learning for Saïd. She is a fan of the television show, *Friends*, and has downloaded all the episodes and shown Saïd how he can access them online to watch with English captions. Saïd struggled at first in English but by practicing with Sophía, taking notes and asking some of his friends in the *lettres* track at his lycée for help with some grammar, his fluency has rapidly developed. He and Sophía now regularly discuss the different characters on *Friends* and joke about some episodes (the "Smelly Cat" song is a favorite), in addition to comparing notes on their classes (she is also in the *ciencias* track at her school). Saïd's pronunciation and fluency have improved to the point where, after he entered a speech contest at the *lycée* in English, his friends and teacher were shocked that he, a science student, was able to discuss the dangers of global warming in English, winning second place in the contest.

Dietrich Hoffmann: Beta Reader/Editor for FanFiction.net

Dietrich Hoffmann is a second-year student at a university in northwestern Germany. He is studying chemical engineering but as a hobby he writes screenplays based on television series and posts them on the site, FanFiction.net. Dietrich's first language is German, but he has near-native proficiency in English as well, due to studying the language from primary school and summers visiting his uncle's family in Albuquerque, in the southwestern United States. Dietrich's favorite series is *Breaking Bad*, which was filmed in and around

Albuquerque. For years he has imagined sequels and alternative directions for the series and has written more than seven full stories and posted them on the FanFiction site.

Early in his career as a FanFiction writer Dietrich received important feedback from a beta reader on the site that improved both the structure of his stories and his English. A beta reader is a more experienced writer of FanFiction who volunteers to read and give feedback to new authors before they publicly post their work. For Dietrich, having someone with a positive approach read and comment on his writing completely changed the quality of his work and inspired him to think of himself as an English author, not just a student of English. After publishing multiple stories and reading many more by other authors, Dietrich decided that it was time for him to become a beta reader himself. He quickly met the criteria and completed the profile and preference pages on the site and soon was receiving requests to beta read other authors' stories based on *Breaking Bad* and other edgy television series.

One very positive outcome of Dietrich's experiences as an author and beta reader on FanFiction, beyond the impact this has had on his own ability to structure a story and write in English, is the impact it has had on his ability to write papers for his university courses. Dietrich has found the experience so powerful that together with some classmates he has created a site for them to share each other's papers, some in English but others also in German, in a wide range of course subjects before they submit them to their professors.

Discussion

The three vignettes that introduce this chapter, based on our personal experiences and research, illustrate some of the many ways that young people use social networking daily to participate in youth culture globally and develop personal relationships safely and responsibly, as they also acquire important skills in English. The broader term "social media" is often used as a catch-all term to describe any interactive use of media online, including YouTube, streaming services, and even email, but this chapter focuses on platforms that provide individuals with the capacity to network and interact with others about personal topics, sometimes in relatively intimate ways. These platforms include Twitter, Facebook, Instagram, Weibo, SnapChat, Discord, QQ, TikTok, Pinterest, and Reddit, to name the most popular. Some of these, like Twitter, are more publicly focused than others; some, like Facebook, Instagram, or SnapChat, are less structured and offer a balance of public posting and private chat; and some are more topical, such as FanFiction, Reddit, or Pinterest. All share three common features: (1) they do not charge membership; (2) they offer individuals unprecedented, 24/7 access to other individuals around the world; and (3) as a result, they carry the potential for a wide range of abuses, including theft, bullying, defamation, and other serious and traumatizing acts.

Adolescents, Social Media, and Mobile Devices Globally

- 97% of teens, aged 12–15 in the UK, use mobile phones.
- 80% of young people in Tunisia, aged 18–29, have a mobile phone.
- 75% of children in Spain, aged 9–16, access the internet with their mobile phones at least once a day.
- Only 3% of young people in Vietnam, aged 18–29, use WhatsApp, but 98% in Lebanon use it.

Source: Adapted from vom Orde and Durner 2021

As discussed in Chapter 2, the freedom and opportunities of the internet also make it a dangerous space, and youth may become prime targets for abuse, and in some cases, abusers themselves. However, it is also our position that these dangers, while they do exist, are frequently exaggerated by the media, or are not caused by social media but rather are reflected and at times amplified by features of digital communication, such as the capacity to broadcast a message to limitless numbers of people, and the speed and ease of digital messaging. Gossiping, bullying, identity theft, and other deviant behaviors were not invented by the internet; they have always been present in human society. In addition, major platforms now regularly scan posts for inappropriate remarks and images using both algorithms and human content moderators, and it is possible for users to manage not only what they post but also who is allowed to see and comment on posts.

The youths described in the three vignettes that open this chapter all demonstrate ways to take advantage of the opportunities for authentic, responsible, and safe interpersonal communication that social media offer. Lanh, for example, used a Twitter handle and avatar that captured her interests but did not reveal her identity, allowing her to both view and contribute posts about her favorite K-pop idols. Saïd and Sofia's meeting was mediated through a third person who was mutually trusted, minimizing the danger that either adolescent would reveal too much personal information before trust was established. Finally, Dietrich's entry into beta reading/editing was mediated through his own experience as an author with a beta reader/editor who had been vetted through FanFiction, as had he.

By using devices to protect identity or, in the case of personal interaction, to vet and sometimes oversee relationships before and as they form, these youths found ways to protect themselves while reaping the benefits of building relationships with peers internationally through English. Their example is the model on which English teachers may begin to imagine and to teach authentic, safe, and responsible uses of social media in their own classrooms. We will return to this theme again in the three scenarios that conclude this chapter.

Chapter Objectives

The central goal of this chapter is to explore the potential of social networking for the development of English language proficiency by adapting learners' informal uses of social networking platforms for classroom practice. As subgoals, readers will learn about recent research in the use of social networking generally and on major platforms, identify the affordances of each for language learning, and consider ways to safely, ethically, and effectively use social networking to extend learning within and beyond the classroom. By the end of this chapter, readers should be able to:

1) Define social networking and the features that distinguish it from social media generally.
2) Explain the general features of social networking as a platform for extending language learning within and beyond the classroom.
3) Identify challenges to adapting social networking safely and ethically within classrooms.
4) Identify the major learning theories that apply to learning through social networking.

(Continued)

(Continued)

5) Define key terms in social networking, such as avatar, beta reader/editor, and tandem language learning.
6) Describe the benefits of social networking for language learners.
7) Apply research findings to adapt social networking to formal instruction while respecting the differences between informal and formal use of networks.
8) Describe three approaches to adapting learner-driven strategies for learning from social networking to classroom contexts.
9) Consider how the research, theory, and the three scenarios in this chapter can be applied to the reader's pedagogical context.

Key Words

social media; social networking; microblogging; avatar; beta reader/editor; zone of proximal development; tandem language learning; English as an international language (EIL)

Research and Theory

Theories of Social Networking

An extensive body of research documents the efficacy of social networking in language learning in both IDLE and classroom contexts (Jabbari et al 2015; Jones 2015; Lomicka and Lord 2016; Reinhardt 2019). Theoretically, researchers draw from psycholinguistic perspectives (e.g., Krashen 1994; Long 1985; Schmidt 1995), but more frequently from sociocultural theory (e.g., Lave and Wenger 1991; Vygotsky 1978) to explain the power and efficacy of social networking.

Psycholinguistically, researchers focus on the capacity for authentic interpersonal communication that social network platforms afford, in which two or more persons voluntarily engage in exchanges that are highly motivating and that require an exchange of information about both the content of a message and its linguistic features. Within IDLE settings, participants self-select each other and are therefore presumed to be communicative at some level. Pragmatically, each is also assumed to be striving to understand the other(s) and so strives to generate output that is comprehensible, which in turn serves as comprehensible input for their partner.

Researchers taking a sociocultural perspective assume the psycholinguistic aspects of language learning but take a more situated, contextual, and culturally focused view of learning. From this perspective, cognition and language learning are themselves situated in time and space, real-life contexts, and language is a tool used not only to produce linguistic meaning but also tangible material and social outcomes, such as transformations in identity and social status. One of the most interesting features of this research is its documentation of the ways that learners use social networking not only to learn language but to use the virtual features of technology to experiment with identities quite different from their real lives. By changing their names, assuming avatars, and creating alternative worlds through images and writing, these users imagine themselves and the world as very different from "real life." In the process, they also learn to use language in increasingly sophisticated and highly imaginative, empowering ways.

Research on Social Networking Platforms

Much of the research on social networking and language learning is not focused on exploring the general characteristics of social networks but rather the specific features of one platform and their implications for language learning and education. Most research has focused on four major platforms—Facebook, Twitter, Instagram, and FanFiction platforms—with a few studies as well on WhatsApp, WeChat, and other platforms.

Facebook. Dressman (2020), in his study of the informal English learning practices of Moroccan university students, found that students used multiple features of Facebook in English. First among these was the feature, Facebook Zero, which allowed students to use a text-only version of the platform, even on "stupid phones" (mobile phones without a video screen) to chat with friends locally and abroad, comment on posts, and by organizing themselves through the Group feature to post announcements about class meetings and assignments, and to share information about English—to use Facebook as an "invisible university" for studying English.

Surveys conducted in New Zealand (Alm 2015), Japan (Gamble and Wilkins 2014) and Malaysia (Kabilan, Ahmad, and Abidin 2010) indicated that students in these countries viewed Facebook favorably for L2 learning both informally (Alm 2015) and formally (Gamble and Wilkins 2014). In New Zealand, students' use of Facebook in the target language depended largely on their level of proficiency (the greater it is, the more use), and students in Japan reported interest in the possibilities of Facebook but also expressed doubts about the mixing of informal, personal contexts for interaction with formal instruction. Similarly, students in Malaysia reported positive attitudes about the use of Facebook in English classes but stressed the need for it to be integrated meaningfully with in-class learning.

The tension between informal, unsupervised uses of Facebook and school-based uses is a recurring theme in research on its educational uses, as indicated in a review of studies by Barrot (2018). Lantz-Andersson and her associates (Lantz-Andersson 2016, 2018; Lantz-Andersson, Vigmo, and Bowen 2013) studied interactions in English among secondary students in Colombia, Finland, Sweden, and Taiwan who shared a single Facebook platform as part of a class assignment in their respective schools. They found that students were quite conscious of the presence of teachers in their interactions, adopting personas that were constructed for the assignment. Students tended to chat in more extended and informal sequences with classmates in their own countries and to engage in exchanges that seemed to be designed as performances for students in other countries. Over time, Lantz-Andersson and her associates reported that boundaries began to be crossed and communication became more open, allowing for more language play and the development of sociopragmatic competence in English. In conclusion, Facebook was theorized as a potential "third space" (Gutierrez 2008) that negotiated the more conventional spaces and opportunities of self-directed and school-directed learning.

Most studies focusing on the uses of Facebook have taken place in university settings. Studies in Vietnam (Rensburg and Thanh 2017) and Belgium (Peeters 2015) noted increased motivation by students to study English out of class and to build community among learners. Akbari, Pilot, and Simons (2015) compared the learning of Persian-speaking doctoral students enrolled in two English courses in the Netherlands, one which was face to face and one that used Facebook. They found that students in the latter were more self-determined and outperformed the students who were taught face to face. They concluded that "Teaching ... on Facebook can have important effects on learning, because students can conquer their shyness, start to learn together with other students, gradually feeling more competent ... (making) their own choices and (choosing) their own time and ways of learning" (132).

Top Seven Social Networking Platforms and Youth

1) **Instagram.** Most frequently used site worldwide for posting photos and messaging, popular among youth.
2) **YouTube.** Video only with strong youth demographic; 73% of people in the United States use YouTube regularly.
3) **Facebook.** Largest platform globally nearly everywhere except China. However, in many countries Facebook is not preferred by youth.
4) **Twitter.** A site for posting short messages. Among the least used sites by youth (largest demographic is 35- to 65-year-old males).
5) **TikTok.** Music and video posting are prevalent. Most recent and fastest growing platform, high usage by those aged 16–24.
6) **Pinterest.** Used for posting photos on specific lifestyle topics, most popular among adult women.
7) **SnapChat.** Brief messages and images that disappear. Hugely popular among youth (78% of users are 18–24 years old).

Source: Adapted from Robinson 2021

Twitter. Studies of Twitter in language learning frequently discuss its "microblogging" aspect, in which short messages (originally limited to 140 characters) are sometimes combined with images, as its distinguishing feature. This feature may explain why the use of Twitter both informally and in formal settings suggests a broader array of targeted uses for language learning compared to studies of Facebook, which was more often used as a means of organizing course content and building general communicative competence. For example, a review of seventeen studies of Twitter in formal learning by Hattem and Lomicka (2016) found eleven separate uses of Twitter in language classrooms. These included interacting with native speakers, developing motivation and autonomy, and building community as well as a developing a wide range of linguistic subskills such as writing, pronunciation, vocabulary, grammar, and pragmatics, and also assessment, language play, and communicative competence. More provocatively, a study of informal language learning of English through Twitter fansites internationally (Malik and Haidar 2020) found that non-English speaking users learned to communicate with each other by mimetically copying short phrases in English. In other words, these informal learners first acquired some English not by learning to combine words syntactically but rather by copying phrases, presumably learning their meaning, and then repeating them in response to posts or in their own posting.

Instagram. Similar to Twitter, the microblogging aspect of Instagram, in which users post photos or videos with short captions, holds strong potential for language learning (Berti 2020; Wagner 2021). Junior (2020) reported findings from a study of Instanarratives, an Instagram-based group of 360 language learners ranging in age from 18 to 65+ (the modal group was 24–35 years old). The participants came from a broad range of backgrounds and professions, and most seemed to speak Portuguese as an L1 and had joined to learn and practice English. Users were encouraged by the group administrator to post a photo of themselves or some aspect of their lives and to tell their story of English language learning. Junior categorized participants' use of the learning network, Instanarratives, in eight ways to: (1) interact with foreign speakers; (2) explore multimodality; (3) make connections between native and foreign language; (4) interact with technologies and cultural artifacts; (5) practice repetition; (6) find personal connections with the foreign language; (7) participate in fandoms; and (8) pay attention to foreign language speakers.

FanFiction. Whereas a critical affordance of most social networking platforms is their "micro-ness," which encourages or requires users to write short sentences or paragraphs, often paired with a meme or other image, FanFiction is strikingly different in that it encourages users to write extended passages of multiple paragraphs often extending to a thousand or more words. In addition, FanFiction platforms are not commercial enterprises but are typically user-supported and funded privately, and there are many different platforms that focus on different genres of fiction (Lopez 2022). In most cases, FanFiction stories are "spin-offs" of popular novels, movies, or television series, in which authors write additional episodes or imagine "what if" a character or event in a storyline were changed.

Despite these differences, FanFiction is categorized as a form of social networking because it is highly interactive. Before a new story or episode is posted, it is read first by a beta reader or editor, who is more experienced and able to make suggestions for revision, such as tightening some descriptions or resolving inconsistencies and non sequiturs in plot, character actions, or setting. After authors blogpost stories on FanFiction sites in recurring cycles, additional readers comment on them. Some authors develop extensive and loyal readerships, boosting the confidence and motivation of the authors (Black 2005, 2006).

FanFiction is a powerful medium for developing second-language writing proficiency, especially among intermediate and advanced language learners (Sauro and Sundmark 2018). The use of beta editors and the distancing feature of the online medium which allows authors to adopt identities and creates a safe space in which to experiment with language, has been well documented, especially among Asian English Language Learners (Black 2006; Choi 2009; Zheng, Yim, and Warschauer 2018). Zheng and Lin (2020), in their review of digital writing among language learners noted four aspects of FanFiction that promoted the development of second-language writing: opportunities for identity development; motivation and autonomy; interaction and feedback; and language development, including language use and multimodality across genres.

FanFiction also has great potential for the teaching of writing in second-language classrooms. Sauro and Sundmark (2018) analyzed the writing of collaborative FanFiction, based on *The Hobbit*, by intermediate and advanced English learners preparing to be secondary teachers in Sweden in two settings: an online FanFiction blogging setting and a class FanFiction setting (with no online posting). They found that allowing students to choose their own formats and sites on which to post (i.e., to choose a site whose technology they were familiar with and could master) was critical to the success of the activity and that the online FanFiction writers were more innovative whereas the classroom writers tended to stay closer to the text of the original novel.

WhatsApp and WeChat. A last group of social networking platforms consists of multiple apps that are used mainly for messaging, but also allow the posting of images and video. Tragant et al. (2021) used WhatsApp to provide students with supplementary lessons and information in a summer English course in Spain. They reported great success in encouraging students not only to message the teacher in the class but also to message each other in English, extending their use of English well beyond class time. Sung and Poole (2017) reported a preliminary study of tandem learning in a US university, in which beginning students of Mandarin whose primary language was English were paired with intermediate and advanced students of English whose primary language was Mandarin, using the app, WeChat. The students were given learning tasks matched to their levels of L2 proficiency and interacted with their counterparts, whose primary language was their target language. They reported that even though the Chinese students were better at English than the US students in Mandarin, the exchanges were relatively symmetrical. The authors noted multiple benefits of the tandem learning process with WeChat, including the authenticity of the communication, improvement in grammar, vocabulary, and speaking (when voice texts were used), and increased cultural learning and the making of social connections with students other than of their own nationality.

Discussion: The Power of Social Networking in Classrooms

Social networking platforms and applications offer many possibilities for classroom teaching, including extending the use of English beyond class time, organizing activities, connecting with speakers abroad, writing, and creating a safe space in which learners can experiment with identities as users of English for authentic, communicative purposes without fear of undue criticism. The research on social networking and language learning also suggests some caveats for teachers to consider when incorporating social networking into their curriculum.

Social Media and Data Mining

"Data mining" refers to the ways that businesses and governments use cookies (code) stored on your browser to collect and analyze information obtained from people's social media accounts.

There are two basic types of data mining. The first is anonymous and aggregate, as when information is collected without identifying the individuals it came from (although demographics like age, gender, and ethnicity may be recorded), and analyzed to determine trends and associations for marketing and policy-making purposes.

(Continued)

The second and more invasive type is individual, as when specific details of information provided by users is collected and used to track their movement, preferences, and associations. If you've ever shopped for a product online and then found an ad for that product on your Facebook feed immediately afterward, you've been tracked by a data miner, who is also likely selling information about you to businesses.

Some individual data mining is relatively benign, as in the case of businesses trying to market their products. Other times it is a veiled form of identity theft, as when you are "innocently" asked to name three cities you've lived in or your favorite movie and where you first saw it or describe where you've vacationed, or fill out a survey to win a prize. In these cases, data miners can be trying to find your address or personal details that can be used in some nefarious and sometimes criminal ways.

First, the tension between informal uses of social networking and possible in-school uses must be acknowledged. Students often make a clear distinction between their private lives and their school lives, and this must be respected. The use of social networking to extend English learning may not always be welcomed by students, especially if the tasks required of them are inauthentic and/or simply a way of digitizing worksheets or language drills. Keeping the tasks as authentic and engaging as possible, perhaps by focusing on popular culture or self-expression, is critical. In addition, for safety and ethical reasons it is not advisable for students to use the same accounts for school tasks as in their personal lives. Instead, students should be advised to create separate Facebook or Instagram accounts for language-learning activities.

Second, it is important to match the affordances of a platform with the language proficiency of users. Instagram and Twitter, for example, lend themselves to activities for beginning speakers of English, but the demands of FanFiction for extensive writing may work better for intermediate or advanced learners. In addition, allowing learners to have a great deal of autonomy in choosing the platforms and deciding how they will use them, also makes a significant difference in students' engagement with a platform. For example, students in some Asian countries may prefer Asian platforms over ones originating in the United States; and students writing FanFiction may choose to post on a platform they are more familiar with rather than the one selected by a teacher.

Third, rather than stress correctness when using social networking, it is more in keeping with the spirit of Facebook, Twitter, and other sites to focus on self-expression and participation. Students will likely use many acronyms such as LOL or IDK rather than write these out; and this should be allowed. The focus of participation on social networking sites should be on developing sociopragmatic skills, practice, and fluency rather than on academic conventionality.

Fourth and last, it is important for teachers to seek students' feedback about the use of networking sites before, during, and after an activity. Again, the tension between uses of social networking in and out of school must be acknowledged, and the best way to do this is to seek the input of students about what is appropriate, what they find useful for them as learners, and how far (and long) activities can reasonably extend.

Practical Applications in the Classroom

Scenario One: Instagram for Italian Teens

The Scene. Louise Holcomb teaches English part time at a language center in Milan, Italy, while she is studying art history at a university. The course she teaches is for teenagers, mostly between ages 12 and 15, and it supplements the instruction they are receiving in their *scuole medie* (public middle school). They have described their English classes as "boring" and filled with grammar lessons, and this attitude carries over into her class.

Louise has been looking for ways to change her students' general attitude about English. In the lobby of the center one day before class she saw a few of her students gathered around a smartphone, laughing and chatting. Louise approached the group and asked them first in English and then in Italian what they found so interesting. One of the girls showed her the screen of the phone, on which there was an Instagram post on the site, Italy Loves K-Pop (n.d.). "Oh, do you all love K-pop?" she asked. "Yes!!" the girls chorused.

Later, Louise opened her class by asking how many students had Instagram accounts. Three-quarters of the students raised their hands. "And how many of you post to fan sites?" she asked. All hands remained raised. Louise then began to ask what the students' favorite groups and sites were, and learned that there were many different preferences, from K-pop to movies, television series, and the sites of particular actors or singers, many of them in English. However, she also learned that most of the students' posts on these sites were in Italian.

After class, Louise mentioned what she had learned to an Italian English teacher, and he laughed, telling her that most of his students were ardent Instagrammers, but "unfortunately they only post in Italian." Louise suggested an idea to him to assign students to post a photo and a paragraph in English on their Instagram account as an assignment. They began to brainstorm how they might do this and visited the director of the center, who warned them about safety concerns and parental permission. It was agreed that if the students created a separate private account for the assignment and used an avatar that wouldn't identify them, keeping the posts within the class, and wrote a letter home to parents in Italian informing them of the assignment, that they could try this activity, "to change the students' attitudes about English."

Analysis: Challenges and Opportunities. The opportunities for authentic language development through social networking are potentially limitless for learners of all levels of proficiency, and across nearly all aspects of learning, from pronunciation to fluency to writing in a wide array of genres. However, as discussed in this chapter, the challenges are also great for teachers hoping to adapt learner-driven strategies for their classrooms. The first challenge is safety, and to respond to threats, both perceived and real, to students' identity and well-being. But a second challenge, and one that is often in conflict with the first, is to remain as authentic and true to the social networking sites and practices within them that make them attractive for students. This is especially true, of course, when working with children and adolescents.

In this scenario, a teacher in a language center in Italy decides to take advantage of her students' inherent interest in pop-cultural posts on Instagram as well as that platform's affordances for beginning language learners. As a responsible teacher, she understands the risks involved and the need to follow her center's policies, and so consults with her director first. Her plan both to inform parents before beginning the activity and to require her students to use a new, private Instagram account in which they do not identify themselves but instead use an avatar, should respond to the challenge to remain authentic and to responsibly guard her students' privacy.

Instructional Plan. Louise's students were very excited when they heard the news that they would be using Instagram to post photos about their favorite pop culture icons and programs. They were less excited to hear that they needed to create a new, private Instagram account, to not share it outside of class, and to know that their parents would learn about this by email and that Louise would be monitoring their activity on the account. However, they also accepted these limitations for the chance to research their favorite "idols" and share posts in English within the class.

To make the activity engaging and authentic, Louise kept the assignment's guidelines as open as possible. Students were instructed to select one short photo or video of any aspect of pop culture they liked and to write a short paragraph of at least 50 words exclusively in English about the image they selected. In addition, the students were required to read and write at least one sentence in response to five of their classmates' posts. Louise also announced that the time used in class for this assignment would be limited to two sessions, but that the assignment and responses would not be due until the following week.

Of the fifteen students in the class, only three did not have smartphones. These students were lent tablets from the center's library to return within a week, but two of the students decided instead to borrow the phone of an older sibling for the assignment or to use a computer at home. By the end of the session, the students had all opened a new account, chosen a name and an avatar that disguised their identity, and were looking for image or video to post. The students also added each other and Louise to their new accounts. At the next session, Louise supervised the prewriting and warned the students not to use Google Translate, but to do their best to write in English on their own, writing first on paper. She reminded the students that she was "grading for expression and originality" and would not "take off points" for mistakes.

Within a few days of the second session, Louise was surprised to see that every student in the class had posted, and that students were beginning to comment on each other's posts in English. She also posted a photo and a short paragraph and was pleased to see that five students responded almost immediately to her post. Louise noted that the English in the paragraphs and comments was far from perfect, but it was usually intelligible and that the meaning authentically reflected the passion of the students for their topics. At the next session, she projected each student's post and the students enjoyed reading and laughing about the comments and the assignment. After class, one of the quietest boys in the class, Alberto, told her that on his "other account," he had started reading comments in English about World Cup qualifying teams and had responded to several in English himself. Louise shared the class's posts with her director and decided to make this a regular out-of-class activity for her students.

1) Materials:
   a) Student smartphones
   b) Tablets for students without smartphones

    c) Wi-Fi or internet connection

    d) Instagram account (private).

2) Learning Mode: Whole class and individual

3) Time: Two 50-minute sessions

4) Sequence of Activities:

    a) Prior to Day 1, send email to parents informing them of the activity

    b) On Day 1, announce the project

    c) Explain the restrictions (private account; classmates only)

    d) Students create accounts and avatars; teacher supervises

    e) Students select pop cultural topic

    f) On Day 2, students select image or video

    g) Students prewrite and compose a paragraph

    h) Out of class: Students post and comment on classmates' posts

    i) On Day 3, share and discuss postings in class.

Assignments and Assessment. This activity has one assessment: Student post and comments (see Table 6.1).

Table 6.1 Rubric for student post and comments.

Achievement level	Descriptor
Excellent	The student chose an appropriate topic and image or video. The written caption related closely to the image or video and provided supporting information and conveyed the author's perspective on the topic with inventiveness and clarity. The caption consisted of several sentences and was coherent and well structured. Vocabulary was appropriate and well chosen, and there were few errors in grammar. The student's comments on five or more posts were thoughtful and clear.
Very good	The student chose an appropriate topic and image or video. The written caption related to the image or video. It provided some information and conveyed a sense of perspective with clarity. The caption consisted of two or more sentences and was coherent. Vocabulary was appropriate and there were some errors in grammar but these did not inhibit meaning. The student's comments on five posts showed some effort at thoughtfulness and were clear.
Satisfactory	The student chose an appropriate topic and image or video. The written caption was related in some way to the image or video. It provided some information and demonstrated a point of view. The caption was one or two sentences and was intelligible. Vocabulary was appropriate and although there were multiple grammatical errors, the caption was intelligible. The student commented on five posts in more than a single word or phrase.
Unsatisfactory	The student's post was off-topic or the image/video was not clear. The written caption did not explain the image or video and provided little information. The point of view of the author was unclear. The caption was very short and consisted of a single sentence or few words. Vocabulary was limited and there were many grammatical errors, inhibiting meaning. The student commented on fewer than five posts, or in a single word or phrase.

Relation to TESOL Technology Standards for Learners and CEFR Reference Level Descriptors

TESOL Technology Standards:

- Goal 1 (Demonstrate foundational knowledge and skills)
  - Standard 3 (Exercise appropriate caution)
- Goal 2 (Use technology in socially appropriate and ethical ways)
  - Standard 2 (Demonstrate respect for others)
- Goal 3 (Critically evaluate tools in language learning competence)
  - Standard 5 (Recognize the value of technology to support autonomy, creativity, and collaboration).

CEFR Reference Level Descriptors:

- Global Scale: A2 (Can understand and use familiar expressions/ Can communicate in simple and routine tasks)
- Overall Reading Comprehension: A2 (Can understand short, simple texts)
- Reading Correspondence: A1 (Can understand short, simple messages)
- Reading for Information and Argument: A1 (Can get an idea of the content of simple informational material)
- Correspondence: A1 (Can write a short, simple postcard)
- Overall Written Interaction: A2 (Can write short, simple, formulaic notes)
- Overall Written Production: A2 (Can write a series of simple phrases and sentences)
- Creative Writing: A1 (Can write simple phrases and sentences)
- General Linguistic Range: A2 (Can use basic sentence patterns)
- Vocabulary Range: A2 (Has a sufficient vocabulary for the expression of basic communicative needs)
- Grammatical Accuracy: A2 (Uses some simple structures correctly)
- Propositional Precision: A2 (Can communicate what he/she want to say).

Analyzing and Extending the Lesson: Application to Additional Contexts. In this scenario, a teacher of young adolescents at a language center uses Instagram to improve her students' attitudes about English and provide them with an authentic writing context. Her principal challenge in this situation was balancing the need for safe and ethical use of social networking by the adolescents in her care with the need to provide as authentic and open an experience as possible for learning.

In this case also, the setting of a language center as opposed to a public-school classroom allowed the teacher to find a way to use Instagram as a platform. Many public-school teachers may be more restricted in the use of public networking platforms, even if they use privacy controls, and may find sites like Instagram and Facebook administratively blocked at school. In these cases, teachers might want to use educationally sanctioned sites or even have students simply find a photo or video, paste it into a Word doc or PPT, and write a caption for sharing with the class.

Finally, although this scenario is written for users at the A1/A2 CEFR Reference Level, it could easily be adapted for learners at intermediate and advanced levels, by having them blog (using Blogger or WordPress) and writing more extensive reviews of their favorite authors, musicians, or movies.

Scenario Two: High School Students Investigate Social Networking

The Scene. Marc Wilson teaches third-year English at a private high school in Abu Dhabi, in the United Arab Emirates. His students are culturally and linguistically diverse and have parents who are midrange professionals—medical technicians, teachers, and business managers—from the Gulf Region, the Middle East, Africa, and across South and East Asia. Although his students do not speak English as a first language at home, in class and in the halls he has been frequently surprised by their fluency, their near-native accents, their currency in North American, British, and Australian English slang, and has observed that their talent in these areas far outshines their proficiency in writing and speaking formally.

Marc attributes his students' grasp of informal English to their engagement with English language websites and social media. Before class and in the lunchroom, he frequently sees students gathered around a smartphone, laughing at a YouTube video or chatting about photos posted on Instagram or SnapChat. Sometimes these are in another language—an Arabic dialect, written in Arabizi, or Gujarati or Tagalog—but mostly in English, as a lingua franca.

He was pleased that his students had found opportunities for learning English outside the classroom until, in a lunchtime conversation with a counselor, he was warned of the negative consequences of social media, such as the exposure of students' identities, possible bullying, disinformation campaigns, and "darker things." Clearly, there was a need to alert his students to these issues without being alarmist or causing them to dismiss his warnings.

His solution was an assignment in which the students would explore their public personas on social media and present a report to the class using PowerPoint or another multimodal medium, called "Who Am I Online?" The goal of this project was first, to raise his students' awareness of how much information they were sharing not only with friends but strangers online; second, to provide a forum in which he could both learn about the extent of students' use of social media and provide information about possible negative consequences; and third, to create an engaging, authentic opportunity for students to use English in all four communication modes: listening, speaking, reading, and writing.

Analysis: Challenges and Opportunities. The challenges of social media today are as, or perhaps more, critical for adolescents than for adults, and they come from multiple sources: From within one's circle of acquaintances, as in the case of cyber bullying or predation; and from without, as in the case of identity theft or through manipulation of users through scams and misinformation (Palfrey 2010). Because many students now interact with English language media as much or more than with their first-language media—on Netflix, through online games, YouTube, and on social media platforms with friends and strangers in other countries—and acquire much of their vocabulary and fluency through these exchanges (Jung 2014), it is the responsibility of English educators to raise their students' awareness not only of the opportunities for pleasure and learning but also the dangers of trusting others too much.

An equal challenge for educators is how to raise the awareness of adolescents without frightening them or turning them away from the message. Developmentally, students in their teenage years are becoming increasingly independent thinkers who insist on making their own decisions and who believe in their own judgment and capacity to "take care of themselves" (Coleman 2008). Making extreme statements or forbidding adolescents to do certain things, especially when adults have little actual control over their behavior on the

Internet, can have the opposite effect intended, and may serve as an invitation to students to "go there" and "try that," if just once (Nolan, Raynes-Goldie, and McBride 2011).

A more subtle and likely more effective approach is to engage students in their own exploration of issues, leading them through discussion and example to come to their own conclusions about the possibilities and dangers of having a social presence on the Internet (Gleason and von Gillern 2018). An English teacher who acknowledges their students' use of social media in English and other languages and encourages them to step back and look at their personas in these venues will not only have great influence in shaping students' values and behavior, but will offer an engaging, authentic, and powerful lesson in the use of the English language online.

Instructional Plan. Marc began by introducing the assignment as a general topic of discussion, asking the whole class which social media they used, how often they were online, why they preferred some media over others, and what their experiences, positive and negative, had been. He recorded the students' ideas on a whiteboard and then distributed instructions for the assignment in which he outlined the topics and subtopics for students to explore as they researched their own use of social media. He explained that over the following two weeks, the class would be studying themselves as "Internet personalities," weighing the impact of their activities on others and on themselves and gathering data for a presentation to the class supported by a PowerPoint or other multimodal medium.

Marc did not expect the students to fully "come clean" or confess all their activities on social media, but he did hope that the activity of observing themselves would begin to raise their self-awareness. Over the next week as the students used their smartphones and the school's computer resources to inventory and analyze their presence online, he took time in class to have students read and discuss in small groups articles he'd found online about the ways that social media platforms gathered information about them, sold them products and ideas, and sometimes opened them to exploitation by others. In the last few days of the assignment period, the students created reports in PowerPoint and shared them in short, three-minute presentations to the class. In the final phase of the assignment, students discussed what they'd learned about social media and its effects in small groups and then used their notes from these discussions in a summative whole-class discussion about the opportunities and perils of social media.

1) Materials:
   a) Students' smartphones and/or school computers
   b) Open access to the Internet, at home or in school
   c) Teacher-developed Project Planner
   d) PowerPoint or other presentation tool
   e) Projector.
2) Learning Mode: Whole class (for discussions); small group (for analysis); individual (for self-research and presentations)
3) Time: Two weeks (ten days); 50-minute periods
4) Sequence of Activities:
   a) In Week 1, Day 1, the topic of social media use is introduced in whole-class discussion
   b) Students are paired and interview each other about their use of social media using a teacher-made questionnaire
   c) On Day 2, students present their partner's use of social media; teacher records information using a chart or spreadsheet

d) Teacher leads whole-class discussion summarizing students' media use

e) On Day 3, instructions for the assignment, "Who Am I Online?," which builds on the interview questionnaire, are distributed

f) On Day 4, students begin to research their online identities, researching their own pages to answer questions about the details of information about themselves that can be found online

g) On Day 5, students read and annotate in small groups the article, "Social Media: The Good, the Bad, and the Ugly" (n.d.)

h) As a homework exercise, students are instructed to review their own social media use and compare it to the points made in the article

i) In Week 2, Day 1, the teacher conducts a whole-class discussion using information from the homework assignment

j) Students begin to write their multimodal reports, using either PowerPoint or Word combining images (edited screen captures of their social media sites) written analysis and captions for images, in support of their presentations on their online identities

k) Teacher cautions students to select images to protect their and others' privacy

l) On Day 2, report composition continues

m) On Day 3, students share their reports in small groups of 4 or 5 students

n) In their groups, students combine and summarize their findings

o) On Day 4, groups present to the class

p) On Day 5, teacher conducts a whole-class discussion summarizing what they learned about their use of social media and shares a concluding article, "Protecting Your Social Media Presence" (n.d.)

q) As an in-class or homework assignment, students are instructed to check their own social media settings against the article and report on how they are working to protect themselves on social media.

Assignments and Assessment. This activity has two assessments: (1) the multimodal report, "Who Am I Online?"; and (2) the homework assignment on Week 1, Day 5 (see Tables 6.2 and 6.3).

Table 6.2 Rubric for multimodal report.

Achievement level	Descriptor
Excellent	This report is an insightful and extended description of the student's use of social media. It includes multiple images from the student's media sites, selected to protect the privacy of self and others. The images are carefully captioned. The written text is detailed, has few errors, and demonstrates significant insight into the positive and negative aspects of social media. Images, text, and captions are carefully composed to produce a positive, informative effect.
Very good	This report is an insightful description of the student's use of social media. It includes multiple images, selected to protect the privacy of self and others. The images have descriptive captions. The written text has some detail and may have errors but is readable and demonstrates some insight into the positive and negative aspects of social media. Images, text, and captions have been composed to produce an informative effect.

Table 6.2 (Continued)

Achievement level	Descriptor
Satisfactory	This report provides some insight into the student's use of social media. It includes some images with attempts to protect the privacy of self and others. The images have captions. The written text may be short but is readable with errors. It indicates some awareness by the student of the positive and negative aspects of social media. The images, text, and captions show evidence of composition.
Unsatisfactory	This report provides little insight into the student's use of social media. It contains few images with missing captions. The written text is short and has significant errors. It indicates little awareness of the positive and negative aspects of social media. The images, text, and captions show little evidence of composition.

Table 6.3 Rubric for homework assignment.

Achievement level	Descriptor
Above expectations	Responses to the handout are complete and extended. They indicate the student has carefully considered each point and compared their use of social media to the issues listed in the reading.
Meets expectations	Responses to the handout are mostly complete and consist of one or two written phrases or sentences. They indicate the student has considered most points and compared their use of social media to the issues listed in the reading.
Below expectations	The assignment is incomplete or demonstrates a short, cursory response to questions. The student has considered only a few points and has either not compared or minimally compared their use of social media to the issues listed in the reading.

Relation to TESOL Technology Standards for Learners and CEFR Reference Level Descriptors

TESOL Technology Standards:

- Goal 1 (Demonstrate foundational knowledge)
  - Standard 3 (Exercise appropriate caution when communicating on the Internet)
- Goal 2 (Use technology in appropriate ways)
  - Standard 2 (Demonstrate respect for others)
- Goal 3 (Critically evaluate technology-based tools)
  - Standard 4 (Use and evaluate research tools appropriately).

CEFR Reference Level Descriptors:

- Global Scale: B2 (Can understand the main ideas of complex text)
- Overall Reading Comprehension: B1 (Can read straightforward factual texts)
- Reading for Information and Argument: B2 (Can understand articles and reports concerned with contemporary problems)
- Reading Instructions: B1 (Can understand ... straightforward instructions)

- Overall Spoken Interaction: B1 (Can communicate with some confidence)
- Overall written production: B2 (Can produce clear, detailed texts)
- Formal Discussion, Meetings: B2 (Can participate actively in routine and non-routine discussion)
- Goal-Oriented Cooperation: B1 (Can explain why something is a problem)
- Interviewing and Being Interviewed: B1 (Can use a prepared questionnaire)
- Overall Spoken Production: B1 (Can reasonably fluently sustain a straightforward description)
- Sustained Monologue: Describing Experience: B1 (Can give straightforward descriptions on a variety of familiar subjects)
- Addressing Audiences: B1 (Can give a prepared straightforward presentation)
- Cooperating: B2 (Can summarize and evaluate the main points of discussion)
- Processing Text: B2 (Can synthesize and report)
- General Linguistic Range: B1 (Has enough language ... to express themselves)
- Thematic Development: B1 (Can reasonably fluently relate a straightforward narrative)
- Coherence: B1 (Can link a series of shorter, discrete simple elements)
- Propositional Precision: B1 (Can explain the main points in an idea or problem with reasonable precision).

Analyzing and Extending the Lesson: Application to Additional Contexts. In this two-week activity, a high school teacher works with his students to explore their online identities as a means of developing awareness of the positive and negative aspects of participating in social media.

As it is described in this scenario, this lesson is an intensive process with a relatively short time frame for developing insight into the implications of social media. Another approach might be to distribute the activity and readings over multiple weeks, interspersed with other activities to give students more time to think about the implications of the information they are receiving from readings about social media.

In closing, we want to emphasize the importance of avoiding the impulse to become alarmist about the dangers of social media. Facebook, Instagram, Snapchat, and other social media platforms are a major feature of students' lives and they are highly unlikely to give them up regardless of what adults might think of them or communicate about them. Forbidding activities is more likely to make these more attractive to students, not less. The better strategy is to explore the possibilities and pitfalls of social media with students, gain their confidence, and help guide them to become responsible participants in what online social media has to offer.

Scenario Three: Developing Multimodal Writing Skills at the University Level

The Scene. Ms. Flora Debora has been teaching a "media and intercultural communication" course for seven years at Indonesia's state university. Her students are training to become English teachers, but they still find writing with expression and precision a major challenge for them. As modest writers, they use a limited range of vocabulary and have a weakness in expressing themselves with clarity. Ms. Debora attributes this to a lack of opportunity to write in English for meaningful purposes. For instance, students primarily receive language input by reading a textbook, but they seldom practice writing in the classroom; and when students are required to write, they do so in the context of a class writing assignment that is inauthentic. Above all, students write for teachers, who select the writing topic and evaluate their work, which is focused mainly on grammar and mechanics.

Ms. Debora is also an enthusiastic supporter of English as an International Language (EIL), a view that challenges the "ownership" of English by countries in which it is the first language. She has urged her students to see themselves as specifically Indonesian English speakers rather than imitators of the varieties of English spoken in North America, Great Britain, or Australia and New Zealand, but her students have resisted this idea. Recently, however, her university has become a partner in a virtual teacher exchange program, and this has opened opportunities for her to emphasize her students' participation in this program as representatives of Indonesia. A few days earlier, her students were in the computer lab on an assignment to survey the exchange program's website. One of her students, Hidayat, came across a series of blogs created by students in a teacher education program in Turkey, in which the students had presented many photos of their lives and surroundings with captions and an accompanying text, and narrated with a recording of the students speaking English with a Turkish but completely intelligible accent. Hidayat was captivated by the photos, the captions, and the recording. "We should do this, too," he suggested.

Analysis: Challenges and Opportunities. As is discussed in more detail in Chapter 12, the global role of English as a lingua franca in many international contexts has led in recent years to a recalibration of the role of L1 English speaking countries as the arbiters of what is "correct" English. In this case, Ms. Debora's Indonesian students could be alerted to this shift in perspective through increased engagement with students who speak English not as a "foreign" but second language in their daily lives, for example in India, Kenya, or Singapore. In addition, this could also be an opportunity for Ms. Debora to create a writing activity that is both multimodal and culturally relevant and engaging for her students.

Instructional Plan. Ms. Debora immediately grasped the implications of Hidayat's suggestion. After class she reserved the computer lab for the following week and set about designing an assignment based on the Turkish students' blogs. At the following class meeting she announced to the class that they would be introducing themselves to other pre-service teachers on the virtual exchange website through three-person blogs that would be linked to the website, just as the Turkish students had done. She allowed the students to choose their own groups, knowing that they would work on this very personal assignment better if they were with friends, and then laid out some very specific guidelines. First, the photos the students included could be of the school and the city, but they were told not to photograph their homes or family members. They were also instructed to only use their first names and to avoid providing personal information such as email addresses or specific information about themselves or their families. Their job in this blog, they were tols, was to represent Indonesia more than themselves.

To this end, as a class the students brainstormed topics to be included in the blogs. These included religion, customs, food, music, and other unique aspects of Indonesian culture and daily life, with a focus on the role of English in Indonesia. Each three-person group created a blog using WordPress and set about collecting photographs and capturing video. They decided to write captions for each image and to write a narrative that they would include as text and as recorded narration. Ms. Debora gave the students one week to complete collecting all the materials they would need and writing the text and devoted two class sessions to designing the blogs and posting all materials on them. In a final session, each group presented to the class and received feedback about minor editing and proofreading details. As a final step, Ms. Debora collected the urls of all the blogs and had them uploaded to the exchange program website. In addition, the students spent a class session reading the blogs of students in other countries and commenting on them, inviting students there to read and comment on their own blogs.

1) Materials:
   a) Student smartphones for recording images, video, and audio narration
   b) Word Press accounts (free)
   c) University computer lab and facilities
   d) Internet connection.
2) Learning Mode: Whole class for discussion; small groups of three for blogging
3) Time: Four 90-minute sessions
4) Sequence of Activities:
   a) In Session 1, teacher introduces the blogging assignment and provides guidelines
   b) Students self-choose blogging groups, register for WordPress accounts, and begin to brainstorm topics
   c) As homework, the students begin to capture photos and videos representing Indonesian culture and education
   d) In Session 2, the students begin to design their blogs, choosing photos, writing captions, and writing a narrative for their blog
   e) Teacher circulates among the groups, troubleshooting and sharing good ideas from the groups with the class
   f) In Session 3, the students meet in the computer lab to upload their materials to the blog
   g) Teacher circulates among the groups, troubleshooting and sharing good ideas
   h) In Session 4, the students share their blogs and help to proofread and edit each other's work
   i) Students share their urls with the teacher, who posts them to the virtual exchange website.

Assignments and Assessment. This assignment has one assessment to evaluate the quality of the three-student blogs (see Table 6.4).

Table 6.4 Rubric to assess the quality of each three-student blog.

Achievement level	Descriptor
Excellent	All three students worked collaboratively to create a blog that is highly representative of multiple aspects of Indonesian culture and of the students' voices as English speakers. The photos and videos in the blog are well composed and highly illustrative. The overall design of the blog is attractive and engaging. Captions and the main text of the blog are grammatical and closely related to the images. The narration of the blog is clear and fully represents Indonesian culture. All three student voices are heard in the narration. Overall, the blog is coherent, cohesive, and represents Indonesian culture in an engaging and original way.

Table 6.4 (Continued)

Achievement level	Descriptor
Very good	The three students collaborated to create a blog that is representative of several aspects of Indonesian culture and of the students' voices as English speakers. The photos and videos are illustrative of Indonesia. The overall design of the blog is attractive and invites exploration. There were few errors in the written portions of the blog, and captions are clearly related to the images. The blog's audio narration described important aspects of Indonesian culture. All three students' voices are heard. Overall, the blog represents Indonesian culture positively.
Satisfactory	The three students worked together with few conflicts to create a blog that focused on one or more aspects of Indonesian culture, and that presented the voices of the students speaking English. The photos and images on the blog related to Indonesia. The overall design of the blog was attractive. Errors in the written portions of the blog do not impede understanding and the captions describe the images. The blog's audio narration related directly to aspects of Indonesian culture and was recorded by the students. Overall, the blog was representative of Indonesian culture.
Unsatisfactory	The three students struggled to work together with multiple conflicts to create a blog that lacked focus or that in some way misrepresented Indonesian culture without including the voices of all three members of the group. The photos and images were poorly chosen and did not represent Indonesian culture. The overall design of the blog lacked planning or organization. Multiple errors impeded understanding and some images lacked captions or were poorly described. The blog lacked an audio narration or the narration was not comprehensible. Overall, the blog failed to represent a student's view of Indonesian culture.

Relation to TESOL Technology Standards for Learners and CEFR Reference Level Descriptors

TESOL Technology Standards:

- Goal 1 (Demonstrate foundational knowledge and skills in technology for a multilingual world)
  - Standard 2 (Use available input and output devices)
  - Standard 3 (Exercise appropriate caution when communicating on the Internet)
  - Standard 4 (Demonstrate basic competence as users of technology).
- Goal 3 (Effectively use and critically evaluate technology-based tools as aids in the development of their language learning competence)

  - Standard 1 (Effectively use and evaluate available technology-based productivity tools)
  - Standard 2 (Appropriately use and evaluate available technology-based language skill-building tools)
  - Standard 3 (Appropriately use and evaluate available technology-based tools for communication and collaboration)
  - Standard 5 (Recognize the value of technology to support autonomy, lifelong learning, creativity, metacognition, collaboration, personal pursuits, and productivity).

CEFR Reference Level Descriptors:

- Global Scale: B1 (Can produce simple connected text on topics, which are familiar, or of personal interest)

- Overall Spoken Interaction: B1 (Can communicate with some confidence on familiar routine and non-routine matters)
- Formal Discussion (Meetings): B2 (an contribute, account for and sustain his/her opinion)
- Goal-Oriented Cooperation: B1/B2 (Can make his/her opinions and reactions understood/ Can outline an issue or a problem clearly)
- Information Exchange: B1/B2 (Can exchange, check and confirm accumulated factual information/ Can synthesize and report information and arguments from a number of sources)
- Overall Spoken Production: B1 (Can reasonably fluently sustain a straightforward description)
- Addressing Audiences: B1 (Can give a prepared straightforward presentation on a familiar topic)
- Overall Written Production: B1 (Can write straightforward connected text)
- Reports and Essays: B1 (Can summarize, report and give an opinion)
- Processing Text: B1/B2 (Can collate short pieces of information/ Can summarize a wide range of factual and imaginative texts)
- General Linguistic Range: B2 (Has a sufficient range of language to be able to give clear description)
- Vocabulary Range: B1 (Has sufficient vocabulary to express themselves)
- Grammatical Accuracy: B1 (Communicate with reasonable accuracy)
- Orthographic Control: B1 (Spelling, punctuation, and layout are accurate enough to be followed most of the time.)
- Propositional Precision: B1 (Can convey simple, straightforward information).

Analyzing and Extending the Lesson: Application to Additional Contexts. In this scenario, a teacher used the occasion of joining a virtual teacher exchange to energize her students' interest in Indonesian English in a group project to represent their country. The blog served to introduce other preservice teachers in the exchange to Indonesia and to the use of English in that country. This activity can be extended across a wide variety of contexts in which students are asked to provide information in a multimodal format about some aspect of their own city, nation, or culture, and to engage in exchange with similar others.

Let's Discuss

1) What has been your personal experience with social networking? Are you on any sites? Why have you chosen these over other sites? Have you used social networking for language learning yourself?
2) How would you deal with concerns about protecting the identity of users, especially students in secondary education? What is your school or program's policy with the use of social media and social networking in school?
3) Which of the three scenarios for adapting social networking to classroom instruction do you think is most appropriate for the context in which you are teaching or will teach? What adaptations will you make, and what other possible uses of social networks do you see being adaptable to your classroom context?

References

Akbari, Elham, Albert Pilot, and P. Robert-Jan Simons. "Autonomy, Competence, and Relatedness in Foreign Language Learning through Facebook." *Computers in Human Behavior* 48 (February 2015): 126–134. https://doi.org/10.1016/j.chb.2015.01.036.

Alm, Antonie. "Facebook for Informal Language Learning: Perspectives from Tertiary Language Students." *The EuroCALL Review* 23, no. 2 (September 2015): 3–18. https://doi.org/10.4995/eurocall.2015.4665.

Barrot, Jessie S. "Facebook as a Learning Environment for Language Teaching and Learning: A Critical Analysis of the Literature from 2010 to 2017." *Journal of Computer Assisted Learning* 34, no. 6 (January 2018): 863–875. https://doi.org/10.1111/jcal.12295.

Berti, Margherita. "Instagram in the Foreign Language Classroom: Considerations and Limitations." *Journal of Second Language Acquisition and Teaching* 26 (October 2020): 5–14.

Black, Rebecca W. "Access and Affiliation: The Literacy and Composition Practices of English-Language Learners in an Online Fanfiction Community." *Journal of Adolescent & Adult Literacy* 49, no. 2 (October 2005): 118–128. https://doi.org/10.1598/jaal.49.2.4.

Black, Rebecca W. "Language, Culture, and Identity in Online Fanfiction." *E-Learning and Digital Media* 3, no. 2 (June 2006): 170–184. https://doi.org/10.2304/elea.2006.3.2.170.

Choi, Jayoung. "Asian English Language Learners' Identity Construction in an after School Literacy Site." *Journal of Asian Pacific Communication* 19, no. 1 (March 2009): 130–161. https://doi.org/10.1075/japc.19.1.07cho.

Coleman, Stephen. "Doing IT for Themselves: Management versus Autonomy in Youth E-Citizenship." In *Civic Life Online: Learning How Digital Media Can Engage Youth*, edited by W. Lance Bennett, 189–206. The John D. and Catherine T. MacArthur Foundation Series on Digital Media and Learning. Cambridge, MA: The MIT Press, 2008. https://doi.org/10.1162/dmal.9780262524827.189.

Dressman, Mark. "Informal English Learning Among Moroccan Youth." In *The Handbook of Informal Language Learning*, edited by Mark Dressman and Randall Sadler, 303–318. London: Wiley-Blackwell, 2020.

Gamble Craig, and Michael Wilkins. "Student Attitudes and Perceptions of Using Facebook for Language Learning." *Dimension* 49 (2014): 49–72. https://eric.ed.gov/?id=EJ1080264.

Gleason, Benjamin, and Sam Von Gillern. "Digital Citizenship with Social Media: Participatory Practices of Teaching and Learning in Secondary Education." *Journal of Educational Technology & Society* 21, no. 1 (January 2018): 200–212. https://dr.lib.iastate.edu/handle/20.500.12876/22805.

Gutiérrez, Kris D. "Developing a Sociocritical Literacy in the Third Space." *Reading Research Quarterly* 43, no. 2 (April-June 2008): 148–164. https://doi.org/10.1598/rrq.43.2.3.

Hattem, David, and Lara Lomicka. "What the Tweets Say: A Critical Analysis of Twitter Research in Language Learning from 2009 to 2016." *E-Learning and Digital Media* 13, nos. 1–2 (January-March 2016): 5–23. https://doi.org/10.1177/2042753016672350.

Italy Loves K-Pop. "Instagram Account." n.d. https://www.instagram.com/italyloveskpop/?hl=en.

Jabbari, Nasser, Anna W. Boriack, Elba Barahona, Yolanda N. Padrón and Hersh C. Waxman Padrón. "The Benefits of Using Social Media Environments with English Language Learners." In *Paper presented at the SITE Conference*, Las Vegas, NV, 2015. March 1–6, 2015. https://www.researchgate.net/publication/285356520_The_Benefits_of_Using_Social_Media_Environments_with_English_Language_Learners.

Jones, Ann. "Social Media for Informal Minority Language Learning: Exploring Welsh Learners' Practices." *Journal of Interactive Media in Education*, no. 1 (April 2015): 1–9. https://doi.org/10.5334/jime.ak.

Jung, Sun. "Youth, Social Media and Transnational Cultural Distribution: The Case of Online K-pop Circulation." In *Mediated Youth Cultures*, edited by Andy Bennett and Brady Robards, 114–129. London: Palgrave Macmillan, 2014. https://doi.org/10.1057/9781137287021_8

Junior,JunJunJun Ronaldo Corrêa Gomes. "Instanarratives: Stories of Foreign Language Learning on Instagram." *System* 94 (November 2020): 1–18. https://doi.org/10.1016/j.system.2020.102330

Kabilan, Muhammad Kamarul, Norlida Ahmad, and Mohamad Jafre Abidin. "Facebook: An Online Environment for Learning of English in Institutions of Higher Education?" *The Internet and Higher Education* 13, no. 4 (December 2010): 179–187. https://doi.org/10.1016/j.iheduc.2010.07.003.

Spain, 2016. November 14–16, 2016. https://www.researchgate.net/publication/311364109

Krashen, Stephen. 1994. "The Input Hypothesis and Its Rivals." In *Implicit and Explicit Learning of Languages*, edited by N.C. Ellis, 45–78. San Diego, CA: Academic Press.

Lantz-Andersson, Annika. "Embracing Social Media for Educational Linguistic Activities." *Nordic Journal of Digital Literacy* 11, no. 1 (March 2016): 50–77. https://doi.org/10.18261/issn.1891-943x-2016-01-03.

Lantz-Andersson, Annika. "Language Play in a Second Language: Social Media as Contexts for Emerging Sociopragmatic Competence." *Education and Information Technologies* 23, no. 2 (July 2018): 705–724. https://doi.org/10.1007/s10639-017-9631-0.

Lantz-Andersson, Annika, Sylvi Vigmo, and Rhonwen Bowen. "Crossing Boundaries in Facebook: Students' Framing of Language Learning Activities as Extended Spaces." *International Journal of Computer-Supported Collaborative Learning* 8, no. 3 (August 2013): 293–312. https://doi.org/10.1007/s11412-013-9177-0.

Lave, Jean, and Etienne Wenger. *Situated Learning: Legitimate Peripheral Participation*. Cambridge: University of Cambridge Press, 1991.

Lim, Jungmin, and Charlene Polio. "Multimodal Assignments in Higher Education: Implications for Multimodal Writing Tasks for L2 Writers." *Journal of Second Language Writing* 47 (March 2020): 1–8. https://doi.org/10.1016/j.jslw.2020.100713.

Lomicka, Lara, and Gillian Lord. "Social Networking and Language Learning." In *The Routledge Handbook of Language Learning and Technology*, 1st ed., edited by Fiona Farr and Liam Murray, 255–269. London, UK: Routledge, Taylor & Francis Group, 2016.

Long, Michael. "Input and Second Language Acquisition Theory." In *Input in Second Language Acquisition*, edited by Susan Gass and Carolyn Madden, 377–393. Rowley, MA: Newbury House, 1985.

Lopez, Hillary. "Best 13 Fanfiction Sites of All Time." 2022. https://www.epubor.com/best-fanfiction-sites-of-all-time.html.

Malik, Zunera, and Sham Haidar. "English Language Learning and Social Media: Schematic Learning on Kpop Stan Twitter." *E-Learning and Digital Media* 18, no. 4 (July 2020): 361–382. https://doi.org/10.1177/2042753020964589

Nolan, Jason, Kate Raynes-Goldie, and Melanie McBride. "The Stranger Danger: Exploring Surveillance, Autonomy, and Privacy in Children's Use of Social Media." *Journal of Childhood Studies* 36, no. 2 (December 2011): 24–32. https://doi.org/10.18357/jcs.v36i2.15089.

Palfrey, John. "The Challenge of Developing Effective Public Policy on the Use of Social Media by Youth." *Federal Communications Law Journal* 63, no. 1 (2010): 5–18. http://nrs.harvard.edu/urn-3:HUL.InstRepos:4738023.

Peeters, Ward. "Tapping into the Educational Potential of Facebook: Encouraging Out-of-Class Peer Collaboration in Foreign Language Learning." *Studies in Self-Access Learning Journal* 6, no. 2 (June 2015): 176–190. http://sisaljournal.org/archives/jun15/peeters.

"Protecting Your Social Media Presence." n.d. https://www.umsystem.edu/ums/is/infosec/protect-social-media-presence.

Reinhardt, Jonathon. "Social Media in Second and Foreign Language Teaching and Learning: Blogs, Wikis, and Social Networking." *Language Teaching* 52, no. 1 (November 2019): 1–39. https://doi.org/10.1017/s0261444818000356.

Robinson, Ryan. "The 7 Top Social Media Sites You Need to Care about in 2022." *Adobe Express*, April 6, 2021. https://www.adobe.com/express/learn/blog/top-social-media-sites.

Sauro, Shannon, and Björn Sundmark. "Critically Examining the Use of Blog-based Fanfiction in the Advanced Language Classroom." *ReCALL*, First View (2018): 1–16. https://doi.org/10.1017/S0958344018000071.

Schmidt, Richard. "Consciousness and Foreign Language Learning: A Tutorial on the Role of Attention and Awareness in Learning." In *Attention and Awareness in Foreign Language Learning*, edited by Richard Schmidt, 1–63. Honolulu, HI: University of Hawaii, Second Language Teaching and Curriculum Center, 1995.

Sung, Ko-Yin, and Fredrick Poole. "Investigating the Use of a Smartphone Social Networking Application on Language Learning." *The JALT CALL Journal* 13, no. 2 (August 2017): 97–115. https://doi.org/10.29140/jaltcall.v13n2.214.

Tragant, Elsa, Àngels Pinyana, Jessica Mackay, and Maria Andria. "Extending Language Learning beyond the EFL Classroom through WhatsApp." *Computer Assisted Language Learning* (January 2021): 1–30. https://doi.org/10.1080/09588221.2020.1854310.

van Rensburg, Henriette, and Triet La Thanh. "Teachers' Use of Facebook Motivating Vietnamese Students to Improve Their English Language Learning." *Education in the Asia-Pacific Region: Issues, Concerns and Prospects* 40 (July 2017): 359–375. https://doi.org/10.1007/978-981-10-4944-6_18.

vom Orde, Heike, and Alexandra Durner. *International Data: Youth and Media, 2021*. UNESCO, Münich: International Central Institute for Youth and Educational Television, 2021.

Vygotsky, Lev. *Mind in Society: The Development of Higher Psychological Processes*, edited by Vera John-Steiner, Michael Cole, Sylvia Scribner, and Ellen Souberman. Cambridge, MA: Harvard University Press, 1978.

Wagner, Keith. "Using Instagram for Language Learning" *Second Language Research & Practice* 2, no. 1 (2021): 154–164. http://hdl.handle.net/10125/69864

Zheng, Binbin, and Chin-Hsi Lin.Digital Writing in Informal Settings Among Multilingual Language Learners." In *The Handbook of Informal Language Learning*, edited by Mark Dressman and William Sadler, 383-393. Oxford: Wiley-Blackwell, 2020.

Zheng, Binbin, Soobin Yim, and Mark Warschauer. "Social Media in the Writing Classroom and Beyond." *The TESOL Encyclopedia of English Language Teaching*: 1–5. https://doi.org/10.1002/9781118784235.eelt0555.

Zourou, Katerina. "On the Attractiveness of Social Media for Language Learning: A Look at the State of the Art." *Alsic. Apprentissage des Langues et Systèmes d'Information et de Communication* 15, no. 1 (March 2012). https://doi.org/10.4000/alsic.2436.

7

Games and Other Virtual Learning Environments

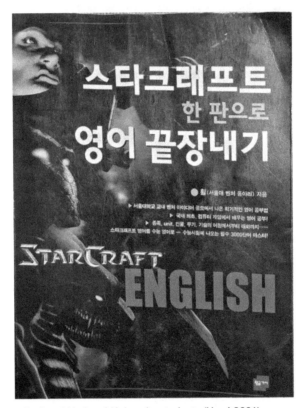

StarCraft English written by Seoul National University students (Hwei 2001).

Introduction

Kim Si Woo: Learning English through MMORPGs

Kim Si Woo is a 21-year-old university student at a private university in Seoul, South Korea. She grew up in a village in a remote part of the country, where her parents were service workers in a nearby larger town. She did not attend a *hagwon*, or private

English Language Learning in the Digital Age: Learner-Driven Strategies for Adolescents and Young Adults, First Edition. Mark Dressman, Ju Seong Lee, and Laurent Perrot.

after-school program, and so spent her afternoons and evenings at home, where she spent much of her time using Korea's high-speed internet system to surf the web, watching videos and playing games.

Like all public-school students in South Korea, Si Woo began studying English in third grade. She was an average student and did not excel at English until she discovered the Massive Multiplayer Online Role-Playing Game (MMORPG), World of Warcraft, at age 10 and began to regularly play after school before her parents returned from work. Si Woo was intrigued not only by the game itself, which offered an immersive fantasy world and complex storyline, but by her co-players, who were from a wide range of mostly English-speaking nations, and who welcomed her on the field of play *in English*. With only a few years of primary-school instruction, Si Woo struggled at first with the game's English instructions, but through repetition of basic phrases, her very basic grasp of English from school, the use of Google Translate, and collaborators who were focused more on communication than correctness, she gradually learned the rules and developed a functional set of vocabulary and phrases in English.

Si Woo's concentration on the game and ability to work with others to achieve goals soon began to win her many friends among the players of World of Warcraft. As she mastered the rules of the game and developed technical expertise in manipulating her avatar, or onscreen cartoon persona, she also became increasingly comfortable using English. At first, she communicated largely through chat, using a repertoire of phrases, but then she began to listen to others as they spoke during the game and synchronized the language with actions on screen, learning terms (e.g., *right/left*; *behind you*; *let's go around*). With some rehearsal on her own, she began to tentatively speak during the games, and she soon mastered many of the commands. Later she watched replays of games, stopping and rewinding to check her understanding, and then to watch additional videos on YouTube in English and to take notes.

By the time Si Woo had reached secondary school, she was an expert player of World of Warcraft with many international friends who admired her skill in play and her basic fluency in English. She had begun to watch television programs and movies in English as well, following along with captions rather than subtitles in Korean, and amazed her teachers in English class, even though she remained an average student in other subject areas. Her next major step came in her first year of high school, when she was introduced to the remastered (and free) version of *StarCraft*, the most popular video game among South Korean university students. A friend introduced her to a guide to learning English through *StarCraft*, written by students at Seoul National University, which contained strategies for playing the game as well as for learning advanced English. The manual was written in college-level academic English and increased her reading comprehension in English as well as her vocabulary.

Si Woo's English score on the CSAT (College Scholastic Ability Test) was the highest in her class, and enhanced her overall score on the test, enabling her to enroll in the English program at a private university in Gwangju. She continued to play *StarCraft* and hoped eventually to work in the growing e-sports industry in South Korea.

Janez Vidmar: Second Life Designer and Bon Vivant

Janez Vidmar is a 17-year-old high school student living in Ljubljana, Slovenia. He dreams of becoming an architect and designer and spends much of his time using Google Sketchup to design buildings. But recently, since his older sister introduced him to the virtual world platform, Second Life (n.d.), Janez's hobby has taken a new dimension. Second Life is an international, build-your-own, free-form gaming platform in which players in the guise of avatars buy "islands" and create their own buildings, complete with furnishings, which are then visited by other avatars for socializing. These avatars are wildly costumed and assume personas that are quite inventive and different from their real-life selves. Janez has been excited to design not only a new environment but a new self to match his virtual space. His sister has given him some property on the island she created and for the last month he has worked to design and build a *kavarna* (cafe) where he and acquaintances can gather.

Janez has also discovered that most of the visitors to his *kavarna* are not Slovene. They come from all over Europe, Asia, Africa, and the Americas, and to communicate they mostly speak English. Janez has been learning English in school since the first grade and regularly watches English language television programs and movies in English with captions and sometimes subtitles in Serbo-Croatian. His reception of English is at an intermediate to advanced level, but he has had few opportunities to speak or write it. When he meets people in Second Life, he has found that they typically address him in English, requiring him to reply to them in English. The questions in chat are initially simple and he has found that within the Second Life community, more than half are non-native speakers who are very forgiving and helpful in speaking. He has recently begun to try speaking with people verbally rather than through written chat and has found this very helpful in improving his pronunciation.

Nubia Gamil and Chess.com

Nubia Gamil is a 22-year-old student at a university in Egypt, with a passion for playing chess. As a young girl, Nubia watched her brothers play on tables in the park or outside her house and picked up the moves from them. However, she struggled to find other female players, and the boys in her neighborhood would not play her for fear of being beaten by a girl.

However, things began to change for Nubia when she turned 18. Her aunt gave her an old smartphone, and Nubia soon discovered that she could find all the players she could imagine through the Chess.com app. She created an alias for herself on the site and soon was playing with others all over the world, regardless of gender. Nubia discovered that she might also chat with these players, and usually in English, which she had studied in school and with which she was familiar from satellite television programs, but had never had much practice in speaking or writing. Soon, however, she began to pick up more and more words and expressions, and soon she was also reading articles about chess in English posted on other players' blogs. She began to study strategy and classic games, and soon found that she was becoming an authority whom others consulted at times.

This gave Nubia an idea to start her own platform about chess, in English and Arabic. With some of her friends she began to video record games and give lessons, and posted these to her YouTube channel, marketing it as an Arab women's chess channel. Her subscribers are slowly growing, and Nubia is beginning to think that perhaps she might have a future as an entrepreneur in digital marketing and communications.

Discussion

For learners in countries or regions with high-speed internet, virtual reality programs are often a gateway for IDLE. Virtual reality platforms differ from conventional Web 2.0 videos and webpages in that they typically create three-dimensional (usually on a two-dimensional screen) environments that are immersive in that they offer a perspective in which users are "in the scene," using computer controls or, in some advanced cases, their own bodies to move about, turning, walking, and even flying through computer-generated space.

The most prevalent form of virtual reality today are MMORPGs. These games evolved from CD- and DVD-based games played on desktops and then on consoles like X-Box, Nintendo, and Playstation by small groups of individuals in homes in the 1990s to online versions today, in which thousands or even millions of players globally gather to play in teams. Some games require subscriptions or initial downloads that are expensive; others are free. These games feature fantasy worlds or sometimes, as in the case of the SIMS (n.d.), simulated contemporary worlds with storylines and a vast array of characters and settings, and all require a player to become a character within the game. The games are also highly social and require players to communicate with others using language. Although it is possible to play exclusively in German or Korean or Arabic, the global nature of the games and players often requires a lingua franca, usually English.

In addition to MMORPGs, there are many other types of virtual platforms. These include open-ended simulated worlds like Second Life, which offers free and fee-based options, and sites that require head-mounted devices (HMDs), or virtual reality (VR) headsets like Oculus or Google Cardboard that offer a highly immersive (and often dizzying) experience for users. One of the most intriguing of these is Google Earth VR (n.d.), which permits users to tour a 3D version of Google Earth.

Opportunities for incorporating some form of virtual reality into English language classrooms are vast, but they depend on the quality and speed of the internet and equipment that is available. While MMORPGs and Second Life require fast processors and high-speed internet, fully immersive technologies using VR headsets require special equipment and exceptionally high-speed processing to be effective. A humbler but in most cases more feasible approach is to use the street-view (where available) of the regular, two-dimensional version of Google Earth. However, not all experiences of Google Earth are real-time, and so do not allow for social interaction with others online.

Chapter Objectives

The central goal of this chapter is to review the research and theory on the use of games and other virtual learning platforms in language learning and consider their applications for classroom instruction. In this review, concepts such as gamification, intrinsic motivation and immersive learning will also be discussed. Readers will also learn how these concepts may influence new instructional designs through three scenarios in the second half of the chapter. At the end of this chapter, readers will be able to:

1) Explain the four elements of gamification and why these need to be adopted as a whole and not individually within educational applications.
2) Distinguish between games and play and other types on online practice platforms.
3) Describe the affordabilities of MMORPGs and other virtual platforms that encourage language learning.
4) Describe the challenges of games and virtual reality platforms for classroom environments.
5) Explain three ways that the principles of gamification and virtual platforms can be applied responsibly and practically within classrooms.
6) Discuss how the research, theory, and three scenarios in this chapter can be applied to the reader's pedagogical context.

Key Words

games; gamification; MMORPG; avatar; intrinsic motivation; virtual reality; immersive learning

---

Research and Theory

Games and Gamification

Research on the use of digital games and other forms of virtual reality in language acquisition and learning spans a wide range of platforms and contexts, but it is nearly always grounded in the theoretical principles of games and gamification. Many explanations of what a "game" is have been proposed (Kramer 2000), and nearly all share at least four elements: (1) it is a form of play; (2) it has a set of rules; (3) it involves a challenge or test of skill or knowledge; and (4) its outcome is at stake (i.e., it has potential value to the players and is not assured). Some theorists posit a fifth element, that it is *social*; however, there are also games with single players where the challenge is against oneself, i.e., against one's own prior skill level or record of achievement.

Most theorists define play as an activity that is not work, although the distinction is sometimes ambiguous (Huizinga 1970). Generally, play is always pleasurable and engaged in freely, for its own sake, and not out of necessity. The rules of games provide both direction (a goal) and structure to the play, making it an ordered but not ritualistic form of cultural activity. The challenge or test of skill or knowledge means that players are always potentially able to improve their play and is a critical aspect of games' application to language learning. Stakes are the motivating force within a game. The stake in a game is typically described as its reward, which can be won or lost, but this is also ambiguous. "Winning" can be its own reward in many games and may not require any token other than an acknowledged gain in skill or the superiority of the player's skills. Oftentimes, even if there is a reward, it is something as simple as a ribbon or recognition by one's peers. One irony of playing games is that the least remunerative rewards can be the most highly motivating for players.

Online Video Gaming Statistics

- There were 2.95 billion active video gamers worldwide in 2022.
- The biggest gaming markets in order are: China, United States, Japan, South Korea, and Germany.
- There are more video gamers in the Asian Pacific than in the rest of the world combined.
- Smartphones account for 40% of market revenue from video gaming worldwide.
- 18–25-year-old gamers average 7.48 hours online per week.
- Males play longer (5.17 consecutive hours) than females (4.02 hours) on average.
- In the United States, 55% of gamers are male and 45% are female.

Source: Adapted from FinancesOnline n.d.

Researchers and designers of games for learning use the term *gamification* to describe the application of the elements of gaming within educational contexts. While different researchers and theorists may use different terminology or include some additional elements, for learning activity to be gamified it must contain *all four* elements listed, not simply one or two, such as stakes, which alone would simply make it another school assignment, or play and stakes, which may or may not require students to test or improve their skills within a rule-bound system. Finally, it should also be noted that the term *game theory* is often mentioned in studies of gaming; however, this term usually refers to mathematically based strategies for playing high-stakes games and is most commonly applied to "games" like playing the stock market and calculating other business decisions. It has little relevance in practice to language learning in or out of classrooms.

Studies of gamification in learning have attempted to identify more specific characteristics that make games successful in learning environments. Stott and Neustaedter (2013) identified four factors in their review of the literature: (1) freedom to fail; (2) rapid feedback; (3) progression; and (4) storytelling. They also found in their analysis of three "best practices" games that "(t)here is no once-size-fits all model for the successful gamification of a classroom" (2013, 7). A more recent review of 32 recent studies in gamification in education found similar ambiguity in precisely how and when to apply principals of gaming within classroom settings, possibly because "there is no agreed definition for the term gamification" (Ofosu-Ampong 2020, 115). A review of 128 studies (Majuri, Koivisto, and Hamari 2018) found that most educational games tend to emphasize achievement and progression and that "social and immersion-oriented affordances of gaming are much less common" (2020, 11).

Studies focusing specifically on the gamification of language learning, for example, Govender and Arnedo-Moreno (2020) and Shortt et al. (2021), have typically focused on the use of mobile-learning devices using apps such as Duolingo or Babbel. These, however, are non-formal rather than informal and do not meet our criteria for a game because they are highly structured with little decision-making required, they are not a true a form of play, and because their outcome is determined. We will discuss these as supplementary additions to classroom learning in Chapter 8.

Research on MMORPGs and Language Learning

Research on MMORPGs has consistently shown gains for players in English language vocabulary (Lee 2020; Liu, Yang, and Huang 2012; Sundqvist 2009), syntax (Yang and Hsu 2013), reading comprehension, writing (Suh, Kim, and Kim 2010), and communicative competence (Adris and Yamat 2015; Peterson 2012). For example, Sundqvist and Wikström (2015) found a positive link between the frequency of digital gaming and English vocabulary knowledge in 88 Swedish 9th graders (aged 15–16 years). Sundqvist (2019) found that playing commercially available games (e.g., *StarCraft* and *Overwatch*) was positively associated with English vocabulary knowledge in 1,069 Swedish middle school students (aged 15–16 years). She found that the more frequently students play games, the higher their English vocabulary test scores.

Lee and Dressman (2018) introduced the case of Su-ja in the Korean context. Su-ja was born and raised in a rural area before moving to Seoul for university. Su-ja had no prior international or private tutoring experience. She did, however, learn English vocabulary through extramural English activities, such as playing online games, from early childhood to adolescence. Su-ja claimed that all the English input she received from online gaming served as a strong foundation for developing English vocabulary.

Jin-Young: Developing English Proficiency Through MMORPG Team Play

The case of Jin-Young (pseudonym), a South Korean university student, provides a detailed case of how MMORPGs contribute to English language development (Lee 2018).

Jin-Young attended public school and private *hagwon* lessons from grades K-12. He did not study overseas. His father pushed him to learn English from an early age, and Jin-Young obliged by becoming an English major at university. Lee (2018) described him as a reflective learner who created strategies and made decisions designed to achieve particular goals. Through these "deliberate" processes, he developed a strong, formal knowledge of English.

However, much of Jin-Young's proficiency as a user of English for communication came through multiple IDLE activities, especially playing one of the most popular MMORPGs in South Korea, *StarCraft*. This game requires team play, and Jin-Young joined a group of American players to improve his English. He also purchased a copy of StarCraft English and using it as a reference enabled him to pick up a wide range of expressions ("You want a piece of me, boy?") and specialized vocabulary (combat physician, barracks). The book also explained how a word like *Terran* (a tribe in the game) could be related to other English words like "territory" and "Mediterranean." By combining the pleasure of team play with research, Jin Young gained both expressive confidence and an extensive range of vocabulary.

Sundqvist and Sylvén (2014) also found that young Swedish English learners (aged 10–11 years) who participated in extramural English activities frequently had a more positive assessment of their English ability. Extramural English, particularly online games, provided English learners with more opportunities to use and monitor their English performance, boosting their confidence in speaking English. According to Sundqvist and Sylvén:

The frequent gamers actually use English to such a great extent outside of school that, in so doing, they more easily realize their own shortcomings in terms of L2 English proficiency in a way that the moderate and non-gamers rarely get a chance to do. In addition, we notice that frequent gamers group clearly was the most confident one in terms of speaking in English. (16)

Additional research has focused on features responsible for English learning within MMORPGs. The chat feature of MMORPGs has been the most frequently cited feature (Won 2015). Suh, Kim, and Kim (2010) identified level of prior knowledge, motivation, and network speed as variables responsible for English learning in primary students. Yang and Quadir (2018) studied the effects of prior knowledge (of English and game experience) on learners' anxiety and English performance in Taiwanese sixth graders. They found that greater knowledge of English was positively correlated with English learning (the more English students knew the more they learned) but also that students with less online gaming experience learned more English, presumably because they needed to focus on learning English to learn to play the game.

Research on Second Life and Other Virtual Platforms

Besides MMORPGs, there are other forms of immersive virtual platforms that can provide an environment for English language learning (Chen 2016). The advantage of these platforms is their malleability: the environments and avatars can be designed by the users and teachers are able to set agendas, rules of play, and design learning activities to meet learning goals. However, these platforms also raise questions for classroom use due to institutional and technological demands (Antoniadou 2011; Kruk 2021; Zhang 2013), the nature of the activity that forms the context for learning (Mayrath et al. 2007), and age-restrictions on platforms like Second Life. For these reasons, virtual platforms are typically used primarily in universities and by older learners.

In his review of the literature on language learning within virtual reality contexts, Sadler (2020) noted two powerful advantages of language learning within virtual worlds: (1) a dramatic reduction in learners' anxiety due to their masked, avatar-based identity; and (2) the collaborative nature of interaction within the worlds, in which players assist each other with directions on how to move and, in task-focused situations, how to create an object or discuss a subject. Sadler cited Oldenburg (1999), who listed eight characteristics of "third places"—public places outside home or work—that reduced learners' apprehension. The most salient of these for language learning were that virtual worlds were "levelers," meaning that there was a lack of social hierarchy within them; that conversation was the main activity within them, requiring players to speak (or write) within them in order to participate; and that the mood was playful and players were free to make mistakes in their communications.

Virtual Reality Sites for Language Learning

- **Second Life.** Although not designed for language learning, this largest of all VR worlds provides many opportunities to chat in a wide variety of languages with other avatars, sometimes in spaces devoted to speaking a particular language. Second Life can be visited for free, but advanced uses are fee-based.

(Continued)

(Continued)

- **ImmerseMe.** Developed in New Zealand, ImmerseMe uses live actors to teach multiple languages through conversation, and supports learning on smartphones, computers, and VR headsets. The interaction is not live, but lessons were recorded in authentic locations with real speakers.
- **Mondly.** This Romania-based site uses interactive chatbot avatars to practice conversations in a range of "real life" settings, such as a taxi, hotel, or restaurant. Learning is supported through smartphones, computers, and VR headsets.
- **Immerse.online.** In this site, the language teacher and the students meet online in a VR setting in the guise of avatars. This is not automated instruction, but a VR synchronous instruction tool for use by a teacher with students to replace Web 2.0 tools like Blackboard, Teams, or Zoom.

Virtual worlds like Second Life or the SIMs are venues for many different types of activities besides education and language learning (Ranalli 2008). However, the international, multilingual nature of the population of these worlds also makes them prime locations for translanguaging (Zheng et al. 2017) and incidental language learning. In a 2012 study, Sadler surveyed 237 players about their language learning via a virtual world environment and found that 48% reported learning language(s) while playing and 26.6% reported that virtual worlds were very helpful in learning language(s).

Sadler concluded his review by noting that the future of language learning within virtual worlds was bright, and that advances in technology permit greater levels of immersion through the use of ocular devices that can "insert" a player/avatar into a three-dimensional space. Whether these advances will increase learning outcomes, however, is unknown. Pollard et al. (2020) found that whether increased levels of immersion improved learning depended on the type of learning task (i.e., learning information vs. learning how to physically perform an action), with greater levels of immersion generally improving the performance of physical rather than intellectual activities.

Discussion: Classroom Implications

In summary, immersive, simulated three-dimensional environments provide powerful opportunities for language learning. A playful environment, use of avatars, and the need to collaborate through language are the principal features that lead to language acquisition and learning. Language learners also report much less anxiety due to the use of avatars, which serve as masks that prevent a loss of face when attempting to speak or write. However, institutional and technological issues (these require high-speed internet and processing) as well as concerns about privacy and inappropriate content may limit their direct application in classroom settings, especially at middle and secondary levels.

We can, however, recommend three appropriate uses of games and other virtual reality platforms within classroom contexts. First, teachers may attempt to adapt or build their own platforms or use lower-level forms of virtual reality such as Google Earth Pro or VR in language learning, but with the caveat that this may require much trial and error and/or heavy use of equipment and software. A second suggestion is to engage students in discussions of how they are informally acquiring a new language online, and to try to build on these strategies to build links between their English learning in and out of school.

A third possibility is not to make use of virtual platforms but rather to adopt elements of gamification in some learning activities. This approach will require teachers to apply all four elements to achieve a true gaming experience, in which the activity must: (1) be recognized by the students as a form of play; (2) have a clear set of rules; (3) involve a challenge or test of skill or knowledge; and (4) have an outcome that is at stake with more than one possible outcome. In addition, research indicates that the "best games" provide: (1) freedom to fail; (2) rapid feedback; (3) progression; and (4) some form of storytelling.

Practical Applications in the Classroom

Scenario One: Gamification for Vocabulary Development in a Korean Middle School

The Scene. Mr. Haru Lee has been teaching English to seventh graders (ages 14–15) in a public school in a rural area of South Korea for two years. This year, he was tasked with teaching 20 students who have been classified as beginners based on their previous English test results. Most of the students began studying English in third grade or later through formal education. They have had fewer opportunities to receive English private tutoring than typical Korean students in larger cities. There has been no international experience among the students.

Mr. Lee uses a textbook that has been approved by an education bureau. His students' vocabulary is lacking, according to previous vocabulary test results and so he starts each lesson with a chapter-based vocabulary test. However, he has been dissatisfied with the test results. Most students receive less than 50% on these tests. He decided to meet with each student after school to learn about how they study English and has found that most students do not have an English learning strategy and that most of them find English classes tedious. They have no compelling reason to study English other than to improve their test scores.

However, he has also learned that his students spend at least one hour after school each day playing English language online games and several spend more than three hours per day playing. If there is no test to study for, his students spend the entire weekend immersed in these games. For instance, Hyun-sung plays *StarCraft* in English with his classmates and other gamers from around the world. He does not write or speak English during the game, but he is repeatedly exposed to a variety of English words and expressions. Shin-young enjoys playing *Overwatch* with his foreign friends. Both Shin-young and Hyun-sung are drawn to the game's storyline and multiplayer, team-based game mode. They have even learned game strategy after playing the game to improve their game skills by watching *StarCraft* and *Overwatch* walk-through videos on YouTube and reading information from *StarCraft* and *Overwatch* online blogs and communities. The majority of the content is provided in English, sometimes with difficult vocabulary. They can, however, comprehend the content by utilizing prior knowledge as well as multimodal information such as images and videos. They also consult an online dictionary or Google Translate to understand the meaning of the content.

Analysis: Challenges and Opportunities. Mr. Lee remembered taking a course in Computer Assisted Language Learning (CALL) as part of his master's degree in TESOL a few years ago. He read several articles about the linguistic benefits of online games for

EFL learners. Sundqvist and Wikström (2015) found a positive link between the frequency of digital gaming and English vocabulary knowledge in 88 Swedish 9th graders (aged 15–16 years). Sundqvist (2019) found that playing commercially available games (e.g., *Starcraft* and *Overwatch*) was positively associated with English vocabulary knowledge in 1,069 Swedish middle school students (aged 15–16 years).

Instructional Plan. Mr. Lee's reading of the research pointed to a highly engaging and motivating way to develop students' vocabulary through gaming and gamification. However, at the same time he was also aware that parents disapproved of their children's online gaming and believed that it was harmful to them academically and perhaps to their safety. He decided to provide parents with a summary of empirical studies as well as a concise guideline on how well-structured gaming and YouTube videos can benefit students' second language acquisition while minimizing students' online safety concerns.

To develop his students' vocabulary, Mr. Lee decided to allow his students to nominate words discovered while playing MMORPGs and to create quizzes of their own for their classmates. These quizzes would consist of five open-ended short-answer questions and five multiple-choice questions. The students were first required to submit the names of the MMORPG they would use for review by Mr. Lee. He then organized them by the games they chose into groups of three or four. The groups were instructed to select one walk-through video of their chosen MMORPG on YouTube (10–15 minutes in length), to select ten vocabulary words that were new or unknown to them and that could be used in many contexts (no proper nouns), and to submit these for review. The students used Edpuzzle (n.d.) to upload the video and create ten questions (5 short-answer and 5 multiple choice). When completed, the groups shared their Edpuzzle links with Mr. Lee, who reviewed them and made comments for their final editing. Mr. Lee then selected one Edpuzzle video per week to use as his vocabulary quiz. In a follow-up exercise, students wrote stories about their favorite MMORPGs using the vocabulary from the quiz.

1) Materials:
    a) School computers, iPads or other devices
    b) School Wi-Fi or landline connections
    c) EdPuzzle
    d) YouTube.
2) Learning Mode: Whole-class for introduction; small-groups of four individual assessment
3) Time: Four 45-minute sessions
4) Sequence of Activities:
    a) Day 1: Teacher introduces the quiz-creation project
    b) Teacher records students' favorite MMORPGs on board and organizes them into groups of three or four
    c) Groups identify a walk-through video on YouTube for playing their favorite MMORPG of 10–15 minutes
    d) Groups identify ten vocabulary words and submit them to the teacher
    e) Day 2: Writing the quizzes
    f) Groups use Edpuzzle to upload their video and compose questions using context clues and other resources
    g) Teacher circulates, offering suggestions and keeping groups on track
    h) Day 3: Taking the quiz

i) Students individually go online to Edpuzzle to take the quiz chosen by the teacher for that week

j) Day 4: Results and debriefing

k) Teacher shares quiz results with students individually and debriefs with them about the vocabulary, their experience writing the quiz, and using Edpuzzle

l) In groups of four, the students use at least seven vocabulary words from the quiz to write a story set within the world of their favorite MMORPG

m) Day 5: Writing and reading the stories

n) Students complete their stories and these are shared with the class

o) In an email to parents, the teacher gives access to their students' Edpuzzle links, as well as a concise guideline on how well-structured gaming and YouTube videos can benefit students' second language acquisition while minimizing students' online safety concerns

p) Subsequent weeks

q) One quiz is chosen per week, with follow-up extension activities.

Assignments and Assessment. This activity has two assessments: 1) the individual quiz score for each student (not included here); and 2) an assessment of each group's performance (see Table 7.1).

Table 7.1 Rubric for assessing group performance.

Achievement level	Descriptor
Excellent	The vocabulary chosen by the groups consisted of relevant, unknown words that could be used in multiple future contexts. The students easily selected an appropriate walk-through video and successfully uploaded it to Edpuzzle. The questions generated were well phrased and answerable, and needed only slight editing. The stories written by them as a follow-up activity were inventive and contained more than seven words that were used accurately. The group worked quickly and collaboratively, staying on task through the entire exercise.
Very good	The vocabulary chosen by the groups consists of relevant, unknown words that could be used in multiple future contexts. The students selected a walk-through video and uploaded it to Edpuzzle. The questions generated were well phrased, answerable, and needed some editing. The stories written by them as a follow-up activity contained at least seven words used accurately. The group worked collaboratively, staying on task through most of the exercise.
Satisfactory	The vocabulary chosen by the groups consisted of mostly relevant, unknown words that could be used in multiple future contexts. The students selected a walk-through video and uploaded it to Edpuzzle with assistance. The questions generated were answerable but needed editing. The stories written by them as a follow-up activity contained at least seven words and most were used accurately. The group collaborated with only a few problems and stayed on task most of the time.
Unsatisfactory	Many of the vocabulary words chosen by the group were either irrelevant or unknown, and needed multiple revisions. The students struggled to find a walk-through video of 10–15 minutes and upload it to Edpuzzle. The questions generated were mostly unusable and needed major revision or rewriting. The stories written by them as a follow-up activity were short, used few vocabulary words, and had many errors in grammar and spelling. The group collaborated poorly and needed to be kept on task.

Relation to TESOL Technology Standards for Learners and CEFR Reference Level Descriptors

TESOL Technology Standards:

- Goal 1 (Demonstrate foundational knowledge and skills in technology for a multilingual world)
  - Standard 1 (Demonstrate basic operational skills in using various technology tools and internet browsers)
  - Standard 2 (Use available input and output devices)
  - Standard 4 (Demonstrate basic competence as users of technology).
- Goal 3 (Effectively use and critically evaluate technology-based tools as aids in the development of their language learning competence)
  - Standard 1 (Effectively use and evaluate available technology-based productivity tools)
  - Standard 2 (Appropriately use and evaluate available technology-based language skill-building tools)
  - Standard 3 (Appropriately use and evaluate available technology-based tools for communication and collaboration)
  - Standard 5 (Recognize the value of technology to support autonomy, lifelong learning, creativity, metacognition, collaboration, personal pursuits, and productivity).

CEFR Reference Level Descriptors:

- Global Scale: A2 (Can understand sentences related to areas of immediate relevance)
- Listening to Announcements and Instructions: B1 (Can understand simple technical information)
- Overall Reading Comprehension: A2 (Can understand short, simple texts)
- Reading for Orientation: B1 (Can find and understand relevant information)
- Reading for Information and Argument: A2 (Can identify information in simpler written material)
- Reading Instructions: B1 (Can understand simply written, straightforward instructions)
- Overall Spoken Interaction: A2 (Can interact with reasonable ease in structured situations)
- Formal Discussion: A2 (Can exchange relevant information)
- Goal-Oriented Cooperation: B1 (Can follow what is said)
- Overall Written Interaction: B1 (Can convey information and ideas)
- Overall Spoken Production: A2 (Can give a simple description or presentation)
- Addressing Audiences: A2 (Can give a short, rehearsed presentation)
- General Linguistic Range: A2 (Has a repertoire of basic language)
- Vocabulary Range: A2 (Has sufficient vocabulary to express him/herself)
- Orthographic Control: B1 (Spelling, punctuation, and layout are accurate enough to be followed most of the time)
- Flexibility: A2 (Can adapt well-rehearsed memorized simple phrases)
- Propositional Precision: A2 (Can communicate what he/she wants to say).

Analyzing and Extending the Lesson: Application to Additional Contexts. In a blended learning mode, a teacher can create and implement game-based presentation activities. Through deeper investigation and reflection of the game, a teacher can also support higher-level and critical thinking. Students, for example, can choose their favorite online games at home. Following that, students can conduct research on the game's plot and background, or they can present their own effective gaming strategy in English. They are getting ready to create a presentation document. Students give a five-minute presentation about the topic in class. The teacher then leads a class discussion about the game's topic and other aspects. This type of lesson can be used in low-resource environments where students can still play online games that do not require high-tech equipment.

Scenario Two: A Google Earth Pro Tour of Dubai

The Scene. Nancie Lang teaches tenth-grade English at an American school in Dubai, United Arab Emirates. Her students are mostly from Emirati and professional expatriate families who speak English in public but mostly Arabic and southeast Asian languages at home and with their friends. Most have been taught in English since primary school and they are conversational but struggle with writing with precision, especially when giving explanations.

This issue has become important to the school with preparations for Expo 2020, the world's fair about to open in Dubai after a year-long delay for the Covid-19 pandemic, because many of the students at the school have been named "Expo 2020 Junior Ambassadors" who would serve as informal guides for visitors to the city during the Expo. In staff meetings, the school director has stressed the need to prepare the students for their duties, and the teachers have expressed concern about the students' ability to give precise directions and about their knowledge of the city in general.

Nancie considered teaching some remedial lessons on direction-giving, but she is not confident that these will help students in practice. Then, in the library one day, she spotted Khalifa, a student in her third-period class, hunched over his laptop, moving his cursor across a digital map. He told her he was working on a geography report in which the class was using Google Earth Pro to trace agricultural sites on the Arabian Peninsula. Intrigued, Nancie asked how he was tracing the sites, and he explained that a feature of the program allowed him to record a narrated tour, moving from street-level site to street-level site, and save it for later replay. He demonstrated the tour he'd been working on for class, and Nancie realized suddenly that here was the tool she needed for her students to both learn about the city and practice giving detailed directions.

Analysis: Challenges and Opportunities. Google Earth (online) and its desktop application, Google Earth Pro, are widely used applications in social studies education but are not frequent in language classrooms. However, these offer an unrivaled and free opportunity for language students make virtual visits to cities and regions of the earth where a target language is widely spoken and to learn from the environmental print on buildings (e.g., signs on buildings).

Both applications offer a "virtual" view of the earth from overhead, or in many (but not all) countries, the ability to "stand" on a street and from that level take a 360-degree view of the surroundings and then, by moving the cursor on the image, to "travel" down that street. These views are not real-time, but the level of coverage of the earth, especially at street level, qualifies them as a virtual and accurate representation of much of the earth's trafficked spaces. An even more immersive version of Google Earth is available through Google Earth VR (n.d.), which uses virtual reality headsets to provide a fully immersive view of some of the world's greatest sites.

In this scenario, a teacher uses the "Record a Tour" button at in the top menu of Google Earth Pro to have her students plan and then record a tour of sites, narrating the tour and providing on-the-ground directions for how to reach locations within Dubai and other areas of the UAE. Directions for how to use this feature are available on YouTube (n.d.) and in print on the Google Earth support site (n.d.).

Instructional Plan. Nancie began her preparation for teaching by visiting the geography teacher at her school to ask about how he was using Google Earth Pro in his classroom. The teacher described a few of the projects his students had completed and their general level of proficiency with the software. They shared class lists and Nancie discovered that more than half her students had used the software before and were reasonably proficient with it. The teacher also told her that the software was already downloaded on the computers in the library and lab, and he showed Nancie how to download and install it on her laptop. Nancie spent a week practicing with Google Earth Pro and made a recording of her own hometown, Chicago, to demonstrate the assignment for her students.

Nancie's students were excited when she explained that they would be working in groups of three to create a recorded tour of 5–7 sites in Dubai, giving visitors clear directions on how to get from one to the other. She left the exact locations each group would visit to the students, but divided the city into seven zones, requiring each tour to visit at least three of these. She showed her students her tour and in creating the groups was sure that each had one member who had previously used the software in geography class. A few of the students who were from other cities in the UAE such as Abu Dhabi or Ras Al Khaima asked if they could give tours of their home cities instead, and Nancie agreed to this.

Nancie also provided her students with an outline of steps for completion of the project. She required the students to research each site they chose before recording and to write a script in which they were sure to give precise descriptions for how to use the Dubai Metro to travel to each site (taking a taxi was not allowed), including what station was closest and even which entrance to the station should be used. At first the students gave vague directions but after Nancie demonstrated that she could not find the site with those directions and provided examples of the level of detail the students needed, they improved. Within two weeks, each group had completed a credible, detailed recording of their tour of Dubai or another city in the UAE and were ready to present them to the school director and a group of teachers for approval before uploading on the Online Guide to Expo 2020 the Junior Ambassadors were creating.

1) Materials:
    a) Laptops or desktops
    b) Google Earth Pro downloaded
    c) Google Earth (optional)
    d) Google Earth mobile (optional)
    e) Internet connection.
2) Learning Mode: Whole class for discussion; small group (three students)
3) Time: Ten days (50-minute sessions)
4) Sequence of Activities:
    a) Day 1: Introduction of assignment
    b) Teacher presents assignment with details

c) Teacher demonstrates use of Google Earth Pro
d) Groups are formed and begin to brainstorm topics
e) Day 2: Site selection
f) Class meets in library or computer lab in small groups
g) Groups begin to select sites using Google Earth (on desktops and/or mobile phones)
h) Groups research their sites and begin to formulate a sequence of visits with directions
i) Day 3: Plan presentations to the teacher
j) Groups write a sequential plan without directions and present it to the teacher for approval
k) Groups use Google Earth Pro to begin tracing a walking path from the closest Metro station to the site
l) Days 4–6: Research, planning, and writing
m) Groups create detailed directions from Metro stations to each site
n) Groups compile their directions into a script describing the entire tour
o) Teacher circulates during these days, supervising
p) Days 7–9: Recording the tour
q) Groups divide parts among members and practice reading through the tour and recording parts
r) Groups record and edit, and finalize their final tours
s) Teacher circulates and supervises the editing of the tours
t) Day 10: Groups present their tours to the class and submit a final version.

Assignments and Assessment. There are two assignments for this activity: (1) a group assessment of the final project; and (2) an assessment of each student's participation in the project for this assignment.

Table 7.2 Rubric for assessing group performance for the final project.

Achievement level	Descriptor
Excellent	The group accurately and completely provided a recorded tour of five or more sites in Dubai or the UAE. The recording was smooth, with clear transitions from one site to the next. Each member of the group recorded a portion of the tour, which was clearly organized. The directions given for the tour were clear, accurate, and could easily be followed from each site to the next or to the next Metro station, including directions for stopping at the next station on the tour. The students' English was fluent and showed few errors in pronunciation, word choice, or grammar.
Very good	The group provided a recorded tour of five or more sites in Dubai or the UAE that was relatively accurate and complete. The recording was smooth, with transitions from one site to the next. Each member of the group participated in the recording, which was organized. The directions given for the tour were clear and could be followed. The students' English was fluent and showed relatively few errors in pronunciation, word choice, or grammar.

(Continued)

Table 7.2 (Continued)

Achievement level	Descriptor
Satisfactory	The group provided a recorded tour of at least five sites in Dubai or the UAE that demonstrated evidence of research. The recording worked with only a few problems in transitions from one site to the next. Each member participated in the recording, but some members participated significantly more, and the tour may have had some problems with organization. The directions given were adequate but might have needed more detail. The students' English was intelligible and errors did not impede meaning.
Unsatisfactory	The group may not have provided a full recording of at least five sites, with little demonstrated evidence of research. The recording played with difficulty and there were several problems with transitions. There was a lack of teamwork during the project that resulted in one or more members not contributing. The directions give were inadequate and needed much more detail. The students' English was barely intelligible with many errors in pronunciation, word choice, and grammar.

Table 7.3 Rubric for assessing individual performance on the project.

Achievement level	Descriptor
Above expectations	The student self-reported and was observed in active participation in every aspect of the project, from selecting sites to researching, writing, and recording the tour. Their contributions were creative and insightful. The student recorded and narrated a significant portion of the tour, and spoke fluently with few errors in pronunciation, word choice, or grammar.
Meets expectations	The student self-reported and was observed to participate in most aspects of the project, from selecting sites to researching, writing, and recording the tour. Their contributions were meaningful. The student recorded and narrated a portion of the tour, and spoke intelligibly.
Below expectations	The student self-reported but was not observed to participate in most aspects of the project, and made few identifiable contributions to selecting sites, researching, writing, or recording the tour. The student may not have recorded or narrated a portion of the tour, or may not have spoken intelligibly.

Relation to TESOL Technology Standards for Learners and CEFR Reference Level Descriptors

TESOL Technology Standards:
- Goal 3 (Effectively use and critically evaluate technology-based tools)
  - Standard 1 (Effectively use and evaluate productivity tools)
  - Standard 2 (Appropriately use and evaluate language skill-building tools)
  - Standard 3 (Use and evaluate tools for communication and collaboration).

CEFR Reference Level Descriptors:
- Global Scale: B2 (Can produce clear, detailed text on a wide range of subjects)
- Overall Reading Comprehension: A2 (Can read short, simple texts)

- Reading for Orientation: B1 (Can find and understand relevant information in everyday material)
- Overall Spoken Interaction: B1 (Can communicate with some confidence on familiar routine and non-routine matters)
- Formal Discussion (Meetings): B1 (Can take part in routine formal discussion)
- Goal-Oriented Cooperation: B1 (Can give brief comments on the views of others)
- Information Exchange: B1 (Can describe how to do something)
- Overall Spoken Production: B2 (Can give clear, detailed descriptions and presentations)
- Sustained Monologue: Describing Experience: B2 (Can give clear, detailed descriptions)
- Overall Written Production: B2 (Can write clear, detailed texts)
- Planning: B1 (Can work out how to communicate main points)
- Note-Taking: B1 (Can take notes as a list of key points)
- Processing Text: B2 (Can summarize the plot and sequence of events)
- General Linguistic Range: B2 (Has a sufficient range of language to be able to give clear descriptions)
- Grammatical Accuracy: B1 (Communicates with reasonable accuracy in familiar contexts)
- Thematic Development: B2 (Can develop a clear description or narrative)
- Propositional Precision: B2 (Can pass on detailed information reliably.)
- Spoken Fluency: B1 (Can express him/herself with relative ease).

Analyzing and Extending the Lesson: Application to Additional Contexts. In this scenario, a teacher in a secondary English Medium of Instruction (EMI) school discovered a student using Google Earth Pro and found a way to repurpose this virtual reality program to have students create and narrate a tour of their home city for visitors. As we noted, using a virtual reality program requires high-speed internet and processing that may not be available in all schools or areas. However, it is also possible to use the street view feature of Google Maps to explore a city and record screenshots that can then be used to illustrate a narrated PowerPoint tour.

The power of using Google Earth or Maps is its authenticity and boundless opportunities to explore either one's own area or, perhaps, an English-speaking city in another country. In addition, the use of technologies such as the Record a Tour feature of Google Earth Pro provides an authentic opportunity for writing and speaking that is well within the ability of speakers at a late beginner or early intermediate level of proficiency. Organizing the resources needed for this activity and mastering the software may take some effort but the motivation and opportunity to "visit" cities around the world makes the exercise very worthwhile.

Scenario Three: Using Second Life as a Virtual Practice Space

The Scene. Sarah Hassan and her colleagues teach English in an American language center in Narita, Japan. A special feature of this language center are its courses on learning to use English in everyday life activities, such as shopping, going to a restaurant or café, or traveling. These short-term courses are very popular with adolescents, college students, and adults who are planning to travel abroad to Hawaii, the Philippines, or perhaps to Europe, and who need to review not only vocabulary and phrases but to practice interacting with others in English. Sarah and the other teachers have found that their students are diligent about learning vocabulary and grammatical structures but are very reticent about speaking and practicing in classroom simulations.

Sarah is a frequent visitor to Second Life, a 3D virtual world in which people create their own spaces on islands and interact with others in real time through avatars. Recently, she met someone in Second Life who revealed to her, after some conversation, that he was a Japanese student at a local university who used Second Life to improve his English. Hideki told her that he was embarrassed and feared losing face when asked to speak in a classroom, but he found it much easier to do so behind the mask of his avatar on Second Life. Sarah reported her conversation to her colleagues, and this has given them an idea for how to solve their instructional problem.

Analysis: Challenges and Opportunities. The exotic nature of Second Life, from the many public spaces that can be visited to the opportunity for students to create a wide range of avatars for themselves, adds interest and opportunities for engagement and autonomy. However, to create specific spaces such as restaurants, post offices, and train or bus stations as scenarios, Sarah and her colleagues may not always be able to rely on public space within Second Life and may need to purchase an "island" of their own on which these spaces can be built to their specifications.

Moreover, the motivational features of gamification that are a critical part of learning within Second Life do not lend themselves to traditional approaches to assessment. The reward of gamified learning is the completion of a challenging task and the sense of achievement that results; evaluation in the form of a traditional grade, therefore, can reduce motivation, making the game seem like work, not play. To evaluate students' progress in learning, Sarah and her colleagues will have to separate practice within Second Life from more traditional, classroom-based forms of assessment.

Instructional Plan. Sarah and her colleagues decided to develop a series of trials to practice everyday communication using Second Life (SL). For their first trial, they selected a visit to a restaurant as their topic. Using an "island" that she had previously purchased, Sarah created a very simple restaurant seating area with enough tables for all the students' avatars to sit at. One of her colleagues, Jim, found an authentic menu from an American-style diner and made copies to distribute to the students.

The teachers decided on a series of three tasks of increasing difficulty for students to practice, over three sessions. To prepare the students, they introduced the menu and useful words and phrases to the students and then announced the practice sessions for the following week. They also gave the students a homework assignment to create a free SL account and avatar over the weekend and to practice moving around in SL and "teleporting" to the restaurant where they would meet the following week. The students used the computer lab in the language center, which had Second Life preloaded for the sessions and allowed one teacher to circulate among the students and troubleshoot face to face while other teachers acted as servers online.

In Session 1, the students were placed in groups of four within the restaurant and given the task to order a simple meal from one of the teachers who was acting as a server. The reward for this first task was an accurate order read back to them by the waiter. In Session 2, the groups needed to enter the restaurant, be seated, and again order; but in this session, the server misread the order back to the students and they needed to correct the order to be successful. In Session 3, the students entered the restaurant, ordered correctly, had a conversation with the server about the food and Japan, and then asked for the cheque, which was incorrect, requiring the students to interact with the server to correct it.

1) Materials:
    a) Computer lab or laptops with a high-speed internet connection
    b) Second Life account
    c) Second Life virtual space.
2) Learning Mode: Small groups
3) Time: Three class sessions of 50 minutes each
4) Sequence of Activities:
    a) Prior to Session 1, students are introduced to Second Life and set up an account and avatar
    b) In Session 1, students and teachers meet virtually online (in computer lab or at home) in a restaurant setting
    c) Students are instructed to "sit" at a table in the restaurant in groups of four
    d) Teacher supervises and troubleshoots as other teachers act as servers, taking the students' orders from menus provided to them
    e) Each student gives her/his order; the server reads the orders back to each table accurately
    f) Teachers and the students debrief about the session
    g) In Session 2, students again "enter" the virtual restaurant and are given a more extensive, complex menu
    h) Teacher supervises and troubleshoots, as other teachers act as servers, taking the students' orders
    i) The servers read back the orders, with errors, requiring students to correct their orders
    j) The teachers and students debrief about the session
    k) In Session 3, the students enter and seat themselves at tables
    l) The students order and the server engages them in a conversation about the food and Japan, asking where they are from, why they are traveling, and so on
    m) At the end of the meal, the students ask for the cheque; it is incorrect, and they must correct the errors with the server
    n) The teachers and students debrief about the session.

Assignments and Assessment. This activity may have two assessments: 1) a survey of students' responses to Second Life; and 2) a summative, in-class assessment, in which the teacher acts as the server for groups of students ordering food.

The survey can be a 5–10 question paper and pencil survey in which students rate their experience and provide feedback on the session and their level of comfort in Second Life (not included here).

The summative assessment occurs in class a week after the three practice sessions. Students re-enact their experience in Second Life, ordering from a menu and correcting simple errors made by the teacher/server (see Table 7.4).

Table 7.4 Rubric for summative assessment of their performance after three practice sessions.

Achievement level	Descriptor
Excellent	The student speaks directly to the server without hesitation in ordering two or more items from a menu. Pronunciation is clear and comprehensible. The student correctly answers questions from the server about the order and is also able to correct any errors made by the server. Overall, exchanges are fluid and require little correction.
Very good	The student speaks to the server with minor hesitation in ordering two or more items from a menu. Pronunciation is clear; the student can restate items that are misunderstood. The student answers questions from the server and corrects any errors that are made. Overall, exchanges are somewhat fluid and errors are corrrected.
Satisfactory	The student speaks to the server with some hesitation but is able to order at least two items from a menu. Pronunciation is comprehensible and the student, with some prompting, can restate items that are misunderstood. The student answers questions from the server and tries to correct errors. Overall, exchanges are completed and most errors are corrected.
Unsatisfactory	The student speaks to the server with great hesitation and struggles to order one item from a menu. Pronunciation is often incomprehensible and the student must be prompted multiple times to restate items. The student is unable or barely able to answer simple questions and errors are not corrected. Overall, exchanges are limited or incomplete, with many uncorrected errors.

Relation to TESOL Technology Standards for Learners and CEFR Reference Level Descriptors

TESOL Technology Standards:

- Goal 2 (Use technology in appropriate ways)
  - Standard 1 (Understand that communication conventions differ)
- Goal 3 (Effectively use and critically evaluate technology-based tools)
  - Standard 2 (Use and evaluate language skill-building tools)
  - Standard 3 (Use and evaluate tools for communication and collaboration)
  - Standard 5 (Recognize value of technology to support autonomy).

CEFR Reference Level Descriptors:

- Global Scale: A2 (Can communicate in simple and routine tasks; can deal with most situations likely to arise whilst traveling)
- Overall Listening Comprehension: A2 (Can understand enough to meet concrete needs)
- Reading for Information and Argument: A2 (Can identify information in simpler written material)
- Overall Spoken Interaction: A2 (Can interact with reasonable ease in structured situations)
- Understanding Native Speaker Interlocutor: B1 (Can follow clearly articulated speech directed at him/her in simple everyday conversation)

- Conversation: A2 (Can participate in short conversations)
- Goal-Oriented Cooperation: A2 (Can understand enough to manage simple, routine tasks)
- Transactions to Obtain Goods and Services: A2 (Can deal with aspects of everyday living such as travel)
- Information Exchange: B1 (Can exchange, check, and confirm accumulated information)
- Asking for Clarification: A2 (Can ask very simply for repetition when they do not understand)
- Compensating: B1 (Can use a simple word meaning something similar to the concept they want to convey)
- Monitoring and Repair: B1 (Can correct mixups)
- General Linguistic Range: A2 (Has a repertoire of basic language)
- Grammatical Accuracy: A2 (Uses some simple structures correctly)
- Phonological Control: A2 (Pronunciation is generally clear enough to be understood)
- Sociolinguistic Appropriateness: A2 (Can perform and respond to basic language functions)
- Flexibility: B1 (Can exploit a wide range of simple language flexibly)
- Taking the Floor (Turntaking): A2 (Can use simple techniques to start, maintain, or end a short conversation).

Analyzing and Extending the Lesson: Application to Additional Contexts. In this lesson, a group of teachers at a language center in Japan experimented with the virtual reality platform, Second Life, to create an opportunity for students to reduce their reticence about practicing English within a restaurant setting. The sessions designed by the teachers correlated with their course curriculum. They avoided directly assessing the students' learning during the sessions to preserve the game-like aspects of the activity, but they did eventually assess their students' learning in an in-class assessment that mirrored the practice sessions.

The activity described here was an augmentation of traditional classroom-based instruction, but SL has also been used to bring students together from around the world to learn English through intercultural exchange. In addition to teaching conversational routines within specific situations, it also has great potential to bring students together in discussion groups focusing on shared readings, videos, music, and so on.

Let's Discuss

1) What has been your experience with learning languages through online gaming or other virtual reality platforms? Have you been able to learn new vocabulary and phrases easily in this manner?
2) Gamification has become a major feature of much educational technology, but it may be overused or not used effectively. What is your view about the use of gaming features to motivate learners?
3) Have you visited a virtual reality site such as Second Life? What was your experience there? As a teacher, how might you use such a site in your classroom practice?

4) The three scenarios in this chapter make use of a range of virtual reality platforms for bringing the world (and virtual worlds) into the classroom. Would your school or classroom accommodate these activities? If not, how might you adapt the activities described for the use of smartphones or more limited uses of technology?

References

Adris, Nadia Balqis, and Hamidah Yamat. "Massively Multiplayer Online Role-Playing Games (MMORPG) as Virtual Grounds for Second Language Learning: Players' Perception." In *Proceedings of the International Seminar on Language Teaching ISeLT 2015*. Bangi, Malaysia, 2015.

Antoniadou, Victoria. "Using Activity Theory to Understand the Contradictions in an Online Transatlantic Collaboration between Student-teachers of English as a Foreign Language." 2011. https://doi.org/10.1017/S0958344011000164.

Chen, Julian ChengChiang. "The Crossroads of English Language Learners, Task-based Instruction, and 3D Multi-user Virtual Learning in Second Life." *Computers & Education* 102 (2016): 152–171. https://doi.org/10.1016/j.compedu.2016.08.004.

Edpuzzle. n.d. https://edpuzzle.com.

FinancesOnline. "Number of Gamers Worldwide 2022–2023: Demographics, Statistics, and Predictions." n.d. https://financesonline.com/number-of-gamers-worldwide.

Google Earth. n.d. https://support.google.com/earth/answer/148174?hl=en.

Govender, Terence, and Joan Arnedo-Moreno. "A Survey on Gamification Elements in Mobile Language-Learning Applications." In *Eighth International Conference on Technological Ecosystems for Enhancing Multiculturality 2020*, 669–676, 2020. https://doi.org/10.1145/3434780.3436597.

Huizinga, Johan. Homo Ludens: A Study of the Play Element in Culture. London: Maurice Temple Smith Ltd, 1970.

Hwel. *Seutakeulaepeuteu han pan-eulo yeong-eo kkeutjangnaegi [Playing a StarCraft game to end English]*. Seoul: Hwalgeumgaji [Golden Bough]. 2001.

Kramer, Wolfgang. "What is a Game?" *The Games Journal*, 2000. http://www.thegamesjournal.com/articles/WhatIsaGame.shtml.

Kruk, Mariusz. "Changes in Self-perceived Willingness to Communicate during Visits to *Second Life*: A Case Study." *The Language Learning Journal* 49, no. 2 (2021): 240–250. https://doi.org/10.1080/09571736.2018.1554692.

Lee, Ju Seong. "Informal, Digital Learning of English: The Case of Korean University Students." PhD dissertation. University of Illinois at Urbana-Champaign, 2018.

Lee, Ju Seong. "An Emerging Path to English in Korea". In *The Handbook of Informal Language Learning*, edited by Mark Dressman and Randall William Sadler, 298–301. John Wiley & Sons Ltd, 2020. https://doi.org/10.1002/9781119472384.ch19.

Lee, Ju Seong, and Mark Dressman. "When IDLE Hands Make an English Workshop: Informal Digital Learning of English and Language Proficiency." *TESOL Quarterly* 2018. https://doi.org/10.1002/tesq.422.

Liu, Lu Ting, Jie Chi Yang, and Ben Gao Huang. "Development of a Massively Multiplayer Online Role-Playing Game for English Learning." In *Collabtech 2012 Conference*. Hokkaido, Japan, 2012.

Majuri, Jenni, Jonna Koivisto, and Juho Hamari. "Gamification of Education and Learning: A Review of Empirical Literature." In *Proceedings of the 2nd International GamiFIN Conference 2018*, 11–19. Pori, Finland, 2018.

Mayrath, Michael, Joe Sanchez, Tomoko Traphagan, Joel Heikes, and Avani Trivedi. "Using Second Life in an English Course: Designing Class Activities to Address Learning Objectives." In *Proceedings of World Conference on Educational Multimedia, Hypermedia and Telecommunications*. Chesapeake, VA, 2007.

Ofosu-Ampong, Kingsley. "The Shift to Gamification in Education: A Review on Dominant Issues." *Journal of Educational Technology Systems* 49, no. 1 (2020): 113–137. https://doi.org/10.1177/0047239520917629.

Oldenburg, Ray. *The Great Good Place: Cafes, Coffee Shops, Bookstores, Bars, Hair Salons, and Other Hangouts at the Heart of a Community*. New York: Marlowe & Company, 1999.

Peterson, Mark. "Learner Interaction in A Massively Multiplayer Online Role Playing Game (MMORPG): A Sociocultural Discourse Analysis." *ReCALL* 24, no. 3 (2012): 361–380. https://doi.org/10.1017/S0958344012000195.

Pollard, Kimberly A., Ashley H. Oiknine, Benjamin T. Files, Anne M. Sinatra, Debbie Patton, Mark Ericson, Jerald Thomas, and Peter Khooshabeh. "Level of Immersion Afects Spatial Learning in Virtual Environments: Results of a Three-condition Within-subjects Study with Long Intersession Intervals." *Virtual Reality* 24 (2020): 783–796. https://doi.org/10.1007/s10055-019-00411-y.

Ranalli, Jim. "Learning English with *The Sims*: Exploiting Authentic Computer Simulation Games for L2 Learning." 21 no. 5 (2008): 441–445. https://doi.org/10.1080/09588220802447859.

Sadler, Randall William. *Virtual Worlds for Language Learning: From Theory to Practice (Telecollaboration in Education)*. Frankfurt: Peter Lang AG, 2012.

Sadler, Randall William. "Virtual Landscapes." In *The Handbook of Informal Language Learning*, edited by Mark Dressman and Randall William Sadler, 85–1000. Hoboken, NJ: John Wiley & Sons Ltd., 2020. https://doi.org/10.1002/9781119472384.ch6.

Second Life. n.d. https://secondlife.com.

Shortt, Mitchell, Shantanu Tilak, Irina Kuznetcova, Bethany Martens, and Babatunde Akinkuolie. "Gamification in Mobile-assisted Language Learning: A Systematic Review of Duolingo Literature from Public Release of 2012 to Early 2020." *Computer Assisted Language Learning* (2021). https://doi.org/10.1080/09588221.2021.1933540.

SIMS. n.d. https://www.ea.com/games/the-sims.

Stott, Andrew, and Carman Neustaedter. "Analysis of Gamification in Education." 2013.

Suh, Soonshik, Sang Won Kim, and Nam Ju Kim. "Effectiveness of MMORPG-based instruction in elementary English education in Korea." *Journal of computer assisted learning* 26, no. 5 (2010): 370–378. https://doi.org/10.1111/j.1365-2729.2010.00353.x.

Sundqvist, Pia. "Extramural English Matters." Dissertation. Karlstad University, 2009.

Sundqvist, Pia. "Commercial-off-the-shelf Games in the Digital Wild and L2 Learner Vocabulary." *Language Learning and Technology* 23, no. 1 (2019): 87–113. https://doi.org/10125/44674.

Sundqvist, Pia, and Liss Kerstin Sylvén. "Language-related Computer Use: Focus on Young L2 English Learners in Sweden." *ReCALL* 26, no. 1 (2014): 302–321. https://doi.org/10.1017/S0958344013000232.

Sundqvist, Pia, and Peter Wikström. "Out-of-school Digital Gameplay and In-school L2 English Vocabulary Outcomes." *System* 51 (2015): 65–76. http://dx.doi.org/10.1016/j.system.2015.04.001.

Won, Eun-Sok. "Analyzing Game Interfaces for Adapting Games in English Learning and Teaching." *Journal of Korea Game Society* 15, no. 2 (2015): 131–144.

Yang, Jie Chi, and Hui Fen Hsu. "Effects of Online Gaming Experience on English Achievement in an MMORPG Learning Environment." In *Conference Proceedings from WorldCALL, Glasgow, 2013*, 379–381. Glasgow: University of Ulster, 2013. https://doi.org/10.1109/IIAI-AAI.2013.10.

Yang, Jie Chi, and Benazir Quadir. "Effects of Prior Knowledge on Learning Performance and Anxiety in an English Learning Online Role-Playing Game." *Educational Technology & Society* 21, no. 3 (2018): 174–185. YouTube. (n.d.). https://youtu.be/iuz6P2ftWB0.

Zhang, Haisen. "Pedagogical Challenges of Spoken English Learning in the Second Life Virtual World: A Case Study." *British Journal of Educational Technology* 44, no. 2 (2013): 243–254. https://doi.org/10.1111/j.1467-8535.2012.01312.x.

Zheng, Dongping, Matthew M. Schmidt, Ying Hu, Min Liu, and Jesse Hsu. "Eco-Dialogical Learning and Translanguaging in Open-Ended 3D Virtual Learning Environments: Where Place, Time, and Objects Matter." *Australasian Journal of Educational Technology* 33, no. 5 (2017).

8

Mobile Apps: Translation, Vocabulary, and Grammar

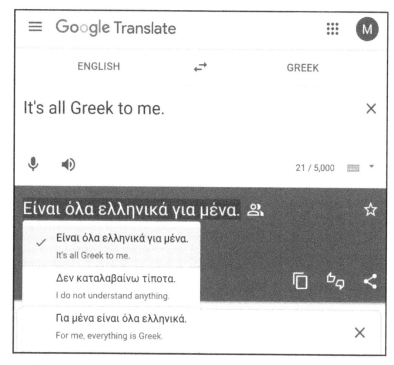

Multiple translations of a common metaphorical saying by Google Translate.

Introduction

Moussa Koné: Google Translate for Gaming and Premier League Football

Moussa Koné is a 14-year-old student living in Montreuil-sous-Bois, a commune in the eastern suburbs of Paris. Moussa was born in a village near Kayes on the Senegal River in Mali, but he came to France when he was 4 and barely remembers his homeland. He speaks Bambara at home with his family but at collège and with his friends in the neighborhood he speaks, reads, and writes French.

English Language Learning in the Digital Age: Learner-Driven Strategies for Adolescents and Young Adults,
First Edition. Mark Dressman, Ju Seong Lee, and Laurent Perrot.
© 2023 John Wiley & Sons Ltd. Published 2023 by John Wiley & Sons Ltd.

Moussa's passion is football. He plays on a local league and is a superfan of Moussa Djénépo, a midfielder in the Premier League, who is also on the Mali national team. Three years ago, his family purchased a computer along with an internet connection. Moussa's older brother introduced him to online gaming, and Moussa discovered that he could connect with friends for multiplayer online football games.

Moussa has discovered an online multiplayer game in which he can play as a member of Southampton, the same team as Moussa Djénépo. However, because the league is British, the game is in English, and most of the players in the game are also English-speaking, he has needed to learn the language. Moussa began studying English recently at school, but his vocabulary and grammar are still very basic. To supplement his knowledge when he plays online, he has learned to borrow his brother's smartphone and use Google Translate to quickly type in and translate phrases he hears or sees in English into French. He has also made a list of basic soccer vocabulary and translated these words, and has also translated a list of common phrases from French to English. By listening to the phrases and repeating them, he has learned many football-related English phrases and can use them in both writing and speech. These activities have given him a new incentive to focus on English at school, and he was complimented recently by his teacher for his pronunciation and participation in class.

Mounir Chafik: Triangulating Among Dictionaries

Mounir Chafik is a Baccalauréat II (final year) student at a *lycée* in a provincial capital in central Morocco. His parents are farmers in a village 50 km from the city, and Mounir has lived away from them for most of his career as a middle and high school student. Early in his life, Mounir realized that his chance to better his life financially and help his family depended on his success in school. He has excelled in languages and now, after three years of English study, he is eager to pass the baccalaureate exam and enter university next fall.

Mounir has also realized that he needs more access to the English language than he receives in school. His teachers for the most part have been very good and helpful to him, offering copies of old books and magazines in English, and these have helped him expand his vocabulary beyond what he has learned at school. Many of the words are completely unknown to him, however. Over the summer, he had a part-time job and was able to purchase a used mobile phone. He downloaded a free dictionary app that has helped him with definitions of words, but he also noted that the definition did not always fit the context of the word he had read, or that it offered a definition that seemed incomplete. To compensate, Mounir downloaded a French–English app, which helped him some more, and then a third, Arabic–English app. He discovered that by triangulating among these apps and his other two languages, he not only arrived at a fairly precise definition of a word in context, he also found that he developed a fuller understanding of the ways the word could be used. Mounir has felt confident enough with these apps to begin to write short essays about his life in English, using both the Arabic and French apps to expand his range of vocabulary and expression.

Maki Suzuki: Instant Translation and Mobile App Learning for Travel

Maki Suzuki is a second-year university student in Osaka, studying marketing. She hopes to work for a Japanese firm when she graduates. Maki was an above-average student in high school and studied English for six years. She understands the principles of

English grammar and has basic vocabulary but has never had to speak the language functionally. She had a business English course at the university for one semester but has not studied continuously since high school.

Maki and several of her friends have been discussing possible vacation trips for the summer. They had planned to go to a southern island, but the summer heat has discouraged them. One of Maki's friends visited Hawaii as a child with his family and is urging the group to go there instead, noting that the temperature will be much cooler than Okinawa in August. Maki is excited about this possibility, but she is also worried about her English. She will be with Japanese friends but expects to order in restaurants and to shop and sightsee. She is aware that the United States is even less multilingual than Japan.

Maki has seen ads on television for instant-translation devices, in which she can speak into the device in Japanese and instantly get a spoken English translation. She borrowed one of these from a friend and has found that it can translate simple phrases but longer or more complex sentences are often a problem. She has also discovered that she can speak into the device in English to see if it translates what she says accurately, to check and improve her pronunciation. To develop her vocabulary for restaurants, shopping, and directions, she has downloaded a mobile language app on her phone. Her family's home in Osaka is on the other side of the city from her university, so Maki has learned to practice vocabulary, grammar, and basic expressions using the app on her long Metro commutes each day. Between the app and her translation device, she is beginning to feel a bit more confident about interacting with people in Hawaii in a few months.

Discussion

This chapter is perhaps the most controversial in this book, for one reason: It seems to promote the use of Grammar-Translation methods in second-language learning. Mobile language-learning apps are mostly digital mechanisms for drill-and-practice. They may introduce some vocabulary and try inductively to teach grammar, but they do so through approaches similar to language textbooks and teach languages as systems without concern for the complexities of real-world communication. Some apps, like Duolingo, Babbel, and Livemocha.com, do offer online chat with more proficient speakers, but this feature is separate from the app itself and is borrowed from other, more authentic, forms of chat that are more authentic and better accessed through social media (see Chapter 6 for a discussion of the uses of written and spoken chat on social media platforms).

Translation devices and apps may seem even worse examples of language pedagogy because they imply that learners may never learn a language if they have an AI-powered device to do the listening and speaking for them. They suggest that the way to learn a language is, again, through translation and not through immersion in the language itself. Digital dictionaries may seem more acceptable (even native speakers use them), but the use of known language–target language dictionaries again would seem to promote a translation-focused approach over more immersion-focused, pedagogically sound approaches.

If mobile apps for language learning are pedagogically and theoretically out of date, then why are we devoting an entire chapter to their use? We admit we are conflicted on this point, but our reason is simple: Because IDLErs (Informal Digital Learners of English) use them, and therefore they are, whether we approve or not, learner-driven and part of the wide repertoire of strategies that constitute informal language learning.

Artificial Intelligence (AI), Machine Learning (ML), and Natural Language Processing (NLP): What Is the Relationship?

According to Microsoft Azure (2022), **Artificial Intelligence (AI)** is defined as "the capability of a computer system to mimic human cognitive functions such as learning and problem-solving." These functions could involve robotic movement, self-driving cars, automated travel booking, and of course many language processes, including automated assistants like Siri and Alexa, machine translation, and so on.

What makes these processes *intelligent* as well as automated is that AI programs are also programmed to improve their efficiency and effectiveness by refining responses over repeated use. This is accomplished through complex mathematical algorithms that analytically identify patterns in response data. These algorithms and the process of updating and refining program outcomes are termed **Machine Learning (ML)**.

When **Machine Learning** involves human linguistic input or output ("listening" or "speaking") by a computer, this is called **Natural Language Processing (NLP)**. NLP translates and coordinates the components of human language—phonemes, vocabulary, syntax, and even increasingly pragmatics—into mathematical formulae, or algorithms. Examples are speech recognition apps, machine translation programs, and virtual assistants, including Siri, Alexa, and automatic answering services.

The best way to understand these three concepts might be to imagine them as three boxes, one inside the other. The largest and most inclusive box would be Artificial Intelligence. Inside it would be Machine Learning, and within it Natural Language Processing. NLP is an aspect of ML, and ML is a part of AI.

The three fictional but reality-based vignettes that introduce this chapter illustrate this point and also suggest how mobile apps can be used productively in combination with other strategies for autonomous language learning. Both Moussa Koné and Maki Suzuki have functional goals that fuel their use of apps. Their focus is not so much learning English as on participating in an online football game or ordering food in a Hawaiian restaurant. As such, their learning through these apps is likely to be very limited and basic, at least at first, but may lead to increased motivation and more focused and advanced study of English in the future. Mounir Chafik, on the other hand, is a more advanced learner who has realized his need to expand his vocabulary and is using three dictionaries in a very sophisticated way that implies his awareness that languages do not translate literally. Finally, in all three cases the learners have also learnt, or are currently learning, English in a formal setting, and so their use of mobile apps extends and helps them to develop their English rather than serves as a comprehensive language program.

The learners in these three vignettes illustrate our position on the use of mobile apps for grammar, translation, and vocabulary learning. We view them as supplements to more comprehensive programs that provide quick support, that boost learners' confidence, and provide opportunities for practice at odd moments. With these purposes in mind, in the remainder of this chapter we will consider the research to date on these apps and devices and present three scenarios in which teachers can make use of them in classroom settings.

Chapter Objectives

This chapter focuses on the use of mobile apps for language learning, translation, and dictionaries in classrooms, using best practices for instruction. Mobile apps typically do not promote best practices because they largely ignore the sociocultural contexts of language use and because they seem to promote ways to use languages without actually learning or acquiring them. However, by repurposing these apps— that is, by using them in ways they were not always intended to be used—they can become powerful tools for developing specific skills and aspects of language. With that repurposing in mind, the main goal of this chapter is to explore the challenges and opportunities of using mobile apps productively. By the end of this chapter, readers should be able to:

1) Explain how mobile apps typically are theoretically out of date and do not reflect best practices in language education.
2) Describe the general benefits of using apps for learning languages, for translation, and as dictionaries.
3) Describe the problems with machine translation (MT) but also how translation apps can be used to teach writing and translation.
4) Describe how gamifying (see Chapter 7) learning with mobile apps can help to repurpose their uses.
5) Consider multiple ways that mobile apps can be applied to classroom instruction in ways that are theoretically and pedagogically sound.
6) Consider how the research, theory, and three scenarios in this chapter can be applied to the reader's pedagogical context.

Key Words

AI (artificial intelligence); grammar-translation method; MT (machine translation); inductive learning; repurposing; NLP (natural language processing)

Research and Theory

Research on Effectiveness and Users' Perceptions of Mobile Apps

Research on mobile applications for language learning can be placed into three categories. The first and most widely researched category is the study of the effectiveness of specific mobile applications, especially the commercial app, Duolingo (Kessler 2021; Klímová 2018; Loewen et al. 2019; Messemer 2021; Moreno and Vermuelen 2015; Pham et al. 2018; Shortt et al. 2021; Teske 2017; Vesselinov and Grego 2012). These studies generally found that language apps were effective for beginners, especially in developing vocabulary (Deris and Shukor 2019). The gamification feature (of Duolingo) was often cited as a motivational feature. In this case, "gamification" referred to the inductive learning process whereby learners needed to figure out a grammar rule through trial and error over multiple examples rather than through explicit instruction in the rule.

However, in these studies, effectiveness was defined as positive reviews from learners and/or simple tests of recall of vocabulary and syntactic rules. Many of the studies also

---

"Almost" Learning Italian with Duolingo: One Learner's Account

David Freeman (2018), a contributor to *The Atlantic* magazine, spent 70 hours trying to learn Italian with Duolingo on his smartphone before a trip to Italy.

Freeman reported that the became "addicted" to the app, which rewarded him with "points" for completing lessons, and that he felt he was actually learning the language. But when his wife challenged him to use what he'd learned to generate sentences for likely contexts during their trip, he was completely lost. Freeman realized that what he'd really mastered was answering Duolingo's multiple-choice questions in Italian.

However, undaunted, Freeman then turned to more traditional Italian language texts and began to work through the exercises in them. He found that what he'd learned via Duolingo did help him complete the exercises, which focused on using the language in realistic contexts. Some more practice with imagined situations and he was ready. Freeman found that during his trip his Italian was not "fluent," but it was functional in a fractured sort of way.

Freeman concluded that Duolingo helps people learn some basic vocabulary and grammar for a language but to make that knowledge functional, learners need to create situations that will enable them to make pragmatic use of their knowledge. The use of languages within flexible, meaningful contexts is one advantage that live teachers will most likely always have over automated learning programs.

---

noted limitations to the learning that resulted from these apps, including the almost complete absence of attention to sociocultural and pragmatic aspects of language use, challenges with motivation and persistence on the app over time, and the lack of theoretical awareness about linguistic communication as opposed to learning languages as pure systems. Lotherington (2018), for example, conducted an autoethnographic self-study of her own processes in learning Italian through four different apps and concluded that "On the whole, MALL apps were found to repackage outdated language teaching pedagogies, and failed to capitalize on the affordances of mobile connection apart from piecemeal incorporation of gamification strategies and social media links" (198).

A second set of studies surveyed users' perceptions of mobile apps in terms of their features and how they were used for learning (Nami 2020; Rosell-Aguilar 2018; Dragonflame, Olsen, and Tommerdahl 2021; Sviķe 2021). These studies report, again, that vocabulary learning was the most frequently cited feature by users. In a study of 4,095 app users, Rosell-Aguilar noted that "many of the features that language app users wish for are already available to language learners through their mobile devices" (Rosell-Aguilar 2018, 871). These included authentic opportunities for chat (through social media), tutorials, and watching authentic content on video.

Repurposing Mobile Apps for Classroom Instruction

A third group of research studies focuses on the "repurposing" of apps for instruction. In these studies, mobile language apps were incorporated into teaching activities rather than used as stand-alone approaches to learning vocabulary or writing skills. The apps themselves were not always used as intended by their designers but rather repurposed to meet the needs of learners and the curriculum.

For example, Little (2019) surveyed families in which maintenance of a heritage language (a language spoken usually by immigrants and passed to their children in a new country) was a priority and found that the use of gamified language apps to encourage children's use of the heritage language was prevalent. Kukulska-Hulme, Lee, and Norris (2017) noted multiple uses of mobile apps to bridge the divide between formal instruction and informal learning, including journaling, the use of apps within heritage language settings, the use of Evernote for documenting images and ideas and sharing these among a group of students, and the use of mobile apps for a range of activities involving more authentic approaches to teaching English in the workplace and for specialized purposes.

Multiple studies have also focused on the repurposing of translation apps for the teaching of writing (Groves and Mundt 2015; Hartono 2017; Tsai 2019). In these studies, students used machine translation apps for automatic translation such as Google Translate either as initial drafts for essays, which they then corrected, or they wrote drafts in English first and then compared them to machine translated versions of their essays written in the L1. In either case, the students and teachers did not regard the translation apps as authoritative but instead used them critically with full awareness of their flaws. In all cases, students benefited from the process because the use of an app introduced alternative vocabulary and expressions or demonstrated how critical context is within the translation process.

Discussion: Classroom Implications

In summary, a review of the literature on mobile applications for language learning indicates very mixed findings. On the one hand, the mobile accessibility of apps would seem to be a boon to in-the-moment learning opportunities, while other features such as the use of artificial intelligence and gamification would seem, if we believe their press releases, to augur a new era of instant translation and effortless language acquisition.

Never Say Never: Machine Translation and the Problem of Pragmatics

Within the field of applied linguistics, a long-standing assumption regarding machine translation has been that without awareness of context, idiomatic expression, and nuanced uses of language, machines will never replace humans. Human translators might then relax and not worry about their jobs.

Such reasoning assumes, however, that context itself cannot be analyzed into discrete parts and converted to a series of algorithms for machine learning. Recently, there have been indications that this may happen. Voita, Sennrich, and Titov (2019) presented a model in which three contextual variables—deixis, ellipsis, and lexical cohesion—were accounted for in extra-sentential contexts (involving more than one sentence). As machine learning and natural language processing progress, it seems that contextual issues in machine translation will gradually be reduced. Consider the example in of how Google Translate handled the ambiguity of the translation of "It's all Greek to me" into Greek into three possible correct choices.

(Continued)

> **(Continued)**
>
> Into the foreseeable future, it is likely that the machine vs. human translation question will not be clearly resolved. A more likely scenario is that human translators will increasingly rely on machine translation to provide a "first pass" or rough draft of translation, to be revised and tweaked by a human translator for context, style, and nuance.

However, the research on these apps tells a more complicated story. Commercial language learning apps such as those offered by Duolingo or Busuu may help users to learn the grammar and vocabulary of a language, but not without significant investments in time and energy equivalent to formal study, and perhaps with reduced outcomes in terms of learning to speak or write a language within authentic contexts. Machine translation through artificial intelligence may gradually improve but still seems to suffer when sentences and the concepts they express are complex and highly contextual and metaphoric.

And yet, there is also significant evidence of these apps' popularity and use by learners, especially in areas such as the use of dictionary apps for vocabulary development, often in conjunction with formal learning. For this reason, educators cannot ignore or dismiss mobile language apps in their classrooms. The most promising use of these apps, it seems, may be to repurpose them within classroom contexts to supplement programs and help to bridge in- and out-of-class learning. In the next section of this chapter we turn to three scenarios that demonstrate how this repurposing can take place.

Practical Applications in the Classroom

Scenario One: A Mobile Dictionary Game in a Munich Middle School

The Scene. Angela Müller teaches English in a Realschule (middle school) in Au-Haidhausen, a district of Munich. Her students are in the mid-tier of performance academically. Some are conversational English speakers with strong listening comprehension acquired by watching television and movies in English, while others' grasp of vocabulary and grammar comes almost exclusively from their textbooks and formal instruction. A recent standardized assessment showed that the students' weakest area of English was vocabulary, and Angela has been looking for engaging ways to expand her students' receptive and productive use of words in English.

Angela has noticed one exception to this pattern in the writing of Anwar, a 13-year-old student from Syria. In a recent assignment to write about a favorite sports team or musical group, Anwar wrote a glowing essay about his favorite football team, FC Bayern München, and peppered it with more than a dozen words like "adroit," "nimble," and "gargantuan." While technically the use of the words was accurate, in some instances they were applied in very original ways, as in the description of an FCB forward as "alacritous like crazy."

Curious about this use of vocabulary, Angela conferred with Anwar about his essay, asking him where he had learned so many "interesting" words. "I used my dictionary app," he told her, and showed her the online dictionary on his smartphone. Angela was impressed and complimented Anwar for his hard work. However, afterward she wondered how she might encourage students to explore new vocabulary with dictionary apps but also be aware of how to choose and use new vocabulary correctly in context. She began to also think about how she had acquired much of her own advanced vocabulary in English and realized that it was through reading and seeing how a new word was used in print. This insight gave Angela an idea for how to engage students' interest in vocabulary-in-context.

Analysis: Challenges and Opportunities. For students at intermediate and advanced levels of proficiency, academic vocabulary development is critical, but often a significant challenge for teachers. Introducing vocabulary out of context through word lists or even "word of the day" activities is also an ineffective approach. Even if students study word lists (and most do not), they are not likely to remember words learned out of context beyond being quizzed, and may never learn to recognize, much less use, these words in proper context.

The preceding scenario is an excellent example of how, even for motivated students, learning vocabulary out of context can be problematic. However, the bright side of this challenge is that it is now possible to both quickly define and study the use of new words through multiple online resources. In addition, research on vocabulary development (Hunt and Beglar 2002) also offers three principles for how words can be effectively acquired. First, it is critical that a "less is more" approach be taken, in which not 25 but at most 5–10 or fewer words be introduced, and that these words be truly unknown and relatively high frequency. Second, it is critical that students invest in the words they are learning. This means that words nominated by students are more likely to be acquired by students than words a teacher would choose. Third, it is critical that once introduced, students should have many recurring opportunities to hear, read, speak, and write the words over time and in context.

We highly recommend two strategies for vocabulary development. The first is the Vocabulary Self-Selection strategy (Ruddell and Shearer 2002), in which students in groups choose their own words from a written passage or elsewhere for development, research the words themselves for presentation to the class, and actively discuss them. The second is the use of interactive word walls (Harmon et al. 2009) that promote long-term use of new words in the classroom. In combination with the use of vocabulary and dictionary apps, these two strategies offer a powerful and effective alternative to the development of vocabulary using lists and drill.

Instructional Plan. Angela decided that the word wall in her classroom needed an interactive, student-nominated makeover. She placed her students into groups of three and announced that the class was having a contest to choose new words for the wall, and that the students would select words they were sure the class did not know and research each word for nomination and selection by the class. Her strategy combined a modification of the Vocabulary Self-Selection process with the use of a word wall for practicing the words after they were introduced to the class.

In Step One, the students were grouped into triads and instructed to use the dictionary apps on their smartphones (or download one if they didn't already have one). Using the synonym/antonym feature, they were instructed to select three common nouns that they were certain the class did not know. For each word, the students were to go to a site such as Wordhippo.com, or search in their browser for "use (word) in a sentence." The students were to select three sentences using the word to present to the class as clues and to write down the definition of the word. Each group shared its words and sentences with Angela for approval.

In Step Two, each group chose one of its words, wrote it on the board and read it aloud, and then read the three sentences to the class (or had them projected for students to see). The first group to correctly give the definition of the word from its context and explain their reasoning received three points. If no group was correct, the students were permitted to "race" to find the word's definition on their dictionary apps and receive one point for the correct definition. Angela then discussed the word and its uses in context. Each group gave one word and saved the remaining words for the following weeks. At the end of the contest, the group with the most points received a classroom privilege (e.g., 15 minutes of free computer time) as a reward.

In Step Three, Angela opened class with a review of the words, challenging students to create a sentence with any of the words on the word wall, discussing successful sentences, and rewarding them with a token (e.g., a sticker or redeemable token). The students were then organized into groups of three and challenged to write a story using at least five words from the previous day's challenge on the word wall. The students were given 20 minutes to compose their stories, which were then read to the class. The students voted on the best story, and the winning group again received a classroom privilege.

1) Materials:
    a) Smartphones (at least one per group)
    b) Internet connection
    c) Wordhippo.com, similar site, or search engine.
2) Learning Mode: Small groups of three
3) Time: Two or three sessions (45 minutes each)
4) Sequence of Activities:
    a) On Day 1, students are placed in triads and contest is explained
    b) Students use smartphones to select three new words and identify three sentences in which they are used correctly
    c) If time remains, each group introduces its word and its use in three sentences
    d) Groups work to define the word
    e) Teacher discusses the groups' responses and the next group presents its word
    f) On Day 2, teacher reviews words and invites students to create original sentences
    g) Groups are formed and challenged to write a story using five words
    h) Stories are shared and the class votes on the best-written story
    i) The following week, the contest is repeated with new words.

Assignments and Assessment. This activity has two assessments: 1) assessment of group performance; and 2) ongoing assessment of the activity as a teaching strategy (see Tables 8.1 and 8.2).

Table 8.1 Rubric for assessment of group performance in vocabulary activity.

Achievement level	Descriptor
Excellent	The group uses multiple resources on mobile phones and/or computers to locate three or more words that are unknown to the class and that are relatively high-frequency in writing and speaking. They also locate and select three sentences. During the contest, the group can explain and give examples spontaneously of the word they are offering to the class as well as accurately define and explain words given by other groups. In the third step of the process, the group writes a clever story that successfully and accurately uses five or more words from the previous day's contest.

Table 8.1 (Continued)

Achievement level	Descriptor
Very good	The group uses multiple resources on mobile phones and/or computers to locate three words that are unknown to the class and used with some frequency in writing and speaking. They also locate and select three sentences with some assistance from the teacher. During the contest, the group can explain the word they are offering to the class and offer definitions and partial explanations given by the other groups. In the third step of the process, the group writes a coherent story that uses five or more words from the previous day's contest with some accuracy.
Satisfactory	The group uses some resources on mobile phones and/or computers with teacher assistance to locate three words that may be unknown to the class and that have some frequency in real use. With teacher assistance they locate and select three sentences in which the words are used in context. During the contest, the group actively participates but may need assistance explaining their word to the class and tries to offer definitions and explanations of other groups' words. The group writes a story using at least five words from the previous day's contest with some accuracy.
Unsatisfactory	The group struggles to use resources on mobile apps and/or computers to locate three unknown words. The group identifies fewer than three words and needs a great deal of assistance identifying sentences in which the words are used in context. During the contest, the group is passive or does not participate in a productive manner. The group needs a great deal of help introducing their word and does not offer definitions of other groups' words. The story written by the group is short and may not incorporate five words.

Table 8.2 Ongoing (formative) assessment of group activity.

Achievement level	Descriptor
Above expectations	Nearly every group in the class is able to use mobile phones and/or computers to identify three or more unknown words, with limited assistance from the teacher. The students select sentences that identify words' meanings in context. During the contest, each group participates with enthusiasm and engagement and offers definitions and explanations of the words. The stories written by all groups are comprehensible and use five or more words from the previous day with relative accuracy.
Meets expectations	Most of the groups in the class are able to use mobile phones and/or computers to identify three or more unknown words, with some assistance from the teacher. The groups select sentences that identify words' meanings in context with assistance from the teacher. Most of the groups participate in the contest with little teacher assistance and can offer definitions and explanations. The stories written by most groups are comprehensible and use five or more words from the previous day.
Below expectations	Most of the groups in the class struggle to use mobile phones and/or computers. The groups identify fewer than three unknown words and need a great deal of assistance from the teacher. The groups struggle to identify three sentences using their words in context. During the contest, only a few groups participate. The stories written by most groups contain parts that are unintelligible and use fewer than five words from the previous day.

Relation to TESOL Technology Standards for Learners and CEFR Reference Level Descriptors

TESOL Technology Standards:

- Goal 2 (Use technology in appropriate ways)
  - Standard 1 (Understand that conventions differ across contexts)
- Goal 3 (Effectively use and critically evaluate technology tools)
  - Standard 1 (Effectively use and evaluate productivity tools)
  - Standard 2 (Effectively use and evaluate skill-building tools)
  - Standard 5 (Value technology to support autonomy and lifelong learning).

CEFR Reference Level Descriptors:

- Global Scale: BI (Can produce simple connected text)
- Overall Reading Comprehension: B1 (Can read straightforward factual texts)
- Reading for Information and Argument: A2 (Can identify specific information in simpler written material)
- Conversation: A2 (Can participate in short conversations in routine contexts)
- Formal Discussion: A2/B1 (Can exchange relevant information/ Can take part in routine formal discussion of familiar subjects)
- Goal-Oriented Cooperation: A2/B1 (Can discuss what to do next, making and responding to suggestions/ Can make their opinions and reactions understood)
- Information Exchange: A2/B1 (Can ask and answer questions/ Can exchange, check, and confirm accumulated factual information)
- Interviewing and Being Interviewed: A2/B1 (Can make themselves understood in an interview/ Can carry out a prepared interview, checking and confirming information)
- Overall Spoken Production: A2/B1 (Can give a simple description or presentation/ Can reasonably fluently sustain a straightforward description)
- Addressing Audiences: A2 (Can give a short, rehearsed presentation)
- Identifying Clues and Inferring: B1 (Can identify unfamiliar words from the context)
- Cooperating: B1 (Can summarize the point reached in a discussion)
- Asking for Clarification: A2 (Can ask for clarification about key words or phrases)
- Compensating: B1 (Can use a simple word meaning something similar to the concept)
- Monitoring and Repair: B1 (Can ask for confirmation that a form used is correct)
- Processing Text: A2 (Can pick out and reproduce key words and phrases)
- General Linguistic Range: A2 (Has a repertoire of basic language)
- Vocabulary Range: B1 (Has sufficient vocabulary to express him/herself).

Analyzing and Extending the Lesson: Application to Additional Contexts. In this scenario, a teacher interested in expanding her students' vocabulary notices a student using a mobile dictionary app and decides to remake her word wall using words nominated by students in a game.

Again, we note that studying vocabulary out of context is a challenging and often ineffective way to learn new words. However, making the process interactive and using student-nominated words followed up by opportunities for students to use the words on a recurring basis offers some productive opportunities. In this case, it is not the technology that drives the learning but rather the innate interest of students in new words facilitated by the opportunity to use dictionary apps and the internet as resources. It is also important that once students encounter new words, they should be given opportunities to use them and perhaps to see them again and again.

Scenario Two: Making Sense and Annotating with Google Translate

The Scene. Mohamed Sadiqi is a Moroccan English teacher working at a private secondary school in Rabat. He teaches students in their third year of secondary school. His students are avid watchers of satellite television, YouTube videos, and TV series. Most also have smartphones with a number of dictionary and translation apps downloaded on them. They are all conversational in English and can usually express themselves when speaking. Their written English is intelligible, but there are often frequent grammatical and usage errors in their writing and many times idioms from French or Arabic are included that do not make complete sense in English.

Mohamed has identified the basic problems that his students have with writing and has conducted many lessons in which he demonstrates and explains uses of tense, homonyms/homophones and other fine points, with little effect. His students seem to value fluency over accuracy in their written expression and resist his direct instruction, with no improvement in their writing. How can he help his students to understand the critical need for accuracy in their writing, not simply to communicate but to communicate with sophistication?

Recently Mohamed has noticed that on the class's Facebook page students often post comments in Arabic that, when automatically translated into English, are barely intelligible and sometimes incoherent. It seems to him that the problems his students are having with writing are similar to the problems of automatic translation.

Analysis: Challenges and Opportunities. In this scenario, a secondary school teacher is frustrated that his lessons on grammar and usage do not seem to be improving the writing of his students. He is challenged by the fact that his students have ingrained habits of usage and grammar likely acquired in part by their tendency to translate when they write from their L1 (Arabic) or L2 (French) into L3 (English). In addition, because the students have few problems understanding the English they encounter online or being understood by others in chat rooms or when they play video games, it does not seem important to them to focus on issues of grammar and usage when they write.

Yet, there are also opportunities lurking in the same technologies that produce his students' false confidence. The problems of automatic translation of Arabic into English on Facebook provide a convincing example of the difficulties associated with translation in general. If Mohamed can use this example, he might be able to persuade his students to look more carefully at their own problems with grammar and usage and to understand the significance of his instruction for them. Moreover, by using the same technologies they are using, he will not only enhance their motivation and engagement but send them a message that he understands how they are learning and using digital resources outside the classroom.

Asking high school students to translate complex song lyrics into English would be a challenging and likely unachievable task if they were working independently and without tools. However, by heterogeneously grouping students and by encouraging them to use dictionary apps and other search tools, the Zone of Proximal Development

(Vygotsky 1978) for this task and these students is expanded to make this a challenging but achievable exercise, within the reach of independent users of English on the B1/B2 CEFR Scale.

Instructional Plan. The observation about automatic translations on Facebook gave Mohamed an idea. On the website Genius.com he found the lyrics to the classic song, *Mahmouma*, by the legendary group, Nass El Ghiwane. He copied and pasted the lyrics into Google Translate, and the translation into English was garbled. The students were then asked to "repair" the Google translation by working in small groups and using dictionary apps on their smartphones in combination with their own knowledge of English grammar and pragmatics.

1) Materials:
    a) Copies of *Mahmouma* in Arabic and Google Translate
    b) Additional paper for writing or laptops/tablets
    c) Projector and/or speakers
    d) Students' smartphones and apps.
2) Learning Mode: Small groups (3–4 students)
3) Time: Three class meetings (50 minutes each)
4) Sequence of Activities:
    a) On Day 1, Students are organized into groups of 3 to 4
    b) Copies of the texts are introduced and projected
    c) Students are instructed to read the Arabic lyrics and English translation from Google; students listen to a recording of the song
    d) There is a preliminary discussion about the problems with the translation; students begin to contribute ideas
    e) A competition is announced, in which students are to "repair" the Google translation in small groups, using their own knowledge, browser searches, and dictionary apps on their smartphones; the winning group will contribute its translation to Google Translate, in order to improve the service
    f) Students are encouraged to "triangulate" word meanings through use of multiple dictionary and other apps
    g) Each group's initial translation is due at the end of the class period
    h) On Day 2, each group is instructed to annotate its translation to explain references to Moroccan culture and language in the lyrics so that a non-Moroccan English speaker would understand them
    i) As the students work, the teacher circulates to prompt students with questions about references in the lyrics and help guide their annotations; as students complete these they begin preparation for presentations the following day
    j) On Day 3, each group presents its translation and answers questions from others in English about references in the lyrics; students take notes about each presentation
    k) The students write a short evaluation at the end of the class of each presentation, and then vote and explain why they chose a particular translation as best
    l) The final annotated translation of each group is collected along with individual students' notes on the presentations.

Assignments and Assessment. This activity has two assessments: (1) the group translation/annotation; and (2) individual student notes (see Tables 8.3 and 8.4).

Table 8.3 Rubric for assessment of group translation exercise.

Achievement level	Descriptor
Excellent	Within their group, all students actively collaborated to produce an accurate translation of the song, which demonstrated knowledge of English grammar and usage as well as sophisticated understanding of word meaning, idioms, and literary references. They were seen to use appropriate apps and to share information with each other in English and occasionally in Arabic. Their presentation was in clear English, was shared among all group members, and accounted for multiple decisions made by the students in repairing the translation.
Very good	Within their group, students actively collaborated to produce an accurate translation of the song and demonstrated basic understanding of English grammar and usage with accurate translation of words and most idioms and references. They were seen to use appropriate apps and share information. Their presentation was comprehensible in English, shared by most group members, and accounted for some decisions made in repairing the translation.
Satisfactory	Within their group, students actively collaborated to produce a translation of the song that was mostly accurate and demonstrated some knowledge of English grammar and usage, as well as word meaning and some idioms. The students were seen to use a few apps and shared some information among themselves. Their presentation was in English, shared, and was comprehensible, with explanation of at least one decision.
Unsatisfactory	Within their group, there was uneven collaboration and participation by members to produce a translation that was minimally accurate. There were significant errors in grammar and word use. Students may have made an attempt to use apps but there was little sharing of information. The presentation was minimal and made by only one student.

Table 8.4 Rubric for assessment of individual student notes.

Achievement level	Descriptor
Above expectations	Notes are extensive and entirely in English, with elaboration and detail; clear organization with references marked.
Meets expectations	Notes are present and mostly in English, with some elaboration and detail; some organization.
Below expectations	Single words without reference or organization, largely in Arabic.

Relation to TESOL Technology Standards for Learners and CEFR Reference Level Descriptors

TESOL Technology Standards:
- Goal 3 (Use and evaluate technological tools)
  - Standard 1 (Use and evaluate productivity tools)
  - Standard 2 (Use and evaluate skill-building tools)
  - Standard 3 (Use and evaluate tools for communication and collaboration)
  - Standard 5 (Recognize use of tools for autonomy and lifelong learning).

CEFR Reference Level Descriptors:

- Global Scale: B2 (Can understand the main ideas of complex text)
- Overall Reading Comprehension: B2 (Can read with a large degree of independence)
- Reading for Orientation: B2 (Can scan quickly through several sources)
- Reading for Information and Argument: B2 (Can understand specialized articles)
- Goal-Oriented Cooperation: B2 (Can help along the progress of the work)
- Overall Spoken Production: B2 (Can give clear, systematically developed descriptions and presentations)
- Addressing Audiences: B2 (Can give a clear, systematically developed presentation)
- Overall Written Production: B2 (Can produce clear, detailed texts)
- Identifying Clues and Inferring: B1 (Can extrapolate the meaning of a section)
- Processing Text: B2 (Can summarize a wide range of factual and imaginative texts)
- General Linguistic Range: B2 (Can express themselves clearly)
- Vocabulary Range: B2 (Has a good range of vocabulary)
- Vocabulary Control: B2 (Lexical accuracy is generally high)
- Coherence: B2 (Can use a limited number of cohesive devices).

Analyzing and Extending the Lesson: Application to Additional Contexts. By having his students "repair" a mangled automatic translation of a classic Moroccan song, the teacher in this scenario not only demonstrates the limitations of Google Translate to his students but engages them to strive for accuracy and attention to detail in their writing. Making this a group activity and challenging students to compete to produce the "best" translation also makes it possible for the students to read, write, and communicate several levels above what some could achieve on their own. Finally, by having students not only repair the translation but present and explain and defend to their peers the reasoning for the choices they made, all four modes of communication—speaking, listening, reading, and writing—have been developed over a three-day period.

An extension activity for this lesson would be to use another translation application for their presentations. Recent versions of PowerPoint for Microsoft Office allow listeners of a PowerPoint presentation to view live translations of the speaker in over 60 languages. The feature provides subtitled translations/transcriptions of spoken text for each slide. A presenter can pre-record the subtitles and repair any errors before a presentation and then play them during the live presentation. However, note that the translator requires an active Microsoft Office subscription and an internet connection.

In this scenario, students might use PowerPoint to present their repaired translation of *Mahmouma* and then use the translation feature to create subtitled transcriptions in English (not a translation but a transcription of their spoken English) presenting their reasons for choosing to repair the song lyrics in a particular way. They would then be able to also repair the errors of the translator and use this process to rehearse their live presentations, extending the speaking activities of the lesson. In addition, because the translator's errors are often due to mispronunciation by speakers, it would serve as a feedback mechanism to the students for their pronunciation.

Google Translate also presents many diverse opportunities for classroom use beyond demonstrations of its inaccuracy with complex, literary texts. Students at lower levels of proficiency can use the app to check simple sentences they have written with much higher accuracy than in the exercise above. Google Translate is also much more accurate with information-based, literal texts such as news reports, and can be used by students to check their reading comprehension of news stories and other English texts. Finally, the pronunciation feature of the app is accurate and provides a quick check on how to pronounce new vocabulary words.

Scenario Three: A Mobile App Phrasebook to Learn English for Special Purposes

The Scene. Jim Johnston is an English for Special Purposes instructor at a language center in Jakarta, Indonesia. His students are mostly young adults working in the tourist industry who are interested in improving their careers or who have been referred by their employers. Most have studied some English in primary and secondary school, where the instruction was mainly focused on memorizing general vocabulary and grammar. As a result, these students also expect to be lectured about hospitality-related English and are hesitant to speak in class. A few have also told Jim they find studying about tourism from their book boring, but they need it for their jobs.

However, during a recent break Jim noticed one of his students, Dewi, speaking into her mobile phone in a language that was neither English nor Indonesian. Curious, he asked Dewi what she was speaking and was surprised when she told him it was Korean. Dewi told Jim she was a serious fan of the Korean K-pop group, SuperM, and was learning Korean "for fun" on Duolingo. Even more curious, Jim asked Dewi if she liked Duolingo and if it was a "good app for learning languages." "Not to speak," she told him. "It helps me understand the songs and it's fun." This was the most spoken English Jim had ever heard Dewi speak. When the class resumed, Jim asked the other students about their interests in other languages and use of Duolingo. He was surprised that nearly half the class was studying Korean or another language on a language app to follow international sports teams or music groups.

Later in the day, Jim described his experience in class to an Indonesian colleague in the workroom. "Yeah," he said. "They're not interested in English for work, but English or Korean or Spanish for fun—that's another thing." This has given Jim an idea: How can he infuse the fun of using mobile apps to learn about sports or music into the learning of English for tourism?

Analysis: Challenges and Opportunities. Jim's conversation with his colleague gave him much to think about. The irony that his students needed English but preferred to learn a language that empowered them to engage more fully as sports and music fans— and had found the means to do so without attending a language center—left him feeling confused as a teacher. Student engagement in English for Special Purposes courses depends on extrinsic sources of motivation and on the degree to which the instruction and materials are authentic and meet both the needs and perceived needs of the learners. The challenge, then, is to find a way to create more authentic and engaging materials and activities for students—activities that speak to their work and life experiences dually and that prepare them to function in daily work and life contexts.

Instructional Plan. After more thought and exploration of different mobile apps, including Duolingo, Jim decided to challenge his students to turn their mobile apps and knowledge of their favorite sports teams and musical groups to the learning of English for hospitality and tourism in an Indonesian context.

Jim announced to his class the following week that instead of studying chapter 7 of the textbook, they would be working in small groups to develop a customized phrasebook for interacting with their favorite international teams or pop groups in both those groups' home language and in English. In the scenario for the assignment, he asked the students to imagine that they had been asked to serve as the chief liaison and guide for their favorite team or group during a visit to Jakarta.

Jim told the students to assume that the manager of the teams and groups for their tour spoke English but that most of the members of the teams or groups would be more comfortable in their home language. In this case, the students as liaisons would need to speak to the manager mostly in English but might have some opportunity and need to speak to individual members. They would therefore need to: (1) develop a tour plan of the various sites the team or group would visit, including a brief description of each site in English; (2) anticipate the vocabulary and phrases they would need to exchange with the manager in English; and (3) anticipate basic vocabulary and phrases they might use with individual members to make them feel welcome and informed. Jim briefly surveyed the students about their favorite teams or groups and put them into groups of three according to their choices.

The students were excited about the idea of combining their knowledge and skills using mobile apps with their favorite teams or groups for an assignment that allowed them to imagine interacting with athletes and idols as professionals. Jim was concerned that the director of the language center would not be happy about using mobile apps or introducing and using languages other than English in class, but she was convinced by Jim's story that the students would be engaged and agreed to allow a trial.

To create the phrasebook, Jim's students downloaded the Google Translate app, which offered a customizable phrasebook option. He suggested the students use their knowledge of the "other" language from Duolingo but also check their phrases with international friends in Jakarta or, via chat rooms, in countries where the target language was spoken. Once organized, the students were given two additional class sessions to work in groups, with the provision that they would work on their own outside of class for homework. In the fourth session, each group presented its tour plan and phrasebook to the class in English.

1) Materials:
    a) Student smartphones
    b) Google Translate app
    c) Duolingo or other language learning app
    d) Internet connection
    e) Teacher laptop and projector or smart television.
2) Learning Mode: Small groups of three students, arranged by interest
3) Time: Five class sessions (90 minutes each)
4) Sequence of Activities:
    a) In Session 1, teacher introduces the project to create a phrasebook
    b) Students are grouped in threes according to their sports teams or music groups
    c) Students begin to plan a tour of Jakarta for their teams or groups
    d) In Session 2, students continue to plan and download Google Translate on their smartphones

e) Students submit plan for tour to the teacher and begin to work on their phrasebooks

f) In Session 3, students continue work on their phrasebooks (one per group; all members copy each other within the group)

g) In Session 4, students complete their phrasebooks and share them with the teacher and class

h) Students comment on each other's phrasebooks and teacher leads a discussion about terms and phrases in English the students learned

i) In Session 5, the teacher meets with each group separately and discusses the terms and phrases they have learned, assessing each student's ability to use what they have learned in speaking.

Assignments and Assessment. Two rubrics can be used to assess learning for this assignment: (1) a rubric to assess the group's phrasebooks (key terms and phrases); and (2) a rubric for assessing individual students' use of these key terms and phrases (see Tables 8.5 and 8.6).

Table 8.5 Rubric to assess key terms and phrases in group phrasebooks.

Achievement level	Descriptor
Excellent	The group plans a tour of Jakarta for their team or group that is logical and takes them to at least four sites, including relevant logistics (meeting, transportation, meals). The group successfully creates a customized phrasebook in English (terms and phrases in the home language of the team or group are not assessed). The terms and phrases used exceed those of the textbook and are comprehensive and realistic. They include more than fifteen new specialized terms and twenty phrases that integrate place names in Jakarta with standard terms in English. In their presentation and discussion, the group describes the tour and the terms and phrases they plan to use in detail and with few errors.
Very good	The group plans a tour of Jakarta for their team or group that is logical and takes them to four sites, including some relevant logistics (meeting, transportation, meals). The group successfully creates a customized phasebook in English (terms in the home language of the team or group are not assessed). The terms and phrases used equal those of the textbook and are complete and realistic. They include at least fifteen new specialized terms and twenty phrases that integrate places names in Jakarta with standard terms in English. In their presentation the group describes the tour and the terms and phrases they plan to use. The presentation may lack some detail and contain errors that do not impede understanding.
Satisfactory	The group plans a tour of Jakarta for their team or group that has few serious lapses in detail and that takes them to four sites, including some mention of logistical arrangements. The group creates a customized phrase book in English (terms in the home language of the team or group are not assessed). The terms and phrases approximate those of the textbook with slight errors. They include more than ten new specialized terms and fifteen phrases that integrate place names and standard English terms. In their presentation the group describes their tour briefly. The presentation lacks detail but provides an overview of the tour.

(Continued)

Table 8.5 (Continued)

Achievement level	Descriptor
Unsatisfactory	The group plans a tour of Jakarta that is incomplete and lacking in relevant detail. Only one or two sites are visited and there is little evidence of concern for logistical details. The group's phrasebook lacks customization and contains only a limited number of key terms (fewer than ten) and only a few phrases. Some of these terms/phrases may be incorrect. The group's presentation is short and without detail.

Table 8.6 Rubric to assess individual student use of phrasebook.

Achievement level	Descriptor
Above expectations	The student demonstrates the phrasebook in full English sentences and can explain and define terms and phrases in some detail. The student's speech is fully understandable, and there are only slight errors, which the student attempts to correct. The use of terms and phrases is accurate and appropriate to the situation.
Meets expectations	The student demonstrates the phrasebook in English using sentences and phrases and can explain terms and phrases in short sentences. The student can be understood, and makes some errors which may be corrected when prompted. The use of terms and phrases is mostly accurate and appropriate.
Below expectations	The student struggles to demonstrate the phrasebook in English. The student speaks in only short phrases, and cannot explain terms or phrases in any detail. The student's speech is difficult to understand and there are multiple errors. The use of terms and phrases may be inaccurate and/or inappropriate.

Relation to TESOL Technology Standards for Learners and CEFR Reference Level Descriptors

TESOL Technology Standards:

- Goal 1 (Demonstrate foundational knowledge and skills in technology for a multilingual world)
  - Standard 4 (Demonstrate basic competence as users of technology)
- Goal 2 (Use technology in social and culturally appropriate ways)
  - Standard 1 (Understand that communication conventions differ across cultures)
- Goal 3 (Effectively use and critically evaluate technology-based tools)
  - Standard 1 (Effectively use and evaluate productivity tools)
  - Standard 2 (Appropriately use and evaluate language skill-building tools)
  - Standard 3 (Appropriately use and evaluate tools for communication and collaboration)
  - Standard 4 (Use and evaluate research tools appropriately)
  - Standard 5 (Recognize the value of technology to support autonomy).

CEFR Reference Level Descriptors:

- Global Scale: B2 (Can produce clear, detailed text on a wide range of subjects)
- Overall Reading Comprehension: B1/B2 (Can read straightforward factual texts/ Can read with a large degree of independence)
- Reading for Orientation: B1 (Can find and understand relevant information in everyday material)
- Reading Instructions: B2 (Can understand lengthy, complex instructions)
- Overall Spoken Interaction: B1/B2 (Can communicate with some confidence/ Can use language fluently, accurately, and effectively)
- Conversation: B1 (Can maintain a conversation or discussion)
- Formal Discussion (Meetings); B2 (Can participate actively in routine and non-routine formal discussion)
- Goal-Oriented Cooperation: B2 (Can help along the progress of the work)
- Transactions to Obtain Goods and Services: B1 (Can deal with most transactions likely to arise)
- Information Exchange: B1 (Can exchange, check, and confirm accumulated factual information)
- Overall Spoken Production: B1/B2 (Can reasonably sustain a straightforward descripition/ Can give clear, detailed descriptions and presentations)
- Overall Written Production: B1 (Can write straightforward connected texts)
- Planning: B2 (Can plan what is to be said and the means to say it)
- Compensating: B1 (Can define the features of something concrete)
- Processing Text: B1 (Can collate short pieces of information)
- General Linguistic Range: B2 (Has a sufficient range of language to be able to give clear descriptions)
- Vocabulary Range: B2 (Has a good range of vocabulary for matters connected to his field)
- Grammatical Accuracy: B1 (Communicates with reasonable accuracy in familiar contexts)
- Vocabulary Control: B2 (Lexical accuracy is generally high)
- Orthographic Control: B2 (Spelling and punctuation are reasonably accurate)
- Propositional Precision: B2 (Can pass on detailed information reliably).

Analyzing and Extending the Lesson: Application to Additional Contexts. This activity is designed to help students develop specific key terms and phrases used in the tourism and hospitality industry, but it must be emphasized that the teaching of English for Special Purposes (ESP) consists of more than learning specialized words and phrases. This activity is not meant to constitute an entire ESP course but is rather meant to capitalize on the interests of students and their mobile devices for motivational and specific learning purposes.

The creation of phrasebooks using a mobile app has a wide variety of applications beyond ESP courses. The activity may also be used in courses focusing on conversation and the teaching of content through the English language. Translation is not always an advisable approach to learning English but the reality is that students do use translation devices in their learning, and this cannot be ignored. Using a task-based group activity and working with students is one way to acknowledge their informal strategies for learning in a productive and motivating way.

Let's Discuss

1) Have you ever used a mobile app for language learning? Have you used a mobile translator or dictionary? What has been your experience with these apps? When do you find these apps helpful and when not? What would you tell students in your classroom who wanted to use these apps for completing assignments?
2) As a language educator, what advice would you give to someone who was interested in using a mobile app to learn a language? How significant, do you think, is the focus on learning vocabulary and grammar without concern for the practical aspects of using a language in live communication? How would you suggest compensating for this problem?
3) What is your position on using programs such as Google Translate to write in English? Is this beneficial, in your view, or does Google Translate suggest to you that direct translation from one language to another is possible and desirable?
4) Which of the three scenarios for adapting social networking to classroom instruction do you think is most appropriate for the context in which you are teaching or will teach? What adaptations will you make, and what other possible uses of social networks do you see being adaptable to your classroom context?

References

Deris, Farhana Diana, and Nor Seha A Shukor. "Vocabulary Learning through Mobile Apps: A Phenomenological Inquiry of Student Acceptance and Desired Apps Features." *International Journal of Interactive Mobile Technologies* 13, no. 7 (2019): 129–140. https://doi.org/10.3991/ijim.v13i07.10845.

Dragonflame, Chrystal Sapphire, Amanda A. Olsen, and Jodi M. Tommerdahl. "Efficacy of Mobile Apps in Teaching Foreign Languages: A Systematic Review." *ORTESOL Journal* 38 (2021): 33–35.

Freeman, David H. "How to Almost Learn Italian." *The Atlantic*, December 2018. https://www.theatlantic.com/magazine/archive/2018/12/language-apps-duolingo/573919.

Groves, Michael, and Klaus Mundt. "Friend or Foe? Google Translate in Language for Academic Purposes." *English for Specific Purposes* 37 (2015): 112–121. http://dx.doi.org/10.1016/j.esp.2014.09.001.

Harmon, Janis M., Karen D. Wood, Wanda B. Hedrick, Jean Vintinner, and Terri Willeford. "Interactive Word Walls: More than Just Reading the Writing on the Walls." *Journal of Adolescent & Adult Literacy* 52, no. 5 (February 2009): 398–408. https://doi.org/10.1598/JAAL.52.5.4.

Hartono, Rudi. "Teaching Translation through the Interactive Web." *Language Circle: Journal of Language and Literature* 9, no. 2 (April 2017): 129–140.

Hunt, Alan, and David Beglar. "Current Research and Practice in Teaching Vocabulary." In *Methodology in Language Teaching*, edited by Jack C. Richards and Willy A. Renandya, 258–256. Cambridge, UK and New York: Cambridge University Press, 2002.

Kessler, Matt. "Supplementing Mobile-assisted Language Learning with Reflective Journal Writing: A Case Study of Duolingo Users' Metacognitive Awareness." *Computer Assisted Language Learning* (September 2021): https://doi.org/10.1080/09588221.2021.1968914.

Klímová, Blanka. "Mobile Phones and/or Smartphones and Their Apps for Teaching English as a Foreign Language." *Education and Information Technologies* 23 (2018): 1091–1099. https://doi.org/10.1007/s10639-017-9655-5.

Kukulska-Hulme, Agnes, Helen Lee, and Lucy Norris. "Mobile Learning Revolution: Implications for Language Pedagogy." In *The Handbook of Technology and Second Language Teaching and Learning*, edited by Carol A. Chapelle and Shannon Sauro, 217–233. Oxford: Wiley & Sons, 2017.

Little, Sabine. "'Is There an App for That?' Exploring Games and Apps among Heritage Language Families." *Journal of Multilingual and Multicultural Development* (July 2019): 218–229. https://doi.org/10.1080/01434632.2018.1502776.

Loewen, Shawn, Dustin Crowther, Daniel R. Isbell, Kathy Minhye Kim, Jeffrey Maloney, Zachary F. Miller, and Hima Rawal. "Mobile-assisted Language Learning: A Duolingo Case Study." *ReCALL* 31, no. 3 (2019): 293–311. https://doi.org/10.1017/S0958344019000065.

Lotherington, Heather. "Mobile Language Learning: The Medium is ^not the Message." *L2 Journal* 10, no. 2 (2018): 198–214. https://doi.org/10.5070/L210235576.

Messemer, Eva Maria. "*Comparing the Effectiveness of One Semester of German Study: Duolingo versus Face-to-Face Instruction.*" MA thesis. Southern Illinois University Carbondale, 2021.

Microsoft Azure. "*Artificial Intelligence (AI) vs. Machine Learning (ML).*" 2022. https://azure.microsoft.com/en-us/overview/artificial-intelligence-ai-vs-machine-learning/#introduction.

Moreno and Vermeulen. "Using VISP (VIdeos for SPeaking), a Mobile App Based on Audio Description, to Promote English Language Learning among Spanish Students: A Case Study." *Procedia – Social and Behavioral Sciences* 178 (2015): 132–138.

Nami, Fatemeh. "Educational Smartphone Apps for Language Learning in Higher Education: Students' Choices and Perceptions." *Australasian Journal of Educational Technology* 36, no. 4 (2020): 82–95. https://doi.org/10.14742/ajet.5350.

Pham, Xuan Lam, Thao Pham, Quynh Mai Nguyen, Thanh Huong Nguyen, and Thi Thu Huong Cao. "Chatbot as an Intelligent Personal Assistant for Mobile Language Learning." In *Proceedings of the 2018 2nd International Conference on Education and E-Learning*, 16–21, November 2018. https://doi.org/10.1145/3291078.3291115.

Rosell-Aguilar, Fernando. "Autonomous Language Learning through a Mobile Application: A User Evaluation of the Busuu App." *Computer Assisted Language Learning* (April 2018). https://doi.org/10.1080/09588221.2018.1456465.

Ruddell, Martha Rapp, and Brenda A. Shearer. "'Extraordinary,' 'Tremendous,' 'Exhilarating' 'Magnificent': Middle School at-Risk Students Become Avid Word Learners with the Vocabulary Self-Collection Strategy (VSS)." *Journal of Adolescent & Adult Literacy* 45, no. 5 (2002): 352–363.

Shortt, Mitchell, Shantanu Tilak, Irina Kuznetcova, Bethany Martens, and Babatunde Akinkuolie. "Gamification in Mobile-assisted Language Learning: A Systematic Review of Duolingo Literature from Public Release of 2012 to Early 2020." *Computer Assisted Language Learning (2021)*. https://doi.org/10.1080/09588221.2021.1933540.

Sviķe, Silga. "Mobile Apps as Language-learning Tools." *AILA Review* 34, no. 1 (2021): 19–36. https://doi.org/10.1075/aila.20006.svi.

Teske, Kaitlyn. "Duolingo." *Calico Journal* 34, no. 3 (2017): 393–401. https://doi.org/10.1558/cj.32509.

Tsai, Shu-Chiao. "Using Google Translate in EFL Drafts: A Preliminary Investigation." *Computer Assisted Language Learning* (February 2019). https://doi.org/10.1080/09588221.2018.1527361.

Vesselinov, Roumen, and John Grego. *"Duolingo Effectiveness Study"* (2012).

Voita, Elena, Rico Sennrich, and Ivan Titov. "When a Good Translation Is Wrong in Context: Context-aware Machine Translation Improves on Deixis, Ellipsis, and Lexical Cohesion." *arXiv preprint arXiv:1905.05979*, 2019. https://arxiv.org/abs/1905.05979.

Vygotsky, Lev S. Mind in Society. Cambridge: Harvard University Press, 1978.

Part III

Language Curriculum in the Digital Age

9

Beyond the Pandemic: Online and Flipped Learning

A live online discussion between students of English in Morocco and the United States before the Covid-19 pandemic.

Introduction

This first chapter in Part III of this book marks a shift in the focus of the following chapters from how learner-driven strategies may inform classroom instruction to the implications of digital technology and informal, autonomous learning for English language curriculum more broadly.

The connection in these chapters between IDLE and formal English language education is less direct but perhaps more profound and signals a slight shift in the structure of the chapters as well. Rather than imagining how the strategies of individual informal learners can inspire classroom instruction, the chapters begin with vignettes featuring teachers who are already knowledgeable about the ubiquitous technologies that power IDLE. Their challenge, then, will be to harness IDLE's features to address issues specific

English Language Learning in the Digital Age: Learner-Driven Strategies for Adolescents and Young Adults,
First Edition. Mark Dressman, Ju Seong Lee, and Laurent Perrot.
© 2023 John Wiley & Sons Ltd. Published 2023 by John Wiley & Sons Ltd.

to formal instruction, such as online learning in the wake of the Covid-19 pandemic in this chapter; learning to write for formal academic purposes in Chapter 10; curriculum and assessment in Chapter 11; and finally, in Chapter 12, the implications of IDLE for English language education into the future.

To this end, the vignettes that begin Chapters 9–11 introduce the detailed scenarios of the Practical Applications in the Classroom section toward the end of each chapter, in which teachers use their existing knowledge of IDLE to address critically important issues outside of informal learning. We hope that the direct connection between the problems introduced at the beginning of these chapters with the solutions found by teachers in conclusion will offer a powerful vision of how IDLE can inform every aspect of English language learning and teaching after the pandemic.

Kip Gallagher: Teaching English Online in a Scuola Media during a Lockdown

Kip Gallagher is an exchange teacher from the United States, teaching English in a *scuola media* (middle school) in Naples, Italy. He has become fascinated by the stories he has heard from students and other teachers of distant relatives who immigrated to the United States and Canada between 1880 and 1924 to escape poverty. After a bit of research online, he has identified seven major North American cities with thriving "Little Italys"—historic neighborhoods where Italians settled in the early twentieth century that are still centers today for history, culture, and food. These are in Toronto; Manhattan, New York City; Philadelphia; Boston; Chicago; San Diego; and San Francisco.

Kip has been planning a unit using Google Earth in which students make a virtual visit to a Little Italy in one North American city and plan a tour for presentation to the class, but just a week before the unit, schools have been locked down again during a new wave of Covid-19. Kip knows that his students have internet access and at least one device— sometimes a smartphone but usually also a laptop—at home, and so he hopes he can arrange to work with his students online on this project.

Michelle Kong: Motivating High Schoolers in the Pandemic

Ms. Michelle Kong has been teaching English to low-achieving secondary school students (10th graders; ages 15–16) in a public school in Hong Kong for over ten years. Her Cantonese-speaking students can generally understand sentences related to their interests, such as family information and places of interest. They can also talk about familiar and routine matters in English, and they frequently code-switch in English and Cantonese. But their academic school report consistently shows low marks in English. They have problems with grammar, especially the second conditional (e.g., "If I could sing, I would/I'd enter the contest"), which they find difficult, and many of them failed their last English test.

And now, suddenly, a wave of infections in the global pandemic has limited face-to-face schooling for students across Hong Kong. Ms. Kong's students were already unmotivated, and she worries that without something more engaging than online lectures she is likely to lose her students' attention completely, causing them to fall even further behind.

Ms. Kong has always known that her students were bright and capable but not meeting expectations. Before online instruction began, she had interviewed some of her students informally about their attitudes toward school in general and English in particular. At first the students were reluctant to tell her the truth, but gradually she won them over. They told her they felt optimistic and excited when teachers taught English with authentic and exciting topics such as diverse cultures and new lifestyles that transcended vocabulary and grammar. They also became more favorable toward learning English when they realized that English was genuine and valuable beyond exams and when teachers used multimodal materials other than traditional textbooks, such as multimedia use of PowerPoint, games, and English songs. Finally, the students said they enjoyed group tasks in which they interacted with peers.

Siobhán O'Byrne: English as Medium of Instruction in a Middle Eastern University

Siobhán O'Byrne teaches a microbiology course in a graduate entry medical school at a university in the Middle East. Her students are a combination of international students, whose first language is English, and Middle Eastern students whose first language is Arabic, although they have had their primary degree through English. The students speak a local dialect of Arabic, and their first literate language is Standard Arabic. Most have studied English from their primary school days and attended English language high schools and completed their primary degree through English, but they are struggling in the English Medium of Instruction (EMI) course, mainly due to the extreme amount of scientific vocabulary of Greek and Latin origin.

These problems have been exacerbated during the pandemic. Although face-to-face teaching has resumed, there have been many interruptions, some students have had to quarantine, and mask mandates and contact rules have meant that students' ability to study with each other and to meet with Siobhán outside class have been limited to meetings on Microsoft Teams. In addition, Siobhán's course is also an intensive, three-week course in which there is little time for study or review. At the end of the course, the students will take a standardized international exam comprising multiple-choice type questions and descriptive clinical vignettes to test their knowledge of microbiology. Siobhán knows from practice exams that vocabulary and reading comprehension in English will place her very bright and capable second-language students at a disadvantage and is searching for a way to provide them more time for study beyond her lectures.

Discussion

Prior to the pandemic, online formal instruction was largely confined to graduate education, usually at the master's level, along with "flipped" learning, in which video recorded lectures or other asynchronous materials were provided to students to free instructional time for interactive classroom discussions and other activities. Primary, secondary, and even undergraduate university instruction was usually assumed to require face-to-face engagement to be effective.

The Covid-19 pandemic has upended all these assumptions. Across the globe and with little or no warning and scant preparation, in the spring of 2020 entire school systems, their students, parents, teachers, and administrators were forced to move the activities of learning, teaching, and assessment online. Every educator we know, ourselves included—and, in the case of primary and secondary teachers especially—was suddenly required to become a master of online teaching, regardless of the subject matter being taught, the grade level of the students, or the level of infrastructure provided by schools or in students' homes; and every student was required to master the practices of distance learning.

Nothing like this had ever happened before in the history of mass education.

As we write in the spring of 2022, the pandemic has raged on and off for two full years worldwide, and its end and outcomes remain uncertain. In many parts of the world, schools are still closed; in others, they are open but for limited times and with many restrictions and absences due to illness. Along with health services, the travel and hospitality industry, and many other areas, the field of education has been severely tested, and the long-term consequences of the pandemic are not at all clear. However, it seems unlikely that things will ever go back to being exactly as they were before.

The Impact of the Pandemic on US Education over Time

According to the US Census Bureau (McElrath 2020), in the first months of the pandemic:
- 93% of children in the US experienced "some form of distance learning."
- Low-income homes relied on paper materials sent from school more than high-income homes, which relied on the internet more.

Two years into the pandemic, the Brookings Institution (Kuhfeld et al. 2022) reported nationwide effects, including:
- Severe staff shortages
- Increased absenteeism (beyond quarantines)
- Rolling school closures
- Mental health challenges for staff and students
- Increased violence and student misbehavior
- Lost instructional time
- Significant drops in math and reading scores
- Higher losses in achievement in low-income than high-income schools
- Continuing losses in achievement over time.

In some cases, the forced experiment in online learning brought by the pandemic has been a dismal failure. We know from our own experience, the anecdotal evidence of colleagues, and emerging data (Lewis et al. 2021; World Bank, UNESCO, and UNICEF 2021), that the quality and quantity of learning has declined across subject areas, along with the quality and quantity of socialization that is also part of schooling. Not only so that parents can go to work again but also so that children can learn both the academic and social skills they will need for life, it appears clear that daily physical interaction with others within structured, formal settings is a necessary condition for living well in our modern world.

We also know from our own experience and anecdotally that it is not only the technological infrastructure of many countries but also the expertise and energy of educators that has been strained, in some cases to the breaking point. Digital technology has made it possible for formal education to continue when buildings close, but not without a severe test on teachers' abilities to adapt instruction and assignments across content areas and grade levels, and at a high cost often to their sense of efficacy and professionalism. Sometimes, teaching has come down to sending students worksheets and hoping they are returned. In other cases, it is unclear if students are actually "tuning in" to live or video recorded lectures or whether real processing of information is occurring in small or whole class online discussions.

And yet, we also know from published research reports that in some cases innovation is occurring, and that there are pockets of success and situations in which the affordances of technology have led to new creativity and enhanced productivity for teachers and students. These innovations, we believe, deserve to survive the pandemic and to enrich learning and teaching in the future. Our focus in this chapter, then, is on what can be taken from the misfortune of the pandemic that is productive and that will increase the autonomy of learners and the efficacy and professionalism of English language education beyond the pandemic and into the future.

Chapter Objectives

The central goal of this chapter is to distinguish among different approaches to online and partially online (flipped, hybrid, and synchronous) learning and teaching of English, with a focus on how IDLE activities relate to formal digital methods of English education, and to acquire practical, scenario-based knowledge of best teaching practices. Subgoals include developing a research-based understanding of the benefits and challenges of flipped and online learning for both teachers and students. A final subgoal is to consider the long-term implications of online instruction for English education in the Covid-19 pandemic. By the end of the chapter, readers will be able to:

1) Distinguish among and describe multiple approaches for flipped/hybrid and online learning.
2) Compare and contrast approaches with respect to their benefits and challenges for learning and teaching.
3) Describe the relationship between the practices of IDLE and online learning and teaching.
4) Describe research findings and their implications for improving flipped/hybrid and online learning.
5) Distinguish and differentiate approaches according to learners' age and grade level (middle school vs. high school vs. university) with respect to the student self-regulation and motivation.
6) Consider how the research, theory, and three scenarios in this chapter can be applied to the reader's pedagogical context.

Key Words

self-regulation; flipped/hybrid instruction; synchronous instruction; asynchronous instruction; task-based language learning

Research and Theory

Comparing Conventional, Flipped/Hybrid, and Synchronous/Asychronous Online Education

Table 9.1 provides a comparison of the teaching and learning characteristics and typical advantages and disadvantages of four curricular modes. From left to right, these are arranged from modes with the greatest and most immediate level of teacher–student engagement to those with the least levels, in which teachers and students are the most separated from each other. From left to right as well, teachers have the greatest control over student learning and students move from the lowest levels of required self-regulation and responsibility, or control over themselves as learners responsible for outcomes, to the highest levels, in which the role of teachers is the most remote and least directive.

Conventional approaches before the pandemic were the most traditional and common from early childhood to graduate education. The core assumption of conventional approaches is that the more immediate and direct the contact between teacher and student, the more high-quality, higher-order learning occurs. In this approach, teachers control the content of what is learned and prepare lessons in a variety of formats (e.g., lecture, projects, discussion) to lead students to acquire information and understanding. Students are the recipients of the teacher's knowledge, although their learning depends on their level of engagement and participation in the lessons. Most new learning takes place in the classroom with time outside class typically reserved for study and completing assignments. The effectiveness of conventional approaches very often depends on the rapport that teachers establish with students and on their ability to engage and motivate students in their delivery of content.

By contrast, *flipped/hybrid* approaches were considered innovative before the pandemic and were typically part of secondary and tertiary (undergraduate and graduate) education, because they assume a greater level of student responsibility and self-regulation that younger students often do not possess. In a flipped/hybrid program, teachers prepare content instruction such as video lectures, games, and self-study guides in advance. Students are required to study these materials before class and to come knowing, or with questions, about the content. More face-to-face time is therefore available for discussions, labs, and projects. Flipped/hybrid approaches are considered to make more efficient use of time for teacher–student interaction and opportunities for students to review and rewatch content, but they can be challenging for both students and teachers. It can be difficult for both students and teachers to adapt to a flipped approach. To be successful, teachers must take extra time to prepare materials such as video lectures and upload these, in addition to creating activities to process and review material during face-to-face sessions. For students, flipping requires greater motivation and self-regulation so the approach often works best in secondary and university classes with highly motivated students.

A *synchronous online* approach is one in which teachers and students meet online, using a video conferencing program usually combined with a Learning Management System (LMS). There can be many variations in this approach, some involving face-to-face

Table 9.1 Comparison of four modes of teaching and learning.

Characteristics of teaching/ learning	Conventional	Flipped/hybrid	Online synchronous	Online asynchronous
Instructional and content delivery	Delivery in-class, face to face (lecture, discussion, problem solving); study and homework outside class	Delivery through videos, self-study outside class; In-class face-to-face meetings for discussion and group work	Live online instruction with remote student attendance and lecture/ discussion; archived materials and student self-study outside class	No meetings between teacher and students or only during office hours; teacher prepares lectures, notes, assignments; self-paced completion of assignments with due dates
Typical conditions for learning	Scheduled physical attendance; some preparation; participation (listening, interacting); outside homework and study	Scheduled physical attendance; greater preparation (watching videos, note-taking); outside homework and study	Scheduled online attendance; some preparation; participation online; outside homework and study	Self-scheduled online study (watching videos, taking notes, completing assignments)
Typical conditions for teaching	Scheduled physical teaching; preparation of activities before class; office hours	Scheduled physical meetings for discussion and supervision; preparation of videos and online instruction and LMS maintenance; office hours online and/or physically	Scheduled online teaching; preparation of activities before class; LMS maintenance; office hours online	Preparation of all materials including lectures in advance; monitoring of student learning through assignments; possible online office hours
Typical advantages	Opportunities for immediate social interaction within physical space and checks for understanding	Increases time for processing, interacting, and checks for understanding; Opportunities to rewatch to prepare videos once and reuse	Retains active live interaction and increases convenience to attend; recorded sessions allow rewatching and review; opportunities for global participation	Within a time frame, allows great freedom to students and teachers for scheduling study and preparation time; materials can be reused and/or updated limitlessly

(Continued)

Table 9.1 (Continued)

Characteristics of teaching/ learning	Conventional	Flipped/hybrid	Online synchronous	Online asynchronous
Typical disadvantages	Attendance is required; miss class and students miss a lesson; scheduling can be difficult; requires optimal infrastructure and engagement for optimization	Increased workload and preparation for teachers or lectures and discussion; requires students to self-regulate and watch videos, prepare for face-to-face instruction	Requires expertise or support to operate online software while teaching/ learning; requires high speed, reliable internet and functional device at scheduled times.	Requires highest level of self-regulation for students; lack of live interaction can be alienating; difficult to check for understanding immediately.

meetings at the beginning and/or end of a course of study and some flipping instruction so that students view lectures asynchronously (on their own schedule) and then attend scheduled online meetings to discuss or review with the instructor and other students. The great advantage of this approach is that it can transcend physical distances, allowing students across geographic regions who are able to "tune in" at a given time to participate. As video streaming became more widely possible In the late 2000s, Massive Open Online Courses (MOOCs) promised to open opportunities for students around the world. Students anywhere would be able to "get a Harvard education" by attending MOOCs developed and taught by professors at the world's greatest universities. Exclusively online universities, like the University of Phoenix, also opened, promising the same quality instruction to students anywhere in the world, at a lower cost than physically attending a university, and since then many graduate programs have migrated to being taught synchronously and online. However, attrition rates for these courses and programs are much higher than face-to-face courses (Gütl et al. 2014). In our experience also, regardless of the reputation of the institution, degrees earned online are often less well regarded and, in some cases, not accepted for employment or admission purposes.

Asynchronous approaches to instruction are those in which there is no face-to-face, and little, if any, direct contact between teachers and students. An asynchronous approach is essentially an online correspondence course, in which individual students work at their own pace to complete assignments or pass exams which are graded remotely by a teacher. Teachers may also make videos that add some personal aspects to the instruction. In some versions, there may be office hours with a teacher, or the student and teacher may email or chat with each other virtually. It is also possible, however, that an asynchronous course could be entirely "teacher-free," in which students read and watch material on their own and take multiple choice exams, which are computer scored. Finally, there are hybrid asynchronous and synchronous approaches, in which much of the instruction is asynchronous and self-paced, but students meet online as a class periodically with a teacher.

Summary Discussion

In summary, approaches to online teaching and learning vary from hybrid combinations which include face-to-face learning to approaches in which everything is online and there is little if any contact with a teacher. The main variables differentiating these approaches are the degree of self-regulation and persistence required for students (the more remote the greater the need for self-regulation and motivation) and for teachers, differences in preparation (the more online and synchronous, the higher the level of preparation and broadcasting skills required).

An additional critical variable in the case of language learning is the type of content being learned. An argument can be made that informational content, in which students learn concepts and facts, is likely much easier to acquire online than content consisting of skills that are applied in practice, as in learning to write and to speak and interact with others. However, we also note that we could add a column on the right of Table 9.1 for an "Auto-Didactic" approach, in which outside the formality of a school or course setting students were completely self-regulated, self-directed, and fully autonomous learners. This column would describe the Informal Digital Learners of English (IDLErs) who are the inspiration for this book.

How, then, do we account for the fact that language learners who rely least on any type of formal instruction are also consistently shown by research to be among the most accomplished learners of English? It is because the full context of IDLErs' learning is more complex than it seems or than Table 9.1 suggests. First, and as we noted in Chapter 1, not all students are as self-motivated or capable of self-regulation as those who use IDLE. Only a percentage of students, which can range from perhaps 10% in some countries to more than 50% in others, acquire English mainly through informal, digital means, and that population is self-selected for higher levels of self-regulation and motivation. Second, the success of IDLE as a language learning strategy is highly dependent on learners' type and degree of engagement with online content. Learners who passively watch television and movies in English with subtitles or captions will incidentally "pick up" some English in the process, but learners who actively watch for the purpose of learning English and who additionally interact with others online in English through chat or commenting on posts or communicating in real time during a video game are likely to learn far more. In these cases, "online" does not mean non-participatory; online learning in these cases may be more interactive than sitting in a classroom listening to others and occasionally speaking.

Third, the reality of IDLE as a strategy for most students is that they are also attending formal classes, and so their context for learning is a naturally hybrid one, in which formal instruction is combined with IDLE. As noted, this appears to be the optimal context for learning outside a totally immersive experience, and in this case, it is teachers and students who find ways to connect and integrate all their opportunities for teaching and learning who are mostly likely to develop greatest proficiency in English.

Research Findings

Research on the benefits and challenges of flipped and online education in general echo the preceding discussion, citing the benefits of increased time for interaction during face-to-face teaching (Akçayır and Akçayır 2018), opportunities for students to rewatch and review materials and to work at their own pace and convenience (Lee and Martin 2020; Mok 2014), but noting the need for students to self-regulate their attention (Shyr and Chen 2017; Wang 2019; Wang and Qi 2018) and in the case of online courses and programs, high attrition rates (Kim et al. 2020; Stone and Springer 2019).

Research focusing on flipped and online instruction in English and additional language-learning contexts is also in alignment with research on other subjects. Flipped/hybrid language education, in which teachers post their own instructional videos or videos from streaming services (e.g., TED Talks on YouTube) as well as games for practicing grammar and simple interaction, are quite common. In these cases, "flipping" has a wide range of meanings, and it generally refers to supplementary activities. Two reviews of flipped language classroom research have shown similar findings. Zhou et al. (2020) reviewed 34 published studies of flipped/hybrid teaching at the university level, noting a wide range of flipped practices, some of which were prepared by eacher and others, such as the use of games and YouTube videos, that were free or commercially available. They reported increases in student motivation, autonomy and self-regulation, confidence, and higher-order thinking along with increased performance, but did not explain fully what the exact increases in performance were. Turan and Akdag-Cimen (2020) reviewed 43 studies specifically of flipped university English classrooms. They noted that in 21 studies in which increases in language ability were measured, 18 showed increases in students' proficiency in English, and concluded that flipping was an effective method of instruction. However, they also noted challenges, which included increased workload for both teachers and students and the need for technological infrastructure that was reliable and sufficient for both teaching and learning.

Flip Your Language Classroom: Ideas from Three Sources

Cambridge University Press provides a start-up guide for flipping a language classroom. Author Philip Kerr (2020) suggests flipping the "less communicative" aspects of language teaching, such as grammar lessons and introduction of vocabulary, providing more in-class time for practice and development of skills.

Panopto (2019) suggests seven possible ways to flip a language classroom. These include video recording classroom demonstrations and uploading them for students to review; linking YouTube videos such as TED Talks for students to view before discussing them in class; and having students create videos on topics they have researched and uploading them for other students to view out of class.

On **Edutopia** (Seynhaeve 2020), a Spanish teacher described a project in which she began with a question about planning a trip to Chile. Her students created blogs to document their planning process and watched videos on grammatical structures out of class that they then used to write when creating their travel projects.

Two findings from these reviews should be noted here. The first is that nearly all the studies reviewed took place in university classrooms, presumably because students at these levels are expected to be more autonomous in their learning and more capable of self-regulation. However, Zou, Luo, Xie et al. found that flipping produced increases in students' autonomy and self-regulation, that is, that flipping actually helped to develop greater autonomy in students, rather than simply building on levels of autonomy that were already there. In other words, flipping itself served as a strategy for helping students to become more active and self-regulatory in their learning practices.

Research on English language education under fully online synchronous/asynchronous conditions prior to the pandemic is scarce, likely because the need for direct contact between teachers and students for language learning was assumed. In one study of the online teaching of business English in Slovenia (Tratnik, Urh, and Jereb 2019), student satisfaction and perceived learning were compared in two classes taught by the same instructor, one traditionally and one exclusively online. Students reported higher satisfaction and perceived gains in learning for the traditional course. They noted lower motivation in the online course, but increased time and effort spent in studying, and missed interacting with peers, although they were satisfied with their teacher interactions and enjoyed the game-related activities of the online course. Actual results for learning measured through exams and grades were not reported in this study.

Research during the Covid-19 Pandemic

The Covid-19 pandemic produced very different conditions for flipped/hybrid and online teaching. With little warning or preparation, teachers worldwide across primary, secondary, and university levels were presented with the need to move their teaching exclusively or at least partly online, often with little instruction in how to do this and inadequate technological resources for them, or, especially, for their students.

As of winter 2022, several studies have been published on how teachers, students, and school systems have managed adjustments to an online teaching and learning environment. Two reports, one global (The World Bank, UNESCO, and UNICEF 2021) and one in the United States (Lewis et al. 2021) of achievement in primary and secondary schools since the start of the pandemic documented declines (globally) or in the United States, lower than normal gains in student learning during the pandemic. In both cases, students from lower socioeconomic backgrounds were more impacted by the pandemic, especially at the primary level, due to lack of access to technology infrastructure.

Three studies conducted at the university level suggest that at this level, students and teachers were better able to adapt and cope in the pandemic. A survey of 158 primary, secondary, and university English teachers in China during the pandemic (Huang, Teo, and Guo 2021) found that under "non-volitional" conditions, teachers indicated that they were prepared to teach fully online, and that their attitudes depended on the perceived quality of the infrastructure allowed them. A study in Hong Kong (Hew et al. 2020) of a flipped/hybrid education course converted to a fully online course found that students performed as well as in flipped/hybrid conditions before the pandemic. At a university in The Netherlands, Veldthuis et al. (2020) found that students in an ICT research course had similar levels of performance and reported higher satisfaction under fully online conditions than when the same course was taught in flipped/hybrid or face-to-face formats. In the last two studies, it should be noted that the courses were both taught by instructors who had significant prior experience with, and materials for, teaching in flipped formats.

Discussion: Beyond the Pandemic

In summary, research on flipped/hybrid learning designs, especially in university and secondary settings, confirms its effectiveness for learning in general and for English language education. However, there is little evidence for the efficacy of fully online teaching of English in either synchronous or asynchronous modes. It seems that some degree of live contact is crucial to keeping students motivated and engaged within the context of formal education, especially at the primary and secondary level.

Silver Linings of the Covid-19 Pandemic

While the Covid-19 pandemic has had a devastating impact on education in many ways, there are also some silver linings, according to Mary Burns (2020), writing for UKFIET. Since the start of the pandemic,

- A culture of experimentation and risk taking with instructional technology has taken hold.
- Teachers' practical knowledge of ICT has soared.
- Educators are more focused on good instructional design.
- Flipped/hybrid learning has gained permanence.
- Digital equity has become a focus of policy making.
- A more holistic view of learners and learning has emerged.
- The relationship between health and digital, online activity has become a concern.
- Educators are learning the importance and power of self-paced learning.
- Physically well-designed (well-spaced and ventilated) classrooms have become a priority.

Studies of student achievement suggest that during the pandemic children and adolescents learned less across subject areas, especially where technological infrastructure was lacking. Anecdotally, we have ourselves struggled as teachers at the university level to adapt to fully online instruction, and to be as present and engaged with students as before the pandemic. We also know many teachers at the secondary and primary levels whose students simply have "dropped out" of classes due to a lack of motivation and the stimulation that comes from school culture as well as physical attendance and interaction with peers and adults, regardless of the quality or quantity of technology and support available. It seems that fully online instruction for children and adolescents, be it synchronous or asynchronous, has not worked well almost anywhere, and at the university level, it has proven to be workable but less than optimal.

However, this does not mean that after Covid, all is likely to return to the way it was before. Many school systems and universities have made significant investments in both hardware and software during the pandemic, and most teachers and administrators have developed at least minimal skills for online instruction. At the very best, the use of flipping/hybrid instruction in primary and secondary schools will increase and educators may be challenged to develop materials that creatively make optimal use of students' study and instructional time. At the least, online formats may serve as back-ups for times when weather and other events do not permit face-to-face meetings. At the university level, it seems likely that trends toward online courses at the undergraduate level and programs at the graduate level will accelerate and that as access to higher education increases so will the stratification of its quality and prestige.

Practical Applications in the Classroom

Scenario One: A Task-Based Google Earth Tour

The Scene. In the first vignette of this chapter, exchange teacher Kip Gallagher was planning to have his students in a middle school in Naples use Google Earth to create a tour of one of the Little Italys that are a feature of many major North American cities as part of his school's focus on Task-Based Language Learning (Ellis 2003). The switch to online teaching during a surge in the pandemic delayed this project while Kip and his students became accustomed to the situation. In the meantime, Kip checked with the lead teacher at his school and was encouraged to learn that she thought this was possible for the students, with some adjustments for time.

Analysis: Challenges and Opportunities. According to Ellis (2003), task-based learning has four characteristics: (1) a focus on meaning; (2) a "gap," requiring learners to problem-solve; (3) open-ended, student-chosen resources; and (4) a clearly defined, non-linguistic outcome. Kip found a topic that was relevant and meaningful for his students and their families. His challenge was to create a task that has a "gap"—that requires students to make inferences and use their own judgment in not merely copying but processing information, to suggest rather than provide resources, and to define a project outcome that presents the findings of the students in a format that is visual and engaging. The tour feature of Google Earth Outreach, combined with additional websites about landmarks in the seven Little Italys, will be a central tool for this learning activity.

An additional major challenge for educators and students during the pandemic has been the need for siblings to share the same hardware at home for classes, leading students sometimes to be absent or to attend using smartphones rather than fully functional computers. In this case, recording lectures or instructions for students to view later and creating flexible schedules and due dates may be one solution to this problem.

Instructional Plan. The shift to online teaching has created additional challenges for the project. After checking to determine that the students had the needed connectivity and computers at home, Kip discovered that the students would be able to complete the assignment. However, he had also learned after teaching online that many students seemed to have trouble attending classes because siblings needed to use the same computer simultaneously.

Kip also realized that he was going to need to provide much more detailed instructions on how to create the tour than he normally would. For the assignment, he created two videos. The first was his detailed description of how to use Google Earth Pro (downloaded version) to create the tour. Kip discovered that by pushing the Windows button and the G key on his PC he could capture video and record his voice while demonstrating how to create a tour, just as he would if he were in his classroom teaching with his computer connected to a projector. Kip reserved one of the Little Italys for his demonstration and created an entire tour as a model for the students. He uploaded this as an unlisted video to YouTube as a demonstration and posted the link on the LMS for the class that he also used for online synchronous instruction.

As a second video that included the full instructions for the assignment, he created a PowerPoint video with all aspects of the assignment, such as number of Little Italy sites to visit, how to plan before recording the tour, details about the narration, the grading rubric, and so on, and inserted his YouTube video into the PowerPoint, remembering to adjust the timing of the video to play automatically. When he was finished, he saved the PowerPoint and then saved it again as an MP4 video. He uploaded this video to YouTube and again added the link to the class's LMS.

In his live, synchronous teaching (which he recorded for students who were not online), Kip introduced the assignment by briefly reviewing the history of Italian immigration from southern Italy in the early twentieth century to his students and inviting them to ask their parents and grandparents if anyone in their family had emigrated, where they immigrated to, and if they had relatives living there now. Based on their answers, he organized the students into groups of four on the LMS and assigned each a Little Italy in one city to investigate.

Kip then showed the students the PowerPoint video he had made for the assignment. They were introduced to the tour feature through Google Earth Outreach (n.d.) and watched videos on YouTube with instructions for creating a Google Earth tour using Google Earth Pro. The tour needed to include directions from Naples to the Little Italy neighborhood, including the use of public transportation if possible, and a tour of the important sites in the neighborhood (a minimum of five), using the touring feature of Google Earth. Students were required to write a narration and then record it to accompany the tour in English.

In their groups, the students needed to organize their home resources to complete the assignment and to download the appropriate version of Google Earth Pro (n.d.) on their smartphones or their home computers or tablets. Kip met with each group synchronously during class and checked to be sure the group had the needed resources. The students began by researching their Little Italy to identify important sites (buildings, statues, monuments, restaurants) and located them on Google Maps. Using the Street View feature, they collected screenshots of each site and then traced a path around the neighborhood, from site to site. Finally, they wrote a short, one-paragraph description of each site and its importance.

The students plotted their tour and recorded their narrations for it as Kip moved from group to group on the LMS, offering suggestions and directing the students to his video and other useful videos on YouTube explaining how to create a tour using Google Earth Pro. The culminating activity was for the students to view each other's tours and then share their impressions of the Little Italys they had toured in the United States and Canada.

1) Materials:
   a) Home computers or other devices
   b) Home wifi or landline connections
   c) Google Earth Pro.
2) Learning Mode: Online synchronous and asynchronous for introduction and concluding presentations; groups of four students on LMS for the task-based project
3) Time: Six 50-minute sessions plus student independent work
4) Sequence of Activities:
   a) On Day 1, introduce the topic and task using live instruction and video
   b) Organize students into groups on the LMS, one per Little Italy
   c) Teacher checks with each group to determine their home resources

d) Students download Google Earth Pro and begin to research and archive websites and screenshots for their Little Italys
e) On Days 2–3, groups continue research and archiving of materials
f) Teacher consults with students on their findings; have a class discussion
g) Students review YouTube tutorials and begin to create their group's tour
h) On Day 4, students write and record narrations for each site visited on the tour
i) On Day 5, students complete their tours
j) One Day 6, students share their tours with the class
k) Teacher conducts a class discussion about the Little Italys.

Assignments and Assessment. This activity has a summative (the tour) and a formative (communication) assessment (see Tables 9.2 and 9.3).

Table 9.2 Summative assessment for student tours.

Achievement level	Descriptor
Excellent	The final tour is complete and includes more than five sites, including narrations. These sites' significance within the neighborhood is well explained in the narration and all information is accurate. The tour demonstrates significant research and analysis of each site and its relationship to the Little Italy. Students were observed to work collaboratively and each contributed to problem-solving and to the production of the tour. The tour demonstrates mastery of the tour feature of Google Earth. The English used in the tour is fluent and contains vocabulary acquired during the research. Sentences are original, complex, and contain only a few errors.
Very good	The final tour is complete and includes at least five sites, including narrations. These sites' significance within the neighborhood is explained in the narration and the information is accurate. The tour demonstrates that the students researched each site and its relationship to the Little Italy. Students worked together and each contributed to the outcome. The Tour demonstrates successful use of the tour feature of Google Earth. The English used in the tour contains vocabulary acquired during the research. Sentences are original but may be simple, with some errors.
Satisfactory	The final tour is largely complete and contains at least five sites, with brief narrations. These sites' significance is touched on in the narration and information is brief and largely accurate. The tour demonstrates some research and a focus on its relationship to Little Italy. All students contributed to the outcome. The tour demonstrates that the students were able to use the tour feature of Google Earth. The English used in the tour contains a few new vocabulary words from the research. Sentences are original but simple; there are mistakes but these do not impede meaning.
Unsatisfactory	The final tour is incomplete and may contain fewer than five sites, with very short of missing narrations. These sites' significance is not apparent, and information may be missing or inaccurate. The tour demonstrates minimal research and a lack of focus on its relationship to Little Italy. Some students may not have contributed to the outcome. The tour demonstrates significant difficulty in using the tour feature of Google Earth. The English of the tour contains few new vocabulary words. Sentences may be copied from websites and/or errors in the narration and writing impede meaning.

Table 9.3 Formative assessment of student communication during the tour project.

Achievement level	Descriptor
Above expectations	The students mostly used English in their searches and were able to read, interpret, and take notes in English using the LMS. They were observed to work collaboratively in English with only a few uses of Italian, and used additional online resources (e.g., Google Translate) to understand difficult passages. The narrations composed for the tour were fluent, extended, and contained few errors in grammar or pronunciation. The overall outcome of the task was complete and engaging to viewers.
Meets expectations	The students used some English in their searches and read, interpreted, and took notes in English using the LMS. They were observed to work together and each student made an effort to contribute in English to the task. They used some online resources to translate information that was not understood in English. The narrations composed for the tour were relatively fluent and errors in grammar or pronunciation did not impede meaning significantly. The overall outcome of the task was complete and comprehensible to viewers.
Below expectations	The students used little English in completion of the task, and relied largely on translation or copying information from other websites. Their note-taking in English was minimal and their collaboration was limited and conducted mostly in Italian. They made limited use of online resources and their narrations were very simple and contained errors that impeded meaning. The overall outcome of the task was incomplete and/or incomprehensible, in part or whole.

Relation to TESOL Technology Standards for Learners and CEFR Reference Level Descriptors

TESOL Technology Standards:

- Goal 1 (Demonstrate foundational knowledge and skills in using technology)
  - Standard 1 (Demonstrate operational skills in using technology tools)
  - Standard 2 (Use available input and output devices).
- Goal 3 (Effective use of tools in language learning competence)
  - Standard 1 (Effectively use productivity tools)
  - Standard 2 (Effectively use language skill-building tools)
  - Standard 3 (Appropriately use tools for collaboration and communication)
  - Standard 4 (Use research tools appropriately)
  - Standard 5 (Understand use of tools for autonomy, collaboration, productivity)

CEFR Reference Level Descriptors:

- Global Scale: A2 (Can understand sentences related to areas of immediate relevance)
- Listening to Announcements and Instructions: B1 (Can understand simple technical information)
- Overall Reading Comprehension: A2 (Can understand short, simple texts)
- Reading for Orientation: B1 (Can find and understand relevant information)
- Reading for Information and Argument: A2 (Can identify information in simpler written material)

- Reading Instructions: B1 (Can understand simply written, straightforward instructions)
- Overall Spoken Interaction: A2 (Can interact with reasonable ease in structured situations)
- Formal Discussion: A2 (Can exchange relevant information)
- Goal-Oriented Cooperation: B1 (Can follow what is said)
- Overall Written Interaction: B1 (Can convey information and ideas)
- Overall Spoken Production: A2 (Can give a simple description or presentation)
- Addressing Audiences: A2 (Can give a short, rehearsed presentation)
- Cooperating: B1 (Can summarize the point reached in a discussion)
- General Linguistic Range: A2 (Has a repertoire of basic language)
- Phonological Control: A2 (Pronunciation is generally clear enough to be understood)
- Coherence: A2 (Can use the most frequently occurring connectors)
- Propositional Precision: A2 (Can communicate wht he/she wants to say).

Analyzing and Extending the Lesson: Application to Additional Contexts. In this task-based lesson, a teacher takes advantage of a connection between his Italian students' family histories of immigration to North America and North American Little Italys to have students research and create a tour of one Little Italy using Google Earth Outreach. When a surge in the pandemic closes schools to face-to-face instruction, he "flips" his instruction with two videos and works in hybrid mode to organize the students to complete the project online.

In this scenario, it is assumed that students have access to high-speed internet resources and devices at home that permit the use of Google Earth Pro. The activity is organized to take six days in this scenario but due to issues with infrastructure and the challenges of online instruction, it could reasonably be extended to ten days (or two weeks). Simpler, less advanced tools such as Google, Bing, or Apple Maps also provide students in classrooms with less bandwidth opportunities to explore and use web-based resources available on smartphones or other devices to create visual presentations using simpler tools such as PowerPoint or other web-based tools such as Book Creator (n.d.).

Scenario Two: Using Book Creator Online to Practice Grammar

The Scene. In the second vignette, Michelle Lee struggled to motivate some under-achieving high school students in Hong Kong. Her students were bright but not academically oriented and had poor results on the grammar portions of the standardized English exam. In her conversations with her students about English, Ms. Lee learned that her students were multimodally oriented and enjoyed using English in contexts that combined their interests in popular culture with technology. When classes were placed online due to a surge in the Covid-19 pandemic, Ms. Lee decided that now was the time to engage her students in an online e-book-making contest in which they wrote and recorded brief paragraphs using second conditional constructions.

Analysis: Challenges and Opportunities. As in Scenario One, a planned activity using digital technologies became even more relevant and needed in the circumstances of the pandemic. Ms. Lee began to consider supporting these unmotivated students by creating e-books. She chose Book Creator (n.d.) as the platform on which the students would compose their e-books. This free online application has many advantages:

1) A teacher can create interactive e-books by utilizing several functions, such as text, image, audio, and different layout.

2) Teachers can easily insert various materials into Book Creator by using the "import" function. Specifically, photos, videos, audio files, webpages, and multiple e-resources can be imported to make the e-book more multimodal and (aesthetically) more attractive.

3) Built-in dictionaries, specifically designed for the target students, can be added to the e-book. For instance, students can click the underlined (unknown) words, check their meanings in the dictionary section, and return to the main story.

4) Teachers can add receptive-oriented activities (e.g., reading comprehension quizzes) or productive-oriented activities (e.g., speaking or writing tasks) to the e-book for self-study. More specifically, a teacher can embed Flipgrid (a free video discussion platform) into the e-book.

5) Students can record a video about the benefits of walking while utilizing the grammar and vocabulary they have learned from the e-book.

6) Students can also view other students' videos and give them a comment on Flipgrid, which can further facilitate peer supports and interaction with others.

Instructional Plan. Ms. Lee announced the project to her students the following week in a synchronous, scheduled class meeting through the school's LMS, and in an email she sent to all the students with detailed instructions. She also recorded the class and placed a link to the recording for her students on the LMS site, along with the link to a tutorial on using Book Creator that she had found on YouTube. The students did not seem excited at first, but after she showed them some examples of books that had been created using Book Creator, they seemed more intrigued.

The assignment for the students was to create an e-book in groups of three in which, on each page, the students wrote one or more sentences using the second conditional to describe what they would do if they won HK$10,000. The book must have at least seven pages plus a cover. Each page should contain one or more sentences describing what they'd do in the second conditional and at least one photograph of themselves illustrating the sentence(s). In addition, the students needed to use Book Creator's recording feature to record themselves reading each page. She also explained that when the books were complete, the class would read all of the books together and vote on the best book.

Ms. Lee assigned students to groups on the LMS. To assist them in the assignment, Ms. Lee conducted a brief review session of the second conditional and included a link to a YouTube video reviewing the second conditional on the assignment page of the LMS. She also demonstrated the use of Book Creator, including how to sign in as a student. Then she let the groups begin to work and met with each group individually in chat to be sure they understood the assignment and were on track.

The students worked on their books over the next three days, uploading drafts to the LMS for Ms. Lee to check in the next class meeting. By Day 4 of the assignment, all groups had completed a draft of their book and were ready to share.

1) Materials:
   a) Student home devices
   b) Home Wi-Fi or smartphone data
   c) Book Creator (n.d.)
   d) School Learning Management System (LMS).

2) Learning Mode: Synchronous online for lecture, discussion, and activity; Groups of three students for making e-books
3) Time: Four 40-minute sessions (160 minutes in total)
4) Sequence of Activities:
   a) In Session 1, the teacher introduces the assignment and demonstrates the use of Book Creator during a synchronous online session
   b) The teacher groups the students and reviews the use of the second conditional
   c) The class brainstorms ideas and the teacher records these for sharing with the students
   d) The teacher records this session for replay on the class's LMS along with other materials such as a YouTube tutorial in using Book Creator
   e) In Session 2, the students begin to work in small groups on their Book Creator e-books synchronously on the class's LMS
   f) The teacher circulates among groups, checking on the use of second conditional and encouraging the use of new vocabulary
   g) In a summative whole-class discussion, the teacher reviews progress with the students and prepares them for the next session
   h) In Session 3, the students and teacher continue working synchronously, following the same procedures as Session 2.
   i) In Session 4, the students complete their e-books and the teacher checks them
   j) If time remains, each group shares their e-book and the class votes on the best one;
   k) If no time remains, the students share in the next session;
   l) Subsequently, the class reviews second conditional and the teacher gives a short test to check individual learning of the target structure.

Assignments and Assessment. This assignment has one assessment for the group e-books.

Table 9.4 Assessment of student e-books.

Achievement level	Descriptor
Excellent	The group's e-book was complete and contained seven or more pages with content that was substantial and original. There were few if any grammatical or spelling errors; vocabulary was advanced and correctly used. The writing was logical, clear, and direct. The group made inventive use of the features of Book Creator (page color, fonts, inclusion of photographs) and included a meaningful photo illustration. Each student in the group recorded the reading of at least one page and read clearly and comprehensibly.
Very good	The group's e-book was complete and contained at least seven pages with content that was mostly substantial and original. The sentences were mostly grammatical and there were few errors in spelling and usage. Some vocabulary was advanced and correctly used. The writing overall was logical, clear, and direct. The group made some use of the features of Book Creator (page color, fonts) and included a photo illustration on each page. More than one student in the group recorded the reading of the pages. The recordings were comprehensible.

(Continued)

Table 9.4 (Continued)

Achievement level	Descriptor
Satisfactory	The group's e-book was complete and contained seven pages with content that was complete and sometimes original. The sentences were mostly grammatical with only a few errors in spelling or usage. A few new vocabulary words were used. The writing overall was logical and intelligible. The group included basic uses of the features of Book Creator and there were photo illustrations. Each page was read and recorded by a member of the group, and the recordings were mostly comprehensible.
Unsatisfactory	The group's e-book was incomplete and contained fewer than seven pages with content that was incomplete on some pages. Some sentences were ungrammatical or incomplete with errors in spelling and usage. Few new vocabulary words were used. The writing overall was not clear and minimal. The group did not use many of the features of Book Creator and there were few photo illustrations. The pages were not read or the recorded reading was poor or incomprehensible.

Relation to TESOL Technology Standards for Learners and CEFR Reference Level Descriptors

TESOL Technology Standards:

- Goal 1 (Demonstrate foundational knowledge and skills in technology for a multilingual world)
  - Standard 1 (Demonstrate basic operational skills in technology tools and internet browsers)
  - Standard 2 (Use available input and output devices)
  - Standard 4 (Demonstrate basic competence as users of technology).
- Goal 3 (Effectively use and critically evaluate technology-based tools as aids in the development of their language learning competence)
  - Standard 1 (Effectively use and evaluate productivity tools)
  - Standard 2 (Appropriately use and evaluate language skill-building tools)
  - Standard 3 (Appropriately use and evaluate tools for communication and collaboration)
  - Standard 5 (Recognize the value of technology to support autonomy, creativity, collaboration).

CEFR Reference Level Descriptors:

- Global Scale: A2 (Can communicate in simple and routine tasks ... Can describe in simple terms aspects of his/her background)
- Goal-Oriented Cooperation: A2 (Can communicate in simple and routine tasks)
- Information Exchange: A1/A2 (Can ask and answer questions about themselves/ Can exchange limited information on familiar and routine operational matters)
- Overall Written Production: A2 (Can write a series of simple phrases and sentences linked with simple connectors)
- Creative Writing: A2 (Can write about everyday aspects of their environment)
- General Linguistic Range: A2 (Can use basic sentence patterns)
- Vocabulary Range: A2 (Has sufficient vocabulary for the expression of basic communicative needs)

- Grammatical Accuracy: A2 (Uses some simple structures correctly)
- Thematic Development: A2 (Can tell a story or describe something in a simple list of points.)
- Coherence: A2 (Can use the most frequently occurring connectors to link simple sentenes)

Analyzing and Extending the Lesson: Application to Additional Contexts. In this project-based lesson, the teacher uses information from interviews with reluctant learners to motivate them to learn and use a basic English grammatical structure. When her school closes due to a surge in Covid, she adapts her lesson to maintain her students' attention and motivation.

The use of e-books has many applications in English language classrooms and can be used to help students practice many different grammatical structures and written genres. The multimodality of the platform is not necessary, but it is especially useful when working with younger students or, as in this case, with those at beginning CEFR levels. In many ways, the hybridity of the activity, mixing synchronous instruction with asynchronous videos and opportunities for student groups to meet outside class works well, but the same activity would also be highly useful post-pandemic, in face-to-face instructional contexts.

Scenario Three: Flipping a Bacteriology Unit for a Hybrid EMI Course

The Scene. In the third vignette that introduced this chapter, a bacteriology unit within a course on microbiology was "flipped" to provide students with additional support in learning many complex scientific terms. Siobhán O'Byrne was aware that her students, who already spoke English at an advanced level, were struggling to learn the extreme amount of Greek- and Latin-based vocabulary required and that this problem was in part responsible for the weak results of practice tests for an international exam.

Analysis: Challenges and Opportunities. Today and into the foreseeable future, it will be highly advantageous for engineers, scientists, and medical students and doctors to have at least a basic reading knowledge of English, because most scientific studies today are published in that language. In many additional cases, English Medium of Instruction courses and programs are becoming an increasing part of STEM graduate and professional programs internationally, especially across the Middle East and Asia (Başıbek et al. 2014; Fenton-Smith, Humphreys, and Walkinshaw 2017).

Content Language and Integrated Learning (CLIL) and Content-Based Instruction (CBI) are two approaches developed by applied linguistics to address the needs of students within EMI contexts (Coyle 2006; Heo 2006). However, in many cases there is little English language instructional support for students (Soruç and Griffiths 2018), and content instructors must consult with colleagues or find their own ways to provide language support.

Instructional Plan. Siobhán consulted with the Chair and several members of the English department at her university. She learned that in the pandemic, they, too, were struggling to support the learning of undergraduates and had turned to "flipping" parts of their instruction, in which they narrated presentations on PowerPoint, saved them as MP4 videos, and then uploaded them to their course LMSs. As an action-research project (Burns 2009), one of the English faculty members agreed to record one of Siobhán's lectures and use it as the audio narration of her PowerPoint for the lecture. In addition, she added captions with vocabulary and definitions that directly connected the vocabulary in the lecture to the images and diagrams on the PowerPoints. Then they saved the augmented PPT as an MP4 video, uploaded it to YouTube as unlisted, and linked the video to the lecture notes on the course LMS.

At first, the video served only as a supplement to the course, and Siobhán continued to deliver her lectures in face-to-face instruction. At the same time, she realized that she could create a comprehensive PPT, narrate and record it herself, and upload it to the LMS on her own. Soon she realized that recording the PPT and then giving the same lecture face to face was redundant. As an experiment, she assigned the lecture video to the class in preparation for the next day's class and used face-to-face time to review the vocabulary and contents with the students and conduct interactive discussions with the students in which she posed questions about vocabulary and concepts to students and so was able to immediately assess what students understood and where they needed additional review.

As the course progressed, Siobhán became increasingly proficient and efficient at producing narrated PPTs and saving them as videos. In the beginning she used the flipped format only once a week; but by the end of the course, she was using it every other day. She also realized that she was rapidly accumulating an entire set of course lectures on PPT and video, and that she could edit the PPT and re-record particular slides to improve the lecture series. Within two semesters, she had an entire library of lectures for her unit on bacteriology and was able to devote her face-to-face meetings with the students to interactive discussions.

1) Materials:
    a) PowerPoint (recent version) and computer for teacher
    b) Internet connection and YouTube account
    c) Home devices and internet connection for students
    d) Learning Management System.
2) Learning Mode: Flipped lectures and whole-class discussion
3) Time: Per video lecture, out-of-class time for students; standard one-hour lecture
4) Sequence of Activities (Note: This describes Siobhán's final procedure):
    a) Teacher prepares lecture notes and a PowerPoint with images, photos, diagrams and target vocabulary for the unit
    b) Teacher uses the "Record" feature of PPT to record the entire lecture
    c) Teacher polishes the recording, saves it as an MP4 video, and uploads it to YouTube with link on course LMS
    d) Students view the video outside class and take notes, including questions about concepts and vocabulary
    e) Class meets face-to-face and teacher briefly reviews contents of lecture
    f) Students ask questions from notes; teacher responds and asks formative questions to assess learning, with a final, short, ungraded quiz
    g) Process repeats for the next lecture.

Assignments and Assessment. This flipped lesson has one formative assessment, to check for student understanding of vocabulary and concepts (See Table 9.5).

Table 9.5 Formative assessment of student understanding of vocabulary and concepts.

Achievement level	Descriptor
Above expectations	Every student in the class watches the video out of class and comes prepared with extensive notes and questions about the concepts and vocabulary covered. The teacher formatively assesses the students' knowledge and finds that all have a basic understanding of the content, which increases with an interactive discussion and review. Students are able to identify and use new vocabulary terms during discussion and in the final minutes of the course are able to accurately identify and define at least 90% of terms.
Meets expectations	Nearly all students report watching the video and 75% take notes and come to class prepared to discuss it. The teacher formatively assesses the students' knowledge and finds that 80% have a basic understanding of the content, which increases with interactive discussion and review. Nearly all students are able to identify and use new vocabulary terms during discussion and in the final minutes of the course are able to accurately identify and define at least 80–90% of the terms.
Below expectations	More than 25% of students report that they "did not have time" to view the video and have come to class unprepared. The teacher formatively assesses the students' knowledge and finds that only 60% have a basic understanding of the content, which increases only slightly with interactive discussion and review. Half the students are able to identify and use new vocabulary terms during discussion and in the final minutes of the course are able to accurately identify and define fewer than 80% of terms.

Relation to TESOL Technology Standards for Learners and CEFR Reference Level Descriptors

TESOL Technology Standards:
- Goal 3 (Effectively use and critically evaluate technology-based tools)
  - Standard 1 (Use and evaluate productivity tools)
  - Standard 5 (Recognize value of technology to support autonomy).

CEFR Reference Level Descriptors:
- Global Scale: B2 (Can understand the main ideas of complex text on both concrete and abstract topics, including technical discussions)
- Overall Listening Comprehension: B2 (Can understand spoken language ...encountered in personal, social, academic or vocational life)
- Listening to Radio, Audio, and Recordings: B2 (Can understand recordings ...likely to be encountered in social, professional, or academic life)
- Watching TV and Film: B1 (Can follow many films in which visuals and action carry much of thee storyline)
- Formal Discussion (Meetings): B2 (Can participate actively in routine and non-routine formal discussion)
- Information Exchange: B2 (Can understand and exchange complex information)
- Note-Taking (Lectures, Seminars, etc.): B2 (Can understand a clearly structured lecture)

- Processing Text: B1 (Can summarize a wide range of factual and imaginative texts)
- General Linguistic Range: B2 (Has a sufficient range of language to be able to give clear descriptions)
- Vocabulary Range: B2 (Has a good range of vocabulary for matters connected to his/her field ...but lexical gaps can still cause hesitation and circumlocution)
- Vocabulary Control: B2 (Lexical accuracy is generally high, though some confusion and incorrect word choice does occur in communication).

Analyzing and Extending the Lesson: Application to Additional Contexts. In this scenario, a teacher in a content area working with students with relatively advanced proficiency in English uses "flipped" lectures to provide additional time for review and teaching of a unit on bacteriology.

As we have noted, situations such as these are increasingly common in countries in which English is the medium of instruction for students who speak it as a second or other language. Within highly technical fields, the use of complex terms of Greek or Latin origin can be very challenging for students, even when they excel in their knowledge of concepts, and can prevent them from excelling on standardized tests. One approach to helping students in this situation is to pre-record "flipped" lessons, allowing students to watch and rewatch a video and then come to class prepared to discuss and process material in greater depth.

However, it should also be noted that "flipping" lectures initially requires at least twice the time a teacher might usually devote to preparing a lecture. Not only must the instructor prepare lecture notes, he or she must also be knowledgeable in the techniques of video recording and set aside time to produce a video lecture, in addition to preparing materials such as formative quizzes and discussion notes for class meetings. Such preparation, especially in the case of classes that meet several times a week, can be overwhelming.

Our advice, in this case, is for teachers not to try to flip an entire class or even unit of study within a single semester but to begin slowly, offering a few flipped lessons the first time a course is taught and then revising and adding new lessons over repeated semesters until an entire unit or course of flipped lectures is produced.

In addition, we caution that students must be helped to adapt to this new approach. Many times, especially in undergraduate or secondary education, students become accustomed to "showing up" for class mostly unprepared, taking notes, and then studying in-depth after class (or sometimes just before an exam). Flipped instruction requires that students watch videos and take notes *before* they come to class, to maximize the quality of their time with the teacher. This is a radical shift in focus for some students and it may take a few weeks of practice before new habits of study take hold. However, once students do begin to prepare before class, their autonomy as learners will begin to grow and their need to "cram" before exams will decrease, leading to improved retention of information and performance on exams.

Let's Discuss

1) As a student or educator, what has been your experience of learning and teaching during the Covid-19 pandemic? What are the main problems you have observed for yourself and others, and how have you addressed these problems? What are the positive outcomes of adaptation that you have noticed?

2) Which of the different teaching/learning paradigms discussed in this chapter—online synchronous instruction; asynchronous online instruction; or hybrid asynchronous with face-to-face instruction—do you think offers the greatest learning potential for students, and why?

3) Of the changes in teaching and learning that you have either witnessed yourself or read about in this chapter, which do you think will survive or deserve to survive the pandemic and become routine in the years to come?

4) Which of the three scenarios for adapting social networking to classroom instruction do you think is most appropriate for the context in which you are teaching or will teach? What adaptations will you make, and what other possible uses of social networks do you see being adaptable to your classroom context?

References

Akçayır, Gökçe, and Murat Akçayır. "The Flipped Classroom: A Review of its Advantages and Challenges." *Computers & Education* 126 (2018): 334–345. https://doi.org/10.1016/j.compedu.2018.07.021.

Başıbek, Nurcihan, Mustafa Dolmacı, Behice Ceyda Cengiz, Burcu Bür, Yeşim Dileke, and Bayram Karaf. "Lecturers' Perceptions of English Medium Instruction at Engineering Departments of Higher Education: A Study on Partial English Medium Instruction at Some State Universities in Turkey." *Procedia—Social and Behavioral Sciences* 116 (2014): 1819–1825. https://doi.org/10.1016/j.sbspro.2014.01.477.

Book Creator. n.d. https://bookcreator.com.

Burns, Anne. *Doing Action Research in English Langauge Teaching*. New York: Routledge, 2009. https://doi.org/10.4324/9780203863466.

Burns, Mary. "Covid Has Cast a Dark Cloud on Education, but There are Some Silver Linings." UKFIET (December 2020). https://www.ukfiet.org/2020/covid-has-cast-a-dark-cloud-on-education-but-there-are-some-silver-linings.

Coyle, Do. "Content and Language Integrated Learning Motivating Learners and Teachers." https://www.academia.edu/21433291/Content_and_Language_Integrated_Learning_Motivating_Learners_and_Teachers.

Ellis, Rod. *Task-based Language Learning and Teaching*. Oxford: Oxford University Press, 2003.

Fenton-Smith, Ben, Pamela Humphreys, and Ian Walkinshaw. *English Medium Instruction in Higher Education in Asia-Pacific*. Multilingual Education 21. Cham: Springer, 2017.

Google Earth Outreach. n.d. https://www.google.com/earth/outreach/learn/creating-a-narrated-tour-in-google-earth.

Google Earth Pro. n.d. https://www.google.com/earth/versions.

Gütl, Christian, Rocael Hernández Rizzardini, Vanessa Chang, and Miguel Morales. "Attrition in MOOC: Lessons Learned from Drop-Out Students." In *Learning Technology for Education in Cloud: MOOC and Big Data from Third International Workshop, LTEC 2014 Santiago, Chile, September 2–5, 2014 Proceedings*, edited by Lorna Uden, Jane Sinclair, Yu-Hui Tao, and Dario Liberona, 37–48. Switzerland: Springer International Publishing, 2014.

Heo, Yook. "Content-Based Instruction." *Hawaii Pacific University TESOL Working Paper Series* 4, no. 2 (2006): 25–31.

Hew, Khe Foon, Chengyuan Jia, Donn Emmanuel Gonda, and Shurui Bai. "Transitioning to the 'New Normal' of Learning in Unpredictable Times: Pedagogical Practices and

Learning Performance in Fully Online Fipped Classrooms." *International Journal Educational Technology in Higher Education* 17 (2020): 57. https://doi.org/10.1186/s41239-020-00234-x.

Huang, Fang, Timothy Teo, and Jiayi Guo. "Understanding English Teachers' Non-volitional Use of Online Teaching: A Chinese Study." *System* (2021): 101. https://doi.org/10.1016/j.system.2021.102574.

Kerr, Philip. "How to Get Your Flipped Classroom Started." Cambridge University Press World of Better Learning (July 2020). https://www.cambridge.org/elt/blog/2020/07/01/how-to-get-your-flipped-classroom-started.

Kim, Dongho, Yongseok Lee, Walter L. Leite, and A. Corinne Huggins-Manley. "Educational Resource-Supported Online Learning Platform." *Computer Education* (2020): 156. https://doi.org/10.1016/j.compedu.2020.103961.

Kuhfeld, Megan, Jim Soland, Karyn Lewis, and Emily Morton. "The Pandemic Has Had Devastating Impacts on Learning. What Will It Take to Help Students Catch Up?" Brookings Institution (March 2022). https://www.brookings.edu/blog/brown-center-chalkboard/2022/03/03/the-pandemic-has-had-devastating-impacts-on-learning-what-will-it-take-to-help-students-catch-up.

Lee, YuYen, and Katherine I. Martin. "The Flipped Classroom in ESL Teacher Education: An Example from CALL." *Education and Information Technologies* 25 (2020): 2605–2633. https://doi.org/10.1007/s10639-019-10082-6.

Lewis, Karyn, Megan Kuhfeld, Erik Ruzek, and Andrew McEachin. *Learning during COVID-19: Reading and Math Achievement in the 2020–21 School Year.* Center for School and Student Progress, 2021.

McElrath, Kevin. "Nearly 93% of Households with School-Age Children Report Some Form of Distance Learning during Covid-19." United States Census Bureau (August 2020). https://www.census.gov/library/stories/2020/08/schooling-during-the-covid-19-pandemic.html.

Mok, Heng Ngee. "Teaching Tip: The Flipped Classroom." *Journal of Information Systems Education* 25, no. 1 (2014): 7–11.

Panopto. "Seven Unique Flipped Classroom Models: Which Is Best for You?" 2019. https://www.panopto.com/blog/7-unique-flipped-classroom-models-right.

Seynhaeve, Lindsey. "How to Flip Your Online World Language Classroom and Boost Engagement." Edutopia (October 2020). https://www.panopto.com/blog/7-unique-flipped-classroom-models-right.

Shyr, Wen-Jye, and Ching-Huei Chen. "Designing a Technology-enhanced Flipped Learning System to Facilitate Students' Self-regulation and Performance." *Journal of Computer Assisted Learning* 34 (2017): 53–62. https://doi.org/10.1111/jcal.12213.

Soruç, Adem, and Carol Griffiths. "English as a Medium of Instruction: Students' Strategies." *ELT Journal* 27, no. 1 (2018): 38–48. https://doi.org/10.1093/elt/ccx017.

Stone, Cathy, and Matthew Springer. "Interactivity, Connectedness and 'Teacher-presence': Engaging and Retaining Students Online." *Australian Journal of Adult Learning* 59, no. 2 (2019): 146–169.

Tratnik, Alenka, Marko Urh, and Eva Jereb. "Student Satisfaction with an Online and a Face-to-face Business English Course in a Higher Education Context." *Innovations in Education and Teaching International* 56, no. 1 (2019): 36–45. https://doi.org/10.1080/14703297.2017.1374875.

Turan, Zeynep, and Birgul Akdag-Cimen. "Flipped Classroom in English Language Teaching: A Systematic Review." *Computer Assisted Language Learning* 33 (2020): 590–606. https://doi.org/10.1080/09588221.2019.1584117.

Veldthuis, Mariella, Hani Alers, Aleksandra Malinowska, and Xiao Peng. "Flipped Classrooms for Remote Teaching during the COVID-19 Pandemic." *CSERC '20: Proceedings of the 9th Computer Science Education Research Conference* 16 (2020): 1–2. https://doi.org/10.1145/3442481.3442512.

Wang, Feng Hsu. "On the Relationships between Behaviors and Achievement in Technology-mediated Flipped Classrooms: A Two-phase Online Behavioral PLS-SEM Model." *Computers and Education* (2019): 42. https://doi.org/10.1016/j.compedu.2019.103653.

Wang, Yuping, and Grace Yue Qi. "Mastery-based Language Learning outside Class: Learning Support in Flipped Classrooms." *Language Learning and Technology* 22, no. 2 (2018): 50–74. https://doi.org/10125/44641.

World Bank, UNESCO, and UNICEF. "The State of the Global Education Crisis: A Path to Recovery." 2021.

Zhou, Di, Shuqiong Luo, Haoran Xie, and Gwo-Jen Hwang. "A Systematic Review of Research on Flipped Language Classrooms: Theoretical Foundations, Learning Activities, Tools, Research Topics and Findings." *Computer Assisted Langauge Learning* (2020). https://doi.org/10.1080/09588221.2020.1839502.

10

From IDLE to Academic Literacy

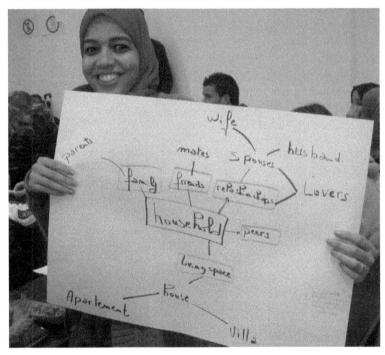

A student creates a semantic map for vocabulary from a short story downloaded from Project Gutenberg.

Introduction

Marina Cole: Teaching Editing and Proofreading Online in Doha, Qatar

Marina Cole has been teaching middle school students (aged 12–15) in a private language center in Doha, Qatar, for two years. Her students come to her in the late afternoon after attending a regular public or private school and sometimes struggle to

English Language Learning in the Digital Age: Learner-Driven Strategies for Adolescents and Young Adults, First Edition. Mark Dressman, Ju Seong Lee, and Laurent Perrot.
© 2023 John Wiley & Sons Ltd. Published 2023 by John Wiley & Sons Ltd.

pay attention in class. Despite rules about keeping smartphones turned off, students often text and sometimes play games on their phones.

The curriculum at Marina's center is fixed and little deviation is allowed, but on occasion she finds space for an activity of her own choice or invention. Generally, the prescribed lessons involve all four communicative modes—listening, speaking, reading, and writing. Her students have stronger receptive than productive skills, but she has found that by making a game of activities, she can sometimes coax students to practice dialogues or even have spontaneous conversations in class.

Marina has learned that her students, as writers, sometimes chat with other teens in English on MMORPGs, but they are shy about writing in more extended, paragraph-long formats. Their writing in English also not only shows the problems that early adolescents have with the conventions of writing in Roman script all over the world such as capitalization and punctuation but also some Arabic-specific features such as problems with the verb *to be* and the present-perfect tense.

These problems came to the fore during a free period in the curriculum when, at the conclusion of a lesson about how US families eat dinner, students were instructed to write a paragraph explaining to a US student what dinner at their home would be like. With some preparation and prompting, the students were able to complete intelligible drafts of 100–150 words, but the number of deviations from standard English left Marina feeling daunted. How could she begin to mark all the errors on these papers, much less begin to show students how to correct them?

Karin Lindgren: Creating a Covid-19 Board Game in Malmö, Sweden

Karin Lindgren teaches English in a *gymnasium* (sixth-form, high school) in Malmö, Sweden. Most of her tenth-year students are university-bound and are academically focused. Their English is remarkably fluent, due largely to habits of playing MMORPGs with international teams where the lingua franca is English and to their taste for US movies and pop music, but it is also very informal and peppered with slang. They are highly literate in Swedish but need to develop their academic English vocabulary. Many of her students anticipate careers in STEM fields, and Karin knows that they will need to learn to read—and eventually write—in English to succeed in these fields.

During the pandemic, Karin began to assign her students to read articles from popular science internet sites on the virology of Covid-19, instructing them to keep a journal with new vocabulary and interesting ideas and quotes to share with the class. Her students dutifully read the articles and took notes but during online class discussions Karin noticed their boredom and lack of enthusiasm for the activity and knew that because of this they were likely to forget everything as soon as the assignment ended. She also knew, however, that the readings she was assigning were at their reading and content knowledge levels, and that they could benefit greatly from reading them. How, she wondered, could she revise her activity to make it more engaging and memorable for her students?

Ji-Hoon (John) Jeong: Teaching Discussion in a Korean University

Ji-Hoon (John) Jeong is a Korean-Canadian assistant professor of English at a private university in Gyeonggi Province, South Korea. He primarily teaches first-year students in courses that focus on developing students' skills in speaking and writing in academic contexts. Dr. Jeong was born in Vancouver, British Columbia. His parents were both born in Korea and he visited many times in his youth, although he lived mainly in Vancouver and attended university there.

Dr. Jeong has struggled with conducting discussions among his students. Many of them, in contrast to stereotypes and their own self-beliefs, are fully conversational in English, although they are more comfortable reading and writing. They have few problems speaking with him one-to-one, but when he has attempted to pose a discussion question to the whole class, they sit quietly, waiting for him either to call on them or for him to lecture. Dr. Jeong discussed this problem with colleagues, who told him that it was because Korean classrooms are lecture-based with little open discussion due to Confucian ideals, which discourage students from speaking unless spoken to by their teacher (DeWaelsche 2015).

Many of the students are interested in international careers in business and are studying English and other foreign languages in anticipation of careers abroad. Dr. Jeong knows that their reticence to speak up within a group will be a problem for them, so he has continued to work with his students to teach them discussion techniques within a formal context, but with little success.

But recently, two things happened that opened an opportunity for teaching. First, the National Assembly passed a bill allowing K-pop stars to postpone military service from age 28 to 30, prompting discussion nationally that top groups like BTS might be exempted entirely if they received international recognition, such as a Grammy award (BBC 2020). Second, the Covid-19 pandemic forced a shift from face-to-face to online instruction. How, Dr. Jeong wondered as he made the transition to teaching online, would this affect his attempts to hold discussions? And could the controversy over mandatory service for K-pop stars be enough to coax his students to discuss the topic in class?

Discussion

In this chapter, we discuss ways to use strategies taken from ubiquitous digital resources to develop the academic literacy of students. By academic literacy, we refer to the choices in vocabulary, expressions, sentence structures, and general tone—the diction—of written and spoken expression characteristic of formal scholarship and conventional print journalism. This is the formal register (version or "dialect") of English—of business, scholarship, and professions—with some variation according to the region of the world in which it is used.

The Registers of English
A register is a mode or way of speaking and writing that is appropriate to a particular context and that signals the user's understanding of the context's linguistic norms. In English, registers signal an understanding of context rather than relationships between speakers. Registers are not formalized but depend on a speaker's cultural knowledge of appropriate choices of words, expressions, and sentence structure. A site from Lund University (2021) in Sweden explains four distinct registers in English: **Familiar.** This is the least formal register of English. It is often used to send short, abbreviated messages to friends through texting or phrases rather than elaborated sentences.

(Continued)

Informal. An egalitarian, public form of address allowing the use of contractions and often dialectic pronunciation and word choice, including slang. It is used among friends and in public settings to express commonality and "plain talk." This is the speech of most YouTubers and social media. It is the register people commonly use in non-professional, everyday settings.

Formal. This is academic English, noted for the use of standardized, formal grammatical rules and conventions and professional jargon. One convention is that the meaning of a message should be entirely contained within the text of the message, rather than relying on any implicit shared meaning between a speaker and their audience. Although there are variations across countries and contexts, these are slight. This is the English of publication and professionalism.

Ceremonial. This is the language of formal addresses and public statements. It is highly elaborated and may include literary allusions, elaborate metaphors, and other poetic devices. It is language that is designed to move an audience both emotionally and intellectually.

We also want to be clear at the outset that although we describe academic literacy as formal English, we do not mean to suggest that it is a *superior* version of the language. It is a register of language like any other, but with connotations of prestige, influence, and power. English, like nearly every language in the world, has many dialects and registers, each of which appears by convention to be appropriate within specific situations. In some languages, such Japanese or Korean or French, formal/informal address is morphologically, structurally built into the language, with specific affixes or suffixes and words conveying a speaker or writer's relationship to (and respect for) the addressed; in others, such as Arabic or Chinese, students learn to speak and write an almost entirely different language (Standard Arabic or Mandarin) from the dialect they use at home or in the street. English is more unified and structurally more egalitarian in some ways, but in others it is stylistically more unforgiving, with arbitrary, seemingly invisible codes that distinguish formal uses of the language from casual ones. These codes are heuristic rules of thumb rather than rules, and they are usually better acquired through practiced engagement than by rote.

Reading, writing, and speaking formal, academic English matters not because it is an objectively better form of the language but because of what its use conveys about a user and his or her message. Formal academic English is the language of power in society and in academia (Delpit 1998; Dressman 1993). It is critical for students because its use or non-use within formal contexts conveys much to others about the user and the message and can have serious consequences for both.

Informal registers of English, often characterized by their use of contractions, slang, colloquial expressions, local pronunciations, and generally non-Latinate vocabulary, are also typically those of IDLE and its texts, but again, these are not linguistically inferior to formal English, only different. In fact, there is evidence that informal language is not a degraded form of English but rather that it is the origin of new words and the expansion of English (Danesi 2010). Our position in this chapter, which is supported by the research literature on English education in both L1 and L2 contexts, is that teaching formal, academic English is not a matter of correcting students' "bad English" but rather a matter of helping students learn to read, write, listen, and speak with appropriate effect across a range of social contexts, and how and when to transition from one register to another.

Register, Dialect, Style: What Are the Differences?

A *register* is a way of speaking or writing a standard form of a language to express an understanding of the linguistic norms of a particular context in which it is used.

A *dialect* is a variation of a language that is mutually intelligible with other dialects. Dialects may vary in pronunciation, vocabulary, and grammar. All dialects are "regular" (follow rules and patterns), but some may be perceived as more or less "educated." Dialects often are used to express regional, ethnic or social class identity (e.g., Jeolla or Busan dialect in Korea or speaking in a Brooklyn [New York] accent). Sometimes dialects are so different (e.g., Moroccan Arabic) from other dialects that they may be considered separate languages.

Style has two meanings, depending on whether the term is used to describe formal or informal uses of a language. Formally, style refers to the precise set of rules used for speaking or writing (e.g., APA style, or, in the case of this book, the Chicago Manual of Style). Informally, it refers to an individual's personalized way of expressing themselves, including the regular use of particular words or expressions, pronunciation, inflection, and use of punctuation and sentence patterns.

The three scenarios that introduce this chapter present classroom contexts in which three savvy teachers work to build on IDLE or IDLE-like practices to lead their students into more formal modes of expression in English. Marina Cole must find a way to teach her Arabic-speaking students the conventions of writing not only in another language but in another script, and to do so in a way that is heuristic and game-like rather than dependent on the memorization of rules. Karin Lindgren sees that she must find a more engaging way to have her students read and study STEM-focused articles with advanced vocabulary. Ji-Hoon Jeong knows that his students, who anticipate careers in business and foreign affairs abroad, must overcome their reticence to speak if they are to succeed overseas. In all three cases, these teachers are also aware of their students' uses of English in more informal contexts online through games, chat, and other interactive formats. How can they build on the skills and affinities of their students to help them develop more formal, academically focused vocabulary and modes of expression?

Chapter Objectives

The central goal of this chapter is to consider the role of IDLE-type practices and activities in the development of more formal, academic uses of English. A major subgoal is to develop an appreciation for differences in informal and formal uses of language in English, and to understand how these differences manifest themselves in English in comparison to other languages and traditions. Readers will also become familiar with research in second-language writing, best practice in writing

(Continued)

assessment, the role of extensive reading, and translingualism as a pedagogical practice. A final subgoal is to learn about the application of IDLE-like digital practices for developing formal, academic literacy through three scenarios. By the end of this chapter, readers should be able to:

1) Explain how the conventions of formal, academic literacy in English differ from other languages.
2) Explain why formal, academic literacy is best acquired through practice and engagement in academic contexts rather than through studying rules.
3) Describe recent research on best practices in teaching academic literacy, with a focus on the work of three major scholars in this area.
4) Describe three scenarios for adapting IDLE-like practices to teaching academic literacy in classrooms.
5) Consider how the research, theory, and three scenarios in this chapter can be applied to the reader's pedagogical context.

Key Words

academic literacy; Language register; contrastive rhetoric; written corrective feedback (WCF); translanguaging/translingualism

Research and Theory

Research on Second-Language Literacy

A full review of the extensive and well-developed research literature on second-language literacy is beyond the scope of this chapter and is the subject of many other books and courses on English language education. In this section, we will focus on providing a very general introduction to trends and issues that relate directly to the role of informal language learning in the development of academic L2 literacy, by discussing the work of three major researchers in this field: Paul Kei Matsuda, Icy Lee, and Doreen Ewert.

Paul Kei Matsuda. Paul Kei Matsuda is a Japanese-born applied linguist educated and working in the United States and Asia. His area of focus is mostly university-level writing in American and East Asian universities. Matsuda has traced the history of second-language writing as an evolving integration of insights from applied linguistics and L1 composition studies (Matsuda 2003). His early area of focus was contrastive rhetoric (Matsuda 1997), an approach in which the focus of instruction is not at sentence level, but rather at the level of structural organization which in turn influences word choice and sentence structure. Matsuda's model of contrastive rhetoric describes how decisions by L2 writers are influenced not only by their L1 and cultural and educational backgrounds but by additional prior experiences of writing in the L1 and the L2. These become salient in the context of producing a text that is shared with a reader, who also has prior linguistic, cultural, educational, and rhetorical experiences in the L2 (and perhaps the same or different L1).

This process is dynamic—it depends on multiple contexts that change with the writing task—and bidirectional, in that it also depends on how a reader understands and responds to the text of the writer. Thus, "In order to mediate the differing backgrounds that the writer and the reader bring to the context of writing, the text must also reflect the writer's understanding of the reader's background and the genres in the discourse community shared by the writer and the reader" (Matsuda 1997, 56). Writing in an L2 in this model is not simply about learning a linguistic code or following a prescribed formula for a written genre; it is about joining a community of discourse as a contributing member with the knowledge and skill to help shape its conversation. This requires not following rules or imitating how others write but understanding their logic and beliefs and how these compare to and contrast with one's own beliefs and processes of understanding.

Informal modes and processes of writing, according to Matsuda and Nouri (2020), have much to contribute developmentally to entering more formal discourse communities. They note that in English the line between informal and formal uses of the language is often blurred, and that within formal settings, much of the daily writing done (writing short notes, messaging, annotating documents) is relatively informal.

They also note that all formal writing is, by definition, high stakes, with lasting consequences for the writer's future education, career, or finances. But, paradoxically, high-stakes situations also provide the least advantageous conditions for learning: Because so much is at stake, learners often "freeze up" or are reluctant to take risks or try new approaches. In low-stakes situations (and there must always be something at stake for activities to be authentic and worthy of engagement), in which consequences are minor and not lasting, learners are released from constraints and are willing and able to push the limits of their knowledge and abilities. These are also precisely the conditions of IDLE. By creating IDLE-like writing activities that are familiar and comfortable and that challenge writers to push themselves to write more, to write in different genres, and to interact with others, writers can begin to move into zones of greater and greater formality in their writing, with confidence, fluency, and a sense of belonging.

Icy Lee. The work of Icy Lee, a Hong Kong-based scholar, focuses on writing assessment, the challenges of working with students on sentence- and paragraph-level composition in English, and especially on the Written Corrective Feedback (WCF) that teachers give to students, that is, marking errors on papers and focusing on issues of grammar, word choice, and mechanics. Lee has conducted research on virtually every area of assessment, feedback, and teacher education in second-language writing. As a single resource on her work on the teaching of L2 writing, we recommend *Classroom Writing and Assessment in L2 Classroom Contexts* (Lee 2017).

Lee's views on the value and best practice of corrective feedback on students' papers can be summarized as: Less is more. She points to the consequences of marking every error on student papers for teachers (exhaustion; burnout; a loss of the big picture of the purpose of writing) and students (a loss of self-efficacy; a sense of failure; anger and resentment; helplessness) and she also notes that typically, after hours of effort by teachers marking up essays, students do not learn from their mistakes. More typically, what they do learn is that writing is an impossibly difficult task that they cannot master and that they must depend on others to fix their errors, rather than develop editing and proofing skills themselves. If teachers must give feedback, Lee recommends focusing on one type of error per paper, focusing on meaning, taking a developmental long view of learning to write, and finally on commenting on the progress and good qualities of students' writing as well as the problems.

Beyond her work on WCF, Lee is a strong advocate for peer editing as a process, for the use of portfolios documenting students' progress as writers over time, and for the use of digital resources, including online and word-processing editors. She also reminds us that these are activities that often must be taught. Because students use Microsoft Word, this does not mean that they are aware of its ability to spell- and grammar-check their work, or to help them with finding alternative words using a built-in thesaurus. Peer-editing is also not a skill that comes naturally to students, who often must learn how to provide criticism and suggestions for editing in constructive ways. Again, the activities of IDLE lend themselves to learning all these editing, proofreading, and feedback-giving tasks.

Doreen Ewert. As we discussed previously in Chapter 5, one of the most powerful tools for building academic literacy is through what Doreen Ewert (2020) terms *extensive reading*. This is a practice in which students are encouraged (and given time and credit) to read a wide range of books of their own choosing, and perhaps to keep a log of their reading with new vocabulary and some notes. By reading in volume and across multiple genres, through the process of statistical learning, students begin to acquire new vocabulary, greater fluency in reading, better comprehension, and as writers they dramatically increase their knowledge of complex sentence structures that, in an informal-to-formal writing program, they will begin to practice.

It might seem that the multimodal digital texts encountered in IDLE are very different in length and informality from the texts of extensive reading, but this is not always the case. As discussed in Chapter 5, many book-length texts are downloadable online, and many can be read aloud using text-to-speech apps. In addition, many videos enjoyed by informal English learners, such as TED Talks and podcasts from the BBC and National Public Radio (NPR) in the United States, have transcriptions available for download and are delivered in a journalistic register that blends some informal English practices (e.g., writing in first person) with discussions of complex, academically oriented subject matter. There are also many blogs and websites on academic subjects ranging from the arts and humanities to social sciences and STEM fields that provide access authentic, academically oriented content written and spoken in an academic/journalistic register. Moreover, these texts can often serve as models for students to create their own podcasts, blogs, and vlogs in which they can practice, develop, and contribute to academic discourse digitally (see Chapters 4 and 5). These activities can be used not only with university students but in both lower and upper secondary levels as well.

Translanguaging and Translingualism

An interesting development in bi- and multilingual research that has implications for improving formal writing ability in English is *translanguaging*, as it is described in primary and secondary settings (Cenoz and Santos 2020; García and Lin 2017; Wei 2017) or *translingualism*, as it is described in literary and university composition contexts (Canagarajah 2013; Kellman 2000). This is the practice of "mixing" languages as they are being learned, integrating structure, vocabulary, and transliterated idioms from an L1 to an L2 (or Ln) and back, in a process of hybridization that makes full use of a learner's and writer's linguistic repertoire in all known languages.

Code Meshing vs. Code Switching

The term *code meshing* is used by scholars of translanguaging and translingualism to describe the integration of two languages within one text. It is based on the assumption that the language resources of bi- and multilingual individuals are not cognitively separate but combined as one resource, and that in speaking or writing translingually, the goal is to integrate the resources of all one's languages into a single whole.

Code switching, on the other hand, is an older term that refers to the practice of moving back and forth between two (or more) languages as one speaks, often to performatively highlight one's knowledge of multiple languages. In this practice, the assumption is that languages are cognitively separate and that users are highlighting differences among languages as they speak.

Code meshing is typically regarded as a more creative and evolutionary process of pushing the expressive capacity of speakers and cultures forward, whereas code switching is a more conservative process of demonstrating mastery of traditional linguistic boundaries.

Dressman and Mahna (2022) studied the writing of Moroccan university students in their first year of English specialist programs across their three literate languages: Standard Arabic, French, and English. These students were basic writers in these languages and frequent users of IDLE. They were used to engaging online in informal writing in which they intermingled all three languages. Although not prompted, the students incorporated phrases from all three languages into essays written on equivalent topics in Arabic, French, and English. Dressman and Mahna found that the more students engaged in translingual practices, the longer their essays were, the more complex their sentences, and the higher the essays were rated holistically. They argued that writing translingually helped these students to express themselves in greater complexity, length, and creativity, and that translingualism could be a powerful transitional tool for helping students develop academic writing skill across all their literate languages.

Discussion: Academic Literacy in the Digital Age

In summary, distinctions in English between and among dialects and registers are not as clear as in, perhaps, other languages, and are often marked by subtle shifts in word choice, sentence complexity, and organizational patterns rather than structural elements such as morphology or syntax. Even within a single discipline such as language and literacy studies, a register or style of writing that would be appropriate and considered relatively formal within one journal might seem colloquial and inappropriate in another. The conventions and style of writing necessary to participate in the academic discourse of a community are best acquired through engagement with that specific community rather than through imitation or the learning of rules, because very often there are no formal rules. Similarly, learning to write formally at the sentence level and to follow the conventions of written language comes best through extensive reading and writing in low-stakes contexts rather than through having errors constantly marked down. Formal writing will not easily develop in high stakes writing assessments where points are lost for errors rather than gained for what was done well. In the end, assessments are evaluative, not instructive. No student ever learns anything constructive from exams or their scores, but rather through practice in constructive, supportive contexts.

In the digital age, distinctions among informal and formal registers in English are frequently blurred, and the focus is increasingly on communicating effectively within a specific discourse community. Even in print-focused communications, it is more accurate to describe the distinction between writing formally and informally as a continuum—a glide rather than a divide—with many gradations between the slangy, acronym-laden, translingual discourse of chat rooms and video games and the jargony, acronym-laden, Latinate discourse of academic and professional meetings and publication. In this way, students who come to English through IDLE have an advantage when it comes to acquiring formal, academic English. Just as they "picked up" and learned to use informal English by hanging out on the internet and watching television, so, too, they can "pick up" and learn to use academic English by hanging out with books and blogs, listening to podcasts and watching videos where more formal, extended uses of English are the norm. It is only a matter of pointing out and helping them to transfer their own practices from informal to formal venues.

Practical Applications in the Classroom

Scenario One: Teaching Editing and Proofreading Online in Doha, Qatar

The Scene. Marina Cole has been working to teach editing and proofreading to early adolescents in a language center in Doha, and in the pandemic, she has been faced with the additional problem of keeping her students engaged and focused during online sessions. After some delay, she has finally received essays from her students explaining to students in the US how Qatari families eat dinner, and now she is looking for a way to teach them proofreading and editing skills.

Remembering how much her students enjoyed competitive activities and using their smartphones when they didn't think she was looking, Marina had an idea: She would write a composite essay of the major problems students were having, put students into teams, and have them compete to find and fix all the errors in the essay.

Analysis: Challenges and Opportunities. English teachers in both L1 and L2 contexts face similar challenges in giving corrective feedback to students on their writing. As Lee (2004, 2017) and others (Bitchener and Knoch 2009; Hillocks 2008) have noted, excessive correction of students' essays not only has the opposite intended effect on students' confidence as writers, sending a message that they can never "get it right" when they write and forcing them to focus more on form than on substance in their writing, it is also time-consuming and professionally debilitating for teachers. Yet, the challenge of finding ways to help students improve the mechanical and grammatical accuracy of their writing persists, and most teachers believe they are not "doing their jobs" if they don't point out students' errors in their essays.

Another way to view this challenge, however, is to see it not as one of correcting students' mistakes but of finding ways to help them monitor and self-correct their own errors as they write and to become more independent writers. Viewed from this perspective, when teachers correct students' errors for them it leaves the students depending on the teacher's knowledge instead of learning how to find and correct errors themselves.

One possible response to this challenge is to use software programs like Grammarly or Scribens or even the spelling and grammar checker on Word for feedback. However, our review of these programs (at least of the free versions) has found that the feedback they provide is limited and sometimes inaccurate. Moreover, dependence on these programs does not build independence for students in the long run.

An alternative approach relies on two things—the power of "group thinking," or cooperative problem-solving and learning through peer editing (Alharbi 2019), and the fact that the most consistent errors in students' writing are also consistent across essays within the same linguistic and cultural context—to alert students to errors and ways to "fix" their own writing through an activity that is both engaging and face-saving. In this approach, groups of writers are challenged to find and correct the errors of a fictional student writer whose essay (composed by their teacher) contains a composite of the most common errors made by students in a writing assignment. A competition among the groups adds a gaming aspect that is highly motivational, and students are prompted to use online resources and their smartphones as well. Once alerted to the mistakes they have generally made in their essays, the students are then instructed to peer-edit each other's essays to find and correct the types of errors targeted by the teacher.

Finally, allowing students to use their smartphones for learning when they are at home (e.g., during the pandemic) instead of laptops shared by siblings frees devices for families and encourages students to use their phones for more than playing games, messaging, and watching videos. Students are also typically more accustomed to using phones, and this adds an informality to the task of proofreading and editing that can build confidence.

Instructional Plan. In preparation, Marina read through all her students' essays and identified the five major problems she saw across them. She composed an essay, fictionally written by the class mascot, Caesar, that imitated the students' essays and contained the five types of errors, and then organized her class into groups of four with each group receiving a link to a different Google doc containing the essay. To make the activity more engaging for the students she also used the "suggestion" feature of Google Docs (each team had the same essay but a different link) to track the students' progress on their smartphones.

Marina prepared a short introductory lesson and PowerPoint with the five errors to project as a reference for the class and shared the PPT on her screen during live, whole-class instruction. She also uploaded it to the course's Learning Management System (LMS). The students were excited to use their smartphones for the editing and to work together on Google Docs. When they were finished, Marina shared each group's editing of the essay with the whole class synchronously and they voted on the best revised essay.

To follow up, Marina reviewed the five major problems across the essays and their revisions. She then instructed the groups to proofread and edit each other's essays on Google Docs and then the students revised their own essays using their peers' proofreading suggestions. In the end, the essays were not "perfect" but they were much improved and Marina was delighted that the students had been able to edit their own work and learn much from the experience that could be applied to future writing activities.

1) Materials:
    a) Google docs
    b) Students' smartphones
    c) Learning Management System (LMS)
    d) Students' home internet.
2) Learning Mode: Small groups of four students each, connected through the LMS and Google Docs
3) Time: Two class periods (45 or 50 minutes each)
4) Sequence of Activities:
    a) On Day 1, students are organized into groups of four students each
    b) Introduce five patterns of error in essays written by students
    c) Sharing the teacher's screen, show the example of the essay written by the fictional student, Caesar
    d) Explain the task for each group as a competition to find and correct the errors in Caesar's essay
    e) Give each group their link to the essay on Google Docs
    f) Show students the editing "suggestion" feature on Google Docs
    g) Allow students 20–25 minutes to make the corrections to the essay
    h) If time remains at the end of class, begin to share with the whole class each group's revision of the essay; discuss decisions that were made in revising as a whole class, and discuss any problems the students had
    i) On Day 2, begin with a quick review and then complete the review of all the groups' revisions
    j) Discuss with the students their processes for finding the errors and what they learned
    k) Return students' own essays to them and instruct them to work together to revise each other's essays
    l) Collect revised essays and discuss the project
    m) After class, review the revisions made by students on their essays and evaluate the process.

Assignments and Assessment

This activity has two possible assessments: 1) an assessment of students' ability to find errors on their individual essays and correct them; and 2) A formative assessment by the teacher of the success of the exercise (see Tables 10.1 and 10.2).

Table 10.1 Assessment of student peer-editing.

Achievement level	Descriptor
Excellent	Nearly all errors in the text are identified and revised appropriately. The revisions retain or enhance the meaning of the text and stylistically add to the fluency of the writing, its informational content, and its aesthetic quality. Additional errors or problems not specifically named among the five errors are also identified and appropriately corrected.
Very good	Most of the errors in the text are identified and revised appropriately. The revisions do not significantly change the meaning of the text and are stylistically appropriate. They may add to the essay's fluency, informational content, and aesthetic effect. Some additional errors may also be revised appropriately.

(Continued)

Table 10.1 (Continued)

Achievement level	Descriptor
Satisfactory	Examples of all five errors are identified and corrected in the revision, indicating that students were able to compete the task successfully. Revisions may be awkward stylistically but meaning is retained. Overall, the essay shows evidence of improvement, but some additional revision may be required.
Unsatisfactory	Only a few errors are identified and corrected. Some attempts to correct and revise the essay alter the meaning of the text, indicating that the students' have either not understood the task or the grammatical and mechanical principles to be applied. Overall, there is little improvement in the essay. Additional instruction and assessment are required.

Table 10.2 Formative assessment of assignment for student engagement and productivity.

Achievement level	Descriptor
Above expectations	Students were enthusiastic and all groups were able to complete the task with little coaching from the teacher. All groups' revisions were at the Excellent or Very Good level. Students made productive use of online tools on their smartphones. When questioned, students could explain their reasoning for revisions made to the essay by their group.
Meets expectations	Students worked cooperatively and completed the task with some hints and additional instruction from the teacher, for the whole class and/or individual groups. Students made use of online tools and their smartphones. Most groups' revisions were Satisfactory or above. Students could give appropriate reasons for their revisions.
Below expectations	The groups struggled and needed additional instruction and whole-class review by the teacher. Some groups found few errors and struggled to correct those they found, and were unable to obtain assistance from online resources. Additional instruction in the basic principles of grammar and mechanics will be needed.

Relation to TESOL Technology Standards for Learners and CEFR Reference Level Descriptors

TESOL Technology Standards:

- Goal 1 (Demonstrate Knowledge of Basic Technology and Internet tools)
  - Standard 4 (Demonstrate basic competence as internet users)
- Goal 3 (Use and Evaluate Tools for Developing Language Competence)
  - Standard 2 (Use and Evaluate Skill-Building Tools)
  - Standard 3 (Use and Evaluate Tools for Collaboration)
  - Standard 5 (Recognize use of tools for autonomy and lifelong learning).

CEFR Reference Level Descriptors:

- Global Scale: A2 (Can understand sentences and frequently used expressions related to areas of most immediate relevance)
- Overall Reading Comprehension: A2 (Can understand short, simple texts on familiar matters of a concrete type)

- Reading for Orientation: A2 (Can find specific, predictable information)
- Goal-Oriented Cooperation: A2 (Can understand enough to manage simple, routine tasks)
- Overall Written Production: A1 (Can give information about matters of personal relevance)
- Reports and Essays: A2 (Can produce simple texts on familiar subjects of interest)
- Identifying Clues and Inferring: A2 (Can deduce the meaning and function of unknown formulaic expressions)
- Asking for Clarification: A2 (Can ask for clarification about key words or phrases)
- Processing Text: A2 (Can pick out and reproduce key words and phrases or short sentences)
- General Linguistic Range: A2 (Has a repertoire of basic language)
- Grammatical Accuracy: A2 (Uses some simple structures correctly, but still systematically makes basic mistakes)
- Orthographic Control: B1 (Spelling, punctuation, and layout are accurate enough to be followed most of the time.)
- Flexibility: B1 (Can exploit a wide range of simple language flexibly)
- Coherence: A2 (Can use the most frequently occurring connectors to link simple sentences).

Analyzing and Extending the Lesson: Application to Additional Contexts. The use of Google Docs and group editing processes before peer and teacher editing of essays is a powerful and flexible tool for addressing persistent grammatical and mechanical problems with student writing, for developing independent habits of self-monitoring in students, and for reducing the wear-and-tear of giving corrective feedback by teachers.

In this scenario, teacher Marina Cole chose to focus on basic grammar usage and mechanics at the middle-school level, but the same instructional approach could be adapted for high school or university students and adjusted, depending on the proficiency of the writers, to a broad range of stylistic and organizational issues. However, naming a class mascot as the fictional author may be inappropriate for older students, and not appreciated by them; in this case, a fictional student "in another class" may be more appealing.

We conclude that while this approach to giving writers feedback and teaching them to self-monitor via peer editing and Google Docs is highly effective, when combined with teacher feedback focused on broader and often more sophisticated issues of rhetorical style it is even more effective. There is, in our view, an important role for teacher feedback and encouragement in the writing process, but this energy is better spent by teachers on higher-order writing skills than on matters like spelling, grammar, and mechanics.

Scenario Two: Creating a Covid-19 Board Game in Malmö, Sweden

The Scene. Karin Lindgren teaches in an academically focused *gymnasium* in Malmö, Sweden. During the Covid-19 pandemic she has tried to increase her students' academic vocabulary and literacy by having them read and take notes from articles focusing on the virology of Covid-19. Her students have dutifully done the work but without enthusiasm and Karin knows this means they are less likely to process and remember the language they are learning.

Analysis: Challenges and Opportunities. Karin Lindgren and her students have a problem with learning in advanced academic contexts that many teachers and students in the same situation around the world face. The students are academically talented and motivated to achieve, but many times the information or tasks they are presented are not inherently engaging for them, and this leads to loss of learning as soon as the assignment itself passes or exams are completed.

One possible solution to this problem, as discussed in Chapter 7, is to "gamify" the learning and review process, requiring students to solve a range of problems and, where possible, take part in the actual design of games using content from their reading. Gamification sounds simple but its successful achievement depends (again as noted in Chapter 7), on the presence of four elements. It must:

1) Be recognized by the students as a form of *play*
2) Have a *clear set of rules*
3) Involve a *challenge or test of skill or knowledge*
4) Have an outcome that is *at stake* with more than one possible outcome.

In this case, creating a game is also highly motivating because it appeals to the students' sense of their academic capability and to some extent competitiveness within the class. If Karin can find a way to spur her students to challenge each other, they will study and retain far more than they could if the stakes were merely passing another exam.

Instructional Plan. After some conversations with the students' biology teacher, Karin searched online to select three core sites for her class. One site focused on the virology and structure of the virus (Physiopedia n.d.); the second focused on methods of studying the virus (Centers for Disease Control 2020); and the last one focused on the history of the pandemic (Centers for Disease Control n.d.). An additional link to the World Health Organization traced the history of the virus in charts (World Health Organization n.d.).

Karin decided that she would have heterogeneous groups of students in her class—balanced for gender, expertise, and academic skill—create an online board game that would trace the history of the virus as well as have students create challenging questions based on information in the readings. Because the readings contained links to additional articles and materials, she decided to allow students to use these as well, if they referenced them. As a check on the students' reading and to increase engagement, she also gamified her assignment by creating rules of play for the games that included point values for correct and incorrect answers on the games and the opportunity for one group to challenge the accuracy and sources of information. Students would need to provided citations for their game questions and submit them to her; she would provide these sources to groups that decided to challenge the accuracy of a question or source. There would be penalties for inaccurate questions and answers.

Karin discovered through a search on YouTube that Google Sheets could be used to create the board games. She found one instructional video that was very clear and posted a link to it on the class's LMS site (YouTube 2020) but with the instruction that students were to make the path of their game more representative of the timeline of the pandemic. Students would need to compose at least seven multiple-choice questions for their game. The questions would need to require information from the articles she supplied and were to be accurately worded and as challenging as possible.

The students were very excited to be placed in teams (groups of four) when Karin introduced the assignment during online teaching, and quickly began to work. Karin instructed the students to write seven multiple-choice questions with information from the readings. She gave them a brief lecture on how to write a good multiple-choice question and showed them a YouTube video on the topic (YouTube 2020). They were somewhat challenged by using Google Sheets to create a board game, but Karin had been careful to place one student whom she knew to have strong digital media skills in each group, and after a weekend of practice at home, each group soon had a workable board game under development. Early in the process, she realized that in addition to engaged reading, note-taking, and question writing, the students were also learning to collaborate in English and to develop advanced skills in using spreadsheets that were critical to their academic futures.

Karin was a member of every group and had access to all board games. She spent most of the sessions for the assignment visiting each group during each meeting and making suggestions. Within five class meetings, the groups had completed their games and were ready to play. Each group played each other's game over three days, keeping score of the points and refereeing challenges to questions. After another three days, play was concluded and Karin declared a winner, offering the winning team school-wide recognition and the opportunity to participate in planning the class's next assignment.

1) Materials:
    a) Home internet
    b) Student home devices
    c) Google Sheets
    d) YouTube (for video)
    e) Relevant online articles
    f) Learning Management System with synchronous video component.
2) Learning Mode: Online whole-class for introduction and closing discussion; online small groups for activities
3) Time: Ten fifty-minute synchronous sessions
4) Sequence of Activities:
    a) In Session 1, teacher introduces the activity and readings
    b) Students view YouTube video on making a board game on Google Sheets and discuss with teacher;
    c) Students are organized into heterogenous groups of four
    d) Students read articles, taking notes on Google Docs
    e) Teacher circulates online among groups, checking progress
    f) In Session 2, students continue to read and take notes;
    g) Teacher circulates online among groups, checking progress
    h) Students begin to discuss readings and outline questions
    i) In Session 3, teacher conducts a brief lesson on how to write a multiple-choice question with four possible answers and distributes a one-page example of strong and poor questions
    j) Students watch YouTube video to review the teacher's points and begin to write questions
    k) Teacher reviews each group's questions as they write them and makes suggestions for revision

l) In Session 4, the students continue writing multiple-choice questions under the teacher's supervision

m) In Session 5, students begin to construct their board game using Google Sheets

n) The students re-view the YouTube video on creating a board game (YouTube 2020) and consult with the teacher

o) The students begin to create a path that represents their reading of the history of the pandemic

p) In Sessions 6 and 7, the students continue to work on revising their questions and designing their board game

q) The teacher supervises each group's activities and discusses questions with them

r) In Sessions Eight and Nine, the groups play each other's games

s) The teacher acts as score keeper and referee

t) In Session 10, the teacher debriefs with the class in a whole-class session about their process and their reading, and announces the winning group

u) To demonstrate/evaluate individual student learning, the students take a quick ten-question multiple-choice quiz compiled by the teacher with rewritten questions based on the groups' board game questions.

Assignments and Assessment. This activity has two assessments: (1) an assessment of the groups' performance in reading the online information, note-taking, writing questions, and creating the board game (See Table 10.3); and (2) a ten multiple-choice question to assess the learning of each individual student, not included here.

Table 10.3 Assessment of student performance.

Achievement level	Descriptor
Excellent	The group worked collaboratively to create a board game based on the core articles that was challenging, creative, and effective. The group read and took clear, comprehensive notes on the readings, recording key vocabulary and concepts and using these to generate seven challenging questions that covered all three readings. The stem question was well-phrased and among the four alternatives there was only one clear answer. The distractors were plausible and of equivalent length, indicating that the students understood and applied principles from the teacher's lesson and the video. During play, all students participated and referred to the readings to answer correctly. Challenges to question accuracy were legitimate and well-grounded.
Very good	The group collaborated to create a board game based on the core articles that was relatively challenging, creative, and effective. The group read and took notes on the readings, recording key vocabulary and concepts. They used these to generate seven questions that covered the readings. The stem question was clearly phrased and among the four alternatives there was only one clear answer. The distractors were plausible and suggested the students understood and tried to apply principles from the lecture and/or video. During play, all students participated and demonstrated some reference to the readings. The group could give reasons to support any challenges to questions.

Table 10.3 (Continued)

Achievement level	Descriptor
Satisfactory	The group generally collaborated to create a board game based on the core articles that in some cases was challenging, creative, and effective. The group read and took notes on the readings, recording vocabulary and concepts. They used these to generate seven questions that covered parts of the readings. The stem question was generally clear and there was a clear answer. The distractors were relatively plausible. During play, most students in the group participated and could give reasons for their answers.
Unsatisfactory	The group was non-collaborative and only one or two members participated, or the board game was incomplete with questions that were not challenging. The group did not fully read or take notes. There were fewer than seven questions written and these did not represent the content of the readings. The stem question was not clearly phrased and there was not one clear answer. Distractors were confusing. During play, only one or two students participated.

To assess individual student learning, the teacher may select ten questions from the board games representative of the content and/or rewrite them to assess learning of the material from reading and discussion.

Relation to TESOL Technology Standards for Learners and CEFR Reference Level Descriptors

TESOL Technology Standards:

- Goal 3 (Effectively use and critically evaluate technology-based tools)
  - Standard 1 (Effectively use and evaluate technology-based productivity tools)
  - Standard 2 (Appropriately use and evaluate language skill-building tools)
  - Standard 3 (Appropriately use and evaluate tools for communication and collaboration)
  - Standard 4 (Use and evaluate technology-based research tools appropriately)
  - Standard 5 (Recognize the value of technology to support creativity, collaboration, productivity).

CEFR Reference Level Descriptors:

- Global Scale: B2 (Can understand the main ideas of complex text on both concrete and abstract topics ... Can produce clear, detailed text)
- Listening to Announcements and Instructions: B2 (Can understand announcements and messages on concrete and abstract topics)
- Overall Reading Comprehension: B2/C1 (Can read with a large degree of independence, adapting style and speed of reading to different texts/ Can understand in detail lengthy, complex texts)
- Reading for Information and Argument: B2 (Can obtain information, ideas and opinions from highly specialized sources)
- Formal Discussion (Meetings): B2 (Can participate actively in routine and non-routine formal discussion)

- Goal-Oriented Cooperation: B2 (Can help along the progress of the work)
- Information Exchange: B1/B2 (Can exchange, check, and confirm accumulated factual information/ Can synthesize and report information and arguments from a number of sources)
- Overall Written Production: B2 (Can write clear, detailed texts ... synthesizing and evaluating information and arguments from a number of sources)
- Identifying Cues and Inferring: B1 (Can identify unfamiliar words from the context)
- Processing Text: B1/B2 (Can collate short pieces of information from several sources/ Can summarize a wide range of factual and imaginative texts)
- General Linguistic Range: B2 (Has a sufficient range of language to be able to give clear description)
- Grammatical Accuracy: B1/B2 (Communicates with reasonable accuracy/ Good grammatical control)
- Vocabulary Control: B2 (Lexical accuracy is generally high)
- Propositional Precision: B2 (Can pass on detailed information reliably).

Analyzing and Extending the Lesson: Application to Additional Contexts. Gamification is a very effective way to move students from the more informal uses of language learned through IDLE activities to more formal, academically powerful uses of English. In this scenario, a teacher gamified a reading assignment for her academically talented students, trusting in their English language literacy and technical skills to create a board game from scratch in ten sessions.

As designed, the assignment required a higher than usual skill and motivational level for the students. However, the assignment could be modified for students at lower levels of English and technological skills. For example, the teacher could read the first (or all sites) with the students, modeling appropriate note-taking skills and working with the class to identify key vocabulary and concepts, and more time could be spent on teaching students how to write multiple-choice questions. To reduce time and effort on the board game, the teacher could provide a template and all students would have to do is write questions and upload them, or the teacher could supply key elements of the game such as the die and question cards and students could design a game path and obstacles.

Scenario Three: Teaching Discussion in a Korean University

The Scene. Korean-Canadian Professor Ji-Hoon (John) Jeong has been searching for a way to teach discussion skills in his classes. His students anticipate careers overseas and he knows they will need to learn how to join discussions and argue for their point of view. However, the students are reluctant to speak up in class due to long-standing norms of interaction in Korean classrooms. When a controversial bill is passed in the National Assembly, he realizes that this issue might give students a reason to speak up. But then the Covid-19 pandemic shuts down face-to-face instruction and Dr. Jeong and his students must learn to navigate teaching and learning online.

Analysis: Challenges and Opportunities. The reluctance of Korean students to participate in class discussions is well documented in the research literature (Choi 2015; Kim 2013: Yun and Kim 2015), especially in US universities. The reason most typically cited is that Korean classroom culture is teacher-centered, with teachers lecturing most of the time, perhaps stopping to call on students, but seldom promoting student participation. This is compounded for Korean students in the United States by their insecurity in speaking English and culturally different conversational norms.

At the same time, research also shows that it is often easier for some individuals to participate in online chat than in face-to-face discussions (Ho and McLeod 2014; Lipinski-Harten and Tafarodi 2013; Pierce 2009), and that anxiety is reduced even further if users adopt an avatar, or disguise (Song, Kim, and Lee 2014; York et al. 2021). If Dr. Jeong can create a context for online discussion that lowers students' affective filters (Krashen 1982) and that they are interested in, he might be able to coax students into practicing—and then reflecting upon—the norms of classroom discussion.

Instructional Plan. Dr. Jeong was aware that his students were fans of the television series, *Squid Game* (IMDB n.d.). All over the university, he repeatedly heard students use "Squid Game" as a metaphor for all sorts of brutal, do-or-die, rule-bound situations, and so he knew the students would be intrigued and very motivated if he posed his activity as a Squid-Game exercise.

But he was also troubled by the idea of *eliminating* students if they made a mistake or of legitimizing the "ethics" of Squid Game through his assessment practices. He discussed his idea (in hypothetical terms) with some older, upper-class students and they agreed that grading students by Squid Game standards would increase anxiety, but they also thought that the comic-book violence of the series was not disturbing if it had no real consequences and that students might find playing a game with *virtual* Squid-Game consequences amusing.

Dr. Jeong decided that he would have his students write an essay of 400–500 words on the topic of the National Assembly's recent decision to postpone K-pop musicians' mandatory military service to age 30 (Yonhap 2020), and that as a pre-writing discussion he would open up the topic for discussion among the students in a whole-class chatroom of the class's LMS. He would have each student create an avatar as a guest to the class, disguising themselves from everyone but him, and just as in Squid Game, he would create different game tasks for each round of the discussion, from writing short position statements (with elimination for students who did not respond in time) to tasks requiring students to reply to each other's comments, and so on. He would briefly explain the tasks and rules of each round with reference to an article on to how make effective online comments (Davenport 2010) before the round was played.

One difference between Squid Game and his discussion activity was that students would be "eliminated" for breaking a rule during a phase but return in the next round. Each student, like the players in Squid Game, would begin with a fictional amount of "money" (₩1,000,000) and a percentage would be subtracted and placed in the winner-takes-all "jackpot" if they were eliminated in a round, and extra would be won if their post was commented on by a classmate. At the end of the game, the player with the most money remaining would win the fictional jackpot.

At the end of each round, Dr. Jeong held a live discussion session with his students online, in which he spoke about the discussion norm that had been the focus of the round, used examples from the chat, and asked students for their feedback. At the end of five rounds, he reviewed the discussion comments and then assigned the students to write an essay in which they used ideas from the chat (citing each other's comments) to argue their position on K-pop stars and mandatory military service. He formally assessed the students' essays but only informally assessed their participation in the discussion.

Dr. Jeong found that using the Squid Game to encourage discussion online helped to "break the ice" in his class. Many students individually expressed their excitement and enjoyment of the activity to him after class. The following week he opened another topic of discussion for the students ("Is Squid Game too violent?") without gamifying the activity (but using their avatars) and found that students were less reluctant to interact and were more likely to respond to each other's comments instead of merely stating their own positions.

1) Materials:
    a) Learning Management System chatroom
    b) Webpost on National Assembly decision (Yonhap 2020)
    c) Internet connection
    d) Teacher and student devices.
2) Learning Mode: Online whole-class synchronous chat
3) Time: Three class sessions, 50 minutes each
4) Sequence of Activities:
    a) In Session 1, teacher introduces the topic and shares an article or webpost
    b) Teacher explains that the class will have a discussion about this topic, following a modified version of Squid Game
    c) Teacher shares and explains the general rules regarding the jackpot and elimination
    d) Students create an avatar as a guest to the chatroom
    e) Teacher shares the game for Round One: "In 50–100 words and within five minutes, state your position on the National Assembly's decision to postpone mandatory service for male K-pop stars. Do not change the topic"
    f) Students begin to post comments in the chatroom;
    g) As students post, teacher "eliminates" students who stray from the topic or do not post within five minutes;
    h) Teacher debriefs with students, discussing successful comments and calling on students for their feedback.
    i) In Session 2, students play two rounds.
    j) Teacher reviews the game with the students, who are playing as their avatars
    k) Round Two: "In 50–100 words and within seven minutes, disagree politely with the position of one of your classmates. You will receive extra money if a classmate disagrees with your position"
    l) Students begin to post comments in the chatroom with same procedures as Round One.
    m) Round Three: "In 50–75 words and within five minutes, agree with one of your classmate's comments today. You will receive extra money if a classmate agrees with your previous comment"
    n) Students begin to post comments in the chatroom with same procedures as previous rounds
    o) In Session 3, students play a final round and review the entire discussion
    p) Round Four: "In 50–100 words and within ten minutes, summarize the discussion and your position, citing at least two classmates' comments. You will receive extra money if a classmate cites any of your comments"

q) Students begin to post comments in the chatroom with same procedures as previous rounds

r) Teacher conducts final discussion and assigns students to write an essay of 500–750 words stating their position on the issue and citing the comments of other students in the discussion

s) Future session: Teacher announces winner and shares best essays.

Assignments and Assessment

This activity has 2 assessments: (1) a formal assessment of the student essays; and (2) an informal assessment of the activity and subsequent online discussions (see Tables 10.4 and 10.5).

Table 10.4 Assessment of student essays about National Assembly policy.

Achievement level	Descriptor
Excellent	The student's essay is focused clearly on agreeing or disagreeing with the National Assembly's policy to delay military service for K-pop stars. The essay is well organized and contains multiple points and references to other students' comments in agreeing or disagreeing with the policy. Its tone is polished and academic and contains few errors in word choice, spelling, grammar, or mechanics. It meets the requirements for length (500–750 words) and contains appropriate headings and/or paragraph breaks. Vocabulary and choice of phrases are academic in tone and contain ideas taken from the discussion. The author cites all quotes and ideas, attributing them to the appropriate source.
Very good	The student's essay is focused on agreeing or disagreeing with the National Assembly's policy to delay military service for K-pop stars. The essay is organized and contains multiple points as well as some reference to other students' comments, both pros and cons. The tone is academic and contains relatively few errors in word choice, spelling, grammar, or mechanics. These do not interfere with the reading or meaning of the essay. It meets the requirements for length and includes paragraphing. Vocabulary and choice of phrases are mostly academic in tone and contain ideas taken from the discussion. The author cites quotes and ideas, attributing them to the appropriate source.
Satisfactory	The student's essay is mostly focused on agreeing or disagreeing with the National Assembly's policy but may speculate on other issues. The essay shows some sign of organization and contains multiple points as well as some reference to other students' comments. The tone is academic but may contain some slang. There are errors in word choice, spelling, grammar, or mechanics but these do not impede meaning, and the essay barely meets the length requirement. Some sentences may be run-on or incomplete, and there may be a few problems with paragraphing. Vocabulary and choice of phrases are mostly appropriate and contain ideas from the online chat discussion. The author cites some quotes and ideas, attributing most to sources.
Unsatisfactory	The student's essay is incomplete and/or wanders off topic. There is minimal organization and may not present both sides of the issue, with little or no reference to other students' comments. The tone is very informal and the author makes statements that are not referenced to evidence or other students' comments. The essay does not meet the length requirement. There are multiple errors throughout the essay that impede meaning at points. There are no quotes or quotes are not cited.

Table 10.5 Formative assessment of activity process and online discussions.

Achievement level	Descriptor
Above expectations	Evidence of the online chat sessions is clearly present in essays written by the students following the activity. In subsequent online discussions, a greater percentage of students contribute than before, and without encouragement respond to each other's comments, agreeing or disagreeing in a formal and polite tone. In live, spoken interaction, students are more willing to participate than before, by at least 30%.
Meets expectations	Evidence of the online chat sessions is present to some degree in essays written by the students following the activity. In subsequent online discussions, several additional students participate who previously did not. When encouraged, students respond to each other's comments as well as the teacher's. In live, spoken interaction, students are more willing to participate than before, by at least 20%.
Below expectations	There is little evidence of engagement with the online chat session in student essays following the activity. In subsequent online discussions, few students participate who previously did not. Although encouraged, students do not "follow" conversations and respond to each other's comments. In live, spoken interaction, nearly all the students still seem unwilling to participate, even if called on.

Relation to TESOL Technology Standards for Learners and CEFR Reference Level Descriptors

TESOL Technology Standards:

- Goal 2 (Use technology in socially and culturally appropriate ways)
  - Standard 1 (Understand that communication conventions differ across cultures)
  - Standard 2 (Demonstrate respect for others in use of information)
- Goal 3 (Effectively use and critically evaluate technology-based tools)
  - Standard 2 (Use and evaluate technology-based language skill-building tools)
  - Standard 3 (Appropriately use tools for communication and collaboration).

CEFR Reference Level Descriptors:

- Global Scale: B1/B2 (Can understand main points and produce simple, connected text .../ Can produce clear, detailed text on a wide range of subjects)
- Overall Reading Comprehension: B1 (Can read straightforward factual texts on subjects related to his/her field and interest)
- Reading for Information and Argument: B1 (Can recognize the line of argument in the treatment of the issue presented)
- Formal Discussion (Meetings): B1/B2 (Can put over a point of view clearly/Can participate actively in routine and non routine formal discussion)
- Goal-Oriented Cooperation: B2 (Can outline an issue or a problem clearly)
- Information Exchange: B1/B2 (Can exchange, check, and confirm accumulated factual information ... Can summarize and give an opinion)
- Overall Written Interaction: B1 (Can convey information and ideas on abstract as well as concrete topics)
- Notes, Messages, and Forms: B1 (Can write notes conveying simple information)

- Overall Written Production: B1 (Can write straightforward connected texts on a range of familiar subjects within their field of interest)
- Reports and Essays: B1/B2 (Can summarize, report and give an opinion about accumulated factual information/ Can write an essay or report which develops and argument)
- Taking the Floor (Turntaking): B1 (Can intervene in a discussion on a familiar topic)
- Cooperating: B2 (Can help the discussion along on familiar ground)
- Asking for Clarification: B1 (Can ask someone to clarify or elaborate what he or she has just said)
- Planning: B2 (Can plan what is to be said and the means to say it)
- Compensating: B1 (Can convey meaning by qualifying a word meaning something similar)
- Monitoring and Repair: B2 (Can correct slips and errors)
- Processing Text: B2 (Can summarize extracts from news items)
- General Linguistic Range: B2 (Has a sufficient range of language to be able to...express viewpoints)
- Sociolinguistic Appropriateness: B1/B2 (Can perform and respond to a wide range of language functions/ Can express themselves appropriately)
- Coherence: B1 (Can link a series of shorter, discrete simple elements into a connected, linear sequence)

Analyzing and Extending the Lesson: Application to Additional Contexts. In this scenario, a university professor in South Korea combined elements of a popular television series, gamification, and the use of avatars to practice discussion in an online chat setting. The product of this activity was a topical essay in which students incorporated points from the online discussion.

In addition to the controversial issues of Squid Game's violence and Darwinian ethos, we also discussed the "elimination" of students within rounds who did not "follow instructions" for the round carefully. Because the students in this situation were of university age and aware of the playful (and instructional) intention of the game (and lack of any real sanction for "losing" in a round), the risk of psychological injury in this case was minimal. However, among high-school and especially middle-school students, we do not recommend the use of the Squid Game metaphor in teaching.

Another concern with this activity might be that although its focus was building student confidence and teaching the basics of formal, polite discussion, these objectives were only indirectly measured through the essay. Our concern was that by giving the activity a "high-stakes" (get it right or you're eliminated) grade, we would achieve the opposite of building confidence and reducing students' anxiety about classroom discussion. We would also argue that the essay, while indirect, is a good measure of students' participation in the discussion, and in the rubric for the essay we specifically indicated that students were expected to write in response to the discussion.

Let's Discuss

1) As a student, what has been your best experience in acquiring academic literacy? How have you learned to read, write, speak, and participate in academic and professional conversations in English?

2) Does your experience align with the approaches to best practice described in this chapter? If yes, how has your experience aligned? If not, how is it out of alignment?

3) If your first language is not English, how would you compare the differences between formal and informal registers of your first language with English?

4) What is your opinion about using translingualism as a transitional practice for helping basic English writers extend and improve their formal writing?

5) In this chapter, differences between informal and formal English have been described as falling along a continuum rather than being clearly divided. If you had to create categories with examples and place them along that continuum, what categories would you create and how would you describe the differences between those categories?

6) As a student, what is your favorite go-to digital resource for writing and reading in formal, academic modes? As a teacher, what digital tools do you, or would you, introduce to your students to help them write more formally?

References

Alharbi, Mohammed Abdullah. "Exploring the Potential of Google Docs in Facilitating Innovative Teaching and Learning Practices in an EFL Writing Course." *Innovation in Language Learning and Teaching* (2019). https://doi.org/10.1080/17501229.2019.1572157.

BBC. "BTS: South Korea Passes Law Allowing K-Pop Stars to Postpone Military Service." 2020. https://www.bbc.com/news/world-asia-55147970.

Bitchener, John, and Ute Knoch. "The Value of a Focused Approach to Written Corrective Feedback." *ELT Journal* 63, no. 3 (2009). https://doi.org/10.1093/elt/ccn043.

Canagarajah, Suresh. Translingual Practice: Global Englishes and Cosmpolitan Relations. London: Routledge, 2013.

Cenoz, Jasone, and Alaitz Santos. "Implementing Pedagogical Translanguaging in Trilingual Schools." *System* 92 (2020): 10373.

Centers for Disease Control and Prevention. "Severe Acute Respiratory Syndrome Coronavirus 2 from Patient with Coronavirus Disease, United States." 2020. https://wwwnc.cdc.gov/eid/article/26/6/20-0516_article.

Centers for Disease Control and Prevention. "CDC Museum COVID-19 Timeline." n.d. https://www.cdc.gov/museum/timeline/covid19.html.

Choi, Jung Yun. "Reasons for Silence: A Case Study of Two Korean Students." *TESOL Journal* 6, no. 3 (2015): 579–596.

Danesi, Marcel. "The Forms and Functions of Slang." *Semiotica* no. 182 (2010): 507–517. https://doi.org/10.1515/semi.2010.069.

Davenport, Thomas H. "Six Ingredients for a Good Online Comment." Harvard Business Review, March 5, 2010. https://hbr.org/2010/03/six-ingredients-for-a-good-onl.

Delpit, Lisa D. "The Silenced Dialogue: Power and Pedagogy in Educating Other People's Children." *Harvard Educational Review* 58, no. 3 (1998): 288–299.

DeWaelsche, Scott A. "Critical Thinking, Questioning and Student Engagement in Korean University English Courses." *Linguistics and Education* 32 (2015): 131–147. http://dx.doi.org/10.1016/j.linged.2015.10.003.

Dressman, Mark. "Lionizing Lone Wolves: The Cultural Romantics of Literacy Workshops." *Curriculum Inquiry* 23, no. 3 (1993): 245–263.

Dressman, Mark, and Mohamed Mahna. "Across Three Languages: The Translinguistic Writing Practices of 113 University Students." In *AAAL Conference*. Pittsburgh, PA, March 20, 2022.

Ewert, Doreen E. "Extensive Reading for Statistical Learning." In The Handbook of Informal Language Learning, edited by Mark Dressman and Randall William Sadler, 395–404. Hoboken, NJ: John Wiley & Sons, Inc., 2020.

García, Ofelia, and Angel M. Y. Lin. "Translanguaging in Bilingual Education." In Bilingual and Multilingual Education, edited by O. García, A. Lin, and S. May, 117–130. Cham, Switzerland: Springer, 2017.

Hillocks, George. "Chapter 20: Writing in Secondary Schools." In Handbook of Research on Writing: History, Society, School, Individual, Text edited by Charles Bazerman, 381–404. New York. Lawrence Erlbaum Associates, 2008.

Ho, Shirley S., and Douglas A. McLeod. "Social-psychological Influences on Opinion Expression in Face-to-face and Computer-mediated Communication." *Communication Research* 35, no. 2 (2014): 190–207. https://doi.org/10.1177/0093650207313159.

IMBD. "Squid Game." n.d. https://www.imdb.com/title/tt10919420.

Kellman, Steven G. The Translingual Imagination. Lincoln, NB: University of Nebraska Press, 2000.

Kim, Jungyin (Janice). "Oral Communication Needs of New Korean Students in a US Business Communication Classroom." *Global Business Journal* 18, no. 7 (2013).

Krashen, Stephen D. Principles and Practice in Second Language AcquisitionOxford Pergamon Press Inc, 1982.

Lee, Icy. "Error Correction in L2 Secondary Writing Classrooms: The Case of Hong Kong." *Journal of Science and Langauge Writing* 13 (2004): 285–312. https://doi.org/10.1016/j.jslw.2004.08.001.

Lee, Icy. Classroom Writing Assessment and Feedback in L2 School Contexts. Singapore: Springer Singapore, 2017.

Lipinski-Harten, Maciek, and Romin W. Tafarodi. "Attitude Moderation: A Comparison of Online Chat and Face-to-face Conversation." *Computers in Human Behavior* 29 (2013): 2490–2493. http://dx.doi.org/10.1016/j.chb.2013.06.004.

Lund University. "Register Types." Academic Writing in English (June 2021) https://www.awelu.lu.se/language/register-and-style/register-types.

Matsuda, Paul Kei. "Contrastive Rhetoric in Context: A Dynamic Model of L2 Writing." *Journal of Second Language Writing* 6, no. 1 (1997): 45–60.

Matsuda, Paul Kei. Second Language Writing in the Twentieth Century: A Situated Historical Perspective. Cambridge University Press, 2003.

Matsuda, Paul Kei, and Melika Nouri. "Informal Writing and Language Learning." In The Handbook of Informal Langauge Learning, edited by Mark Dressman and Randall William Sadler, 75–84 Oxford: John Wiley & Sons, 2020. https://doi.org/10.1002/9781119472384.ch5.

Physiopedia. "Coronavirus Disease (COVID-19)." n.d. https://www.physio-pedia.com/Coronavirus_Disease_(COVID-19).

Pierce, Tamyra. "Social Anxiety and Technology: Face-to-Face Communication versus Technological Communication among Teens." *Computers in Human Behavior* 25 (2009): 1367–1372. https://doi.org/10.1016/j.chb.2009.06.003.

Song, Hayeon, Jihyun Kim, and Kwan Min Lee. "Virtual vs. Real Body in Exergames: Reducing Social Physique Anxiety in Exercise Experiences." *Computers in Human Behavior* 36 (2014): 282–285. http://dx.doi.org/10.1016/j.chb.2014.03.059.

Wei, L. "Translanguaging as a Practical Theory of Language." *Applied Linguistics* 39, no. 1 (2017): 9–30.

World Health Organization. "WHO Coronavirus (COVID-19) Dashboard." n.d. https:// covid19.who.int.

Yonhap. "National Assembly Passes Bill on Allowing Recognized Pop Stars to Defer Enlistment." 2020. http://www.koreaherald.com/view.php?ud=20201201000856.

York, James, Koichi Shibata, Hayato Tokutake, and Hiroshi Nakayama. "Effect of SCMC on Foreign Language Anxiety and Learning Experience: A Comparison of Voice, Video, and VR-based Oral Interaction." *ReCALL* 33, no. 1 (2021): 49–70. https://doi.org/10.1017/S0958344020000154.

YouTube. "Create a Multiplayer Interactive Board Game with Google Sheets." 2020. https:// youtu.be/VbwWdPZ1H2k.

Yun, Sun Mi, and Heui-Baik Kim. "Changes in Students' Participation and Small Group Norms in Scientific Argumentation." *Research in Science Education* 45 (2015): 465–484. https://doi.org/10.1007/s11165-014-9432-z.

11

Curriculum, Assessment, and Professional Development in the Age of IDLE

Two IELTS Test Prep Superstars on a billboard in Hong Kong.

Introduction

Jacoba Willems: Design-Based Curriculum for *Basisvorming* in The Netherlands

Jacoba Willems teaches English to early adolescents in the *basisvorming* (first three years) of an Hoger algemeen voortgezet onderwijs (HAVO), or high school, in Groningen, The Netherlands. Her students are likely to progress to some form of higher education after their HAVO years and will need to speak and become literate at a relatively high level (CEFR B2/C1) of English for their studies and future careers. English-language television and movies in The Netherlands are subtitled rather than dubbed, and the proximity to the UK and close trading relations means that her students are exposed to a great deal of English in their daily lives, especially in terms of entertainment and media, even though most speak Dutch exclusively at home and among themselves.

English Language Learning in the Digital Age: Learner-Driven Strategies for Adolescents and Young Adults, First Edition. Mark Dressman, Ju Seong Lee, and Laurent Perrot.

Schools were closed during the Covid-19 pandemic and now, as they slowly reopen, researchers are documenting the general lack of progress made by students in The Netherlands during that time (Engzell, Frey, and Verhagen 2021). Test scores for most subject areas show a clear lack of progress if not loss during the period. However, Jacoba and her colleagues have been surprised to see that their students' spoken English seems more fluent than it was before, although rather than aligning with the norms of British English, according to school practice, students seem to have adopted pronunciation and idioms that are clearly from the United States. For example, a few days ago, Jacoba suggested reading a novel and asked her students for their opinion about her choice. "Oh, I'm down!" (I agree), Jeroen laughed from the back of the room. Jacoba shared this anecdote with colleagues, who told her of similar experiences in their classes. This has given them an idea for an action research project in design-based curriculum.

Park Hae-in: Reading Comprehension Test Review with Quizlet

Park Hae-in teaches 11th grade English in a high school in Daegu, South Korea. His students, their parents, and his fellow teachers and school administrators are beginning to feel the pressure of the upcoming College Scholastic Ability Test (CSAT). Most of his students are enrolled in a *hagwon*, or after-school program focused on test prep, and discussion in meetings has begun to turn to appropriate strategies, practice exams, and best techniques for review. This pressure has become even greater in the pandemic, as face-to-face review sessions have become nearly impossible. However, the test is still more than a year away for his students, and Mr. Park is concerned that too much heavy review this early will reduce his students' motivation and engagement and unduly increase their anxiety.

During the pandemic, Mr. Park realized that he needed to reduce anxiety and yet find ways to productively practice for the CSAT. He decided to combine the teaching of reading in English with activities similar to the reading comprehension passages and questions his students would face on the test. He also wanted to teach his students to understand the logic of the test questions and believed that if students had an "insider's view" of how multiple-choice test questions are written, they would be at an advantage when it came time to read short passages and answer questions on the CSAT. Finally, to reduce the tension of studying and build students' confidence, he decided to gamify the review activities, and to add an online component.

Radovan Kadlec: Redesigning English at a Technical Institute in the Czech Republic

Dr. Radovan Kadlec chairs the English department at a technical institute in the Czech Republic. His students are mainly undergraduates in STEM programs, and English is a required subject in the first two years of their studies. Just before the pandemic forced undergraduate instruction to go online, the Dean of Engineering complained to Radovan that English courses were not preparing students adequately to read or write in technical areas of English. He requested that Radovan offer more instruction in technical vocabulary and writing. However, Radovan's faculty, who had no background in STEM, suggested that perhaps instead the few instructors who were interested could offer special courses in English for Special Purposes or co-teach with faculty in a Content and Language Integrated Learning (CLIL) context.

When teaching at the institute went online for undergraduates in the spring of 2020, the English faculty found themselves and their students struggling. They noticed that student attendance was dropping and that when students were logged on during synchronous instruction, they often failed to respond when called. Radovan also noticed that his faculty were beginning to lose morale, and that there was need for a project that would keep them energized.

At the same time, however, two faculty members in the department began to make the best of the situation and then to become truly innovative in their use of the technology available to them and to their students at home. They realized that if they created assignments that were realistic approximations of the type of writing and reading they would do in STEM fields and that combined writing with spoken presentations and the use multimodal texts such as video, PowerPoint, and webpages, students responded creatively, especially if they were allowed to choose topics and how they worked. As Radovan received reports of their progress and then reviewed student work, he was sure he'd found a way to energize his faculty and respond to the Dean of Engineering.

Discussion

In this final methodological chapter, we turn our focus to the ways that learner-driven strategies and IDLE-like practices relate to curriculum and assessment. These two terms are conceptually broader than individual classroom concepts and practices and often exert great control over teaching and learning, depending on the national context. The term *curriculum* is used mostly in anglophone countries and so may be unfamiliar to some readers. It refers to all the influences that shape what and how students learn. These include materials (textbooks, technology) but also temporal conditions such as scheduling and how a student progresses through a system, teacher preparation, teaching practices, the design of spaces for learning and teaching, and how subject matter is defined and organized, and its learning assessed. Traditionally, curriculum and schooling were viewed as largely self-contained, but in recent decades the influence of cultural and societal values (the *hidden curriculum*; see Giroux and Penna 1979) and policy making on classroom practice and life outcomes for students has become a central focus of debate and discussion.

Curriculum typically has two views: a macro, top-down view of all the parts and their integration, and a micro, bottom-up view of subject organization and classroom learning. From the macro, administrative view, the integration of the parts of a curriculum is usually viewed very mechanically, with concern for how to maximize the efficiency and smooth operation of schooling placed in the center. From the micro, instructional view, curriculum is typically viewed holistically, with all the parts (including administrative oversight and assessment) perceived as a single, organic entity.

Similarly, assessment can be viewed broadly, as the total ways that the product, or outcome of curriculum practices is measured; or more narrowly, and from two levels: (1) official, national-level assessments, which are typically "objective," paper-and-pencil exams; and (2) local, typically teacher-made instruments that summatively (at the end of a unit of study) or formatively (during instruction) measure student achievement and progress. These two levels are related in two ways: first, through curriculum guides that determine what will be learned and assessed at both levels; and second, through test preparation in classrooms for national exams. Exactly how these parts relate varies across countries and cultural traditions. In some countries, high-stakes exams, especially those that determine university and post-secondary admission, exert a great deal of control over English-language curriculum in the final years of secondary school; indeed, in some cases preparation and review for the national exam has effectively become the curriculum for those years.

It might seem that IDLE and its practices would have no influence or role to play in the national and institutional, macro aspects of English language curriculum and policy, but that is not always the case. For example, Dressman (2020) found that students in Moroccan public universities compensated for their institutions' lack of listservs and learning management systems by creating Facebook pages for sections (cohorts) of English students. All the students in a section joined the same page, which was created and coordinated by one student in the section. They posted meeting times for classes, updated students if an instructor rescheduled a class, and shared information about assignments, due dates, and content (including links to resources). In interviews with individuals, students typically described a wide range of internet-based, self-coordinated resources that they used for coursework to compensate for a lack of textbooks and other materials (e.g., websites and YouTube videos for learning grammar, sites for downloading reading materials, dictionary apps). Dressman described these online materials as an "invisible university" that enabled students, instructors, and the university itself to succeed in conditions (course enrollments of 100–150 beginning English students per class; no textbooks; no electronic means of communication) that would have otherwise led to systemic collapse.

The rise of English Medium of Instruction (EMI) courses and programs in universities across Europe and Asia may also be supported, albeit invisibly, by IDLE. An EMI class or program of study is one that is offered in English to non-native speakers of English with little or no support for students' English levels. Instruction and materials are provided in English, sometimes with and sometimes without translation or other enabling features, and students are expected to use their own initiative to learn the material and to be assessed in English. In Japan, for example, despite relatively low levels of proficiency in English, which is taught beginning in middle school, the number of undergraduate and graduate courses and programs offered to Japanese university students is on the rise across the country (Hino 2017). The Japanese government is currently working to extend and modernize the teaching of English in schools with hope for future improvement in proficiency, but this cannot account for the growth and success of EMI curriculum in the present. At the beginning of the twenty-first century, the widespread development of EMI programs would have been inconceivable in Japan or many other Asian and European countries, and yet it is common today. Although it is never stated explicitly, the revolution in digital communications, the World Wide Web, and the practices of IDLE are certainly enablers of EMI's development.

With respect to assessment, the influence of IDLE is narrower. Certainly, developments in digital technology and especially the use of artificial intelligence (AI) to assess student performance may affect the authenticity of future assessments by allowing machines to measure students' productive ability to write and speak more efficiently and "objectively" than is typically possible with human evaluators at national levels. This may in turn affect teaching and test preparation, but it is currently only speculative. The greater influence of IDLE-like practices in the present and near future is in review and test preparation activities, through apps for creating test items and other practice activities. These may be highly collaborative and require students to generate their own items for practice, allowing teachers in turn to use student-generated questions as formative assessments of students' strengths and weaknesses. In addition, in the wake of the pandemic, action research, which has much in common with IDLE in terms of its focus on autonomy, autonomous learning, and authenticity, may be seen as one way to assess, in personal and formative ways, the effects of online learning and teaching on English-language proficiency.

Internet Connectivity Increases in the Covid Pandemic

A report by the International Telecommunication Union (ITU 2021) noted that in the first year of the Covid-19 pandemic, internet connectivity increased by 782 million new users, mostly in developing countries. However, 37% of the world's population (and 96% of these were in developing countries) had still never used the internet.

The report also noted that worldwide there are major discrepancies in speed and access between urban and rural areas. A gender gap also remains but it has narrowed: 62% of males used the internet in 2021 compared to 57% of females. There is also an age gap: 71% of 15–24-year-olds use the internet, but above 24 years, only 57% use it.

These figures show an improvement in internet connectivity worldwide during the pandemic, but also show how far there is to go. The figures have clear implications also for the integration of IT with educational services and the development of curriculum to reach every student globally.

The three scenarios that introduce this chapter and that continue in its "Practical Applications in the Classroom" section provide fictional but reality-based examples of the implications of IDLE at the levels of curriculum and assessment. Jacoba Willems is a teacher at a HAVO (middle school) in The Netherlands and will collaborate with her fellow English teachers to investigate shifts in their students' use of English during a period of online instruction during the pandemic. Their story provides an example of how action research can be used formatively to assess student learning through IDLE. At the secondary level, Park Hae-in is a high school teacher in Korea under pressure during the pandemic to find a way to engage his students' attention in studying for the CSAT. His solution will be to gamify his review practices through the online app, Quizlet. In the Czech Republic, Radovan Kadlec, the chair of English at a technical institute, finds in the crisis of the pandemic (and two of his faculty's response) the opportunity to redesign the English curriculum, using ubiquitous digital resources that bring the institute's students and English and Engineering faculty into alignment with multimodal developments in scientific communications.

Chapter Objectives

The central goal of this chapter is to consider how informal digital learning of English (IDLE) may interact with curriculum and assessment at school and policy levels. A subgoal is to understand distinctions between macro curricular issues at the policy level and curriculum at the micro, or classroom level, along with levels of assessment at the policy and classroom level. An additional subgoal related to evaluation is the use of Action Research at the classroom level, and to investigate the impact of IDLE on classroom learning, especially during the Covid-19 pandemic and its aftermath. By the end of the chapter, students will be able to:

1) Explain the difference between curriculum at macrostructural and microstructural levels.
2) Explain the progression of modern language education from 1900 to the present in terms of theory, learning, teaching, context of instruction, and assessment.
3) Describe IDLE as a continuation of theory and practice over the last century.
4) Describe possible uses of IDLE-like practices in assessment.
5) Describe the role of action research in assessing and integrating IDLE into classroom curriculum.
6) Explain three ways that the principles of IDLE can be applied to curriculum and assessment within classrooms.
7) Discuss how the research, theory, and three scenarios in this chapter can be applied to the reader's pedagogical context.

Key Words

curriculum; English as a medium of instruction; design-based curriculum; content and language integrated learning (CLIL); High stakes assessment; speech recognition software; natural language processing; action research

---

Research and Theory

IDLE's Place in English Second-Language Curriculum

Although IDLE may seem at first glance to be a radical departure from traditional curricular approaches to English language teaching, a look at the progression of research, theory, and practice since 1900 suggests that this is not the case. Table 11.1 provides an overview of the history of major approaches used to teach English as a second and foreign language from the beginning of modern language pedagogy to the present. Across the top row of the table, the major methods of this period are listed chronologically from left to right. Down the left column, these methods are described by their constituent elements: theory, learning, teaching, context of instruction, and typical forms of classroom assessment.

Briefly, before 1900, modern languages (spoken by people in their daily lives) were first taught formally using the same philological, pre-linguistic methods of grammar and translation by which classical languages such as Greek, Latin, and Sanskrit were taught.

Table 11.1 Progression of English language education methods x language theory, teaching, learning, contexts, and assessments.

	Grammar-translation	Direct method	Audiolingual method	Communicative Language Teaching (CLT)	Computer-Assisted Language Learning (CALL)	Task-Based Language Teaching (TBLT)	Informal Digital Learning of English (IDLE)
Language theory	Philological, pre-linguistic	Atheoretical; reaction against grammar-translation	Applied linguistics; syntax is central	Applied linguistics; communication is central	Multiple: linguistic, sociolinguistic	Applied linguistics; language as a tool for action	Applied linguistics; language as social practice
Teaching	Lecture; supervision of translation exercises	Demonstrating language; designing speaking exercises	Applying linguistic principles using machines and drill	Dialogically engaging students in speaking	Shift from programmed learning to students using computers in a range of activities, AI	Creating and supervising completion of authentic tasks	Integrating student-driven strategies within formal learning contexts; co-learning with students
Learning	Explicit instruction in grammar and vocabulary; deductive practice in trans.	Inductive learning through observing and interacting with teacher	Inductive learning through repetition and practice	Inductive learning through engagement with teacher and peers	Shift from programmed learning to autonomous use of digital tools	Inductive learning through engagement with others in completion of complex tasks	Autonomous learning in coordination with formal classroom instruction
Contexts	Teacher-directed classroom use of literary texts, grammar texts, dictionaries	Teacher-directed instruction in classroom	Teacher coordinated use of machines; use of audio laboratories	Teacher-directed teacher-student and peer interaction in classroom	Use of computers, language software, games, AI, digital communications	Teacher-directed classroom-based problem solving	Integration of out-of-school and classroom learning; use of digital technology
Typical assessments	Written exams and translation	Rated demonstration of speaking, conversation	Speak tests; written tests	Speak tests; written exams; essays; presentations	Machine-scored tests; game scores; digital comm. texts	Written group projects and presentations	Multimodal, digital products and presentations
Historical progression							

Teacher-Centered; Controlled Language Materials → Learner-Driven; Authentic Language Sources

The Direct Method, in which teachers taught exclusively in the target language, using realia and gestures to lead learners inductively and systematically into knowledge of the language, was largely a reaction against grammar-translation, and became the main method of private language schools such as Berlitz in the early twentieth century. In the 1940s, the formal study of language teaching began with the application of "applied" linguistic approaches and the use of highly structured audiolingual methods and the development of language labs. A turn to Chomskian linguistics in the 1960s and 1970s laid the groundwork for Communicative Language Teaching (CLT), in which teachers taught by interacting with students in dialogue and other communication activities (Canagarajah 2015). In the 1980s, research in situated cognition (Lave and Wenger 1991), language as a social practice (Gee 1992), and a renewed interest in problem-based learning (Stepien and Gallagher 1993) supported the development of Task-Based Language Teaching (TBLT).

The rise of computing in the 1970s and then personal computing devices in the 1980s gave new life to the promise that learning languages through machines might provide limitless, efficient opportunities for practice and learning of foreign languages, and led to the rise of Computer-Assisted Language Learning, or CALL (Kenning 1990). As the speed and sophistication of computing increased, different approaches and uses of computing in language education multiplied rapidly in the twenty-first century, from the uses of AI and natural language processing (NLP) to provide more naturalistic and personalized learner–machine interactions to the uses of computing to connect learners through social networking sites.

As Table 11.1 also shows, there is both continuity and progression in the history of modern language education. In the first half of the twentieth century, teachers were considered active transmitters of language to students who had relatively little agency or control over their learning. By midcentury, as language itself came to be described in more dynamic terms, its teaching became more interactive, and learning became a process of give and take, of initiating and responding to meaningful utterances. By the end of the twentieth century, shifts in the conceptualization of learning from an exclusively cognitive perspective to one that was practically and socially situated in the solving of problems led to a growing focus on learner autonomy. Advances in digital technologies and communications in the early 2000s opened new opportunities for autonomous language learning and its research. The focus of this book on IDLE and the integration of learner-driven strategies for learning within language classrooms is thus the logical, not aberrant, or revolutionary, outcome of more than a century of pedagogical and technological progression.

Research on Assessment and IDLE-Related Technology

The practices of IDLE are unlikely to have an influence on high-stakes assessment of English proficiency or policy at national levels because learner-driven strategies are a means to learning rather than ends in themselves. More locally, IDLE-like approaches that include the use of flashcard and quiz apps such as Quizlet and Kahoot can have a role to play in review (see Chapter 7 for a discussion of these). One possible area of overlap is in the use of speech recognition software to assess and give feedback on pronunciation accuracy using programs such as the Microsoft Speech SDK (Software Development Kit; Microsoft 2022). Research in the branch of AI related to language,

NLP (Sun, Anbarasan, and Kumar 2020; Xiaohong and Yanzheng 2021), may in time make the machine scoring of high-stakes exams using electronically written and recorded samples produced by test takers possible (Bernstein et al. 2000; Franco et al. 2010; Tao et al. 2016). Presumably, it may then also be possible for learners to access this service through personal devices and use it for review and practice.

AI Language Assessment in the Here and Now

Here are three recently developed language assessment tools that already make use of AI and NLP to provide quick assessments of language proficiency. All are online and promise nearly immediate results.

Language Confidence (n.d.) is a service that provides quick, formative assessment results for students and classroom teachers called the LCAT, with a focus on speaking and pronunciation.

Duolingo English Test (n.d.) provides a cheaper and quicker alternative assessment than the IELTS or TOEFL iBT for individuals applying to universities and for employment. Results are scored on a scale of 10–160 for speaking, listening, reading, and writing.

Emmersion (2022) is a service for employers needing language certification of proficiency in nine languages. Results are provided in CEFR levels and on a 100-point scale on a variety of measures for speaking, listening, reading, and writing.

Research on Action Research in English Language Education

A final, IDLE-like approach to curriculum assessment and professional development in language education is action research. Action research has a long history in education (Cano 2004; Glassman, Erdem, and Bartholomew 2013) but it is a more recent development in English language teaching (Banegas et al. 2013; Burns 2005; Thorne and Qiang 1996). It is not necessarily technologically grounded, but in its do-it-yourself spirit and focus on the autonomous learning of teachers about their practice and their students' learning, as well as its use of local, personalized setting and use of ubiquitous tools, it has much in common with the practices of IDLE, especially when it is used by teachers to study their students' use of digital technology in learning.

Discussion

In summary, a review of the history of language instruction in modern times indicates that the integration of IDLE and its practices into classroom instruction, which is the central theme and goal of this book, is not a revolutionary or aberrant concept at all, but the logical continuation of a trend toward learner autonomy and the development of progressively more authentic materials and learning tasks since at least the advent of CLT in the 1960s. The revolution in digital computing devices and software in the last five decades has also supported an increase in autonomous learning.

IDLE is not likely to have a direct impact on national curriculum goals and the use of high-stakes assessments in the near future, but developments in NLP may in time influence the format of high-stakes assessments, allowing for the machine scoring of authentic samples of students' speech and writing. These same developments may make it possible also for students to receive instant feedback on their language skills through smartphones and other devices. Finally, in the wake of the pandemic, the use of action research to evaluate the impact of online language instruction on students' language development is a practice in line with the principles of IDLE.

We will argue in conclusion that although IDLE is unlikely to directly impact policies regarding national curriculum or high-stakes assessment practices, this does not mean that it has no impact on students' learning. Curriculum is not an exclusively top-down or bottom-up process, but rather what emerges at the level of teaching and learning for both teachers and students is a negotiation between the two. As we have demonstrated throughout the previous chapters of this book, IDLE is a powerful phenomenon with enormous implications for the development of students' proficiency in English, even if its informality and its idiosyncrasies make it difficult for policy makers to take seriously. The challenge for teachers in the coming years will be to take advantage of IDLE's affordances without formalizing them, and to build creatively on its learner-driven strategies and outcomes. That will take a delicate hand, and one better left to teachers at the classroom level.

Practical Applications in the Classroom

Scenario One: Design-Based Curriculum for *Basisvorming* in The Netherlands

The Scene. As schools reopen after the Covid-19 pandemic, Jacoba Willems and her colleagues at a HAVO (middle school) in Groningen have discovered that their students' spoken English seems to be more fluent than it was before and that they are using more "Americanisms" in their speech. They suspect that this is due to their students' increased television viewing and online activities, but they do not know the details of why or how this is happening. In response, they've decided to conduct a collaborative action research project and to involve their students.

Analysis: Challenges and Opportunities. In contrast to research conducted by academics in formal sciences, in which researchers attempt to establish "objectivity" by removing themselves from the collection and analysis of data, in action research the researchers themselves are considered an integral part of the process. Action researchers are also interested in "objectivity," that is, in obtaining the accurate facts of the phenomenon they are studying, but they assume that as actors themselves within the research setting, they are part of what is happening and that their perspective is critical to understand a situation fully. Most action research projects are therefore also very practical and local in their focus. The knowledge produced is specific to the situation studied and not usually generalizable, although it may contribute to general knowledge collectively.

During the pandemic, action research can be seen as a critical part of teachers' documentation and evaluation of the effects of the pandemic and online instruction on their students' learning. At this time, when teachers were challenged simply to keep up with the demands of transforming instruction from in-class to online, it was likely impossible in most situations to design a study and collect and analyze data as events unfolded. But in its wake, there is much data in the form of lesson plans, student assignments, recorded lessons, and student interviews and surveys that could be analyzed and that would add an emic, insider perspective to one of the most significant educational events in history.

Instructional Plan. Jacoba and three of her colleagues decided that they would create an assignment for their students they called the "Two Week Challenge." They based this idea on Sundqvist and Sylvén's (2016) "30-Day Extramural English Challenge," but reduced the length to accommodate their early adolescent participants. In this challenge, students would fill out a chart, either in hard copy or on Google Sheets, in which they reported any exposure to English in their lives outside school. The teachers brainstormed categories of English language exposure with their students to make the chart. These included: (1) environmental print (signs, etc); (2) television series programs; (3) movies (on video); (4) video games; (5) YouTube or other video sharing services; (6) social media (Facebook, Instagram, etc.); (7) chat rooms in English (name the chat room); (8) music and music videos; (9) other websites; (10) other (specify). For categories in which students "watched" or "listened" for an extended period, they were instructed to log the amount of time and list specific titles of programs, videos, or songs.

The teachers distributed hard copies of the charts and sent the link for the Google Sheets page to the students. They reminded the students daily by email and an automatic text-messaging system to complete their logs and at the beginning of every class they collected students' hard-copy data and reviewed the growing compilation of information. At the end of two weeks, they had compiled data sheets on student IDLE activity for each class and combined these data into a master sheet for all classes. Within individual classes, students were placed in groups of three or four and instructed to analyze the findings for their class. The teachers showed the students how to create data charts and graphs on Google Sheets to visualize their findings and provided a YouTube video in support. In whole-class discussion, students shared their charts and selected those which were most interesting. The classes discussed interpretations of the findings. They compared their class's findings to the total findings of all classes and noted differences and similarities.

As the students were conducting their analyses, the teachers analyzed equivalent short writing samples that students had written before schools closed and just after they reopened. They counted the number of words and the number of t-units (Larsen-Freeman and Strom 1977) in each writing sample. They also identified and counted any words or phrases in each sample that they knew informally were not part of the school curriculum. Once they had these counts, they compared the language of the writing samples before and after the school was closed and found that there was a slight gain for the students in the average length of t-units and new vocabulary used. One of the teachers had knowledge of statistical analysis and used a t-test to determine whether the means of the before and after samples were "significantly" different. She found that they were different at the $p < .05$ level. This was not hugely significant, they knew, and could have been explained simply by growth over time, but the finding suggested that students' ability to write in English had improved during the period of school closure and online instruction, in contrast to other subject areas. When they reviewed their lists of new vocabulary and phrases, they found that more of the items in writing after reopening were traceable to the United States than before closing.

Findings from the students' reports of their IDLE activities showed that they had spent two to three times as many hours "IDLE-ing" as they had in formal instruction in English. They found that in terms of music, they listened to as many British or Australian groups as they did from North America, but the overwhelming majority of their television and movie viewing came from sources in the United States. Students were divided on whether they turned subtitles on and/or paid attention to them. The groups' reports were much longer than expected (300–400 words) and consisted of reports of charts and interpretations that were more detailed than any writing the teachers had seen before.

As Jacoba and her colleagues discussed among themselves afterwards, their action research project had not only demonstrated how much English students were learning out of school but also its power and the power of action research to teach students to write about a meaningful topic in a mindful way. In the process the students had also developed new skills in taking notes, recording data, using spreadsheets, and collaboratively analyzing data and writing up their findings. They brainstormed new projects that would involve students' interests in popular culture, such as writing reviews of new and favorite programs and music artists and perhaps integrating mathematics (statistics) with English-language writing and presenting.

1) Materials:
    a) Student computing devices
    b) Home and school internet connections
    c) Google Sheets
    d) Learning Management System for classes.
2) Learning Mode: Action research; whole-class, small-group, individual
3) Time: Ten days (two weeks, 50 minutes per day) for data collection; five days for data analysis and report writing and sharing
4) Sequence of Activities:
    a) On Day 1, teachers introduce and explain the "30 Day Extramural English Challenge" to students in each class, including the online Google Sheets.
    b) On Days 2–10
        i) Students turn in their logs to their teacher (if not recorded on Google Sheets)
        ii) Teachers remind students about keeping logs daily by email and text message
        iii) Instruction in regular curriculum takes most of the remainder of class time
        iv) Teachers meet to analyze short written samples collected before school closed and just after school opened.
    c) On Day 11, data collection concludes
    d) Teachers organize students into small groups and demonstrate making charts and graphs on Google Sheets
    e) Students begin to analyze class data using Google Sheets
    f) On Days 12–13, groups continue to analyze data

g) Teachers circulate among groups, supervising
h) As groups finish analysis, they begin to write reports of their findings and interpretations
i) On Day 14, students share their charts and discuss within the whole class
j) On Day 15, students conclude writing of reports
k) Teachers share whole-class analysis and their study of student writing before and after
l) Outside class meeting time: Teachers meet to discuss implications of the project for future teaching assignments.

Assignments and Assessment. This activity has two assessments: (1) an assessment of the student group analyses and reports; and (2) an informal assessment of individual student participation in the research project (see Tables 11.2 and 11.3).

Table 11.2 Assessment of group analyses and reports.

Achievement level	Descriptor
Excellent	The group demonstrated solid collaboration across all stages of the project. Each student was observed to collaborate on the creation of charts and graphs from the data collected. In their analysis, the group chose variables that were significant and original (e.g., compared male vs. female students; looked for relations among categories). The group selected relevant charts that comprehensively described the data and took notes on findings. Their reports were also comprehensive and focused on relevant details. The writing was clear and formally phrased, with good word choice and phrasing, and met or exceeded the 300–400-word limit.
Very good	The group demonstrated collaboration across all stages of the project. Each student was observed at some point collaborating on parts of the assignment and in the creation of charts and graphs. In their analysis, the students chose significant variables and selected relevant charts that described the data comprehensively. Some students took notes. The report was relatively comprehensive and mostly focused on relevant details. The writing was clear and formally phrased, with some errors that did not impede meaning, and met the 300–400-word limit.
Satisfactory	The group demonstrated some degree of collaboration across most stages of the project, Each student was observed to collaborate at some part of the assignment and to contribute to creating charts and graphs, although there were clear leaders in this task. In their analysis, the students chose variables that were important to them and selected charts that described most of the data. The report was complete and reported factual findings but with limited interpretation. It was clearly written with errors, but these did not prevent understanding. The report met the 300–400-word limit.
Unsatisfactory	The group demonstrated limited or very little collaboration across stages of the project. Some students were seen to contribute in very limited ways and only one or two students created data charts. The report was incomplete and limited in its reporting of facts with little interpretation. There were many errors and some impeded meaning. The report did not meet the 300–400-word limit.

Table 11.3 Informal assessment of individual student participation.

Achievement level	Descriptor
Above expectations	The student was an active participant across all stages of the project, including daily reports of exposure to English, which were complete and comprehensive. The student actively participated in class discussions and planning in English and collaborated with group members, contributing insight. The student created charts and graphs and shared these with the group in English. The student took notes in English and shared these in the writing of the group's report.
Meets expectations	The student was an active participant across most stages of the project and contributed daily reports of their exposure to English. The student participated in class discussions and planning, usually in English, and was observed to collaborate with group members, sometimes offering suggestions in English. The student helped with creating charts and graphs in English. The student may have taken some limited notes in English as the group worked, and was seen to actively contribute to the writing of the report.
Below expectations	The student was a mostly passive participant across multiple stages of the project and missed multiple daily reports of their exposure to English. The student showed limited engagement in class discussion and planning as well as limited collaboration with the group, offering few suggestions in English or another language. The student did not participate in creating charts and graphs and took few if any notes. The student was not seen to contribute to the writing of the paper and using English.

Relation to TESOL Technology Standards for Learners and CEFR Reference Level Descriptors

TESOL Technology Standards:

- Goal 1 (Demonstrate foundational knowledge)
  - Standard 4 (Demonstrate basic competence)
- Goal 3 (Effectively use and critically evaluate technology tools)
  - Standard 1 (Use and evaluate productivity tools)
  - Standard 2 (Use and evaluate skill-building tools)
  - Standard 3 (Use and evaluate tools for communication and collaboration).

CEFR Reference Level Descriptors:

- Global Scale: B1 (Can produce simple connected text on topics, which are familiar, or of personal interest)
- Overall Spoken Interaction: A2/B1 (Can interact with reasonable ease in structure situations/ Can exchange, check and confirm information)
- Conversation: B1 (Can enter unprepared into conversations on familiar topics)
- Formal Discussion (Meetings): A2/B1 (Can exchange relevant information and give an opinion on practical problems/ Can take part in routine formal discussion)
- Goal-Oriented Cooperation: A2/B1 (Can discuss what to do next/ Can make opinions and reactions understood)

- Information Exchange: A2 (Can ask and answer question about habits and routines)
- Overall Written Production: B1 (Can write straightforward connected texts on a range of familiar subjects)
- Reports and Essays: B1 (Can summarize, report and give an opinion about accumulated factual information)
- Cooperating: B1 (Can summarize the point reached in a discussion)
- Processing Text: B1 (Can collate short pieces of information from several sources)
- General Linguistic Range: B1 (Has enough language to get by, with sufficient vocabulary to express themselves)
- Vocabulary Range: A2 (Has sufficient vocabulary to conduct routine, everyday transactions)
- Grammatical Accuracy: B1 (Communicates with reasonable accuracy in familiar contexts)
- Coherence: B1 (Can link a series of shorter, discrete simple elements)
- Propositional Precision: B1 (Can express the main point he/she want to make comprehensively).

Analyzing and Extending the Lesson: Application to Additional Contexts. In this scenario, a group of teachers at a HAVO in Groningen, The Netherlands was curious about gains in their students' English during a school closure for the pandemic. They decided to organize an action research project, in which students would report their IDLE activities daily over two weeks and then analyze and interpret their findings in a report, using the charts and graphs feature of Google Sheets.Action research is an excellent professional development activity for collaboration and teamwork among teachers, which also improves student–teacher rapport. Although findings are typically not generalizable and may not meet standards for publication in peer-reviewed journals, they can provide powerful insights for teachers about their students' learning and their own teaching, and lead to important changes in curriculum and teaching.In this scenario, a group of teachers decided to collaborate, but individual teachers can also conduct studies within their classrooms. The design of the study and the data collected can be adapted to any situation or research question, and teachers need not share findings with others. One important point is that if I teacher decides to conduct an action research study in which they collect data from students, they should communicate with students and parents about the information to be collected and the goals and objectives of the data collection.

Scenario Two: Reading Comprehension Test Review with Quizlet

The Scene. The anxiety felt by Mr. Park Hae-in's eleventh-grade students over the College Scholastic Ability Test (CSAT) has only increased during the pandemic, because the students' sense that they cannot focus or learn as well online as in face-to-face instruction. He recognizes he will have to address the students' need to study in ways that are effective and reduce their stress.

Analysis: Challenges and Opportunities. Test review poses many challenges for high school teachers worldwide, but especially in countries where a single final examination determines a student's future academic life and possible career. The pressure to teach for the test from parents and administrators can be intense, with consequences that increase students' anxiety rather than preparing them, and it can also lead to "teaching" that is nothing more than having students answer practice questions on worksheets and review them over and over in class—a practice that, in the end, doesn't teach much that is useful.

Yet, the pressure to engage in such practices far too early, and well before they might be appropriate, can be intense. An alternative strategy is to begin to work test preparation into meaningful reading and writing activities, and by "gamifying" the process (see Chapter 7, "Games and Other Virtual Learning Environments") to make it more interesting and engaging for students. In addition, focusing on authentic texts and teaching students the logic of item construction on the test will build confidence and teach them how to read not only texts but test questions with greater insight.

Mr. Park's response to this dilemma has been to combine the teaching of reading in English with activities similar to the reading comprehension passages and questions his students will face on the test. He also wants to teach his students to understand the logic of the test questions and believes that if students have an "insider's view" of how multiple-choice test questions are written, they will be at an advantage when it comes time to read short passages and answer questions on the CSAT. Finally, to reduce the tension of studying and build students' confidence, he has decided to gamify the review activities, and to add an online component.

Instructional Plan. To meet his goal of curriculum-based, low-pressure review, Mr. Park has decided to have his students read short articles from periodicals such as *Scientific American*, *The Smithsonian*, and the *Economist*, and write their own multiple-choice comprehension questions, after he teaches them some basics about writing them. In addition, he will place these questions on Quizlet, an online and free review/game platform. And to add an element of gaming and competition, he has organized his students into teams and assigned different point values for questions according to whether they are literal, interpretive, or critical in their focus.

He began by selecting three appropriate articles and photocopying them for his students. The articles contained many challenging vocabulary items and complex sentence structures, similar to passages that might be found on the CSAT. Mr. Park organized his students into heterogenous groups of three, gave one of the three articles to each group and challenged them to read, annotate, and then write multiple-choice comprehension questions for the passage.

He additionally showed them three types of questions: Literal, in which the answer is stated in the passage; Interpretive, in which the reader must draw a connection between two points of information in the passage that is not directly stated; and Critical, in which the reader must draw a connection between one or more points in the passage and information outside the passage. To illustrate these differences, he selected a passage the class had read a week before he had written for the passage. He also discussed the need to have one clear correct answer and to write three clever but incorrect "distractors."

Mr. Park then announced that this activity would be completed as a comprehension game, in which groups or teams would be awarded points both for writing questions and for successfully answering questions from the other groups. Literal questions would be worth 1 point; Interpretive questions 5 points; and Critical questions 10 points. To receive points for writing the questions, they would have to be well formed and approved by Mr. Park in advance. The prizes for winning the game would be recognition on the class's

Wall of Fame, an advantage in future competitions, and free time in the school library for the top three groups, or teams.

To play the game, Mr. Park selected Quizlet, an online program that teachers can sign up for and whose basic membership is free. He created an assignment on the class's learning management system with groups for students to upload a minimum of four original questions totaling at least 20 points within two days. As the students began to work, Mr. Park circulated in the class, offering advice and supervising question writing. As students uploaded their questions, he reviewed them and provided feedback.

The gaming aspect of the assignment was very motivating for the students. They initially struggled with the distinctions among the types of questions, but with some trial and error soon began to write increasingly sophisticated questions. By the end of two days the groups had completed the process and Mr. Park worked quickly to upload all viable questions for their article onto the Quizlet site. The following day, the students went to the computer lab to play the game. In groups, they sat in front of one computer and read through all three articles, answering all the comprehension questions for them, minus their own questions.

Mr. Park recorded the correct answers of each group (Quizlet does this automatically), added their points from writing the questions, and announced the top three teams, with prizes chosen by the teams in descending order. As a debriefing exercise, he selected one Literal, one Interpretive, and one Critical question from the three passages and asked students individually to write a short paragraph explaining the answer they chose and why they thought it was correct.

1) Materials:
   a) Free teacher membership on Quizlet (or other online system)
   b) Computers (in a lab or laptops) for each group
   c) Photocopies of three downloaded journalistic articles.
2) Learning Mode: Whole class for introduction; small groups (teams) for writing and playing the game
3) Time: Four days; 50-minute class periods
4) Sequence of Activities:
   a) On Day 1, Introduce the activity and announce there will a competition among groups
   b) Announce and place students in heterogenous (equivalent ability) groups
   c) Describe and demonstrate the differences among Literal, Interpretive, and Critical questions, using a practice essay and test questions, and explain point values for questions
   d) Distribute one of three readings to each group and assign reading for homework
   e) On Day 2, check each group to make sure students have read and annotated their essay
   f) Students begin to write questions in groups as teacher circulates to check for understanding of Critical, Literal, and Interpretive distinctions
   g) On Day 3, students continue writing questions and teacher checks their work
   h) Students upload their questions on the class Learning Management System as the teacher checks for accuracy and copies questions to Quizlet
   i) On Day 4, students play the game and debrief at the end of the class (or the next day).

Assignments and Assessment. This activity has 2 assessments: 1) an assessment of the groups' question writing; and 2) an individual assessment of students' ability to explain their answer choices (see Tables 11.4 and 11.5).

Table 11.4 Assessment of group question writing.

Achievement level	Descriptor
Excellent	The group successfully wrote questions at all three levels totaling more than 20 points. All questions were usable in the game. The questions focused on significant points of the article and were cleverly phrased, with a clear correct response and three well-written distractors.
Very good	The group successfully wrote questions on at least two of the three levels, totaling at least 20 points. Some questions required rewriting before they could be used for the game. The questions focused on important points of the article and were well phrased, with a clear correct response and three distractors.
Satisfactory	The group successfully wrote questions on at least two of the three levels, totaling 15–20 points. One or two questions may have been unusable for the game. The questions focused on some points in the article and were understandable, with a correct response and three distractors.
Unsatisfactory	The group was unable to write questions totaling 20 points and failed to distinguish among levels. Most questions were unusable for the game. Some questions may have been off-topic or incomplete.

Table 11.5 Individual assessment of students' ability to explain their answer choices.

Achievement level	Descriptor
Above expectations	The student could explain in some detail and accurately how they arrived at a correct answer. The response indicated a clear understanding of the logic of item construction.
Meets expectations	The student could briefly explain how they arrived at a correct answer. The response indicated a basic understanding of test item construction.
Below expectations	The student could not explain how they arrived at a correct answer with any accuracy. The response indicated weak understanding of test item construction.

Relation to TESOL Technology Standards for Learners and CEFR Reference Level Descriptors

TESOL Technology Standards:
- Goal 3 (Effectively use and critically evaluate technology-based tools)
  - Standard 1 (Effectively use productivity tools)
  - Standard 3 (Use and evaluate tools for communication and collaboration).

CEFR Reference Level Descriptors:

- Global Scale: B2 (Can produce clear, detailed text on a wide range of subjects)
- Overall Reading Comprehension: B2 (Can read with a large degree of independence)
- Reading for Information and Argument: B1/B2 (Can recognize significant points in straightforward newspaper articles/Can understand articles and reports concerned with contemporary problems)

- Goal-Oriented Cooperation: B1/B2 (Can make his/her opinions and reactions understood/ Can outline an issue or a problem clearly)
- Information Exchange: B1/B2 (Can exchange, check and confirm accumulated factual information/ Can synthesize and report information and arguments from a number of sources)
- Overall Written Production: B1/B2 (Can write straightforward connected text/ Can write clear, detailed texts on a variety of subjects)
- Processing Text: B1/B2 (Can collate short pieces of information/ Can summarize a wide range of factual and imaginative texts)
- General Linguistic Range: B2 (Hass a sufficient range of language to be able to give clear descriptions)
- Grammatical Accuracy: B1 (Communicates with reasonable accuracy in familiar contexts)
- Vocabulary Control: B1 (Shows good control of elementary vocabulary)
- Orthographic control: B1 (Can produce continuous writing, which is generally intelligible throughout)
- Flexibility: B2 (Can vary formulation of what they wants to say)
- Coherence: B1 (Can link a series of shorter, discrete elements)
- Propositional Precision: B1 (Can explain the main points in an idea or problem with reasonable precision).

Analyzing and Extending the Lesson: Application to Additional Contexts. In this scenario, a teacher finds a way to use an online flash-card activity using authentic texts and gamification to teach reading comprehension and the logic of test item construction while reducing anxiety in his students.The first or second time that teachers attempt to teach their students about testing by having students write test items, some students may struggle, and others may be frustrated, because learning to understand testing from the inside-out is initially a very new concept for students. In some situations, it may be useful to break the activity into smaller components, teaching students to write only Literal questions on simpler texts first, then moving to Interpretive questions with more difficult texts and finally to Critical questions with complex texts. Although the process of learning how to write test questions is challenging, it is critical to students' ultimate success as test takers; and the confidence and insight that comes from mastering this activity is powerful and well worth the effort.Finally, it may seem that the use of technology in this activity is peripheral and that the same results could be achieved simply with word processed and printed questions, or even with paper and pencil. Avoiding the use of Quizlet or another online flash-card program is possible, but the automation of the process and the attractiveness of the online format improve the efficiency and the game-like quality of the activity for both teachers and students. Using Quizlet also allows teachers to more easily archive questions and to manage the process over successive texts and classes.

Scenario Three: Redesigning English at a Technical Institute in the Czech Republic

The Scene. Dr. Radovan Kadlec chairs the English department at an advanced technical institute in the Czech Republic, where the Dean of Engineering has asked for courses that are less focused on generally learning to use English and more on reading and writing in technical areas. Radovan agrees with the Dean. He has noticed over the past five years that his students speak increasingly better English and suspects this is because they engage in IDLE activities in their free time, and he knows that students need to be more challenged in their English classes. However, his faculty are not technically focused and have resisted developing new courses until recently, when two teachers showed him a multimodal assignment they had developed. This has given Radovan an idea for redesigning the core courses of his program.

Analysis: Challenges and Opportunities. The situation at this fictional technical institute in the Czech Republic reflects a very real challenge for English instruction globally, especially in higher education today, and where English is either the medium of instruction or specific courses and programs are taught exclusively in English by content specialists. As we noted earlier in this chapter, across Europe and Asia, EMI programs have increased rapidly since the 2010s, not only for international students who do not speak the standard language of instruction at the university, but for students who have enough knowledge of English to study advanced content in the language.

In response, the field of TESOL has developed several programs to address the needs of English users in advanced and specific contexts. These include English for Special Purposes (ESP); English for Academic Purposes (EAP); Content Language Integrated Learning (CLIL); and Content Based Instruction (CBI), among others. The first two of these describe English instruction tailored to specific purposes, usually with an emphasis on learning terminology and the genres of writing and speaking specific to one discipline or area of study. The second two describe conditions in which the learning of content and English are integrated. From an English learning perspective, all of these approaches assume a focus on language as the medium of communication and that the goal of instruction is to address limitations in students' knowledge of the English language.

Conditions at the technical institute where Radovan is chair are somewhat different from what standard TESOL responses imply but they are not at all unique. Radovan must continue to staff courses within the English program and does not have faculty for integrated English engineering courses or with the engineering knowledge to teach highly technical vocabulary and concepts. At the same time, he can also see that the demands of communication within STEM fields are changing, from solely print-based formats to multimodal communications combining video, interactive charts, audio, and print, and that the students are themselves becoming increasingly sophisticated users of communication platforms in English. His goal is not simply to respond to the request of the Dean of Engineering to teach more technical English but to lead the institute in its response to advances in digital communications in STEM.

Instructional Plan. Radovan knew that to redesign the core courses for engineering students at his institute he would need the support of his faculty and the administration. He also knew that several faculty members were already doing innovative work with multimodal communications activities, and he asked them and their students if he could use some of their assignments as examples. He met with the Dean of Engineering and other university administrators and showed them several of the student projects, describing course assignments that were general but that allowed students to apply their knowledge of engineering from their courses to activities such as responding to a Request for Funding (RFP; a call for grant proposals; see RFP360 n.d.) or writing a report comparing the technical specifications of three brands of equipment (e.g., smartphones, laptops, or electric vehicles). Administrators were impressed and agreed to support the redesign.

Radovan's next step was to recruit a steering committee from his faculty to design new course syllabuses, write new assignments, and pilot them. He chose the two faculty members who had submitted innovative student projects, three others who were open to trying new approaches in their teaching, and one faculty member who had previously resisted changes to the program. He charged them with redesigning two course syllabuses and developing articulated assignments that moved from relatively simple (but multimodal) tasks to increasingly sophisticated and complex assignments. The committee met over a six-month period. They discussed and suggested changes to the syllabuses, and Radovan chaired the committee and reported regularly to his faculty and Dean about their progress.

By the following semester, the committee had developed syllabuses and assignments for the new courses, and they agreed to pilot their teaching. As the Covid-19 pandemic moved most classes online at the institute, faculty staff were required to become increasingly competent in the uses of instructional technology and became more open to ideas for creating instructional videos and having students experiment in their writing and presentations with new multimodal formats. At the end of the semester, they selected student assignments to share among themselves, discussing challenges and how they were solved.

In the next stage of the redesign, Radovan sought approval for the course changes through the institute's curriculum committees. The members of the steering committee divided the two courses and assignments between them and acted as workshop coordinators, holding faculty development workshops with the rest of the faculty and introducing the new syllabuses and course assignments. They invited faculty members to develop additional assignments that responded to course guidelines and reported to Radovan about faculty innovations and challenges. Within a semester, the redesign of the courses was established, and Radovan urged the faculty to conduct some action research projects to assess their effectiveness and practicality. Faculty who had resisted gradually understood the importance of the redesign and began to adapt their instruction. Radovan knew that some faculty staff still had concerns and that there was some unevenness in the redesign across faculty and courses, but he trusted that in time the new approach would become more and more standardized and refined.

1) Materials:
   a) Request for Proposals (RFP) assignment
   b) Digital devices for students (laptops, tablets, smartphones)
   c) Learning Management System
   d) Internet connection
   e) Free website development platform (Wix.com or Weebly.com)
   f) Student-created YouTube accounts
   g) PowerPoint
   h) Additional online software programs

2) Learning Mode: Whole-class online and individual
3) Time: Five weeks, three 50-minute instructional periods per week
4) Sequence of Activities:
   a) Week One:
      i) Teacher introduces the assignment (introductory video is optional) and outlines the tasks for individual students
      ii) If possible, teacher shows examples of previous student projects to set the standard
      iii) Students begin to brainstorm as a whole class and then individually grant project proposals
      iv) Day 3: Students submit a proposal idea with a rough estimate of costs, materials, and timeline.
   b) Week Two:
      i) Students begin to research their topic, list materials, research prices, and create a general timeline for completion of the proposed project
      ii) Teacher demonstrates how to customize the Gantt chart template provided by Microsoft Office (Simple Gantt Chart n.d.) and provides an Excel spreadsheet for budgeting (Budgets n.d.)
      iii) Teacher meets individually with students during class and office hours to offer suggestions and keep students focused
      iv) Day 3: Students submit a progress report and rough budget for their project.
   c) Week Three:
      i) Students begin to write, reserving the abstract/executive summary of the proposal for last
      ii) Teacher meets with students individually, checking the progress of their writing and making editorial suggestions
      iii) Day 3: Students complete drafts of their Gantt charts and budgets for review by the teacher, along with rough drafts of their full proposals.
   d) Week Four:
      i) Students begin to create websites for the proposal using Wix or Weebly and a video using PowerPoint in which they summarize and "pitch" their proposal to a funding committee
      ii) Teacher supervises the work and meets with students individually
      iii) Day 3: Students submit links to their developing websites with materials posted on them.
   e) Week Five:
      i) Students work to complete and polish their written proposals, websites, and videos
      ii) Teacher supervises and offers editorial suggestions
      iii) Days 2 and 3: Students present their videos and websites to the class.

Assignments and Assessment. This assignment has one individual assessment of student performance on their multimodal, web-based response to the RFP (See Table 11.6).

Table 11.6 Individual assessment of student response to RFP.

Achievement level	Descriptor
Excellent	The proposal is complete and fully uploaded to a website. The design of the website is user friendly and matches the topic of the proposal. All links are correct and functional, and the video plays on the website. The video is creative and engaging for viewers and clearly summarizes the proposal. The proposal is logical and persuasive, and contains an executive summary, a narrative of the proposal, its budget, and timeline, along with relevant references in the appropriate style. Planning and budgeting are reasonable and detailed and reflect true estimates of costs and timeline. The idea of the proposal is clever and well phrased. The student used appropriate technical language and tone in the writing. Overall, the proposal indicates that the student thought clearly and used all resources, including the English language, very effectively.
Very good	The proposal is complete and uploaded to a website. The design is usable and relates to the topic of the proposal, but may not be elaborate or original. Most links are correct and functional, and the video plays on the website. The video summarizes the proposal. The proposal is logical and mostly persuasive, and contains all required elements. Planning and budgeting show some detail and are reasonable. The idea of the proposal is clear and consistent. The student used some appropriate technical language, and the tone of the writing was relatively formal. Overall, the proposal indicated that the student understood the assignment, thought clearly about it, and used most resources, especially the English language, with positive effect.
Satisfactory	The proposal is largely complete and was uploaded to a website. The design of the website was acceptable and showed some attempt at customization but was minimal. There were few links but most worked, and the video played. The video was in English and simple but conveyed the idea of the proposal. The proposal contained all parts and all required elements, but some were limited in their content. There was a budget and a Gantt chart, but these needed more detail. The idea of the proposal was clear but not original. The student used technical language but there were some errors, and the writing was incomplete or informal. Overall, the student completed the assignment fully.
Unsatisfactory	The proposal is incomplete and lacking some important parts on its website. The website is also incomplete and may not show signs of customization for the assignment. Some parts of the proposal, such as the Gantt chart, the video, or the budget, may not be uploaded or play and links do not work. The video had significant technical problems and the student's speech and slides were difficult to understand. The idea of the proposal was confused or not well developed; the Gantt chart and budget were unrealistic and/or poorly developed. The written proposal had significant errors and a lack of technical language that impeded meaning. Overall, the proposal was incomplete and demonstrated a lack of command of English in the field.

Relation to TESOL Technology Standards for Learners and CEFR Reference Level Descriptors

TESOL Technology Standards:

- Goal 1 (Demonstrate foundational knowledge)
  - Standard 4 (Demonstrate basic competence as users of technology)
- Goal 3 (Effectively use and critically evaluate technology-based tools)
  - Standard 1 (Use and evaluate language productivity tools)

- Standard 3 (Use and evaluate tools for communication)
- Standard 4 (Use and evaluate research tools)
- Standard 5 (Recognize the value of technology to support creativity and productivity).

CEFR Reference Level Descriptors:

- Global Scale: B2 (Can produce clear, detailed text on a wide range of subjects/ Can use language flexibly and effectively for social, academic, and professional purposes)
- Overall Reading Comprehension: B2 (Can read with a large degree of independence)
- Reading for Information and Argument: B2 (Can obtain information, ideas, and opinions from highly specialized sources)
- Reading Instructions: B2 (Can understand lengthy, complex instructions in his field)
- Addressing Audiences: B2 (Can give a clear, systematically developed presentation, with highlighting of significant points and relevant supporting detail)
- Overall Written Production: B2/C1 (Can write clear, detailed texts/ Can write clear, well-structured texts of complex subjects)
- Reports and Essays: B2 (Can write an essay or report that develops an argument systematically)
- Processing Text: B2 (Can summarize a wide range of factual and imaginative texts)
- General Linguistic Range: B2 (Has a sufficient range of language to be able to give clear descriptions)
- Vocabulary Range: B2 (Hs a good range of vocabulary for matters connected to his field)
- Grammatical Accuracy: B2 (Shows a relatively high degree of grammatical control)
- Orthographic Control: B2 (Spelling and punctuation are reasonably accurate)
- Sociolinguistic Appropriateness: B2 (Can express him- or herself confidently)
- Thematic Development: B2 (Can develop a clear description or narrative)
- Propositional Precision: B1 (Can explain the main points in an idea or problem with reasonale precision)
- Spoken Fluency: B1 (Can express him/herself with relative ease).

Analyzing and Extending the Lesson: Application to Additional Contexts. This scenario has provided a description of the redesign of two core English courses in a technical institute. The design has focused on developing students' communication skills in technical English and features the example of one assignment in the redesigned program, which combines written text with charts, a video presentation, and website design multimodally.

This design departs from conventional TESOL approaches to teaching specialized, technical English in that it focuses less on teaching the English language than on *using* English within authentic technical contexts as a tool of communication. We have argued in this chapter, and in keeping with the focus on IDLE throughout this book, that such approaches are more congruent with learner's digital orientation to learning English, and that this scenario represents the future of English language instruction, at least within intermediate and advanced contexts.

The teaching assignment included in this scenario was, in fact, based on an assignment developed by one of the authors of this book in a university in which English was the medium of instruction. The timeline and materials are identical. Students were required to complete much of the work outside class independently. We recognize that some instructors might find the use of Gantt charts and other materials daunting, as was the author initially. But the incorporation of these features was important in developing the technical literacy skills required for students' success in STEM-focused professions. We recommend that instructors might begin more simply, incorporating one or two aspects of the assignment described here and perhaps organizing students into small groups rather than individually, at least for beginning assignments.

Let's Discuss

1) What is your response to the argument that IDLE and its assumptions about learning, language, and materials are the logical outcome of an historical trend dating back to the middle of the twentieth century? As a pre-service or practicing teacher, where would you place your own experience as a learner within the progression described in Table 11.1? Where would you place the curriculum of your school or program?

2) What is your view of high-stakes assessments and their relation to curriculum? Do you think that tests and testing should drive the teaching and learning process? What is the tradition of your region, city, or country?

3) If you had the power to reform the official English language curriculum of your school, city, or country, what would your reform look like? Would it incorporate IDLE-like strategies, and how? Would you include high-stakes assessments to measure your curriculum or how else might you measure student learning?

4) What do you think the lasting effects of the Covid-19 pandemic will be on the curriculum and teaching practices of your school, city, or country? If you were a teacher during the pandemic, what changes did you have to make to your curriculum? Will you retain any of these?

5) What is your view on using action research as a possible way to evaluate the effects of the pandemic on teaching and your students' learning? Is this a practical approach, or do you think that using test scores will tell you enough about students' learning during this period?

6) Which of the three scenarios for adapting IDLE-like strategies to curriculum and assessment in this chapter do you think is most appropriate for the context in which you are teaching, or will teach? What adaptations will you make, and what other possible uses of social networks do you see being adaptable to your classroom context?

References

Banegas, Dario, Anahí Pavese, Aurelia Velázquez, and Sandra María Vélez. "Teacher Professional Development through Collaborative Action Research: Impact on Foreign English-Language Teaching and Learning." *Educational Action Research* 21, no. 2 (May 2013): 185–201. https://doi.org/10.1080/09650792.2013.789717.

Bernstein Jared, J.H.A.L. De JongDavid Pisoni, and Brent Townshend. "Two Experiments on Automatic Scoring of Spoken Language Proficiency." In *Proceedings of InSTIL2000: Integrating Speech Technology in Learning*, pp. 57–61. Dundee,UK: International Speech Communication Association, 2000.

Boog, Ben W. "The Emancipatory Character of Action Research, Its History and the Present State of the Art." *Journal of Community & Applied Social Psychology* 13, no. 6 (September 2003): 426–438. https://doi.org/10.1002/casp.748.

"Budgets." n.d. https://templates.office.com/en-us/budgets.

Burns, Anne. "Action Research: An Evolving Paradigm?" *Language Teaching* 38, no. 2 (April 2005): 57–74. https://doi.org/10.1017/s0261444805002661.

Canagarajah, Suresh. "TESOL as a Professional Community: A Half-Century of Pedagogy, Research, and Theory." *TESOL Quarterly* 50, no. 1 (March 2015): 7–41. https://doi.org/10.1002/tesq.275.

Cano, Jamie. "The Role of Action Research in Effecting Educational Change." *The Agricultural Education Magazine* 76, no. 6 (May–June 2004): 2.

Dressman, Mark. "Informal English Learning among Moroccan Youth." In The Handbook of Informal Language Learning, edited by Mark Dressman and Randall William Sadler, Hoboken, NJ: John Wiley & Sons, Inc., 303–318, 2020. https://doi.org/10.1002/9781119472384.ch20.ed.

Duolingo English Test. n.d. https://englishtest.duolingo.com.

Emmersion. 2022. https://emmersion.ai.

Engzell, Per, Arun Frey, and Mark D. Verhagen. "Learning Loss Due to School Closures during the COVID-19 Pandemic." *Proceedings of the National Academy of Sciences* 118, no. 17 (February 2021): https://doi.org/10.1073/pnas.2022376118.

Franco, Horacio, Harry Bratt, Romain Rossier, Venkata Rao Gadde, Elizabeth Shriberg, Victor Abrash, and Kristin Precoda. "EduSpeak(R): A Speech Recognition and Pronunciation Scoring Toolkit for Computer-Aided Language Learning Applications." *Language Testing* 27, no. 3 (August 2010): 401–418. https://doi.org/10.1177/0265532210364408.

Gee, James Paul. The Social Mind: Language, Ideology, and Social Practice. South Hadley, MA: Bergin & Garvey, 1992.

Giroux, Henry A., and Anthony N. Penna. "Social Education in the Classroom: The Dynamics of the Hidden Curriculum." *Theory & Research in Social Education* 7, no. 1 (March 1979): 21–42. https://doi.org/10.1080/00933104.1979.10506048.

Glassman, Michael, Gizem Erdem, and Mitchell Bartholomew. "Action Research and Its History as an Adult Education Movement for Social Change." *Adult Education Quarterly* 63, no. 3 (March 2013): 272–288. https://doi.org/10.1177/0741713612471418.

Hino, Nobuyuki. "The Significance of EMI for the Learning of EIL in Higher Education: Four Cases from Japan". In English Medium Instruction in Higher Education in Asia-Pacific, edited by Ben Fenton-Smith, Pamela Humphreys, and Ian Walkinshaw, 115–131, 2017. https://doi.org/10.1007/978-3-319-51976-0_7.

International Telecommunication Union. "2.9 Billion People Still Offline." 2021. https://www.itu.int/en/mediacentre/Pages/PR-2021-11-29-FactsFigures.aspx.

Kenning, Marie-Madeleine. "Computer-Assisted Language Learning." *Language Teaching* 23, no.2 (1990): 67–76

Language Confidence. n.d. https://languageconfidence.ai.

Larsen-Freeman, Diane, and Virginia Strom. "The Construction of a Second Language Acquisition Index of Development 1." *Language Learning* 27, no. 1 (January 1977): 123–134.

Lave, Jean, and Etienne Wenger. Situated Learning: Legitimate Peripheral Participation. Cambridge: Cambridge University Press, 1991.

Microsoft. 2022. "Pronunciation Assessment." https://docs.microsoft.com/en-us/azure/cognitive-services/speech-service/how-to-pronunciation-assessment?pivots=programming-language-csharp.

RFP360. "RFP Meaning: A Definitive Guide to the Request for Proposal." n.d. https://rfp360.com/rfp-meaning.

"Simple Gantt Chart." n.d. https://templates.office.com/en-us/simple-gantt-chart-tm16400962.

Stepien, William, and Shelagh Gallagher. "Problem-based Learning: As Authentic as it Gets." *Educational Leadership* 50, no. 7 (1993): 25–29.

Sun, Zhuomin, M. Anbarasan, and D. Praveen Kumar. "Design of Online Intelligent English Teaching Platform Based on Artificial Intelligence Techniques." *Computational Intelligence* 37, no. 3 (May 2020): 1166–1180. https://doi.org/10.1111/coin.12351.

Sundqvist, Pia, and Liss Kerstin Sylvén. Extramural English in Teaching and Learning: From Theory and Research to Practice. New York: Springer, 2016.

Tao, Jidong, Shabnam Ghaffarzadegan, Lei Chen, and Klaus Zechner. "Exploring Deep Learning Architectures for Automatically Grading Non-native Spontaneous Speech." In *2016 IEEE International Conference on Acoustics, Speech and Signal Processing (ICASSP)*, 6140–6144, 2016. https://doi.org/10.1109/ICASSP.2016.7472857.

Thorne, Christine, and Wang Qiang. "Action Research in Language Teacher Education." *ELT Journal* 50, no. 3 (July 1996): 254–262. https://doi.org/10.1093/elt/50.3.254.

Xiaohong, Wang, and Wang Yanzheng. "The Application of Artificial Intelligence in Modern Foreign Language Learning." In *2021 4th International Conference on Big Data and Education*, 34–37, June 2021. https://doi.org/10.1145/3451400.3451406.YouTube. 2016 https://youtu.be/pxIDuag7Np8

Zawacki-Richter, Olaf, Victoria I. Marín, Melissa Bond, and Franziska Gouverneur. "Systematic Review of Research on Artificial Intelligence Applications in Higher Education – Where Are the Educators?" *International Journal of Educational Technology in Higher Education* 16, no. 1 (October 2019): 1–27. https://doi.org/10.1186/s41239-019-0171-0

12

Autonomous, Informal Learning and the Future of English Language Education

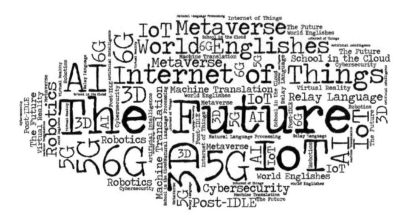

The digital world of English language education in 2035.

Introduction: Imagining English Learning and Teaching in the 2030s

It's 2035, and you are just beginning your second decade of teaching communication arts. In the 2020s you studied to be an English language teacher, but already in that time advances in digital technologies were beginning to make the teaching of English to beginning speakers obsolete. Through a wide variety of media available on the internet 24 hours a day, your students were rapidly picking up vocabulary, common phrases, and developing accents with a decidedly international flair. With a bit of instruction, they quickly gained basic competence in writing (and, with some encouragement, speaking) simple sentences.

Over time, with increased use of digital media and some practice, your students developed enough proficiency to read non-technical texts in English with comprehension, to write simple paragraphs, to watch videos without captions or subtitles, and to hold a simple conversation. You still met with your students at school at regularly scheduled times and followed standard course schedules, and you considered yourself an up-to-date

English Language Learning in the Digital Age: Learner-Driven Strategies for Adolescents and Young Adults,
First Edition. Mark Dressman, Ju Seong Lee, and Laurent Perrot.
© 2023 John Wiley & Sons Ltd. Published 2023 by John Wiley & Sons Ltd.

teacher because you understood the role of IDLE in your students' learning and had worked to integrate it into your teaching. You challenged your students to expand their repertoire of skills digitally to make videos and post them on YouTube in English and to create web pages and become competent users of Web 2.0 technologies in English.

But, in the mid-to-late 2020s, several developments began to challenge the foundations of your profession. The Covid-19 pandemic that began in 2020 led to enhanced digital infrastructure in schools and to increased interest in online and flipped learning in governments all over the world. Flipped learning became a common tool for teachers and schools to transmit content, with the intention of providing more time for classroom interaction. However, soon the amount of face-to-face time was reduced to around half of what it had been before, as students complained that they couldn't both come to class five or more hours per week and complete all those videos and exercises. Your role as a teacher shifted to developing materials for flipping and meeting many more students per week to interact with them. Universities began to rely less and less on formal English courses and moved to English Medium of Instruction (EMI) courses, with some integration of English instruction on the side.

By the late 2020s, advances in automatic machine translation had eliminated the need for the teaching of basic writing and speaking. Being able to speak without an automatic translator was still a valued skill, but learners began to realize that with some knowledge of English as a base, they could use a translator to learn and practice basic conversational phrases and patterns in real time. With practice, they could gradually reduce their reliance on the translator and eventually hold conversations on their own. The confidence they gained led to being able to deliver extended monologues and then to speak spontaneously in a wider and wider range of circumstances. Your task as a teacher became to create opportunities for this to happen.

By 2030, the need for basic, and in some countries intermediate, instruction in English had all but disappeared. Students learned English through highly sophisticated packages that combined virtual 3D "visits" to English-speaking countries, simulated conversations with L1 speakers, and augmented instruction using video, captions, and inserted lessons in grammar and pronunciation, all available at a click when needed. Their proficiency was assessed automatically through writing samples and recordings of them speaking in these environments. New and merged genres of digital entertainment provided immediate captioning and verbal translation (dubbing) for gaming and viewing a wide range of narrative series (i.e., movies and television, which merged as genres in the late 2020s). These included virtual participation in 3D worlds with characters who could speak English or any other language requested.

As a former English teacher, you have constantly needed to update your skills and revise your profile over the years. You and your educational institution have found that a strong need remains for the teaching of advanced and specific composition and communication skills. English is still—and will remain so in the foreseeable future—the lingua franca of academia and of business, and for individuals who can communicate effectively and persuasively across multiple genres, from the writing of advertising copy to news reports and articles to legal communications and publishing in scholarly journals. Each of these genres has its own conventions and requires the use of specific terms and structures that still defy automatic translation. In addition, complex genres that combine speaking with writing, graphic images, and video are needed more than ever, so the need for teaching these also remains. This has required you to master an increasingly sophisticated range of digital composition tools as well as to constantly improve your own proficiency in English.

As a teacher, then, your day is much more varied than you expected it to be when you started in 2023. You still spend some of your day in a classroom environment with students, but you spend more time working in your office or from home, creating materials for learning and advising your students much more than teaching or evaluating them. Your students, especially the younger ones, still need to see you personally and your relationships with them and your colleagues are just as strong, but you are together fewer hours per week, and you have many more students than you did before. There are, of course, schools and places where traditional English language instruction continues, but, increasingly, these are in areas that are marginalized economically, culturally, and politically.

Despite the promise of democratization and equity that the World Wide Web promised some 60 years ago, the world has become more stratified, with some regions and countries far ahead of others in terms of the speed and efficiency of their digital communications infrastructure (OECD 2021). You consider yourself fortunate indeed to be able to keep pace with change, but you also wonder how long you will be able to do so, and whether, beyond 2050, there will be a need for English or communication arts teachers at all.

The Timeless Need for Access, Authenticity, and Interaction

The preceding scenario is, we believe, an accurate projection of the ways that advances in technology and changes in education in the post-pandemic world are likely to affect English language education in the next 15 or so years. To many readers, this scenario may seem a discouraging or even pessimistic one, in which the role of teaching is gradually reduced as more and more functions of learning that were formerly under the control of teachers become automated or placed under the control of learners.

However, as we noted in Chapter 11 and have intimated throughout this book, this trend is consistent with developments in English language education since the beginning of the twentieth century. Figure 12.1 provides a chart tracing the paths of seven developments in English language education since 1900. It shows that with each new development, previous approaches did not fade away but continued in some settings, even as they might have been dismissed as "out of date" in others. Even today in many parts of the world, the grammar-translation approach remains the de facto method of teaching English, even if in teacher education programs it is dismissed as ineffective; the direct method survives beginning English courses in some language centers; and versions of the audiolingual method persist in some language labs.

More important, Figure 12.1 illustrates the ways that some aspects of older approaches influence the development of newer ones. Thus, the direct method's focus on interaction and inductive learning reappears in the rise of CLT in the 1960s and 1970s and continues in the rise of TBLT in the 1980s, with its focus on authentic communication and learner agency, which also appears in the evidence of studies of IDLE after 2010. In a different but related pattern of inheritance, the focus on technology of the audiolingual method is recapitulated in the rise of CALL in the 1980s and then IDLE in 2010. These two patterns of influence converge in IDLE, in which learners use technology and English in the

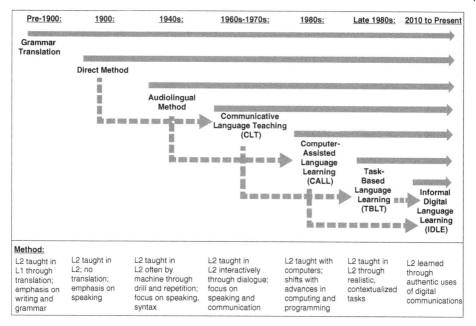

Pre-1900:	1900:	1940s:	1960s-1970s:	1980s:	Late 1980s:	2010 to Present
Method:						
L2 taught in L1 through translation; emphasis on writing and grammar	L2 taught in L2; no translation; emphasis on speaking	L2 taught in L2 often by machine through drill and repetition; focus on speaking, syntax	L2 taught in L2 interactively through dialogue; focus on speaking and communication	L2 taught with computers; shifts with advances in computing and programming	L2 taught in L2 through realistic, contextualized tasks	L2 learned through authentic uses of digital communications

Figure 12.1 Overview of the history of methods in English language education, pre-1900 to the present.

service of performing authentic tasks, and in the process become functional users of the language. If we were to extend the trends of Figure 12.1 into the 2030s, they would logically lead to the scenario that introduced this chapter.

Nearly all developments in English language education from the direct method in 1900 to the present and beyond are in many ways a reaction against the first method of language education, grammar-translation. That method, which originated in the teaching of classical, "dead" languages no longer actively spoken, ignored the need for spontaneous communication in a modern setting and focused on the learning of grammar and vocabulary within an ancient historical context. Modern language educators over the years have progressively understood that learning to use a new language in the here-and-now requires at least three additional components: access to the target language; authenticity of contexts, materials, and learning tasks; and opportunities for meaningful interaction. Over the last century, these were the challenges of language education that methodologists and technology continually worked to address.

The need for access, authenticity, and interaction is a timeless one, and this should give current and prospective English language educators some hope for their future. We are at the beginning of a golden era for autonomous language learning, one that realizes and then exceeds the promises of IDLE, but it will not be an era without need of teachers. During the Covid-19 pandemic we have learned how critical it is for people to come together physically and have real, not exclusively virtual, interactions. Although it may initially be novel to learn English by interacting with a robot, no robot into the foreseeable future is likely to be as fully interactive (and unpredictable or as engaging) as live humans can be. As discussed in Chapter 8, we also know that current non-formal programs for language learning such as Babbel and Duolingo have high attrition rates and that motivation to continue beyond a few lessons is a great problem for learners and program developers. In the end, language learning will necessarily remain, at least to some degree, a highly social and human process requiring most learners to come together with others and a knowledgeable human instructor.

Finally, translation and autocorrection may be appropriate starting places for writing but they will never add the nuance, the personality, or the elements that make a text individual and convincing for readers; and as compositions become increasingly multimodal, the need to learn new skills to combine and juxtapose images, video, audio, and written text will become more important than ever. These complex and highly individualized skills will demand greater levels of instruction than a program can provide.

What, then, will English language teaching look like 15 or 20 years into the future? What will learning look like? And how about curriculum and assessment? Before considering these further, we need to look first at how communication technologies may develop in the next decades and to consider what place English itself is likely to have in the world.

Chapter Objectives

The central objective of this chapter is to provide a research-based context for anticipating the future of English language education into the first half of the twenty-first century. A major goal is to consider five major advances in digital communications technologies that are likely to have an impact on both English as a global language and on language education, with a focus on curriculum, assessment, teaching, and learning. A subgoal is to consider how English may develop as a global language and what impact this may have on education. Additional subgoals are to imagine classroom practices in 2035, to examine the role of teaching in highly automatic contexts, and to consider the future of English language teaching as a profession. By the end of this chapter, readers should be able to:

1) Describe lines of continuity in approaches to English language education over the past century and into the present.
2) Identify five advances in digital technology and their possible impact on English language education in classrooms.
3) Describe the possible development of English as a global language in the twenty-first century and its impact on English language learning and teaching.
4) Describe in detail how advances in digital technology and increased learning autonomy will optimally affect English language teaching across multiple contexts and age levels.
5) Describe major changes in the role of teachers likely to occur in the next two decades.
6) Evaluate possible scenarios for English language education in 2035.
7) Describe the consequences of not developing new skills and learner-driven approaches to English language education in the future.

Key Words

5G network technology; internet of things (IoT); robotics; metaverse; relay language

Digital Technology in 2035: Five Advances in Technology

5G Networks, the Internet of Things (IoT), and Beyond

Although 5G networking is already in place in parts of North America, Europe, and East Asia, its progress has been slowed by the pandemic and its full potential is yet to be realized. Readers with new mobile devices in areas with 5G are likely to notice greater reliability, faster speeds, and minimal lag time than with their old 4G devices, but 5G promises new possibilities for networking that were almost inconceivable in the past (Godwin-Jones 2021; Lei 2020; Li 2021).

5G technology uses a cloud-based networking architecture that is far less centralized than a 4G network. This allows for signals to travel more quickly and efficiently and increases the ability of devices to "talk among themselves" separately from human intervention or control, facilitating an "Internet of Things" (IoT) in addition to an internet of people interacting with each other or an internet of people interacting with things. In an IoT environment, communication among devices is nearly fully automated, requiring minimal human direction (Cohen 2020; Kumar 2021).

Imagine, for example, a warehouse that is fully automated, in which all parts of the process of both filling orders and restocking the warehouse are achieved through a series of robotic devices communicating and coordinating activities among themselves. Or imagine someone with a serious heart condition having a device implanted which monitors in real time not only heart rhythm but blood flow and oxygen level, and that continually sends this information to another device operated by a medical service, which may also be partially automated. In the event of arrythmia or other anomaly, a signal is sent to the device in the patient that stimulates the heart or even releases precisely and automatically calculated doses of drugs and alerts a physician that there is a problem. In these scenarios, human judgment and intervention are not eliminated, but much of the physical labor of moving goods or of a patient making regular visits to a doctor's office is reduced, improving service levels, and allowing managers and physicians to work more efficiently and effectively.

Now imagine the application of IoT technology to English language education. Researchers in Valencia, Spain created a task-based learning scenario for teaching English to young children (de la Guía et al. 2016). Each child wore an IoT device (a watch or smartphone) that had an app for reading IoT-tagged objects in a scenario in which the students within a classroom setting were required to shop for tagged food items and then use tagged utensils to prepare a recipe. The objects and the students' devices were linked by Bluetooth to a server that coordinated and recorded the students' activities, thus monitoring their progress and learning. The server also directed the students to perform specific subtasks and gave them feedback as they progressed, letting them know, for example, if they had identified the correct food item in English. The teacher led the task, instructing students when to begin and circulating among the students as they worked. The authors noted that using IoT technology in this case had three advantages over reproducing the task in a standard setting: (1) the devices helped keep track of progress through the activity; (2) the system automatically recorded each child's participation; and (3) the children seemed more focused on following instructions than if the teacher were trying to direct them all by voice. Overall, the teacher was more able to focus on "guiding and encouraging" (de la Guía et al. 2016, 370) the students rather than struggling to manage many things at once.

Note that in this example from 2016, the system used Bluetooth and Wi-Fi technology rather than 5G to accomplish its goals, and that it was relatively complicated to set up. In a 5G environment, much of the technology interface for the activity would pre-exist and teachers would only need to tag relevant objects. A 5G environment would also presumably allow for more complicated IoT English-learning tasks requiring more complex uses of English at more advanced levels of learning, and might even extend beyond classroom or school walls to community-based learning, all automatically recorded by teachers remotely (Cohen 2020).

Beyond 5G

As 5G advances globally, the planning and design of 6G networking has already begun (Davis 2020). Plans currently call for an increase in speed from 10 gigabits per second to 100, which will allow self-driving automobiles to instantly communicate with each other on the road, doctors to perform surgery remotely with no lag time between the surgeon's movement and an in situ robot's, and people to meet holographically in virtual space.

But these advances will require new technologies beyond those used for 5G. Current problems with overheating 5G phones requiring more power than assumed, and the need for increased base stations has slowed 5G's rollout and will need to be addressed first. Solving these problems and developing new 6G technologies are not likely to happen until 2030 or later.

5G technologies will also provide a more stable and efficient interface for game-based learning and for 3D virtual environments, and 6G networks which are now being envisioned for introduction in the next 25 or so years will take immersive virtuality to even greater lengths (Piran and Suh 2019). Imagine taking students for a projected walk down a street in an English-speaking city like Sydney or San Francisco and having them "bump into" a pre-arranged stranger on the street who answers their questions about the city and gives them directions to the Opera House or the Golden Gate Bridge.

Artificial Intelligence, Robotics, and Machine Translation

Uses of AI, machine translation, and speech recognition applications are already commonplace worldwide, although their application within English language classrooms remains limited. As early as 2018, a review of 33 research articles on robotic language learning reported studies in which robots were used to teach vocabulary, some basic grammar, and speaking skills to students from pre-school to adult, with mixed results (van den Berghe et al. 2018). Other uses of AI in language education are also common, but not necessarily in language classrooms. For example, mobile language apps use AI not only to adjust levels of questions but also to assess pronunciation. One study using Amazon Alexa as a practice activity found significant gains for speakers (Hsu, Chen, and Todd 2021). Readers who have a subscription to Microsoft Office will find a feature of PowerPoint that allows them to have their spoken presentation translated and presented in subtitles as they give it into more than 60 languages (Pairaphrase 2022). This works by sending everything a presenter says to Microsoft, where it is immediately translated and sent back to the PowerPoint slide. At the time of writing, hand-held translation devices that take spoken sentences and automatically translate them into speech and text through a Wi-Fi or 4G connection are on the market for less than USD $300; one even uses a pair of ear pods which two conversants share so that they don't need to keep passing a device back and forth. Finally, the use of machine translation to teach L2 writing, as noted in Chapter 8, is well-researched (Groves and Mundt 2015; Hartono 2015; Lee 2019).

If the future already appears to be the present, then why hasn't the use of AI, machine translation, and robotics become more prominent in classrooms and informal digital contexts? The reason is first that many programs using these applications remain rudimentary and are sometimes inaccurate. Second, most current mobile applications rely on 4G technology, which is unreliable if the signal is weak, causing lag time and drops in service in many contexts. In combination, these issues can be very frustrating for users.

However, the introduction of 5G networking will address issues of lag time and provide faster and more reliable service to users, spurring advancements in AI, machine translation, and robotics. For example, Google Glass premiered to thunderous hype, but in fact its needed connection to Wi-Fi or to a smartphone through a 4G connection rendered it clunky to use and unreliable. But imagine a 5G version of augmented glasses equipped with a camera and audio receiver connected to a 5G smartphone with negligible lag time and high speed and reliability, worn by a user with perhaps a B1 CEFR level—someone able to participate in most conversations but who struggled at times with words or phrasing in English (Hong and Choi 2018). The glasses would "read" the visual and audio context of the wearer's setting and anticipate words or phrases in the conversation as the wearer spoke, scaffolding not only immediate conversations but, through an AI feedback loop, helping the wearer to become a more independent, fluent, and proficient speaker of English.

3D (Virtual) Multimodal Composition

Combining written text with images, video, animation, and narration within a PowerPoint presentation or web page has been possible for more than a decade, but fully multimodal compositions within academic and commercial publishing remain rare, due to curent limitations in storage space and infrastructure. However, advances in 5G technologies are likely to create new opportunities for more efficient creation and storage of multimodal texts (Chandler, O'Brien, and Unsworth 2010; Lim and Toh 2020; Wardle 2014).

Imagine, for example, a middle school English class in which the students produce a play or short skit with dialogue written by themselves or another author, or perhaps they create a new episode of one of their favorite series, in the style of fanfiction (see the example of Dietrich Hoffmann in Chapter 6). The students write a script and then, to perform it, use animation software that is far more advanced than what is currently available. Alternatively, perhaps they perform it in a 3D virtual environment similar to Second Life (see the example of Janez Vidmar in Chapter 7), wearing sensor-suits that direct the actions of the avatars in the 3D environment, record their performance, and upload it to a next-generation YouTube-like platform for viewing. In a final scenario, imagine a student studying chemistry in an EMI program who creates a 3D model of a molecule for a report, which she then narrates and records along with the longer written paper (Limniou, Roberts, and Papadopoulos 2008). These are only a few possible ways that L2 writing in 2035 might be combined with speech and virtual imagery.

The Metaverse

Closely related to 3D multimodal composition is the concept of the Metaverse, a fully realized virtual world in which, through VR headsets and perhaps sensor-suits, individuals can become fully immersed (Chen 2022; Duan et al. 2021; Kye et al. 2021; Lee et al. 2021). Partial versions of virtual worlds already exist in programs like Second Life, but these experiences currently come through two-dimensional computer screens. In a fully immersive environment, users would be "in" the world itself, walking (or perhaps flying) around, interacting with others, and having real-time conversations.

Another possibility is that rather than being immersed in an artificially created world, virtual 3D worlds could be constructed from video captured by 360-degree cameras. In this scenario, one could wear a VR headset and sensor-suit to "visit" a famous site such as the Great Pyramids or the Grand Canyon and have a "real" experience of it, along with others. Imagine, then, a group of high school students in Busan, South Korea meeting with students in Brisbane, Queensland in a Metaverse exchange program; or a university instructor in Abu Dhabi taking a class on a Metaverse field trip to a virtually recorded Washington, DC or Vancouver, British Columbia.

Cybersecurity, Privacy, and Ethics

As the transition from 4G to 5G technologies progresses, new threats to security, individual privacy, and ethics will also evolve. Cloud-based systems and the Internet of Things provide many, many more points of entry for hackers, so that connected objects like printers or even coffee makers could be hacked (Forge and Vu 2020; Pezoa et al. 2021). Opportunities for plagiarism and other forms of cheating may also increase. Developers of the new technologies are of course aware of the problems but just as there are problems with security, privacy, and ethics now, these will surely persist in the future (CISA 2021; Wheeler and Simpson 2019; Yeruva 2021).

Ironically, it seems that the more technology opens opportunities for global communication and connection through virtual contact, the greater the need becomes for individuals and organizations to shield themselves and safeguard their privacy. By 2035, it is likely that new modes of authentication and walling will be needed. Using a VPN or similar shield is likely to become a necessity online, and we may all need to create avatars and take other steps to mask our identity and protect our assets. In the future, when online we may never project ourselves openly without serious risk, nor ever really know the people with whom we are interacting.

Transforming Roles for English and Its Education

The Global Role of English in 2035

At the beginning of the twenty-first century, the future of English as the world's foremost global language seemed assured. Globalization, an often ill-defined buzzword for the increasing economic interdependence of nations, was assumed to require a global lingua franca whereby governments, corporations, and international agencies would be able to coordinate among each other. English, as one of the most widely spoken languages—and almost certainly as the most widely spoken second and foreign language—in the world, seemed the most logical candidate to fill that need.

Two well-known, and to this day, frequently cited books celebrated and yet also raised concerns about the globalization of English: *English as a Global Language, 2nd Ed.* by David Crystal (2003) and *The Future of English?* by David Graddol (1997) both published in the UK. Both books assumed a Kachru-like model (Kachru 1990) to describe the distribution of English speakers in the world, consisting of three concentric circles: an inner circle of "native" speakers; an outer circle of second-language speakers; and an expanding circle of speakers of English as a foreign language. In this model speakers in the first circle continued to have the most (if not complete) control over the standardization of the language and its development, while speakers in the outer circles remained dependent on the inner circle in some way.

Both authors also saw English in competition with other world languages and within itself among its varieties, or "Englishes," for domination. Crystal in particular expressed concern for the development of Englishes, or different dialects of English originating not only in inner circle countries like the United States and Australia but outer circle countries like India and Singapore. Grounding his argument in the dissipation of Latin into varieties that eventually became French, Italian, Romanian, and so on, he suggested that, in time, the Englishes of the world could also become separate languages, implying that the English of the inner circle might become eventually less dominant than currently. He also suggested that English might be rejected in some regions and countries due to past histories of colonialism or a reluctance on the part of populations, not governments, to incorporate English into business and daily activities.

Was English Ever a Single Language?

Much of the modeling to describe the growth of English globally depends on the image of a unified language originating in England and then spreading throughout Britain and Ireland, into North America and Australasia, and beyond. But an argument can be made that English was never a unified language, even in England.

According to some estimates, there are likely dozens of dialects of English in the UK alone, and many more worldwide, all (mostly) intelligible to one another (Laperre 2020). It is a historical fact that English began in England, but even there it has never been a unified language—there has never been an "English Academy" defining English as there is an Académie Française.

The mutability of English has been one of its defining features, present at its creation, and arguably the feature that has enabled its service as the global lingua franca. Does it matter, then, if one speaks it as a first, second, or other language? Is there, in fact, a unified "Indian English" or a unified "Nigerian English?" And if not, then what does it mean to speak any of these varieties or even British English "well?"

Crystal did not take technological developments or the revolution in global communications of satellite television and the internet into account in his analysis. Graddol, on the other hand, provided an analysis of English's global rise to prominence consistent with our analysis in Chapter 2 of this book, in which he described globalization in general and digital technologies especially as responsible for national policy decisions worldwide to prioritize English-language instruction in schools and EMI programs, in some cases at secondary levels, and in many others, university programs.

In *The Future of English?* (Graddol 1997) and a subsequent book, *English Next: Why Global English May Mean the End of 'English as a Foreign Language'* (Graddol 2006), both published by the British Council, Graddol focused on the rise of English-language media, the internet, and advances in machine translation in continuing English's preeminence as a world language, although he also noted the rise of media in other world languages as well. However, he underestimated the implications of advancing technologies and missed almost completely the role of the informal learning of English through digital technologies in the spread of English. From his perspective, English would continue to be taught—and learned—mostly in school, although he also noted for his inner-circle readers that the advantages of being a "native speaker" might dissipate over time. He also considered the rise of EMI globally and saw this as a clear sign that in the future English teachers would need to adapt and to acquire new skills and models of teaching, but his discussion of the direction English teaching would take was framed in acronyms, such as CLIL (Content and Language Integrated Learning), ELF (English as a Lingua Franca), and EYL (English for Young Learners).

In the intervening years between the early 2000s and early 2020s, our review of the research indicates little challenge to patterns or issues in the globalization of English described by Kachru, Crystal, and Graddol. Most research published in this period focused less on global patterns and more on local and national concerns about the rise of English, for example, in India (Graddol 2010), South Korea (Joo, Chik, and Djonov 2020), China (Fang 2018), Japan (Takahashi 2021), Indonesia (Lestari and Setiyawan 2020; Zein 2018), Bangladesh (Rahman and Pandian 2018), and so on, framed by the assumptions of those authors. Our reading of that literature in early 2022, following a global pandemic that could not have been foreseen, is that while they were correct to note the globalization of English and its continued influence well into the twenty-first century, they radically underestimated the spread of digital communications technologies and the implications of that spread for learning and teaching, or for the plurilingualism that advances in machine translation might bring.

Consider the implications of the image in Figure 12.2. This window popped up as we were searching for articles for this chapter on the site for the journal, *Language Teaching*, published by Cambridge University Press, stating that the scholarly article we were searching for could be translated for us into one or more of 20 languages. In other words, in this case English was used as a "relay language" in Graddol's (1997, 31) terminology, that is, as the nominal language among many in which the content of the article might

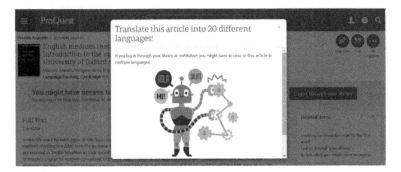

Figure 12.2 Some journal publishers now offer translations of articles in multiple languages.

be accessed. This development in machine translation shatters all the presumptions about World Englishes of Kachru, Crystal, and Graddol, and indeed, many of their presumptions about the need for a global lingua franca, if, at the push of a button, a paper or any text written in Indian English can be automatically "translated" into Australian or British or American English, or indeed, if any text written in any of 20 or more major world languages can be translated into English, or Hindi, or Japanese. It also renders Kachru's three-circle model irrelevant and realizes Graddol's (2006) prediction that soon distinctions among native, second-language, and foreign-language speakers of English will become increasingly irrelevant.

From our perspective, English is likely to remain the world's lingua franca (or at least its relay language) into the coming decades, but Kachru's model and its assumptions are likely to appear anachronistic as time goes by. No doubt the ability to speak English with a high degree of proficiency and creativity will continue to be highly valued, but the parameters for its acquisition and learning are likely to change, and the roles of curriculum and assessment in classrooms as well as teachers may undergo transformation, especially within settings where technological infrastructure keeps pace in schools. In the remainder of this chapter, we outline our vision of how the elements of language education may transform by 2035 and beyond.

Classrooms, Curriculum, and Assessment in 2035

A recurring theme of this chapter has been that the present and future of English language education are not the result of a rupture or revolution but rather a continuation and refinement of a long line of theory and practice traceable to the early decades of the twentieth century. In education as in many other fields of practice, the past is always active, for better and for worse, in its present and in its future.

Although digital technologies clearly have revolutionized global communications, their impact on the design of classrooms or schools is not likely to be outwardly different in 2035 from the classrooms and schools of today, which have changed little in the past century and are remarkably similar across the globe. Almost anywhere in the world, a classroom is a rectangular space for 30–40 desks usually placed in rows, with a central station for a teacher in front and a set of surfaces on one or more walls that can be written on. A school is a collection of these classrooms organized by a central hallway, with some ancillary spaces for other activities such as a library, a gymnasium, an administrative office, and lunchroom. This pattern has been remarkably stable for over a century and there is no reason why it is likely to change by 2035.

Changes between now and 2035 are therefore more likely to be peripheral than central in the design of classrooms and curricular programs, but, if implemented thoughtfully, their impact on learners may be profound. In terms of infrastructure, the most likely changes will be in the ubiquity, speed, and reliability of the internet, although the extent of these changes will vary depending on the affluence of a school or nation, and whether 4G or 5G connectivity is available. The expense of installing 5G and its requirement of new hardware, along with cybersecurity issues previously discussed, will likely forestall its implementation in less affluent countries for some time.

In terms of curriculum and instructional practices, a realistic forecast is that some basic changes may become endemic in schools and English language classrooms worldwide, while others may be limited to settings with greater resources and/or motivation to innovate. At the level of basic changes, in many countries a beginning, A1 and possibly A2, CEFR level of knowledge about English may be assumed of students through their interaction with English-language media as they enter formal instruction; or beginning English classes may largely be taught through AI programs or by robots, either as physical or on-screen entities. At intermediate and advanced levels, there is likely to be much more flipped learning, with much content in the form of grammar, practice sessions, and cultural lessons assigned to students for homework, with reduced instructional/meeting time for interaction with the teacher and peers. Some content may comprise lectures developed by teachers, but much of it is also likely to be packaged, programmed learning materials that will largely replace hardcopy textbooks. Like art, music, or physical education teachers now, English language teachers may have less contact with more students, seeing each class for only a few hours each week and playing more of a supervisory role guiding and encouraging students and monitoring their progress. During class meetings, activities may be more task-based, with students using the internet to research and solve problems that require practice in particular English skills.

Perhaps the most significant change may be in the use of AI to monitor and assess student progress continuously. Via the Internet of Things, each student could have a dedicated device on which they completed all of their work. The device would be connected to a school server and program that would continuously monitor the quality of a student's writing, and perhaps even speech, in English and provide reports to the teacher and student suggesting possible materials and programs to enhance the student's learning. This would effectively eliminate the need for periodic tests or even the grading of assignments. A summative assessment would be made at the end of each grading period and an English proficiency score would be assigned for speaking and writing. Students who failed to achieve a benchmark level might be assigned additional programs or meet with a teacher for extra lessons. In theory, exclusive use of the device by an individual student would also eliminate the possibility of plagiarism or other forms of cheating like the use of translators, since the device would be monitoring all of a student's spoken and written activity. However, the increased level of surveillance could also have detrimental, anxiety-producing effects for the student as well as raise ethical issues about privacy.

Beyond these basic, endemic shifts in English language education, in settings with greater resources and/or motivation, additional uses of technology might enhance student learning experiences (OECD 2021). Imagine the possibilities of augmented reality for teaching using a Pokemon-Go! type of activity, in which students followed a trail to gather clues and piece together a mystery in English. In another example, students might use VR headsets to travel to an English-speaking country Google Earth-style, moving down the street and perhaps meeting and having a conversation with a pre-arranged English speaker. Enhanced use of computer-mediated communication tools (Godwin-Jones 2021; Li 2021) might include virtual meetings with students in a classroom in another country, or the creation of 3D tours of each other's cities to be watched and commented on asynchronously. Students might even engage in extended "virtual exchanges" where they attended class virtually in another country. The increased use of multimodality to create projects in which students used advanced (and much more intuitive) versions of programs like Blender (Zamudio et al. 2017) to create 3D models and then narrate and write about them is another possibility, as is the extended use of corpora, or large, text-based collections of writing from a particular author or genre that might be "mined" to study the use of words or structural organization sentences within an authentic context (Poole 2018). These are only a few of the possibilities that provide increased access, authenticity, and interaction for learners in English.

Learning and Teaching English in 2035

Learning. The preceding discussion points to the increasing autonomy of English language learning by 2035, although it remains unclear how "autonomy" will be defined. Will it mean, for example, that within classroom settings learners will have more control and greater choice over the means of their learning and that strategies for teaching will be learner-driven and derive from authentic sources of input? Or will autonomous learning be defined as students independently working their way through packages of sophisticated language programs consisting of interactive games and videos, with the support, encouragement, and occasional live sessions with a teacher in a classroom?

With respect to IDLE, by 2035 it is likely that informal learning of English through digital media will become so ubiquitous and taken for granted that in many countries teachers will assume that students enter English programs with basic vocabulary and idioms, even if they lack a formal understanding of grammar or more extended and formal uses of English. "Learning English," then, may consist of being initially introduced to the conventions of formal English, including for early learners, English script, then using English in an ever-expanding circle of contexts, including writing and producing a range of multimodal compositions that are personal and academic within highly social online and in-person contexts. Learning in this context is acquisitional and incidental and simultaneously deliberate and conscious.

Teaching. The preceding discussion also points to major changes in the role of teachers within advanced digital environments. Today as in 2035, best practices in teaching are not characterized by the image of teachers as possessors of knowledge who transmit content to students through highly controlled, teacher-directed lectures and practice exercises. Rather, in a learner-driven and technologically advanced environment, teaching is an intuitive, empathic, and very complex activity in which teachers' primary task is to learn from their students and to integrate insights about their interests and motivations with standardized curricular goals. Teachers become improvisational planners: They have a clear understanding of curricular goals but remain open to the parameters and means of its achievement and are highly sensitive and responsive to input from students.

However, this description would only apply in situations where teachers and students had the ability largely to determine their own practices. In more basic, technology-centered programs using commercially prepared materials, the role of teachers (and learners) would likely be much reduced.

The School in the Cloud. A possible compromise and very intriguing model of learning is "The School in the Cloud," developed by the Indian-British educator Sugata Mitra (2014). Mitra may be best known for a popular series of TED Talks in which he describes his early and current projects in India and the UK. In 1999, Mitra embedded a computer with a high-speed internet connection and a track pad in a wall three feet off the ground in a poor urban area in India. He left no instructions but found that soon children began to congregate around the computer and a little later had learned how to use it to surf the internet for information and games to play. He was astonished by the speed at which the children learned to operate the computer, and began to experiment with simple learning tasks, such as changing their English accents by requiring them to use speech recognition software and then giving them advanced academic tasks in which they were required to learn subjects like biotechnology in English and then were tested. Mitra found that the students in South India were able to teach themselves about biotechnology but they learned more if they were assisted by a "granny"—a retired schoolteacher in the UK who met with the students and knew nothing about the subject but was very warm and encouraging. Mitra expanded the "granny cloud" with a network of retired teachers and found a similar result across multiple learning tasks.

In 2014, with funding from the TED Foundation, Mitra developed the SOLE, or Self-Organized Learning Environment. A SOLE is a room with a series of internet-linked computer stations distributed in a room around which groups of four students stand to do collaborative research in response to a teacher-generated question. It is essentially a task-based learning center that trusts in the ingenuity of students to collaboratively find and report solutions to open-ended and very engaging questions on a variety of topics. In studies of SOLEs in seven different countries on three continents, Mitra has consistently found that students are able to learn complex subjects far more thoroughly when allowed to direct their own learning collaboratively than was previously thought possible.

Mitra's work is highly controversial, however, and he has been criticized for what is seen as his dismissal of the role of teachers and his admonition to them not to guide or even ask leading questions as the children work. However, a recent documentary of his work by Deutsche Welle (2021) shows that teachers play a vital role in the process. They lead and organize students, generate questions for the students to research, evaluate the results of the learning and debrief with students afterwards, and provide support and encouragement. Moreover, the grannies in the documentary are seen being more engaged with the students in discussing their lives in the UK and the lives of the students and offering interesting and engaging activities to them than Mitra's description of them suggests.

The School in the Cloud may not be feasible as an entire language curriculum for students, but as an activity once or twice a week that would supplement a more programmed language curriculum, it could add a significant level of student-driven learning and value to English language programs of the future at primary and secondary levels of schooling. In addition, the technology of SOLEs is relatively simple. It requires a 1:4 ratio of computers to students and a reasonably fast internet connection that can be delivered through a landline, 4G, or satellite connection. As such, it is a workable model of student-driven language learning in the present that would be feasible in many developed and developing countries now rather than in the future; and as 5G and other technological advances become available, new resources would be opened to students that would only enhance their experiences.

Four Scenarios for 2035

A Middle School in Daegu, Republic of Korea. Yeo Hyejin is an English communication arts teacher at a middle school in Daegu, South Korea. In the last decade, K-pop and

K-drama have become major entertainment powers worldwide with the merger of major Korean entertainment companies Studio Dragon and YG with Disney and Fox in the United States and Vivendi in France to form world-pop and world-drama. Korean groups produce a few songs in English, Japanese, or Spanish, but most of their repertoire remains Korean. Although advances in machine translation now allow viewers to watch programs in more than 60 languages, the process is still awkward, and the students often prefer to view with subtitles.

In addition to the growth of Korean entertainment worldwide, Australian telemovies (series with movie-quality production) are also spreading worldwide, and Ms. Yeo's students are as excited about the stars and Australian storylines as students in Australia are about Korean entertainment. Through her virtual master's program, she has met several Australian language teachers and formed close friendships with two teachers of Korean in Melbourne.

Ms. Yeo's school has recently transitioned to an AI assessment system, in which students' speech and writing in class is continuously monitored and evaluated, and she follows a standardized curriculum with a prescribed set of language skills that must be met. Much of her program is automated and Ms. Yeo's job is largely one of monitoring and guiding her students through virtual activities. However, every 10 weeks there is a "free week" in which teachers can develop unique projects. Because there is only a two-hour time difference between Korea and Melbourne, she and her friend have designed a project in which their students will have a series of live video conferences in which the classes meet and students ask each other questions arising after watching each other's telemovies, such as "What does it mean to have a 'small face' in Korea, and why do Koreans like small faces?" from the Australian students, or "What is Vegemite and how do you eat it?" from the Koreans. They will have automatic translators to assist the students, but both teachers are working with their students now to prepare and use these as little as possible. "Natural" communication remains the preferred method of interaction in 2035, even though simultaneous translation has become a possibility in most situations.

A Sixth-Form Program in RAK, UAE. Malika Al Shehhi teaches English at a small, newly established experimental sixth-form program in Ras Al Khaimah (RAK), UAE. Under a recent reorganization of secondary education in RAK by the Ministry of Education that emphasizes global outreach, her school has adopted a British curriculum and paired with a school in London. The London partner has a similar global focus, and a significant percentage of its students are from the Arab Gulf. As part of their agreement, there have been several teacher and student exchanges between the two schools in the past year, and virtual exchanges for all students are planned in the coming school year.

In a bold move, the school's administration has decided to adopt the O-, AS-, and A-level exam system of the British Department of Education in English, maths, and sciences, and Malika has been asked to take the lead in designing curricula for English A levels. She and her colleagues are concerned that their sixth-form students will struggle because although English is introduced in primary grades in RAK, instruction does not begin in English until students reach high school. Her students watch a great deal of world drama on Netflix and other streaming services and their interest in telemovies from Hollywood has helped many of them speak fluently, but they struggle with writing in more formal genres. The literary focus of the A levels will also be challenging, although recent additional requirements for demonstration of skills in digital composition should provide the context for collaborative student work.

There is a four-hour time difference between London and RAK that Malika and her counterparts in London have decided to take advantage of, pairing morning classes in London with early afternoon classes in RAK. Teachers in both locations have decided to share the same subject content and to focus on Arab-British literary texts. As their fictional work, they've chosen *The Book of the Thousand Nights and a Night*, translated by the Victorian explorer and author Sir Richard Burton (1934), and as the nonfiction selection, *Arabian Sands* by the British military explorer and author, Sir Wilfred Thesiger (2007). The classes will meet simultaneously using wall-sized projection screens and conferencing software that will allow for team teaching and discussion of the books. As a project, students will be organized into groups of four (two RAK and two British students) and using advanced teleconferencing software during school and independently, will collaboratively create an interpretive video production of one of the stories from *The Thousand Nights* along with a live presentation of their interpretation of the story, and a short documentary based on one chapter from *Arabian Sands*.

A University in South-Central France. Guillem Albert is a professor of languages and media at a university in South-Central France, working in a program directed on multilingual writing and digital media production, with a focus on journalism. Guillem is a native of Perpignan in French Catalonia and grew up bilingual in French and Catalan, with some knowledge of Spanish and North African Arabic varieties, which he picked up from friends as an adolescent. He attended university in Ottawa on a scholarship and learned English there. He worked formerly for France 24 as a reporter and linguistic consultant before joining the university as director of its multilingual journalism program.

Since 2030, language programs at universities in France have become more focused on communication in specialized areas. The program in multilingual journalism is a response to this initiative. Guillem's students also reflect the changing demographics of France and its universities. Half are ethnically French while the rest are composed of first- and second-generation North and West Africans, refugees from Syria and Hong Kong, and immigrants from other parts of Europe, Latin America, and East Asia.

Many of the students in the program have internships with France 24 and serve as linguistic and cultural consultants. Through Guillem, they also produce multilingual documentary shorts about immigration and other topics for broadcast domestically, as well as longer documentaries for broadcast internationally in multiple languages, using a combination of machine translation and review by first-language students. Students are all expected to become fully proficient in English, French, and Spanish during their program. They meet weekly for language classes specializing in the use of journalistic languages, but most of their learning comes from using these languages. Their proficiency is monitored through submission of periodic reports and podcasts in English, with expectations that they will achieve a professional level of proficiency in each language by the time they graduate. They anticipate careers in broadcast journalism in regions where their first language is spoken as well as internationally.

A Language Center Anywhere. Jorge Torres directs a language center in a major world city that is not predominantly English-speaking. The center is part of a worldwide chain of language centers that merged with a major online language education company and has since emphasized the use of advanced proprietary digital programs for learning languages, combined with live in-person and online instruction. Some of the teachers at Jorge's center are local and work directly with students in the city, while other instructors are online and meet with students for tutorials or more specialized language sessions. The center offers instruction in not only English but in other major world languages and has a wide variety of clientele. Both Jorge and his staff are multilingual and are required to have advanced skills in their instructional languages as well as proficiency in a range of digital composition mediums, including video and web design.

To remain relevant and cost-effective in an increasingly plurilingual world with many opportunities for simultaneous, machine translation, the center offers many specialized programs and services. English is not offered in preschool or early primary grades in the city, and so the center offers programs in English for Young Learners that combine IoT technologies and interaction with caring, enthusiastic teachers at low student–teacher ratios for parents who want their children to have a head start in English. Beginning English courses consist of the use of English instruction in virtual reality settings, using programs created by the home company that are not available elsewhere, combined with live instruction in small classes and a consultation with a teacher once a week. At the intermediate and advanced levels, test preparation courses and courses in English for Special Purposes and digital composition are offered, as well as translation services that used advanced machine translation in consultation with a language specialist who helps a client tailor a composition in multiple languages.

Conclusion

The Alternative: Suppose None of "The Future" Happens for English Language Education?

The preceding scenarios present best-case depictions of English language education in formal settings worldwide, where students are assumed to have a basic knowledge of English. Where they do not, they acquire this through programmed instruction. Technology plays a vital role in all settings, but it is still technology that is recognizable today, and programs make use of convenient time zones and advanced forms of video-conferencing to take advantage of global connections for special projects. Teaching English has become a far more diversified practice, with more focus on communication and the meeting of standards, and teachers have become proficient users of many forms of digital technology.

These practices are in keeping with developments in the practices of English language education identified in Figure 12.1 at the beginning of this chapter, in which automation and increased uses of technology combine with increasing autonomy in language learning from the middle of the twentieth century onward. They are also in keeping with the emergence of IDLE and rapid developments in digital communications in the twenty-first.

However, the horizontal arrows of Figure 12.1 also indicate that new approaches to language teaching add rather than replace old ones, so it is very likely that even in 2035 grammar-translation may still exist as a teaching approach. In many parts of the world teachers and students will continue to meet in classrooms with very little technology and the benefits and opportunities of informal digital learning of English will remain unacknowledged even as many learners acquire as much if not more of their English in this way.

However, opportunities for employment and for building a career in English language education are also likely to contract, especially for teachers without advanced pedagogical and digital skills. As David Graddol (1997; 2006) has noted, distinctions between second- and foreign-language speakers are already blurring, and in future being a "native" speaker of English is likely to provide less of an advantage. As English grows in many countries, its learning will be assumed and the demand for experts will decrease. The growth of EMI programs with little or no language support in Asian and European universities is clear evidence of this trend.

To remain relevant and to build a career in English education over the next decades will require that teachers develop new skills and strategies that enhance opportunities for engaged learning. These skills and strategies are in the five areas that were identified in Chapter 1 as the features of IDLE: (1) social connection; (2) authentic, compelling, and varied input; (3) autonomy; (4) multimodality; and (5) ubiquitous access. In the classroom, three of these are especially critical and have been emphasized in this chapter: opportunities for access, authenticity, and interaction (social connection).

Throughout this book, our argument has been that the best way for the teaching of English to remain vital and relevant for students, their parents and communities, and for policy makers, is to learn from learners themselves in the digital age. This means working to integrate the means and strategies that make English learning engaging and successful for adolescents and young adults through satellite television, the internet, and mobile phones into classroom instruction. These technologies and learner-driven strategies powerfully reduce if not largely eliminate the challenges of relevance, artificiality, and student resistance that language educators have struggled with for more than a century. Their adoption and integration are essential to the prosperity of English language learning and teaching in 2035 and beyond.

Key Points for Teaching English, Now and into the Future

As last words, we offer four key points for the teaching of the English language, now and into the future.

1) **It's Not About Linguistics Anymore.** Yes, of course English is a language and understanding its grammar, either implicitly or explicitly, is key to its use. However, for many decades it has been clear that mastering grammar rules or taking an exclusively linguistic approach to teaching languages is ineffective for learning to use the language proficiently as a tool of communication (Warschauer 2012). In addition, there now exist programs for teaching the elements of English as a language that are more consistent and less expensive and time consuming than live teaching. In future, teaching the linguistic aspects of English is likely to be replaced by robots and programs.

2) **Soon, It May Not Be About English.** The replacement of English as a global language is not likely in the next half century, but advances in machine translation may soon mean that English becomes a "relay" language (Graddol 2006) among many major world or local languages. Teachers who are multilingual may be the best

positioned to take advantage of this change, and teachers who have advanced proficiency in the pragmatics of communication across languages and contexts, as well as those who have advanced skills in multimodal communication and a broad range of digital applications are likely to thrive.

3) **Get to Know Your Students.** It bears repeating that in a digital communications environment, it is adolescents and young adults who lead populations in not only adopting but finding productive ways to use new technologies. The practices of IDLE are not only pedagogically sophisticated but research shows they are extraordinarily effective. Their integration into classrooms is dependent on teachers not only learning about them from books but from their users. Now and into the future, teachers who get to know their students and their learning practices by engaging as co-learners with them will be far more effective in their teaching.

4) **Become Proactive, Not Reactive.** As this chapter has noted, the future of English education is wide open, especially regarding advancements in 5G technologies and translation, but now is not the time to panic or overreact by abandoning all previous practices and adopting a technology-driven approach. The future will be a continuation of the past and present, and teachers who take a proactive approach, beginning now to learn from their students and to build on learner-driven practices with respect to digital technologies, are likely to remain vital and relevant to their students, to the profession of English language education, and to educational policy in their locale far into the twenty-first century.

Let's Discuss

1) What is your response to the opening portrait of English language teaching in this chapter? Do you view the description of an English language teacher's job as "reduced" or "enhanced" in the wake of the Covid-19 pandemic and advances in digital technology? Can you see yourself as a teacher in this scenario?

2) Which of the five advances in digital technology that were discussed do you see as having the most impact on the teaching of the English language in the coming decades? Which of these are you the most excited about or finding the most troubling? What ideas do you have about implementing these technologies as a teacher?

3) What is your response to the future of English as a global language? Do you see the future described here as bright for you? What adaptations do you see yourself making as a knowledgeable user of English or other languages?

4) How do the descriptions of curriculum, assessment, and teaching in 2035 relate to your vision of practice as a teacher? Do you see automated, continual assessment of student learning as a possibility in your current or future school? Do you think that school-in-the-cloud activities are practical or could be applied in your school?

5) Do the four concluding scenarios of teaching at middle, high school, university, or a language center seem feasible to you? At your level of teaching, could you see yourself teaching in that program? What changes might you have to make to your current practice to be successful?

References

Anderson, Don D. "Machine Translation as a Tool in Second Language Learning." *CALICO Journal* 13, no. 1 (January 2013): 68–97. https://doi.org/10.1016/j.esp.2014.09.001.

Burton, Richard F. The Book of the Thousand Nights and a Night. New York: Heritage Press; New York Editions Club, 1934.

Chandler, Paul D., Aine Therese O'Brien, and Len Unsworth. "Towards a 3D Digital Multimodal Curriculum for the Upper Primary School." *Australian Educational Computing* 25, no. 1 (2010): 34–40. https://www.researchgate.net/publication/259568402_Towards_a_3D_digital_multimodal_curriculum_for_the_upper_primary_school.

Chen, Brian X. "What's All the Hype about the Metaverse?" 2022. https://www.nytimes.com/2022/01/18/technology/personaltech/metaverse-gaming-definition.html#after-top.

CISA. "Securing 5G Infrastructure from Cybersecurity Risks." 2021. https://www.cisa.gov/blog/2021/05/10/securing-5g-infrastructure-cybersecurity-risks.

Cohen, Hayden. "IoT Applications in Task-Based and Foreign Language Learning." 2020. https://www.iotforall.com/iot-applications-task-based-foreign-language-learning.

Crystal, David. English as a Global Language. Cambridge: Cambridge University Press, 2003. http://ebooks.cambridge.org/ebook.jsf?bid=CBO9781139196970.

Davis, River. "Forget 5G for a Moment. Instead, Imagine 6G." *Wall Street Journal* (April 12, 2020). https://www.wsj.com/articles/forget-5g-for-a-moment-instead-imagine-6g-11586743200.

de la Guía, Elena, Vicente Lopez Camacho, Luis Orozco-Barbosa, Victor M. Brea Lujan, Victor M. Penichet, and Maria Lozano Perez. "Introducing IOT and Wearable Technologies into Task-Based Language Learning for Young Children." *IEEE Transactions on Learning Technologies* 9, no. 4 (October–December 2016): 366–378. https://doi.org/10.1109/tlt.2016.2557333.

Deutsche Welle. "The School in the Cloud – Virtual Learning as an Opportunity." Deutsche Welle video, 42:35, 2021. https://www.dw.com/en/the-school-in-the-cloud-virtual-learning-as-an-opportunity/av-60147753.

Duan, Haihan, Jiaye Li, Sizheng Fan, Zhonghao Lin, Xiao Wu, and Wei Cai. "Metaverse for Social Good: A University Campus Prototype." In *Proceedings of the 29th ACM International Conference on Multimedia*, October 2021. https://doi.org/10.1145/3474085.3479238.

Fang, Fan. "Ideology and Identity Debate of English in China: Past, Present and Future." *Asian Englishes* 20, no. 1 (February 2018): 15–26. https://doi.org/10.1080/13488678.2017.1415516.

Forge, Simon, and Khuong Vu "Forming a 5G Strategy for Developing Countries: A Note for Policy Makers." *Telecommunications Policy* 44, no. 7 (August 2020): 1–24. https://doi.org/10.1016/j.telpol.2020.101975.

Godwin-Jones, Robert. "Evolving Technologies for Language Learning." *Language Learning & Technology* 25, no. 3 (October 2021): 6–26. http://hdl.handle.net/10125/73443.

Graddol, David. The Future of English? London: The British Council, 1997.

Graddol, David. English Next: Why Global English May Mean the End of 'English as a Foreign Language'. London: The British Council, 2006.

Graddol, David. English Next India: The Future of English in India. London: The British Council, 2010.

Groves, Michael, and Klaus Mundt. "Friend or Foe? Google Translate in Language for Academic Purposes." *English for Specific Purposes* 37 (January 2015): 112–121. https://doi.org/10.1016/j.esp.2014.09.001.

Haristiani, Nuria. "Artificial Intelligence (AI) Chatbot as Language Learning Medium: An Inquiry." *Journal of Physics: Conference Series* 1387 (2019): 1–6. https://doi.org/10.1088/1742-6596/1387/1/012020.

Hartono, Rudi. "Teaching Translation through the Interactive Web." *Language Circle: Journal of Language and Literature* 9, no. 2 (April 2015): 129–140. Semarang: Semarang State University.

Hong, Youngtaek, and Jaehoon Choi. "60 GHz Patch Antenna Array with Parasitic Elements for Smart Glasses." *IEEE Antennas and Wireless Propagation Letters* 17, no. 7 (2018): 1252–1256.

Hsu, Hsiao-Ling, Howard Hao-Jan Chen, and Andrew G. Todd. "Investigating the Impact of the Amazon Alexa on the Development of L2 Listening and Speaking Skills." *Interactive Learning Environments* (December 2021): 1–14.https://doi.org/10.1111/j.1467-971X.1990.tb00683.x

Joo, Sun Jung, Alice Chik, and Emilia Djonov. "The Construal of English as a Global Language in Korean EFL Textbooks for Primary School Children." *Asian Englishes* 22, no. 1 (2020): 68–84. https://doi.org/10.1080/13488678.2019.1627636.

Kachru, Braj B. "World Englishes and Applied Linguistics." *World Englishes* 9, no. 1(March 1990): 3–20. https://doi.org/10.1111/j.1467-971X.1990.tb00683.x.

Kumar, Vinod. "Why 5G Networks Are Disrupting The Cybersecurity Industry." 2021. https://www.forbes.com/sites/forbestechcouncil/2021/10/29/why-5g-networks-are-disrupting-the-cybersecurity-industry/?sh=77637ff71fe9.

Kye, Bokyung, Nara Han, Eunji Kim, Yeonjeong Park, and Soyoung Jo "Educational Applications of Metaverse: Possibilities and Limitations." *Journal of Educational Evaluation for Health Professions* 18 (December 2021): 1–13. https://doi.org/10.3352/jeehp.2021.18.32.

Laperre, Eline. "There Is No Such Thing as Standard English." Cambridge University Press World of Better Learning, 2020. https://www.cambridge.org/elt/blog/2020/02/24/no-such-thing-as-standard-english.

Lee, Lik-Hang, Tristan Braud, Pengyuan Zhou, Lin Wang, Dianlei Xu, Zijun Lin, Abhishek Kumar, Carlos Bermejo, and Pan Hui. "All One Needs to Know about Metaverse: A Complete Survey on Technological Singularity, Virtual Ecosystem, and Research Agenda." *Journal of Latex Class Files* 14, no. 8 (September 2021): 1–65. https://doi.org/10.48550/arXiv.2110.05352.

Lee, Sangmin-Michelle. "The Impact of Using Machine Translation on EFL Students' Writing." *Computer Assisted Language Learning* 33, no. 3 (February 2019): 157–175. https://doi.org/10.1080/09588221.2018.1553186.

Lei, Xu. "The Research on Optimization Strategy of College English Teaching Mode Based on 5G Technology and Artificial Intelligence Technology." In *Paper presented at the 2020 International Conference on Virtual Reality and Intelligent Systems (ICVRIS)*, Zhangjiajie, Hunan, China, 2020. https://doi.org/10.1109/ICVRIS51417.2020.00212.

Lestari, Sri, and Radius Setiyawan. "Technology Era, Global English, Clil: Influence and Its Impact on English Teaching for Young Learners in Indonesia." *IOP Conference Series: Earth and Environmental Science* 469 (2020): 1–8. https://doi.org/10.1088/1755-1315/469/1/012094.

Li, Rui. "Research Trends of Blended Language Learning: A Bibliometric Synthesis of SSCI-Indexed Journal Articles during 2000–2019." *ReCALL* (December 2021): 1–18. https://doi.org/10.1017/s0958344021000343.

Li, Zhi. "Simulation of English Education Translation Platform Based on Web Remote Embedded Platform and 5G Network." *Microprocessors and Microsystems* 81 (2020): 1–7. https://doi.org/10.1016/j.micpro.2020.103775.

Lim, Fei Victor, and Weimin Toh. "Children's Digital Multimodal Composing: Implications for Learning and Teaching." *Learning, Media and Technology* 45, no. 4 (September 2020): 422–432. https://doi.org/10.1080/17439884.2020.1823410.

Limniou, Maria, David Roberts, and Nikos Papadopoulos. "Full Immersive Virtual Environment CAVETM in Chemistry Education." *Computers & Education* 51, no. 2 (September 2008): 584–593. https://doi.org/10.1016/j.compedu.2007.06.014.

Mitra, Sugata. "The Future of Schooling: Children and Learning at the Edge of Chaos." *Prospects* 44, no. 4 (October 2014): 547–558. https://doi.org/10.1007/s11125-014-9327-9.

OECD. 21st-Century Readers: Developing Literacy Skills in a Digital World. Paris: PISA, OECD Publishing, 2021. https://doi.org/10.1787/a83d84cb-en.

Pairaphrase. "Best Way to Translate a PowerPoint Presentation." 2022. https://www.pairaphrase.com/best-way-translate-powerpoint-presentation.

Pezoa, Jorge E., Xu Le, Li Wei, Weixiao Meng, and Gonzalo A. Montalva. "The China-Chile ICT Joint Laboratory: A 5G Standalone Network for Education, Innovation Research and Development." In *Paper presented at the 2021 IEEE 4th 5G World Forum (5GWF)*, 2021. https://doi.org/10.1109/5gwf52925.2021.00096.

Piran, Md. Jalil, and Doug Young Suh. "Learning-Driven Wireless Communications, towards 6G." In *Paper Presented at the 2019 International Conference on Computing, Electronics & Communications Engineering (iCCECE)*, 219–224, 2019. https://doi.org/10.1109/iCCECE46942.2019.8941882.

Poole, Robert. A Guide to Using Corpora for English Language Learners. Edinburgh: Edinburgh University Press, 2018. https://www.degruyter.com/document/doi/10.1515/9781474427180/html?lang=de.

Rahman, Mohammad Mosiur, and Ambigapathy Pandian. "A Critical Investigation of English Language Teaching in Bangladesh." *English Today* 34, no. 3 (February 2018): 43–49. https://doi.org/10.1017/s026607841700061x.

Rahman, Tariq, James D'Angelo, and Anamika Sharma. "English in Pakistan: Past, Present and Future." In Functional Variations in English, edited by Ram Ashish Giri, 127–148. Singapore: Springer, September, 2020. https://doi.org/10.1007/978-3-030-52225-4_9.

Takahashi, Chika. "Developing the Ideal Multilingual Self in the Era of Global English: A Case in the Japanese Context." *The Language Learning Journal* 49, no. 3 (2021): 358–369. https://doi.org/10.1080/09571736.2019.1606272.

Thesiger, Wilfred. Arabian Sands. London: Penguin Books, 2007.

van den Berghe, Rianne, Josje Verhagen, Ora Oudgenoeg-Paz, Sanne van der Ven, and Paul Leseman. "Social Robots for Language Learning: A Review." *Review of Educational Research* 89, no. 2 (April 2018): 259–295. https://doi.org/10.3102/0034654318821286.

Wardle, Elizabeth. "Considering What It Means to Teach "Composition" in the Twenty-First Century." *College Composition and Communication* 65, no. 4 (June 2014): 659–671. https://www.proquest.com/scholarly-journals/considering-what-means-teach-composition-twenty/docview/1545533269/se-2?accountid=14553.

Warschauer, Mark. "The Changing Global Economy and the Future of English Teaching." *TESOL Quarterly* 34, no. 3 (January 2012): 511–535. https://doi.org/10.2307/3587741.

Wheeler, Tom, and David Simpson. "Why 5G Requires New Approaches to Cybersecurity." 2019. https://www.brookings.edu/research/why-5g-requires-new-approaches-to-cybersecurity.

Yeruva, Vinod. "Why 5G Networks Are Disrupting The Cybersecurity Industry." 2021. https://www.forbes.com/sites/forbestechcouncil/2021/10/29/why-5g-networks-are-disrupting-the-cybersecurity-industry/?sh=589c6dd21fe9.

Zamudio, Víctor, María del Pilar Pérez Mata, Victor Callaghan, Shumei Zhang, and Carlos Lino. "Using a Creative Science Approach for Teaching English as a Foreign Language to Postgraduate Students." In *Paper Presented at the EAI International Conference on Technology, Innovation, Entrepreneurship and Education*, 19–25, September 2017. https://doi.org/10.1007/978-3-030-02242-6_2.

Zein, Subhan. "English, Multilingualism and Globalisation in Indonesia." *English Today* 35, no. 1 (May 2018): 48–53. https://doi.org/10.1017/s026607841800010x.

Index

Note: Page numbers followed by "*f*" and "*t*" indicate figures and tables, respectively.

English Language Learning in the Digital Age: Learner-Driven Strategies for Adolescents and Young Adults,
First Edition. Mark Dressman, Ju Seong Lee, and Laurent Perrot.
© 2023 John Wiley & Sons Ltd. Published 2023 by John Wiley & Sons Ltd.

AQ5AQ4AQ3AQ2AQ1